Spirit & Reason

THE VINE DELORIA, JR., READER

FOREWORD BY WILMA P. MANKILLER

EDITED BY
Barbara Deloria, Kristen Foehner, and Sam Scinta

Fulcrum Publishing
Golden, Colorado

OTHER BOOKS BY VINE DELORIA, JR.

Library of Congress Cataloging-in-Publication Data
Deloria, Vine.
    Spirit & reason : the Vine Deloria, Jr., reader / edited by Barbara Deloria, Kristen Foehner, and Sam Scinta.
        p. cm.
    Includes bibliographical references and index.
    ISBN 1-55591-430-6 (pbk.)
    1. Indian philosophy—North America.   2. Indians of North America—Social conditions.   3. Indians of North America—Study and teaching.   I. Deloria, Barbara.   II. Foehner, Kristen.   III. Scinta, Samuel.   IV. Title.   V. Title: Spirit and reason.
E98.P5D45   1999
970'.00497—dc21   99-30110
                                                                                                         CIP

Printed in the United States of America
0 9 8 7 6 5 4

Book design: Bill Spahr
Cover art: "Flying Pipe, Canupa Kinyan, Yankton Sioux," copyright © 1999 Jeralyn Lujan-Lucero/Gathering Flowers Taos Pueblo.

Fulcrum Publishing
4690 Table Mountain Drive, Suite 100
Golden, Colorado 80403
(800) 992-2908 • (303) 277-1623
www.fulcrum-books.com

▼ CONTENTS ▼

▼▼▼▼

PART IV: INDIANS

PART V: RELIGION

▾ FOREWORD ▾

Wilma P. Mankiller

▼▼▼▼

No writer has more clearly articulated the unspoken emotions, dreams, and lifeways of contemporary Native people than Vine Deloria. This collection of Deloria's works takes the reader on a fascinating journey through Indian country as Deloria responds to some of the most important issues of the last three decades. Deloria's literary gift is amply demonstrated in pieces that are a mix of logic, humor, irreverence, and spirituality. But it is his clarity of thought and stunning ability to express complex concepts in a simple, straightforward manner that captivate the reader.

One of the most compelling pieces in the collection, "If You Think About It, You Will See That It Is True," reminded me of the phrase coined by Alice Walker, "looking backward toward the future." With flawless logic and adroit use of language, Deloria examines the way many traditional Native people look at the universe, the connectedness of all living things, and our own insignificance in the totality of things compared to the objective, segmented way scientists in the academy view the universe. Deloria points out that "everything that humans experience has value and instructs in some aspect of life. . . . The real interest of the old Indians was not to discover the abstract structure of physical reality but rather to find the proper road along which, for the duration of a person's life, individuals were supposed to walk." This argues "that the universe is a moral universe."

In "Low Bridge—Everybody Cross," Deloria challenges conventional scholarly arguments that Native people in North America are immigrants just like everyone else because they crossed the Bering Strait, albeit centuries earlier than Columbus. Deloria painstakingly takes apart the arguments of proponents of the Bering Strait theory of migration and attributes their motives to a combination of intellectual slothfulness and "residual guilt . . . over the manner in which the Western Hemisphere was invaded and settled by Europeans."

In "The Turmoil of Ethnic Studies," Deloria illustrates the acceptance of ethnic studies in the academy with a tongue-in-cheek passage, "I realized that some measure of academic respectability had been achieved because I could hardly understand what my colleagues were saying. . . . That kind of behavior is the best measure of academic respectability—a professor can talk for an hour and only his closest colleagues can understand what he is saying." In the same playful mood, he wrote "A Flock of Anthros" to argue in part that anthropology is a field of study with a very dogmatic framework and a nebulous foundation.

Deloria writes poignantly of the struggle of Caucasian people in America to understand why many Native people did not participate in the Bicentennial Celebration, which appeared to commemorate the concept that "the institution of oppression has survived two centuries!" He goes on to argue in "Why Indians Aren't Celebrating the Bicentennial" that placing our current situation in a historical context but, "What is done is done. It is where we go next that is important . . . so that the next hundred years will not force us to look back on mistrust, arrogance, and injustice."

Although all the chapters in this book are instructive, "Higher Education and Self-Determination," an optimistic essay about the future of Indian education, is particularly interesting because it explains in part the reason that some academically qualified Native people simply drop out of college and go home. Deloria says "Non-Indians live within a worldview that separates and isolates and mistakes labeling and identification for knowledge. . . . Indians were completely outside the system and within their own worldview."

There are other equally absorbing pieces, ranging from "Alcatraz, Activism, and Accommodation" to "The Religious Challenge." One of the most engaging minds of our time, Deloria gives the reader a rare glimpse into the world of Native people as we grapple with questions that all come back to the central issue of how to retain a strong sense of who we are as Native people as we walk confidently into the next millennium as whole human beings.

▼ PREFACE ▼

▼▼▼▼

One of the annoying things about living too long is the task of digging out ancient writings that people want to copy. "Didn't you write an article on the BIA about twenty years ago that would be useful in this case?" Even with the excuse of a house fire some time back, I still drop everything, rummage through the remaining files, and try to find the piece. How people can remember phrases I have turned years after I have forgotten about them is a mystery unsolved. So when Sam Scinta proposed a reader that would include some of my more obscure articles, representative pieces from some of my books, and articles I had written but not submitted for publication, the idea had considerable attraction.

Nothing is as heartbreaking as reading massive amounts of your own writings from the past. You remember early morning trips to the post office in the snow to be certain the piece went out in the first mail. Other articles recall hours hammering away at a decent opening sentence, and excerpts from books bring back memories of watching copy editors quarrel with just about everything in the chapter.

There is a frequent temptation to rewrite some of the pieces because you know so much more now than you did then, and when you see the oldest pieces you are appalled at how little you knew about the subject before realizing that no one else knew as much about the subject back then anyway.

You finally surrender to the passage of time and quarrel with your editor about using an old article and volunteer to write a more modern version of the subject. I got so interested in formulating my present views on different subjects that I wrote about ten new articles for this collection in spite of myself. But there was no temptation to rewrite everything, because I was pleasantly surprised to realize that I liked a lot of the things that had been done years ago and would say the same thing if writing on the topic today. This reluctance to change does not, I hope, indicate a brain frozen in time but is rather indicative of the fact that people have not made much progress in resolving issues and the same concepts are still potent and representative of how we feel about things.

Some of my articles have been written to respond to particular problems that were demanding attention at the time, and it was my regret quite often that I did not have time to write a whole book on a topic and make it immediately available to help clarify situations. With each new administration there is a promise of major changes in Indian policy, but after the preliminary publicity whitewash things continue as they once did. This inertia is true whether the new commissioner or assistant secretary is Indian or not. Indeed, each administration seems to appoint people who will make the fewest reforms to avoid any unanticipated publicity on Indians and embarrass the administration. So virtually no new ideas come into the policy field during the course of a person's lifetime. This stalemate makes some of my early articles on Indian policy as fresh as the day I submitted them.

Many years ago Mel Thom, then charismatic leader of the National Indian Youth Council, promulgated the slogan "For a better Indian America," and although everyone teased Mel about the grandiose nature of his idea, there was a certain moral content that has not been equaled in the decades since. When I began writing articles and books it seemed to me that my writing should fall within the scope of that vision—that whatever was written should be both aggressive about Indian rights to inspire Indians and a means of pointing out to the larger society the changes that they should be making if they really wanted to help Indians.

Over the years some people have complained that my writings have had an aggressive edge, and I freely admit that there has been a sharpness not evident in contemporary writing. Looking back at a time when conferences on Indians had no Indians, when buffs and hobbyists made major policy decisions regarding the fate and future of Indians, and when a handful of church representatives conferred quietly with the secretary of the interior about federal programs, it seems to me that the rugged edge was justified if only to get the few Indians on the scene to speak up on their own behalf. In those days we really believed that it was possible to re-create nations but only if people, Indian and non-Indian, honestly dealt with the facts.

In this context law and policy depend on the appearance of morality, if not its substance. Thus any discussion or recommendation that can be made must have some grounding in common decency, if such can be said to exist in the political arena. I have never been able to escape my background as the son and grandson of missionaries mixed with chiefs and political leaders of long ago. My family over the generations always engaged in religious leadership and saw issues in religious terms, so it could be predicted that I would tend to see the underlying religious dimension of political action. Thus *Custer Died for Your Sins*, a theological slogan submerged in a political protest; *God Is Red*, an explanation of contemporary activism that helped to emphasize the need for religious as well as political revival; and *The Metaphysics of Modern Existence*, an effort to sketch out an alternative view of perceived realities, were all the product of a continuing conviction that there were values above the political that must nevertheless be expressed in political terms.

Religion, as I have experienced it, is not the recitation of beliefs but a way of helping to understand our lives. It must, I think, have an intimate connection with the world in which we live, and any religion that promotes other places—heaven and so on—in favor of what we have in the physical world is a delusion, a mere control device to allow us to be manipulated. Science provides us with a reductionist, materialistic perspective on our experiences, but much of our experience is that of the physical world and we do reduce our understandings to a few basic principles. So my interest in science has been a continuing one. I detest bad science, however, and I loathe fakery when it is not necessary to explain things. So the more science I read, the more I come to understand that it is a big hoax in a large number of areas.

My dissatisfaction with orthodox science began after reading *Worlds in Collision* by Immanuel Velikovsky. I was a freshman at the Colorado School of Mines at the time and trying my best to master the theories of the day (Wegner, with his floating continents, was also a heretic in those days), and one sentence by Velikovsky hit me very hard. It was an argument that if fossil footprints were easy to preserve, we would have thousands of them in the rocks. I had done my share of roaming around as a teenager and knew that footprints were always washed out by the next hard rain and that to be preserved, they would have to be semibaked quickly after the person or animal had made them. Catastrophism of some kind was, therefore, the real explanation of geologic reality. It was not possible, for me at least, to look out at the Boulder Flatirons and believe, for example, that they had risen a millimeter a millennium.

Reading voraciously in popular scientific literature, I could never shake off the stories my father and other older Indians told about the way the world had been in ancient times. So for many years I was torn between science and the old stories. Encountering the writings of Dorothy Vitaliano and Henrietta Mertz, I was convinced that earth history and indeed human history were much different from the way scholars described them. So I finally moved completely into the heretical literatures in every field and began to put together my own understanding of things. This task has involved trudging through a ton of nonsense, but it has also alerted me to the woefully deficient articulation of knowledge we are fed by orthodox science.

My writings in the critique of science are always misunderstood, many times deliberately by critics and reporters, so that people I have not seen for a long time frequently accuse me of going "crazy" for advocating certain beliefs. But many of these statements are not beliefs that I would die for, as would many religious people and scientists, but merely points that stick in my craw that I would like smarter people to resolve. I simply bring them to people's attention. People who complain about my so-called beliefs are usually those who have not read a thing since they graduated from college, or academics who read only the writings of their own peer group. I still wait in vain for an anthro to send me a book or an article that offers full and convincing proof of the validity of the Bering Strait theory— and of course there is none.

I hope the selections in this volume will give the reader a reasonably comprehensive idea of the subjects I have written on, the areas of activity I have tried to engage, and the issues that have attracted my attention. It is difficult to anticipate what interests people have, but these selections represent areas in which I have worked and will continue to work. Perhaps these readings will inspire others to voice their opinions and offer their scholarly studies in these areas, pushing the frontiers of understanding much farther than I could manage.

▼ Part I ▼

PHILOSOPHY

PERCEPTIONS AND MATURITY:

Reflections on Feyerabend's Point of View

▼▼▼▼

Among the fallacies that Alfred North Whitehead identified within the Western philosophical tradition was the belief that the principles of philosophy were "clear, obvious, and irreformable."[1] Feyerabend's exploration of method speaks directly to this point, but it also deals with the barriers that cultures raise against foreign critical ideas to protect their central integrity. Can any philosophy transcend its cultural barriers and speak to the larger question of how we perceive and interact with the world around us? What is the potential for a philosophy to help us make sense of our lives? The West has certainly not solved that problem; it has only used its tremendous political and economic power to render the question moot.

Science and technology reign today as the practical gods of the modern age; they give us power to disrupt nature but little real insight into how it functions. We tend to dismiss what we cannot understand by the use of code words—"instinct" for example covers a plenitude of ignorance. Only when we look outside Western culture, or when someone outside looks in, do we discover the glaring inconsistencies and begin to measure the actual changes that science and technology have wrought in our lives. In 1820 George Sibley, the Indian agent for the Osages, a tribe in the Missouri region of the country, tried to convince Big Soldier, one of the more influential chiefs, of the benefits of the white man's way. After enthusiastically describing the wonders of the white man's civilization, Sibley waited expectantly for the old man's response. Big Soldier did not disappoint him:

> *I see and admire your manner of living, your good warm*
> *houses; your extensive fields of corn, your gardens, your cows,*
> *oxen, workhouses, wagons, and a thousand machines, that I*
> *know not the use of. I see that you are able to clothe your-*
> *selves, even from weeds and grass. In short you can do almost*
> *what you choose. You whites possess the power of subduing*
> *almost every animal to your use. You are surrounded by*
> *slaves. Every thing about you is in chains and you are slaves*
> *yourselves. I fear if I should exchange my pursuits for yours, I*
> *too should become a slave.*[2]

If we subdue nature, we become slaves of the technology by which the task is accomplished and surrender not simply our freedom but also the luxury of reflection about our experiences that a natural relationship with the world had given us.

Western civilization seems clear, orderly, obvious, and without possibility of reform primarily because it defines the world in certain rigid categories. The product of this clarity, however, is a certain kind of insanity that can survive only by renewed efforts to refine the definitions and that, ultimately, becomes totally self-destructive. Whitehead also noted that "a system will be the product of intelligence. But when the adequate routine is established, intelligence vanishes, and the system is maintained by a coordination of conditioned responses."[3] That condition is certainly prevalent in modern politics and economics and can be found in many fields of scientific endeavor. Western civilization seems to have a multitude of "commonsense" propositions, and as common sense is such a rarity, what we actually mean by this statement is that we have a certain set of propositions that we have agreed not to question. Further, we have arrived at these propositions through a refining process whereby we throw away the "anomalies"—the facts that do not fit into our definitional schemata. Feyerabend's major contribution to modern philosophy is to insist that these premises and principles that we accept be demythologized and then revised to present increasingly broader understandings of what we are actually doing.

Feyerabend's work is critically important for non-Western and post-Western peoples because he stands within the Western tradition yet has mastered many of its social and political barriers so that he can speak meaningfully and critically to its less intelligent proponents. He is a threat to the routine operation of philosophy, science, and the process of accumulating human knowledge because he asks penetrating and embarrassing questions in fields that most people feel have been laid to rest. Feyerabend is one of the few voices that sees that the body of human knowledge is not merely an instance of adding insights of non-Western peoples to the already constructed edifice of Western knowledge but that the full content of human knowledge must be a discontinuous arrangement of smaller bodies of knowledge derived from the many human traditions represented in planetary history.

It is exceedingly difficult at the present time to break through the mind-set of the West and engage in dialogue and conversation with Western thinkers. The reception that the non-Western thinker receives is frequently one of paternalism, more often a chiding ridicule that a native would presume to enter the lists of educated people, occasionally a deep jealousy and resentment when the non-Westerner appears to have something important to say to the Western scheme of things. Some years ago I wrote a book that sought to take dissident and discredited Western thinkers and show that their ideas, synthesized properly, could produce a pattern suggesting a consistent alternative explanation of what we know about the world. This pattern, moreover, suggested that perception could be a fundamental epistemological principle and that it could produce a knowledge capable of providing a context for human maturity and personality formation.

Unfortunately, I had the word "metaphysics" in the title of the book and was told by the publicity department of Harper and Row, my publishers at the time, that nothing would be done to give the book publicity "because no one will buy a book on metaphysics written by an Indian." Other minority writers have told me of their similar experiences. Thus the potential for engaging in serious philosophical debate between and among the diverse cultures of the world is exceedingly remote, and it is only people such as Feyerabend who are willing to look at the anomalies and inconsistencies of Western philosophy and who are keeping the door open for any future possible discussions.

Of course, there are many ways to pierce the Western intellectual curtain. I could rephrase these same ideas, pass them off in the format of ancient teachings of American Indians, and have Harper's publicity department declare that they were being revealed for the first time. Harper and Row, incidentally, is not averse to publishing any amount of nonsense as long as it is packaged properly. But in adopting that format I would then be attracting hundreds of hippies, disgruntled ex-Christians, and the usual scattering of affluent white youths whose most philosophical moments occurred while backpacking the Continental Divide under the influence of the herbs of the *Cannabis* genus. The ensuing attention would not be philosophical dialogue even though it might qualify/condemn me to appear in the pages of *People* magazine. It is not difficult to manipulate the emotions of Western peoples because their routine lives make them vulnerable to such tactics. It is exceedingly difficult to converse with them because they guard their minds and beliefs rigorously. Thus it is people such as Paul Feyerabend who will prove critical in opening enough breaches in the walls of Western intellectual chauvinism so that some exchange of ideas can occur.

Being more political than philosophical in nature, I have my own agenda for Feyerabend's future writing that originates in the manner in which I discovered his writing and saw its potential. It fits perfectly with my own agenda for raising issues of an ultracultural nature, issues that, with the present ecological breakdown of the planet, have become more pressing with the passage of the years. So my own emotional and intellectual responses to Feyerabend's work bear mentioning. My first encounter was with *Science in a Free Society*. A fellow admirer of Immanuel Velikovsky finished reading the book and called me to recommend it, pointing out that it spoke directly to the problem of allowing dissident and alternative philosophies to flourish. Finishing that work, I set out to master *Against Method* and became an enthusiastic Feyerabend student. My enthusiasm for Feyerabend disturbed some staid academic friends who told me with a certain undertone of chastisement that Thomas S. Kuhn's *The Structure of Scientific Revolutions* was much more respectable, Feyerabend having some rough edges that many academics didn't like.

My rule of thumb in these cases is to rush to embrace the heretical because the rank and file of academia is usually a generation behind the original thinkers within its peer group. Anyone who can raise the eyebrows of academics and evoke that "tut-tut" casual disapproval usually is a serious thinker with a great deal to say. In comparing the two men, I find Feyerabend a much more daring and fundamental thinker than Kuhn. Not only does he reach conclusions similar to those I reached in *The Metaphysics of Modern Existence,* that perceptions are the primary mode of receiving information and that maturity is the ultimate goal of human existence, but I also feel that Feyerabend wrestles with the angels in areas where Kuhn fears to read. A comparison of the two thinkers will indicate that Feyerabend, in advocating anarchism, is in fact asking us to show some intellectual courage. I find this missing in Kuhn and in most of the other writers trying to deal with the same or similar problems.

Both Feyerabend and Kuhn agree that the best advances in science and philosophy are made by the outsider, a conclusion not difficult to reach but exceedingly difficult to accept emotionally. Even the best minds trained in the mythology of Western science, in which the use of numbers, sincerity, and a tenured position in the university equal science, miss the nuances when they compare the two thinkers. Kuhn phrases his analysis as follows: "Almost always the men who achieve these fundamental inventions of a new paradigm have been either very young or very new to the field whose paradigm they change."[4] Feyerabend suggests that "science is advanced by outsiders, or by scientists with an unusual background."[5]

There is a considerable difference here. Kuhn's agent of change is presumed to be approved by the establishment; his creators of the new paradigm presuppose the uniform march of orthodox science with a few exciting changes in perspective. Feyerabend frankly admits that outsiders count. And they certainly do. Albert Einstein was a mere patent clerk, Michael Ventris was an architect when he deciphered Linear B, Heinrich Schliemann was a funny little German merchant who believed in the mythology of ancient Greece. Without the outsider it is difficult to imagine what science and philosophy would have been able to accomplish. Although Kuhn *seems* to be talking about scientific history, the message he conveys is not precise and not useful. Basically it reinforces the old mythology that we are, after all, the priests of a noble tradition and occasionally, by golly, we are shook up by a few youngsters as well we should be.

Feyerabend raises the whole question of what the scientific endeavor really is. And it is the offbeat character who does not pander to his colleagues and has his own perspective of the world who is not always consonant with the respectable people of his time. He is canonized only after his death in many instances and quickly becomes a paradigm figure with virtually no rough edges. It becomes difficult for us to remember that Newton and Kepler were basically astrologers whose by-products were very successful. Alfred North Whitehead pointed out, "The great thinkers of the sixteenth and seventeenth centuries were singularly detached from universities. Erasmus wanted printers, and Bacon, Harvey, Descartes, Galileo, Leibniz, wanted governmental patronage or protection, more than university colleagues."[6] If Kuhn recognizes this dimension of scientific history, he disguises it so completely that he endorses the very situation that he has promised to criticize and explain.

This failure of nerve appears so consistently in Kuhn's work that I suspect his purpose is not discussion of scientific methodology but baby-sitting a generation of minds that need to be reassured that Faustus and Strangelove were not really lurking in their unconscious. We see the radical difference in the two men again when we examine how they believe ideas originate. Feyerabend takes a radical and honest approach:

> *The first step in our criticism of customary concepts and customary reactions is to step outside the circle and either to invent a new conceptual system, for example a new theory, that clashes with the most carefully established observational results and confounds the most plausible theoretical principles, or to import such a system from outside science, from religion, from mythology, from the ideas of incompetents, or the ramblings of madmen.*[7]

For Feyerabend, ideas should be judged by the potential for making a contribution to understanding, not on their origin, former use, or relationship to accepted symbols of contemporary authority. Or, as Alfred North Whitehead observed, "If you have had your attention directed to the novelties in thought in your own lifetime, you will have observed that almost all really new ideas have a certain aspect of foolishness when they are first produced."[8]

Kuhn seems unable to deal with the question of the origin of ideas. He approaches the problem from the perspective of the traditional scientist: "Scientists . . . often speak of the 'scales falling from the eyes' or of the 'lightning flash' that 'inundates' a previously obscure puzzle, enabling its components to be seen in a new way that for the first time permits its solution."[9] This condition is a psychological process to be sure, and the comparison with Feyerabend is not precise. But Kuhn leads us down a particular road and then tells us that he has not misled us: "No ordinary sense of the term 'interpretation' fits these flashes of intuition through which a new paradigm is born. Though such intuitions depend upon the experience, both anomalous and congruent, gained with the old paradigm, they are not logically or piecemeal linked to particular items of that experience as an interpretation would be."[10] So ideas come in an intuitional flash—no one can quarrel with that description, and indeed stories about the intuitional grasping of new concepts abound in science.

What does Kuhn do with his insight? He promptly recants and panders to the old boy network by closing the doors of intuition. "Some readers have felt that I was trying to make science rest on unanalyzable individual intuitions rather than on logic and law," he says. "But that interpretation goes astray in two essential respects. First, *if I am talking at all about intuitions, they are not individual. Rather they are the tested and shared possessions of the members of a successful group, and the novice acquires them through training as a part of his preparation for group-membership.*"[11]

WHAT?

I delight in these little surrenders because the scenarios that they invoke in the mind are too precious to let escape. GROUP INTUITIONS? INTUITIONS ACQUIRED IN A NOVICE'S TRAINING? How now? And where? In the oral examination for the Ph.D.? In writing up the proposal to the National Science Foundation for a research grant? In attending faculty meetings as junior visiting professor? At professional meetings? If science and philosophy advanced via group intuitions for which a person could be trained, why haven't we solved all of our remaining problems? I was under the impression that Descartes was alone that winter evening, that Newton was not in an auditorium but a garden when the apple hit his head, and that Einstein was busy with his office files as he was thinking out the implications of his theory. The scenario that Kuhn invokes is most prominently found in the Acts of the Apostles where the Holy Spirit appears to the disciples in the upper room at Whitsuntide. THAT is group intuition.

The approach of the two men to the question of Western supremacy is important to note because it is intimately tied to each man's epistemology and to their willingness to consider data from non-Western sources. Kuhn feels that Western information gathering is unquestionably superior. "Every civilization of which we have records has possessed a technology, an art, a religion, a political system, laws, and so on," Kuhn admits. "But only the civilizations that descended from Hellenic Greece have possessed more than the most rudimentary science."[12] In this statement Kuhn joins Werner Heisenberg, Teilhard de Chardin and numerous other modern thinkers in echoing a cold war mentality and recommending cultural chauvinism akin to religious fanaticism. But note that the only criterion is science, as if science alone determined the substance of human life and experience.

Feyerabend is certainly no doctrinaire worshiper of Western science. Indeed, he delights in pointing out the many advances made by our ancestors, of all cultural traditions, in the domestication of plants and animals, the creation of language, knowledge of the larger cosmic context, and other major innovations that were fundamental to and underlay all our more recent scientific accomplishments. "True," he remarks, "there were no collective excursions to the moon, but single individuals, disregarding great dangers to their soul and their sanity, rose from sphere to sphere to sphere until they finally faced God himself in all His Splendour while others changed into animals and back into humans again."[13] Here we find the proper mooring for intuition that Kuhn so proudly spread over academic/scientific practitioners.

The inventors of myth, Feyerabend reminds us, *started* culture; scientists merely *changed* it. One might add that the inventors of myth became bards, minstrels, and gods, whereas the scientists have produced such memorable characters as Faustus, Frankenstein, and, in our day, Dr. Strangelove and Edward Teller, all of whom have made the villagers very nervous. But there is a deeper level of discussion to be found here. Our ancestors *observed* nature and perceived sets of relationships in the world. They used obscure correspondences to relate phenomena that appeared to be entirely separate and thereby derived a reasonably predictive knowledge about how the world works. Anomalies interested them and triggered their intuitional abilities. Western science has established wholly artificial experimental settings wherein we can force nature to respond in certain ways and we measure those ways. What doesn't fit the preconceived results in our experiments we often discard as the anomalous and believe that we have captured an ultimate knowledge about the world.

Kuhn and Feyerabend both deal with the discarded anomalies of experience and experiment that science allocates to the rubbish heap of data. But again they take somewhat different approaches to the subject. "No part of the aim of normal science is to call forth new sorts of phenomena," Kuhn observes. "Indeed, those that will not fit the box are often not seen at all."[14] Anomalies, for Kuhn, are often simply oversights, and if one adopts this interpretation, then an important part of the scientific perspective is lost. Feyerabend agrees that "whatever fails to fit into the established category system or is said to be incompatible with this system is either viewed as something quite horrifying or, *more frequently, it is simply declared to be non-existent.*"[15] For Kuhn, science often makes little mistakes; but Feyerabend admits that if something varies substantially from our expectations, we promptly banish it so that we will not have to try to understand it. This practice is hardly what the layperson would expect from scientists who spend a good deal of their time reassuring us that they are in total control of the situation and that they *know* what reality is.

So what is it exactly that Western scientists do that is all that great? They gather data from what appear to be similar entities and circumstances, and after much meditation, and today many computer sequences, they announce the discovery of "laws" that, with some notable exceptions of which we never hear, describe the universe. Sometimes these anomalies become the basis for further research, and when this procedure is followed we have a fruitful situation. But some anomalies are directly contrary to established doctrine and *these* hard facts are often just swept under the rug. That their measuring instruments continue to negate their laws as their tools become more sophisticated seems not to bother scientists. Nor does the fact that they are imposing certain restricted patterns on the natural world, thereby limiting its potential for response, seem to worry them. Scientists are not asking complete questions of nature, and they may not even be asking relevant questions.

The idea of forcing nature to tell us its secrets has an alternative in other cultural traditions of observing nature and adjusting to its larger rhythms. Feyerabend understands this aspect of considering the alternative approach to knowledge. Thus his methodology is open to receiving additional data and to incorporating non-Western insights into the structure of human knowledge. Kuhn would no doubt reject alternatives, first because they are not in line with scientific method and second because they originate from suspect sources that may be tinged with emotion and mysticism. How many people give alternative explanations the respect that allows them to learn from them? Very few, and it is a rare thinker who looks carefully enough to understand the nuances of the alternative. An example of American Indian knowledge may help us to illustrate this point.

Many centuries ago the Senecas had a revelation. Three sisters appeared and informed them that they wished to establish a relationship with the people, the "two-leggeds." In return for the performance of certain ceremonies that helped the sisters to thrive, they would become plants and feed the people. Thus it was that the sisters' beans, corn, and squash came to the Iroquois. These sisters had to be planted together and harvested together, and the Senecas complied with their wishes. The lands of the Senecas were never exhausted because these plants, in addition to sharing a spiritual relationship as sisters, were also a sophisticated natural nitrogen cycle that kept the lands fertile and productive. The white men came and planted only corn and wheat and very shortly exhausted the soil. After exhausting scientific experiments, the white man's scientists "discovered" the nitrogen cycle and produced tons of chemical fertilizer to replace the natural nitrogen. But recently we have discovered that there are unpleasant by-products of commercial fertilizer that may have an even worse effect on us than they do on the soil.

Feyerabend's methodology can incorporate this story and learn something from it. Other methodologies cannot begin to deal with it.

For every scientific "discovery," then, there may exist one or more alternative ways of understanding natural processes. But we cannot know what these alternatives are unless and until we begin to observe nature and listen to its rhythms and reject the idea of artificially forcing nature to tell us about herself. But science carelessly rejects alternative sources of information in favor of the clear idea, an absurd abstraction if ever there was one. Lacking a spiritual, social, or political dimension, it is difficult to understand why Western peoples believe they are so clever. Any damn fool can treat a living thing as if it were a machine and establish conditions under which it is required to perform certain functions—all that is required is a sufficient application of brute force. The result of brute force is slavery, and whereas Big Soldier, the Osage chief, could see this dimension at once, George Sibley and his like have never been able to see the consequences of their beliefs about the world. Reductionism is about the least efficient way to garner knowledge.

Feyerabend shows every indication that he is moving toward a major breakthrough in his thinking. He currently positions himself at the border between epistemology and metaphysics and sometimes seems to cross that boundary a bit to probe possibilities. I am unable to discover how Feyerabend has linked perceptions and maturity, but as every thinker does not detail the steps by which he has arrived at conclusions, I must withhold judgment until I understand how that linkage occurs. My fear is that he flashes from insight to insight and does not always go back over the ground he has covered so that others can follow more easily.

Maturity, in the American Indian context, is the ultimate goal of all human existence. Here we have a good many similarities with Feyerabend's conception of mature understanding. "Maturity," he writes, "is more important than special knowledge and it must be pursued even if the pursuit should interfere with the delicate and refined charades of scientists. After all, we have to decide how special forms of knowledge are to be applied, how far they may be trusted, what their relation is to the *totality* of human existence and therefore to other forms of knowledge."[16] Maturity, in the American Indian context, is the ability to reflect on the ordinary things of life and discover both their real meaning and the proper way to understand them when they appear in our lives. This idea sounds as abstract as anything uttered by a Western scientist but it is not abstract in the Indian context.

Maturity is a reflective situation that suggests a lifetime of experiences that, through an increasing ability to reflect on experience, has produced a personal hierarchy of relationships. This hierarchy has three major components that, because of the intense personal nature of experience, are appropriately related to the experiences of the individual and, on the tribal level, the group. Some components are weighted heavily because of the intensity of their content, others because of their inherent rationality and capability to explain everyday occurrences and others are simply a matter of personal preference, originating in any number of ways, although greatly influenced by the particular environment, social and natural, of the person who has reached maturity. Thus it is possible to hold sophisticated views about technology while verifying them by reference to personal emotional experiences and using them to predict future behavior. Here we have two additional dimensions that modern scientific method rejects or overlooks: the intensity of the experience and the perspective of the observer/participant. With relativity and quantum theory modern science is beginning to introduce the participant/observer, but it is still not capable of integrating the intensity of the experience because it assumes that intensity is subjective and therefore not capable of being measured and controlled.

Within the life history of maturity one can be said to travel from information to knowledge to wisdom. Organisms gather information, and as the cumulative amount begins to achieve a critical mass, patterns of interpretation and explanation begin to appear—even thoughts seem to form themselves into societies at a certain level of complexity. Here it is that Western science prematurely derives its scientific "laws" and assumes that the products of its own mind are inherent in the structure of the universe. But American Indians allow the process to continue, recognizing that premature analysis will produce anomalies and give incomplete understanding. When we reach a very old age, or have the capability to reflect and meditate on our experiences, or even more often have the goal revealed to us in visions, we begin to understand how the intensity of experience, particularity of individuality, and rationality of the cycles of nature all relate to each other. This state is maturity and seems to produce wisdom.

My uneasiness with Feyerabend's suggestion of pursuing maturity is that I don't believe that it can be deliberately accomplished. Unless a whole vision is received in a religious experience—and these visions are not always concerned with holiness because they can frequently reveal ordinary patterns of behavior, unsuspected relationships and correspondences, and rational principles—it becomes a matter of receiving maturity as the result of having possessed both knowledge and information for a sufficient length of time to allow them to arrange themselves so that they can serve us. One of the fallacies of Western civilization is the belief that the ingestion of tremendous amounts of material coupled with the mastery of relatively abstract propositions creates maturity and wisdom. If we merely glance around at Western society, we see that millions of people have performed these tricks but very few have anything approaching wisdom or maturity. Because Western society concentrates so heavily on information and theory, its product is youth, not maturity, and thousands of plastic surgeons in America testify to the fact that we have not yet crossed the emotional barriers that bar us from understanding and experiencing maturity.

What we are discussing when we look at Feyerabend's philosophy is the reemergence in Western philosophy of a rare form of honesty. Having demonstrated that scientific discovery is a process of propaganda, faith, clever phrasing, and sleight of hand to get others to see from a new perspective, I hope that Feyerabend now moves into the examination of what some of the rejected parts of experience really mean. Does their cumulative effect suggest an alternative method for gathering knowledge? I believe so. It may even have sufficient content to suggest a vision of reality that we have not glimpsed before.

An old chief of the Crow tribe from Montana was once asked to describe the difference between his tribe and the whites who lived nearby. Pausing slightly and drawing his conclusions, he remarked that the white man has ideas, the Indian has visions. The true anarchism is the chaos of ideas that must compete against each other without having a context in which relationships can be established between them. Feyerabend does not like this kind of anarchism; he wishes to break the stranglehold of doctrine and preconceived results that at present characterizes Western science. He sees a greater vision of human knowledge that incorporates the many insights of human cultures and provides a context for our better understanding of the planet and its history. This vision is badly needed, and, I believe, Feyerabend will eventually move from epistemology to metaphysics and offer it to us.

NOTES

1. Alfred North Whitehead, *Adventures of Ideas* (New York: Macmillan, 1933), p. 224.
2. Jedidiah Morse, *A Report to the Secretary of War on Indian Affairs* (1822), p. 207.
3. Whitehead, *Adventures of Ideas*, p. 96.
4. Thomas S. Kuhn, *The Structure of Scientific Revolutions* (Chicago: University of Chicago Press, 1962), p. 90.
5. Paul Feyerabend, *Science in a Free Society* (New York: LNB, 1978), p. 88.
6. Whitehead, *Adventures of Ideas*, p. 66.
7. Paul Feyerabend, *Against Method* (New York: Shocken Books, 1975), p. 68.
8. Alfred North Whitehead, *Science and the Modern World* (New York: The Free Press, 1925, 1967), pp. 48-49.
9. Kuhn, *The Structure of Scientific Revolutions*, pp. 122-123.
10. Ibid.
11. Ibid., p. 191.
12. Ibid., pp. 167-168.
13. Feyerabend, *Against Method*, pp. 306-307.
14. Kuhn, *The Structure of Scientific Revolutions*, p. 24.
15. Feyerabend, *Against Method*, p. 298.
16. Feyerabend, *Science in a Free Society*, p. 87.

2

THE TRICKSTER AND THE MESSIAH

▼▼▼▼

More than a quarter of a century ago Paul Radin published his study of the Winnebago trickster myths,[1] a work that complemented his earlier works *Primitive Man as Philosopher*[2] and *The World of Primitive Man.*[3] In his prefatory note, Radin suggested that the best approach to understanding this body of literature was psychological, arguing that "only if we view it as primarily such, as an attempt by man to solve his problems inward and outward, does the figure of Trickster become intelligible and meaningful."[4] Parts 4 and 5 of *The Trickster* consisted of invited commentaries by Karl Kerenyi and Carl Jung, respectively, and it is this essay of Carl Jung's, "On the Psychology of the Trickster-Figure," that suggests and needs further commentary.

Jung, of course, was responding to the materials gathered by Radin, although he had already published some of his major alchemical studies a decade earlier that involved Mercurius the European Trickster figure.[5] Jung's commentary, therefore, is limited by both the sparsity of Radin's vision and the necessity to conform his interpretation of the Trickster to a format that illuminates the Winnebago data while making a connection with the larger and more easily documented European tradition. Nevertheless, Jung's comments on the Trickster are important because they raise important questions regarding the unity of human experience and the possibility of using doctrines of interpretation and therapeutic techniques derived almost wholly from

the symbols and experiences of one cultural tradition in nonconform-
ing communities and traditions. Jung's remarks suggest a unity of human experience underlying the various separate cultural expressions.

Jung describes the Trickster as

> *a primitive "cosmic" being of divine-animal nature. On the
> one hand superior to man because of his superhuman quali-
> ties, and on the other hand inferior to him because of his
> unreason and unconsciousness. He is no match for the animals
> either, because of his extraordinary clumsiness and lack of
> instinct. These defects are the marks of his human nature,
> which is not so well adapted to the environment as the
> animal's but, instead, has prospects of a much higher develop-
> ment of consciousness based on a considerable eagerness to
> learn, as is duly emphasized in the myth.*[6]

This combination of divine–human characteristics led Jung to see
the Trickster as

> *a forerunner of the saviour, and, like him, God, man, animal
> at once. He is both subhuman and superhuman, a bestial and
> divine being, whose chief and most alarming characteristic is
> his unconsciousness. Because of it he is deserted by his
> (evidently human) companions, which seems to indicate that
> he has fallen below their level of consciousness. He is so
> unconscious of himself that his body is not a unity, and his
> two arms fight each other.*[7]

Jung thus chooses the most sublime aspect of the Trickster figure, a
cosmically important savior figure, on which to base his commentary. Although cosmic, the Trickster has important consequences for
human society. Radin suggests that the civilizing process really begins within the framework of the Trickster myth, relying on the Indian traditions of the Pacific Northwest that attribute the origin of
crafts to the Trickster figure, generally Raven or Coyote. During the
civilizing process, "the marks of deepest unconsciousness fall away
from him; instead of acting in a brutal, savage, stupid and senseless
fashion, the trickster's behaviour towards the end of the cycle becomes quite useful and sensible."[8] Jung describes the Trickster as a

psychologem, "an archetypal psychic structure of extreme antiquity. In his clearest manifestations he is a faithful reflection of an absolutely undifferentiated human consciousness, corresponding to a psyche that has hardly left the animal level."[9]

Perhaps the most telling comment Jung makes regarding the nature of the Trickster concerns the function of the myth in the psychic processes of the human mind. "If, at the end of the trickster myth," he notes, "the saviour is hinted at, this comforting premonition or hope means that some calamity or other has happened and been consciously understood. Only out of recognition can the longing for a saviour arise—in other words the recognition and unavoidable integration of the shadow create such a harrowing situation that nobody but a saviour can undo the tangled web of fate."[10]

It is probably not possible, therefore, to separate out the various elements of the Trickster myth and function one from another to insist that Jung saw in the Trickster a substantial prefiguring of the Messiah in a completely cosmic sense. At least we cannot substantiate the idea that the Trickster figure, in its evolution and development, leads directly to the theological Messiah who finds incarnation in human history and provides the psychological archetype for individual salvation.

Jung and Radin seem to suggest that the Trickster represents unstructured primordial unconsciousness as it experiences a civilizing process and that the ultimate, if distant, goal of this process is the emergence of the Messiah who makes the subsequent development of consciousness meaningful. Essentially, this figure is a form of psychological evolutionism that must certainly presume that, apart from cultural and historical variants, most individuals would produce the same basic psychological complexes and understandings in their emotional lives. Indeed, the benefit of Jungian psychology as opposed to other interpretations appears to be that it can more easily resolve crises that occur at midlife and that involve questions of maturity and meaning. Whether or not Jung wished the Trickster-Messiah figure to occupy a prominent place in his pantheon of archetypal figures, it would seem that his system is woefully lacking without it if we assume that Jung's system points toward adult maturity.

The evolutionary format for interpretation of any system of thought or body of data, however, presumes an ignorance and lack of sophistication at the point of origin, with a corresponding increase in complexity, meaning, and value as the process continues. There is certainly a modernistic value judgment involved in the evolutionary framework, and this judgment generally involves an uncritical approval of present knowledge along with an equally uncritical derogation of past knowledge. It further suggests that, apart from cultural quirks and historical accidents, each human society would inevitably march along a civilized incline the goal of which would be a scientific, technological society holding the same beliefs and adhering to the same interpretation of the world as that which we presently enjoy.

There is simply no basis for this belief other than cultural bias or preference—or a lack of a well-rounded education in the humanities. Some thinkers have attempted to avoid this obvious conclusion—Toynbee[11] noting the presence of eight major religions and Niels Bohr[12] suggesting that each human cultural tradition represents a different mode of social reality. Although Jung appears to hold to an evolutionary interpretation in his Trickster figure, he elsewhere recognizes the problem of easy classification in familiar evolutionary terms. In his essay "The Role of the Unconscious," Jung notes,

> *The question of the relations between conscious and unconscious is not a special question, but one which is bound up in the most intimate way with our history, with the present time, and with our view of the world. Very many things are unconscious for us only because our view of the world allows them no room; because by education and training we have never come to grips with them, and, whenever they came to consciousness as occasional fantasies, have instantly suppressed them. The borderline between conscious and unconscious is in large measure determined by our view of the world.* "[13]

I need not add that our view of the world is an inherited view for the most part transmitted to us by elders and relatives, and later by peers, and for the majority of us remains almost wholly unexamined.

The Trickster, therefore, cannot really represent the process of civilizing or the emergence from the unconscious because we cannot determine with any degree of accuracy exactly where the unconscious and the conscious are tangent to each other, or have intimate relations one with another. It is better, in this respect, to examine the two traditions, European and North American Indian, to see the context in which the Trickster of each arose and to determine what social conditions must have participated in the crystallization of the cycle of myths and ceremonies that we have in modern times identified with the Trickster.

Paul Radin's earlier works suggest that he had begun to differentiate between so-called primitive societies on the one hand and major civilizations on the other and was leaning favorably toward primitive societies. In discussing the larger, more sophisticated ancient civilizations, Radin noted that "one of the fundamental traits of these major civilizations was their essential instability, the frequent social-economic crises through which they passed and the amazing vitality of two somewhat contradictory fictions. The first was to the effect that there has never been any instability or change and the second that stability existed eternally, but in the afterworld not in this."[14] There would seem to be plenty of reason for a savior in these major civilizations, and it would certainly appear that achieving a stable mental condition was a major accomplishment.

Radin described the state of aboriginal society in somewhat more positive terms:

> *If one were asked to state briefly and succinctly what are the outstanding positive features of aboriginal civilizations, I, for one, would have no hesitation in answering that there are three: the respect for the individual, irrespective of age or sex; the amazing degree of social and political integration achieved by them; and the existence there of a concept of personal security which transcends all governmental forms and all tribal and group interests and conflicts.*[15]

Perhaps a better form of social existence can be conceived, but surely no greater form can be realized than what we see in aboriginal societies. Why, then, would they create or discern a Trickster figure that attempted to deal with the civilizing process or that projected a messiah to rescue them from the problems of their social condition? As between the two forms of social existence, certainly we can conclude that the major civilizations, the societies in which modern society finds its historical and emotional roots, had great need of both a process of socialization and a messiah, whereas aboriginal societies had no real need of either.

There is a further aspect of this problem that merits our attention. Robert Bellah, in his intriguing essay "Religious Evolution," notes that one of the profound facts of religious history is "the emergence in the first millennium B.C. all across the Old World, at least in centers of high culture, of the phenomenon of religious rejection of the world characterized by an extremely negative evaluation of man and society and the exaltation of another realm of reality as alone true and infinitely valuable."[16] Bellah emphasizes this point in his essay but does not seem to realize the importance of his insight:

> *I want to concentrate on the fact that they were all in some sense rejections, and that world rejection is characteristic of a long and important period of religious history. I want to insist on this fact because I want to contrast it with an equally striking fact, namely the virtual absence of world rejection in primitive religions, in religion prior to the first millennium B.C. and in the modern world.*[17]

Complex, highly organized, sophisticated, scientific—however we characterize the larger civilizations—we see that they have both social-political-economic instability and a negative view of the world, which suggests that the ultimately real and reliable is found far beyond sense perceptions, beyond, in fact, the world as we know and experience it. From this posture we can trace the subsequent development of modern society. We find the scientific frenzy to locate the ultimate constituent of reality, at least physical reality, and we also find the transference of ultimate value religiously to a realm beyond anything we find here on earth. Both the scientific and religious postures produce an extreme individualism, the solitary atomic structure that constitutes the ultimate substrata of our physical world and the solitary sinner who needs first religious salvation and now in our time, therapy. Neither of these beliefs is found as a dominant motif in aboriginal societies and in a majority of so-called primitive societies cannot be found anywhere.

Bellah, on the contrary, says,

> *Primitive religions are on the whole oriented to a single cosmos; they know nothing of a wholly different world relative to which the actual world is utterly devoid of value. They are*

*concerned with the maintenance of personal, social, and
cosmic harmony and with attaining specific goods—rain,
harvest, children, health—as men have always been. But the
overriding goal of salvation that dominates the world rejecting
religions is almost absent in primitive religion, and life after
death tends to be a shadowy semi-existence in some vaguely
designated place in the single world.*[18]

For aboriginal peoples, there is not only no need for a messiah, there
is really no place for him in the cosmos. Whatever interpretation we
may place on the data collected by Radin and discussed by Jung, we
cannot validly find the Trickster as a prefigured messiah except insofar as the figure occurs in the Western cultural tradition. Gathering
together all the Trickster data without regard for the cultural context in
which it originates, then, is a hazardous if not foolish thing to do.

Unfortunately, the Radin–Jung description of the Trickster
myths has become the predominant interpretation of scholars dealing with these data. Mac Winscott Ricketts, in an article in *History
of Religion* entitled "The North American Trickster," adopts the orthodox stance in dealing with this material. "The real religious quest of
man," Ricketts suggests, "is to obtain omniscience, and through it,
omnipotence. The various religions of the world are the many indi-
rect pathways to that goal; the way of the trickster is the direct oath.
The trickster does not yield to the temptation to turn aside to worship
strange gods, but he holds sacred only the struggle itself and the
sum of its past victories: culture, the world-as-it-is, and the world as
it has been arranged and understood by man."[19] This definition of
religion may be Promethean, but it certainly has no relationship to
the North American Indian.

Ricketts notes, "While the trickster is not worshipped, his myths
are. Not the trickster as a living being, but the deeds he does and
what they reveal about man and the world, are the sacred reality.
This is because the trickster is Man Himself, while his actions as
related in the myths disclose man transcending himself."[20] Ricketts
here chooses a particularly inadequate word, "transcendence," to
describe a psychological process. The word implies reaching another
level of reality, one with more substance than that previously experienced. In the North American Indian tradition such generalities can
certainly not be used with any degree of accuracy because individuals

do not transcend themselves, they simply learn additional things about the single reality that confronts them.

Ricketts isolates the factors he considers integral to the Trickster mythology.

> *The essential elements in the structure of the myth figure are these: (a) he is a trickster, a worldly being of uncertain origin who lives by his wits and is often injured and embarrassed by his foolish imitations and pranks, yet who never takes himself too seriously and never admits defeat; (b) he is a transformer, a being of myth times who goes about doing things that set the pattern and form of the world for all time, acting customarily without apparent plan or forethought, and leaving the world as it is today, having thus prepared it for mankind, his "children"; and (c) he is a culture hero, who, unassisted, risks his life and limb in daring entanglements with supernatural powers in order that the world may be a better place for those who are to come."[21]*

There are certainly other aspects of the American Indian Trickster but these major chords of the trickster symphony are sufficient to cover the areas with which we are concerned.

We should deal with these aspects of the trickster in reverse order, as they are more easily comprehended by moving from the immediate cultural context to the more philosophical and abstract conceptions. First, although some Indian traditions attribute the origin of some techniques and crafts to a Trickster figure, the evidence is equally strong, if not stronger, that humans received special knowledge of their environment and a good deal of their immediate physical cultural practices from plants and animals who revealed themselves or through contact with other peoples. In the Pacific Northwest where a significant number of Trickster stories credit Coyote or Raven with inventions, there are other traditions that suggest that new peoples moving into the area taught weaving and other crafts and that plants revealed their uses and purposes to specific Indian individuals in the course of tribal history. In other regions of the country stories dealing with cultural traits quite frequently specify how people learned how to do things. In very few of these cases is the Trickster figure credited with devising the specific trait.

Describing the Trickster as a culture hero in the old classical sense is, I suspect, a mistake made through erroneous generalization. I suggest that a classification of crafts, plants and animals, and other quasi-technological adaptations to the immediate environment in any particular Indian tribe would show a clear and consistent tradition of receiving information from plants and animals, either in visions or in unique daily experiences, and the number of cultural aspects that are attributed to the Trickster is actually far fewer than Radin or Ricketts would admit. In this sense the Trickster is a convenient symbol in which ignorance can be safely deposited, and hence things of cultural importance attributed to him simply had no other historical or social explanation.

The Trickster as transformer is more difficult to describe. Radin suggests that we are dealing actually with two distinct concepts: "the supreme deity, creator of all things, beneficent and ethical, unapproachable directly and taking but little interest in the world after he has created it; and the Transformer, the establisher of the present order of things, utterly nonethical, only incidentally and inconsistently beneficent, approachable, and directly intervening in a very human way in the affairs of the world."[22] When we look specifically at the role and accomplishments of the Transformer, we find that his function was to change specific parts of the world, generally in an effort to reestablish order after what appears to be a catastrophic event, rather than to work in the capacity of a demiurge shaping the physical world that we know from daily experience.

Involved in the conception of the Transformer is the Indian idea of worlds and world cycles. Whereas history in a cosmic sense moves from a specific point of creation toward an undetermined future, many tribes speak either of periodic renewal in which each physical version of the planet differs considerably from its predecessor or of periodic cleansing of the planet with some disruption of landscape and destruction of life followed by the appearance of new life-forms and new networks of responsibility. Western thinkers have generally frowned on this interpretation of planetary history, preferring to believe that planetary history has experienced one continuous and progressive movement from the creation or origination of the cosmos until the present. There does not seem to be much basis for this belief other than personal preference and cultural orientation, and the spate of articles that have appeared in recent times attempting to make the catastrophic theories of Immanuel Velikovsky respectable by suggesting cometary interventions and meteoric collisions as an explanation of the extinction of flora and fauna at the end of certain geologic periods suggests that the Western view of continuous and uniform planetary existence is giving way to a view more compatible with Indian tribal views and beliefs.

The Transformer phase of Trickster mythology, then, suggests the attribution to a personal force or entity of the power to bring order out of a chaos that has disrupted a previously ordered creation. Depending on the number of worlds that each tribal tradition recalls, we find a significant variance in the work of the Transformer and the myths attached to the beings who bring order. The Hopi twins who grasp the poles of the planet while it is in deep, dark, and cold space, frozen as it were, and slowly begin to rotate the planet on its axis must testify to a dimly remembered physical fact about our earth that we cannot yet comprehend. At any rate, I believe that the overwhelming number of stories attributed to the Trickster as Transformer can be placed within a specific geographic context and serve to explain why a certain landscape is *now* the way it is.

Ricketts's final, albeit first, category of Trickster functions is that of the Trickster himself—the worldly being of uncertain origin who lives by his wits and who is often embarrassed. This version is one with which I am more familiar as the Sioux Iktomi stories deal quite heavily with the Spider who seeks shortcuts and almost always becomes the butt of laughter, human, plant, and animal. I suggest that this aspect of Trickster tales is designed to demonstrate the inevitability of cosmic law and teach humility and other virtues by showing the consequences of attempting to be what one is not supposed to be. Here I would like to refer to an old observation on Indian education made by John Heckewelder, who published the "Account of the History, Manners, and Customs of the Indian Nations who once inhabited Pennsylvania and the neighboring States" in 1818. I think, with some variations, that the sequence and content of this education can be found in almost every tribal tradition. Being the major explanation of the purpose of life, and occurring in societies that had the stability and benign outlook that Radin finds in tribal societies and which Bellah confirms, this message must have made a powerful impression on Indian children and must have influenced them and directed them for the major part of their lives.

*The first step that parents take towards the education of
their children, is to prepare them for future happiness, by
impressing upon their tender minds, that they are indebted for
their existence to a great, good and benevolent Spirit, who not
only has given them life, but has ordained them for certain
great purposes.*

*That he has given them a fertile extensive country well
stocked with game of every kind for their subsistence, and that
by one of his inferior spirits he has also sent down to them
from above corn, pumpkins, squashes, beans and other
vegetables for their nourishment; all which blessings their
ancestors have enjoyed for a great number of ages.*

*That this great Spirit looks down upon the Indians to see
whether they are grateful to him and make him a due return
for the many benefits he has bestowed, and therefore that it is
their duty to show their thankfulness by worshipping him,
and doing that which is pleasing in his sight.*

*They are then told that their ancestors, who received all
this from the bands of the great Spirit, and lived in the enjoyment
of it, must have been informed of what would be most pleasing
to this good being, and of the manner in which his favour
could be most surely obtained, and they are directed to look
up for instruction to those who know all this, to learn from
them, and revere them for their wisdom and the knowledge
which they possess; this creates in the children a strong
sentiment of respect for their elders, and a desire to follow
their advice and example.*

*Their young ambition is then excited by telling them that
they were made the superiors of all other creatures, and are to
have power over them; great pains are taken to make this
feeling take an early root, and it becomes in fact their ruling
passion through life; for no pains are spared to instill in them
that by following the advice of the most admired and extolled
hunter, trapper or warrior, they will at a future day acquire a
degree of fame and reputation, equal to that which he possesses;
that by submitting to the counsels of the aged, the chiefs, the men
superior in wisdom, they may also rise to glory, and be called
Wisemen, an honorable title, to which no Indian is indifferent.*

> *When this first and most important lesson is thought to be*
> *sufficiently impressed upon children's minds, the parents next*
> *proceed to make them sensible of the distinction between good*
> *and evil; they tell them that there are good actions and bad*
> *actions, both equally open to them to do or commit; that good*
> *acts are pleasing to the good Spirit which gave them their*
> *existence, and that on the contrary, all that is bad proceeds from*
> *the bad spirit who has given them nothing, and who cannot*
> *give them any thing that is good, because he has it not.*[23]

Heckewelder has obviously mixed some Christian dogma with his observations of Indian education. There are few tribes, for example, that would teach that humans are superior to animals, almost every tribe believing that each species forms a family or a people and has a specific relationship to humans, who merely constitute another species.

Heckewelder notes,

> *When this instruction is given in the form of precepts, it must*
> *not be supposed that it is done in an authoritative or forbidding*
> *tone, but, on the contrary, in the gentlest and most persuasive*
> *manner: nor is the parent's authority ever supported by harsh*
> *or compulsive means; no whips, no punishments, no threats*
> *are ever used to enforce commands or compel obedience. The*
> *child's pride is the feeling to which an appeal is made, which*
> *proves successful in almost every instance.*[24]

If pride is the chief emotional feeling used in the education of children, then it would follow that appearing foolish in the eyes of the community would be the most dreadful experience a young child could have. I suggest, then, that the primary use of Trickster tales is to demonstrate the uniform nature of the physical world and its laws and to show that disobedience of natural laws produces foolishness and opens a person to ridicule.

Ricketts seems to be undecided on this point. He notes,

> *If a man tries to do things for which he was never intended,*
> *the result can be only that he will make a fool of himself and*
> *probably get hurt in the process. Of course the trickster, like*

*man, never learns this lesson; but he keeps on trying again
and again to do everything that others can do: get food by
slicing his thigh like the bear, peck worms out of tree trunks
like the woodpecker, make his children to be spotted like the
deer's fawns, eat grass like the bison, etc.*[25]

But Ricketts also shifts his focus and says, "In laughing at the incredible antics of the trickster, the people laugh at themselves. The myths of the trickster enabled the Indians to laugh off their failures in hunting, in fighting, in romance, and in combatting the limitations imposed upon them by their environment, since they saw in the trickster how foolish man is, and how useless it is to take life too seriously."[26]

This latter explanation must have originated in Ricketts's Trickster mentality as tribal traditions have a multitude of stories dealing with hunting, fighting, romance, and lands that deal not with the foolishness of man but with the presence of a variety of spirits, powers, and prophecies designed to illustrate real-life experiences in these situations. Indeed, most of the stories deal with precise medicines and prophecies that enable nonparticipants to deal with adversity and failure with even more precision and specificity than they did before. Although Indians may use ridicule and stories to ensure personal and communal humility, it is doubtful that Trickster stories were sufficiently precise to accomplish this goal. Residence in an Indian community, even today, will quickly educate a person on the use of stories to maintain social control and standards. Believe me, Trickster tales are the least of a person's worries. Indians hone right in on a person's specific feats and personal quirks and make their point with considerable precision.

The suggestion, then, that the Trickster foreshadows the Messiah is applicable only to the European tradition, and however it is applied there and whatever the apparent parallels, the two traditions and the Trickster symbol or archetype cannot be seen as identical. More important for our discussion is the obvious question regarding the Messiah. Why do the Western European peoples, and by extension before them the Near Eastern peoples, need such a figure? Why is their appraisal of the physical world a negative one? Why do their societies suffer such perennial and continuing crises? Why do they insist on believing that ultimate reality is contained in another, almost unimaginable realm beyond the senses and often beyond the span of human life?

Western religion and many of its predecessors seem to conceive the world as a massive cosmic trial court. Some unpardon-
able cosmic sin has been committed and the world and its people
are eternally damned. In many of these religions a great flood is
sent to purge the earth, and, although this divine intervention would
seem to argue against predestination and the uniformity of cosmic
process, history continues apace toward a mythical and wholly
unfamiliar conclusion that is itself characterized by extreme cosmic
physical disruption. Then there is no more physical world, salvation
is achieved, the elect dwell with the deity, and, depending on the
sect, the damned suffer eternal torture and punishment.

American Indians have this flood and other planetary catastrophes also. The people existing before the flood or other destruction
are often characterized as wicked also. Yet within the smaller dimensions of planetary history, new ceremonies are given, new peoples,
plants, and animals emerge, and laws and ways of life are articulated. Whatever evil existed is either purged or has been sublimated
and is restricted to the former world. The world, the people, and the
ceremonies begin anew and predictions concerning the end of that
world almost always describe the erosion of peoplehood, the cessa-
tion of ceremonies and their powers, and the consequent exhaustion
of possibilities within the world age. Here we have a fully applicable
understanding of entropy that is not regarded as good or evil but
simply a part of cosmic process.

When we examine psychoanalytic theory the burning question
that should occupy our time should concern where the complex of
ideas that constitute Western civilization originated, how they originated, and whether they have any realistic correspondence to what
we can observe and experience in nature. I think they do not correspond, and I wonder quite often and quite profoundly if the Western psyche has been interfered with at some remote time in planetary
history.

Looking at all of planetary history and the many experiences
of the great variety of peoples who have emerged, flourished, and
expired, I sometimes feel that the natural peoples of this planet
have been invaded by alien forces from outside and that, although
these visitors must have long since departed or expired, Western
peoples have never been able to overcome the shock or training that
these aliens impressed on them.

I suggest this possibility because the Messiah, unlike the North American Indian Trickster, comes on the clouds and takes the faithful to a blessed land indescribably different from anything we have here. I therefore conclude this examination with the suggestion that Western culture, including its religious tradition and its derivative schools of psychology, is a long-enduring cargo cult the origins of which must be vigorously uncovered and understood so that the schizophrenia it represents can be finally healed.

NOTES

1. Paul Radin, *The Trickster* (New York: Philosophical Library, 1956).
2. Paul Radin, *Primitive Man as Philosopher* (New York: Dover, 1957).
3. Paul Radin, *The World of Primitive Man* (New York: Grove Press, 1953).
4. Radin, *The Trickster*, p. x.
5. "Paracelsus as a Spiritual Phenomenon" was published in 1942; "The Spirit Mercurius" was published in 1918.
6. C. G. Jung, "On the Psychology of the Trickster-Figure," in *The Archetypes and the Collective Unconscious*. Collected Works, vol. 9, i (Princeton, N.J.: Princeton University Press, 1959), p. 264.
7. Ibid., p. 263.
8. Ibid., p. 266.
9. Ibid., p. 260.
10. Ibid., p. 271.
11. Arnold Toynbee, *An Historian's Approach to Religion* (New York: Oxford University Press, 1956), p. 141
12 As cited in Claude Lévi-Strauss, *Structural Anthropology* (New York: Harper Torchbooks, 1963), pp. 295-296.
13. C. G. Jung, "The Role of the Unconscious," in *Civilization in Transition*. Collected Works, vol. 10 (Princeton, N.J.: Princeton University Press, 1970) p. 27.
14. Radin, *The World of Primitive Man*, pp. 7-8.
15. Ibid. p. 11.
16. Robert Bellah, *Beyond Belief* (New York: Harper & Row, 1970), p. 22.
17. Ibid., p. 23.
18. Ibid.
19. Mac Winscott Ricketts, "The North American Trickster," *History of Religions*, vol. 5, no. 2 (Winter 1966), p. 347.
20. Ibid., p. 344.
21. Ibid., p. 343.
22. Radin, *Primitive Man as Philosopher*, p. 347.
23. John Heckewelder, *History, Manners, and Customs of the Indian Nations* (New York: Arno Press, 1971), pp. 113-114.
24. Ibid., p 115.
25. Ricketts, "The North American Trickster," p. 338.
26. Ibid., p. 347.

3

RELATIVITY, RELATEDNESS, AND REALITY

▼▼▼▼

It was not so long ago that Newtonian physics and mathematics described a world of absolute space, time, and matter and people believed that understanding the universe completely was simply a matter of policing up the obscure subjects that had not received much attention in the past. Then the Michaelson-Morley experiments to detect and measure, if possible, the "ether" that was thought to exist between large bodies in the solar systems returned a blank and thinkers went back to their solitude to try to understand what this failure actually meant for cosmology—and by extension for science itself.

The result of deliberations by many of the best minds of the age was a theory put forth by Albert Einstein, then a patent clerk in Germany, and certainly not a luminary of the academic establishment. Einstein's thesis, viewed from our present perspective, is hardly revolutionary and probably just a simple corrective to the centuries of belief that human beings could know the innermost workings of the larger cosmos by examining phenomena on one tiny planet on the edge of a galaxy.

Space, time, and matter, Einstein argued, are concepts whose measurement should be in relationship to the context in which they are to be used. That is to say, these ideas are not part of the eternal structure of the universe in and of themselves but are how we describe this universe, and therefore as we do have experiences, we can use these ideas and they have substance as long as we remember that we are part of the process of gathering information.

Nearly three generations have been required to work through the implications of relativity, and physics and mathematics have prospered immensely in their ability to probe the micro and macro levels of cosmic existence once freed from the idea of absolute time and space. Other "sciences" have not fared as well because many of their practitioners adopted the idea that everything was "relative," which is to say, there is no absolute truth or description of reality, it all depends on the action of the observer and the nature of the experiment or investigation. In the social sciences in particular, the idea of including the observer meant a reduction of certainty almost to the point of personal preference. Americans, as we are likely to do, have reduced relativity to a form of psychobabble.

WE ARE ALL RELATIVES

A positive by-product of the entrenchment of relativity in the nonmathematical sciences and disciplines has been the willingness of people to look at non-Western cultures and give them a measure of respect for their knowledge of the natural world. In a previous article I reviewed the tendency of pioneer thinkers to begin to bring separate fields of inquiry together by merging ideas and concepts and in effect create new sciences that weld together the bodies of knowledge that should not have been separated in the first place. Strangely, there has been very little attention paid to Indian methodologies for gathering data, and, consequently, the movement is primarily an ad hoc, personal preference way of gathering new ideas and attempting to weld them to existing bodies of knowledge. We cannot expect fundamental change in the manner in which Western scientists interpret their data until massive changes in individual items occur and a paradigm shift is forced by the failure of the established doctrines in the field to explain the materials.

The Indian perspective of the natural world is not subject to this limitation because it already has a fundamental principle of interpretation/observation that pervades everything that Indians think or experience. Thus verification of existing knowledge and the addition of new knowledge is simply a matter of adding to the already considerable body of information that Indians possess. An unfortunate aspect of the Indian knowledge is that so much data have been lost in the last century as Indians have been prevented from roaming freely over their traditional homelands, gathering plants and animals for food and ceremonies, and performing those ceremonies that ensured the prosperity of the earth and its life-forms. Nevertheless, the information that we formerly had remains available to us if we can return to the traditional manner in which we related to lands and life.

The Indian principle of interpretation/observation is simplicity itself: "We are all relatives." Most Indians hear this phrase thousands of times a year as they attend or perform ceremonies, and for many Indians without an ongoing ritual life, the phrase seems to be simply a liturgical blessing that includes all other forms of life in human ceremonial activities. But this phrase is very important as a practical methodological tool for investigating the natural world and drawing conclusions about it that can serve as guides for understanding nature and living comfortably within it.

"We are all relatives" when taken as a methodological tool for obtaining knowledge means that we observe the natural world by looking for relationships between various things in it. That is to say, everything in the natural world has relationships with every other thing and the total set of relationships makes up the natural world as we experience it. This concept is simply the relativity concept as applied to a universe that people experience as alive and not as dead or inert. Thus Indians knew that stones were the perfect beings because they were self-contained entities that had resolved their social relationships and possessed great knowledge about how every other entity, and every species, should live. Stones had mobility but did not need to use it. Every other being had mobility and needed, in some specific manner, to use it in relationships.

HARVEST BY OBSERVATION

Materials illustrating kinds of relationships are plentiful, but it is necessary when speaking to them to ponder their meaning very seriously in order to understand the body of knowledge that they represent. I will use some examples from the Plains, but the same kind of demonstrative process could be done by using the knowledge of the Pacific Northwest tribes, the desert tribes of the Southwest, and the woodlands tribes of the eastern United States. It is my hope that the present generation of Indian students will adopt some version of this methodology as they are studying Western science, particularly social and biological science, and leapfrog into prominence in their fields by writing and teaching from an Indian perspective. In this way science will move very quickly into a more intelligent understanding of the natural world.

The tribes who lived along the Missouri River and its tributaries grew corn and vegetables but also conducted a summer hunt for buffalo, deer and antelope. It was their practice to plant the crops, do one hoeing to reduce the weeds and grasses around the corn hills, and then depart for the high plains and Rocky Mountains for July and August to prepare meat for the winter. We might think there was great concern about the condition of the corn crops as corn would provide the major food supply during the winter. But the tribes had already perceived plant relationships and so had what we might call "indicator plants" that told them how their corn was coming.

The Pawnees simply examined the seed pods of the milkweed, and when these pods had reached a certain condition and were at maturity, they packed up everything and headed for home, arriving in time to harvest their corn and hold a corn dance. At first glance this information seems like an interesting tidbit but with nothing to do with relatedness or relativity. In fact, the Pawnee had been able to discern, through observation or by information given to them in a ceremony, that corn and milkweed had about the same growing season. To be more precise, milkweed was a bit faster growing than corn because it would take several weeks to return to their villages after having examined the milkweed. Western science might run across the similarity between the two plants, but the chances of making the linkage and being able to use it predictively for practical purposes are minimal.

Standing Bear said, "Away from the woods grew the sand cherries on little low shrubs. Around and over the sand hills, and patches so barren that not a blade of grass grew, these bushes flourished, yielding a luscious fruit which we were very careful in gathering. We picked this fruit only against the wind, for if we stood with our body odors going toward the fruit its flavor was destroyed." Here we see that scope of relatedness in a surprising context. Unquestionably, we have a human-plant relationship but one in which the human is the less sensitive participant. The human had to be particularly aware of the bush and pay unusual respect to it in order to use its fruit.

I would be curious to learn how an anthropologist or botanist trained in Western science would explain how the Sioux discovered this fact of plant life. People would have to harvest the fruit for a reasonably long time in order to have enough experiences with it to formulate the most constructive way to relate to the bush. But what on earth would inspire anyone to look into the direction of the wind when picking fruit? Annual harvests would occur for a very short time each summer. The variance in rain, heat, and other climatic factors would appear to be so much more important in determining the condition of the fruit that it would seem unlikely that anyone could identify human body odor as the critical factor in the relationship. Yet the Sioux were able to identify this element from everything else that needed to be considered.

Some information must have come directly from observations made by the people, and once this knowledge was gained, it was put to good use. Standing Bear noted that gophers and other small animals cached their food for the winter and

> *our women knew the likely places of these caches, usually near a low bank, and went hunting for them with long, sharp-pointed sticks. They poked in the ground until they came to a soft spot in the earth, and there, ten or twelve inches under the soil and carefully covered with fine dry shredded grass, would be a nice lot of vegetables lying in a heap as fresh as when they were gathered. Some of these caches would lie three feet in diameter and would hold as much as one person could carry.*

I suppose it is not good public relations to recount how the Indians used to steal from the gophers, but from this bit of information we can derive two things. First, Indians had the knowledge of the natural world necessary to sustain themselves in spite of any misfortune that might befall them. Thus a person lost on the prairie would not starve because of this knowledge. Second, and more important, by watching how the animals preserved food, the people learned that they could use the same techniques to preserve their foods. Standing Bear says that the gopher caches were "models of neatness. . . . There would be no sign of the tops and roots, both being cut clean from the vegetable, whereas when the women stored they left both attached, tying bunches together by the long string-like roots." The Indians, of course, did not have large bags and boxes for carrying vegetables and therefore had to keep the roots so they could tie the food to poles and harnesses in order to carry them.

BUFFALO, BULRUSHES, AND SUNFLOWERS

Not all information about the natural world came as a result of careful observation based on the principle of relatedness. If we greatly expand our understanding of the sense of being relatives, we discover that plants, birds, and animals often gave specific information to the people. Standing Bear described one such instance: "A food that had an interesting history for us was the tall plant that grew in the swamps, commonly called the bulrush. The duck, who brought many good plants and roots to the tribe, told the Duck Dreamer medicine-man about it and named it psa. In the early spring and summer we welcomed this plant, which was pulled up by the roots, and the white part eaten like celery." Here is a bird-human relationship that involves information about the plant and its use. We do not know what the subsequent plant-human relationship was or might have become, but we can assume that at some point the tribe had more knowledge than what Standing Bear relates.

An observation that always struck me as critically important for understanding the plant and animal relationship, although I have no good explanation for it, regarded the buffalo and the sunflower. I briefly mentioned this behavior in my previous article, and I would like to expand my comments on it. Standing Bear wrote, "The buffalo loved the simple and odorless sunflower just as did the Lakota. These great beasts wandered through the sunflower fields, wallowing their heads among them. Sometimes they uprooted the plants and wound them about their backs, letting sprays dangle from their left horns."

I suspect that we have here an observation of a buffalo ceremonial, perhaps even the buffalo version of the Sun Dance performed by human beings. Or we may have a form of buffalo recreation. There is no question that this kind of behavior enabled the sunflower seeds to be scattered over a much greater distance than they would otherwise be able to reach, but the benefit to the buffalo, other than enjoyment, was not explained. Nevertheless, we have to recognize that the buffalo, bear, and the cottonwood tree were the three dominant nonhuman entities on the Great Plains, that they engaged in purposeful action, and that they dominated even the ceremonial relationships of humans. Therefore, it is highly probable that we have in this behavior a much deeper meaning than we can presently explain.

These examples are only the anecdotal data that are most easily retrieved today in a library. Information about the buffalo could be multiplied a thousandfold by talking with the people who are now raising buffalo and are now coming back to a knowledge of this animal. At a recent meeting of the Intertribal Bison Cooperative in Rapid City, speaker after speaker related observations on the intelligence and knowledge of this animal, affirming in many instances information that had been passed down in the oral tradition but never verified by the Sioux people because of being on the reservation for the last 120 years. Each speaker at this training session, however, once again confirmed the ancient understanding that these creatures are more like humans in their behavior than they are like other animals if you know how to interpret their behavior.

REALITY BY THE SENSES

The theory of relativity dislodged Western science in its belief that humans could not obtain absolute truth about the constitution and processes of the natural world. What this theory really did was eliminate the naive belief that by using one particular methodology, that of reducing everything to mechanical form, we could completely understand the world around us. This old belief saw reality as something beyond our senses and means of apprehension, and Western people have held this belief since the time of the Greek philosophers. For American Indians, however, it was not necessary to postulate the existence of an ideal world of perfect forms untouched by space or time or to suggest that space, time, and matter were inherent and absolute qualities of the physical world, which, when properly described in mathematical terms, could accurately explain the universe.

For most Indian tribes it was enough that they understood the manner in which living things behaved. Recognizing that the universe was alive, they began to accumulate knowledge about how every other entity behaved in various situations. Once this knowledge had begun to expand beyond the ability of anyone to remember, various people would come to be experts in how entities would behave in certain kinds of circumstances. Thus there was specialization somewhat like present academic subdivisions of bodies of knowledge, but the major principle of relatedness always remained as the critical interpretive method of understanding phenomena.

Reality for tribal peoples, as opposed to the reality sought by Western scientists, was the experience of the moment coupled with the interpretive scheme that had been woven together over the generations. If there were other dimensions to life—the religious experiences and dreams certainly indicated the presence of other ways of living, even other places—they were regarded as part of an organic whole and not as distinct from other experiences, times, and places in the same way that Western thinkers have always believed. Indians never had a need to posit the existence of a "real" reality beyond the senses because they felt that their senses gave them the essence of physical existence in enabling them to see how the other creatures behaved. Life in other dimensions was not thought to be much different from what had been experienced already.

GIVING SCIENCE A SENSE OF PURPOSE

The next generation of American Indians could radically transform scientific knowledge by grounding themselves in traditional knowledge about the world and demonstrating how everything is connected to everything else. Advocacy of this idea would involve showing how personality and a sense of purpose must become part of the knowledge that science confronts and understands. The present posture of most Western scientists is to deny any sense of purpose and direction to the world around us, believing that to do so would be to introduce mysticism and superstition. Yet what could be more superstitious than to believe that the world in which we live and where we have our most intimate personal experiences is not really trustworthy and that another, mathematical world exists that represents a true reality?

The idea of a relatedness of all things is not new, but it may seem to be outmoded to some Indian students who have been trained in Western scientific thinking. A good way to test this idea would be to talk with elders about what they know of plants, animals, and the natural world. If the student keeps the methodology of trying to relate bits of information to all elements in the scenario, that is to say, to regard information about plants as relevant to the birds and animals who use them and the location where they are found, there is no question that a great deal of important knowledge will be achieved. Taking these diverse bits of understanding and working them into the Western scientific format will be a little difficult at first, but eventually the student will discover that he or she is the possessor of a knowledge much broader, deeper, and more comprehensive than what is being taught in the classroom.

4

IF YOU THINK ABOUT IT,
YOU WILL SEE THAT IT IS TRUE

▼▼▼▼

The movement toward a "science of wholeness" depends in large measure on the ability of philosophers and scientific thinkers to move beyond their comfortable and presently accepted categories of arranging and interpreting data—to glimpse and grasp new unities of experience and knowledge. In order to do this, we must first ask fundamental questions about the goals of science. Do we wish to predict or describe? At what level do we wish to do either of these things? What does it mean to have knowledge that is applicable to the world around us and to have it arranged in a systematic manner? What systems are applicable to the different kinds of data derived at the different levels at which scientific inquiry can be conducted? How are data derived from a causative-dominated methodology to be combined with insights or information created by simple observation or intuitive visions?

Some Western thinkers have recently begun to examine the knowledge and insights that non-Western peoples had about the natural world. Part of this movement is a popular fad that romanticizes the primitive and his relationship to his pristine environment, but part is also a sincere attempt to reach out and gain new insights and perspectives.

Even with the flexible scientific paradigm of relativity and indeterminacy, there are strong indications that we have reached a dead end in many sciences and perhaps need new insights derived from other sources. So why not tribal knowledge?

Most recent efforts have been limited to gathering specific information: plant knowledge, fishing practices, forms of pottery making, and irrigation and forest management burning techniques. In psychoanalysis, the Jungians are exploring similarities between Western archetypal figures and tribal legends and folk heroes. More recent efforts have been made to gain knowledge of the use of plants that have certain curative powers. Jurisprudence is examining new kinds of mediation techniques and different victim compensation theories for minor offenses to replace retribution as the theoretical basis for criminal law, thereby even modifying the concept of the social contract itself. Many approaches are being taken to incorporate tribal values and knowledge into Western thought systems, but as yet no systematic comparison of tribal and scientific knowledge of the natural world has been made.

One reason that scientists examine non-Western knowledge on an ad hoc basis is the persistent belief held by Western intellectuals that non-Western peoples represent an earlier stage of their own cultural evolution—often that tribal cultures represent failed efforts to understand the natural world (the Incas had wheels, why didn't they make cars?). Non-Western knowledge is believed to originate from primitive efforts to explain a mysterious universe. In this view, the alleged failure of primitive/tribal man to control nature mechanically is evidence of his ignorance and his inability to conceive of abstract general principles and concepts.

Tribal methodologies for gathering information are believed to be "prescientific" in the sense that they are precausal and incapable of objective symbolic thought. This belief, as we shall see, is a dreadful stereotypical reading of the knowledge of non-Western peoples, and wholly incorrect.

In fact, tribal peoples are as systematic and philosophical as Western scientists in their efforts to understand the world around them. They simply use other kinds of data and have goals other than determining the mechanical functioning of things. A good way to determine the relevance of tribal knowledge and illustrate its potential for providing insights for the present body of scientific knowledge is to examine some of the knowledge of a particular tribe and discuss what they knew and how they gathered this information. I would like to take a few selections from a historical report on the philosophy of the Western Teton Sioux to illustrate my points.

THE INDIAN PERSPECTIVE

In late August 1919, A. McG. Beede, a missionary on the Standing
Rock Sioux Reservation in North Dakota, sent Melvin Gilmore, the
curator of the State Historical Society, a manuscript that discussed
the beliefs of the Western Teton Sioux. This paper is regarded as an
early and accurate account of the knowledge of the Western Sioux
and Chippewa Indians. Beede's discussions with the Indians reveal
their basic attitude regarding the knowledge they possessed and their
response to the scientific knowledge that Beede and his friend Harry
Boise discussed with them. The conversations have a startlingly
modern ring to them.

Beede wrote:

> The Western Sioux believed that each being, a rock for
> instance, is an actual community of persons with ample
> locomotion among themselves, and such locomotion not
> regarded as circumscribed or restricted, save as the maker
> (oicage) of the whole gives to each species his own sphere.
> And, they reasoned, this limitation is merely in body (tancan),
> the mind, intelligence, and spirit of each is privileged to
> range, through and blend with totality by gaining a right
> attitude toward Woniya (Spirit) . . . .[1]
>
> And, I should have said, the fact of a rock, or any object,
> being a community of locomotive persons, was based on, or
> concomitant with, the belief that not a few of their people
> actually had the ability to see into and through a rock
> discerning its make-up, similarly as we look into a community
> or grove of trees. I have known many Indians believing they
> possessed this ability—and not regarding it as anything
> remarkable—and there was no occasion for doubting their
> sincerity. . . .[2]
>
> Of course, the history of any people contains mythology
> (which is, perhaps, not quite so simple or invaluable as many
> a "scientist" might assume), but is such a mythology composed
> entirely of myths added one to another, or is there beneath all
> and through all and in all an all-compelling something
> unexplained by our "scientific" "force and energy" which the
> Western Sioux thought of, sincerely claimed to know of, as

*Woniya (Spirit)? It does not bother the old Indians to under-
stand, in an elementary way, what we mean by "the modern
scientific attitude." . . .*[3]

*There is no difficulty in leading an old Teton Sioux Indian
to understand the "scientific" attitude, and that the processes
that give rise to phenomena may be more and more known by
man and may be, to some extent, controlled by man, and that
in this way the forces of nature may become a mainspring of
progress in the individual and in the human race. The idea of
atoms and electrons is easy and pleasing to an old Indian, and
he grasps the idea of chemistry. Such things make ready
contact with his previous observation and thinking. . . .*[4]

*In the Turtle Mountains, North Dakota, Harry Boise . . .
was with me eight months. At his request I allowed him to
teach the old Chippewa and Cree Indians there the modern
scientific attitude with its view of things. . . . The chief among
his pupils was old Sakan'ku Skonk (Rising Sun). . . . But
Rising Sun, speaking the conclusion of all, pronounced "the
scientific view" inadequate. Not bad or untrue, but inadequate
to explain, among many other things, how man is to find and
know a road along which he wishes and chooses to make this
said progress unless the Great Manitoo by his spirit guides the
mind of man, keeping human beings just and generous and
hospitable. (Emphasis added.)*[5]

THE SIMILARITY OF CONCLUSIONS

These passages give something of the flavor of the knowledge of the
old Indians, people who had known the life of freedom before they
were confined to the reservations and subjected to Western religious
and educational systems. Substitute "energy" for "spirit" in some of
these passages, and we have a modern theory of energy/matter. But
the similarity, although profound, hides a deeper truth that we must
examine. For these two groups, the old Indians and the modern scientists, reach their conclusions in entirely different ways, using data
that are completely incompatible if placed together.

The old Indians, as Rising Sun noted, were interested in finding
the proper moral and ethical road upon which human beings should
walk. All knowledge, if it is to be useful, was directed toward that

goal. Absent in this approach was the idea that knowledge existed apart from human beings and their communities, and could stand alone for "its own sake." In the Indian conception, it was impossible that there could be abstract propositions that could be used to explore the structure of the physical world. Knowledge was derived from individual and communal experiences in daily life, in keen observation of the environment, and in interpretive messages that they received from spirits in ceremonies, visions, and dreams.

In formulating their understanding of the world, Indians did not discard any experience. Everything had to be included in the spectrum of knowledge and related to what was already known. As the general propositions that informed the people about the world were the product of generations of tradition and experience, people accepted on faith what they had not experienced, with the hope that during their lifetime they would come to understand.

The Nebraska poet John Neihardt interviewed Black Elk, the Oglala Sioux medicine man, about the beliefs and practices of the old days. During their conversations, Black Elk told Neihardt how the Sioux received the sacred White Buffalo Calf Pipe, the central religious object of the Plains Indians. The story involved the appearance of a woman who instructed the people in moral, social, and religious standards and showed them how to communicate with the higher powers through the use of the pipe in ceremonies. After finishing his story, Black Elk paused, was silent for a time, and said: "This they tell, and whether it happened so or not, I do not know; but if you think about it, you can see that it is true."[6] This is not only a statement of faith: It is a principle of epistemological method.

If the Western Sioux obtained their knowledge by accepting everything they experienced as grist for the mill, Western science has drawn its conclusions by excluding the kinds of data that the Western Sioux cherished. Western science holds that ideas, concepts, and experiences must be clearly stated, and be capable of replication in an experimental setting by an objective observer. Any bit of data or body of knowledge that does not meet this standard is suspect or rejected out of hand. Thus most emotional experiences of human beings are discarded as unsuitable for the scientific enterprise, or are pushed to the periphery of respectability and grudgingly given a bit of status.

Science further limits itself by insisting that all data fall within the reigning interpretive paradigm of the time. According to Thomas

Kuhn, a paradigm primarily enables scientists to classify data and verify whether or not it falls within the acceptable mode of interpretation. One of the things a scientific community acquires with a paradigm, Kuhn explains,

> is a criterion for choosing problems that, while the paradigm is taken for granted, can be assumed to have solutions. To a great extent these are the only problems that the community will admit as scientific or encourage its members to undertake. Other problems, including many that had previously been standard, are rejected as metaphysical, as the concern of another discipline or sometimes as just too problematic to be worth the time.[7]

If science works within this severely restricted arena in which statements have such limited validity, how can we have faith that it is presenting to us anything remotely approaching reliable knowledge about the world? And why do scientists, knowing these limitations, act so dogmatically about what they know?

Scientific knowledge also has the problem of internal politics, in which prominent scholars can force acceptance or rejection of theories based on wholly extraneous considerations, often a matter of personal preference or the desire for professional status. New research on the relationship between Charles Darwin and Alfred Wallace, for example, shows that it is quite possible that Darwin simply stole Wallace's idea of natural selection and had the right political connections within the English scientific establishment to make good his theft.[8] Such revelations would indicate that there is considerable reason to be skeptical about the findings of Western science, because it excludes a substantial amount of data and allows cliques to determine what is acceptable theory and doctrine.

But how do we explain the Indian perspective on knowledge, which saw no need to engage in the process of developing interpretive frameworks, producing many anomalies, creating ad hoc theories, and finally formulating new explanations? How do Indians handle anomalies, for there surely must have been anomalies in a worldview of such relative simplicity.

Indians believed that everything that humans experience has value and instructs us in some aspect of life. The fundamental premise is that we cannot "misexperience" anything; we can only misinterpret what we experience. Therefore, in some instances we can experience something entirely new, and so we must be alert and try not to classify things too quickly. The world is constantly creating itself because everything is alive and making choices that determine the future. There cannot be such a thing as an anomaly in this kind of framework: Some things are accepted because there is value in the very mystery they represent.

Because, in the Indian system, all data must be considered, the task is to find the proper pattern of interpretation for the great variety of ordinary and extraordinary experiences we have. Ordinary and extraordinary must come together in one coherent comprehensive story line. Sometimes this narrative will deal with human behavior and sometimes with the behavior of higher powers. But it will have a point to it and will always represent a direction of future growth. Finally, with the wisdom that old age brings, there will be time for reflection and the discovery of unsuspected relationships that make themselves manifest in consciousness and so come to be understood.

THE MORAL UNIVERSE

The real interest of the old Indians was not to discover the abstract structure of physical reality but rather to find the proper road along which, for the duration of a person's life, individuals were supposed to walk. This colorful image of the road suggests that the universe is a moral universe. That is to say, there is a proper way to live in the universe: There is a content to every action, behavior, and belief. The sum total of our life experiences has a reality. There is a direction to the universe, empirically exemplified in the physical growth cycles of childhood, youth, and old age, with the corresponding responsibility of every entity to enjoy life, fulfill itself, and increase in wisdom and the spiritual development of personality. Nothing has incidental meaning and there are no coincidences.

The wise person will realize his or her own limitations and act with some degree of humility until he or she has sufficient knowledge to act with confidence. Every bit of information must be related to the general framework of moral interpretation as it is personal to them and their community. No body of knowledge exists for its own sake outside the moral framework of understanding. We are, in the truest sense possible, creators or co-creators with the higher powers, and what we do has immediate importance for the rest of the universe.

This attitude extends to data and experiences far beyond the immediate physical environment, including the stars, other worlds and galaxies, the other higher and lower planes of existence, and the places of higher and lower spiritual activities. If many Indian legends appear to be geocentric, to be restricted to the conditions existing on this earth, it is because they are formulated in this manner to make the transmission of information easier. But there are many accounts of people traveling to other worlds, of people becoming birds and animals, living with them, and experiencing the great variety of possible modes of existence.

In the moral universe all activities, events, and entities are related, and consequently it does not matter what kind of existence an entity enjoys, for the responsibility is always there for it to participate in the continuing creation of reality.

What the Western Sioux sought was the moral content of entities and relationships; they tried to understand their role and function in the natural world, and to come to an understanding, often revealed by the entities themselves, of the actual physical composition of things. Coming from the opposite ends of the spectrum of knowledge and methodology—the Indian representing perhaps the extreme of subjectivity and the Western scientist the extreme of objectivity—these views suggest a middle meeting ground where contradictions can possibly be resolved. But the content of whatever configuration may exist in the middle would seem to be, following the Western Sioux and Plato, a knowledge of the physical universe arranged or understood in such a manner as to call forth some form of moral response.

This conclusion is anathema to most scientists, whose fear (well justified considering the history of warfare between sacred and secular forces in Western civilization) is that if such ethical dimensions are admitted, it would once again allow ecclesiastical authorities to gain control of social and political institutions and so prevent or inhibit investigative scientific activities. Thus introducing purpose and morality suggests for many people the existence of a higher entity that can become an object of worship and thereafter a source of continuing social conflict.

In fact, the old Indians did not see a specific higher personality who demanded worship and adoration in the manner in which we find deity portrayed in the traditions of the Near East. Rather they saw and experienced personality in every aspect of the universe and called it "'Woniya" (Spirit), looking to it for guidance in a manner quite similar to Socrates obeying his "daemon."

I do not believe this perspective is pantheistic in the traditional sense that frightens scientists and religious people alike. Even those tribes that projected from the experiences of birds, animals, and plants and personified these experiences did not make any particular entity a deity alone and apart from everything else. Most of the tribes were content to stop their description with a simple affirmation of the existence of Spirit. The Sioux, in fact, simply said the "Great Mysterious." Only later, when Christian missionaries attempted to link Sioux traditions to their own religious systems, did this mysterious presence begin to take on human forms and demand a groveling, flattering kind of worship.

THE STRUCTURE OF THE TRIBAL UNIVERSE

The Plains Indians arranged their knowledge in a circular format—which is to say, there were no ultimate terms or constituents of their universe, only sets of relationships that sought to describe phenomena. No concept could stand alone in the way that time, space, and matter once stood as absolute entities in Western science. All concepts not only had content but were themselves composed of the elements of other ideas to which they were related. Thus it was possible to begin with one idea, thoroughly examine it by relating it to other concepts, and arrive back at the starting point with the assurance that a person could properly interpret what constituted the idea and how it might manifest itself in concrete physical experiences.

The purpose of such an arrangement was to be certain that all known aspects of something would be included in the information that people possessed and considered when making decisions and reaching conclusions. There were, therefore, almost limitless ways of describing snow, rain, wind, or other natural phenomena, as each particular manifestation of the general concept needed to be described accurately and placed properly within a spectrum of the possibilities of realization. Indian languages, and the Dakota/Lakota language that the Western Sioux used, had a very large vocabulary that enabled people to be specific in remembering and describing the ways that a concept could be realized within human experience.

In the rest of this section, I will try to unravel some aspects of the Sioux circle of knowledge and make a list of the most important components of the Indian universe. Other interpreters of the Sioux worldview may differ considerably in the emphasis they place on certain concepts. I feel certain, however, that these principles would emerge if a consensus of the interpreters was achieved.

The Universe Is Alive

It cannot be argued that the universe is moral or has a moral purpose without simultaneously maintaining that the universe is alive. The old Indians had no problem with this concept because they experienced life in everything, and there was no reason to suppose that the continuum of life was not universal. The belief in a living universe raises hackles among many scientists today because it raises the specter of subjectivity and calls to mind the religious perspective, in which the universe is seen as divine. On the other hand, within the Western religions, the idea of the "living universe" is often dismissed as "merely pantheism," as if labeling a belief could thereby explain it.

Recent controversy over the living universe has been particularized within science in the debate over the "Gaia hypothesis," which I consider in detail in the final section of this article (see *A Reexamination of the Metaphysical Foundations of Modern Science*).[9] James Lovelock and a bevy of colleagues, admirers, and followers have raised the question of whether it is helpful to view the planet as a living organism.[10] But the debate has often centered on false arguments, with both the advocates and the opponents of the theory restricting the definition of "life" to reactive organic phenomena that are observed primarily in the higher organisms.

Traditional Indians are quite amused to see this revival of the debate over whether the planet is alive. Long ago in ceremonies and visions Indians came to experience this truth. The practical criterion that is always cited to demonstrate its validity is the easily observable fact that the earth nurtures smaller forms of life—people, plants, birds, animals, rivers, valleys, and continents. For Indians, both speculation and analogy end at this point. To go further and attribute a plenitude of familiar human characteristics to the earth is unwarranted. It would cast the planet in the restricted clothing of lesser beings, and we would not be able to gain insights and knowledge about the real essence of the earth.

Nor was there any reason to suppose that other forms of life did not have the same basic intelligence as humans. The Sioux, as well as other tribes, interpreted the scheme of life as leading eventually to the production of human beings. Unlike Western religion and philosophy, however, the fact that humankind had been the final product of the purposeful life force did not make them the crown of creation.

Coming last, human beings were the "younger brothers" of the other life-forms and therefore had to learn everything from these creatures. Thus human activities resembled bird and animal behavior in many ways and brought the unity of conscious life to an objective consistency.

This idea that everything in the universe is alive, and that the universe itself is alive, is knowledge as useful as anything that Western science has discovered or hypothesized. When understood and made operative by serious and sensitive individuals, it is as reliable a means of making predictions as anything suggested by mathematical formulas or projected by computer programs. There are, however, substantial differences in the manner in which predictions are made. Because the universe is alive, there is choice for all things and the future is always indeterminate. Consequently, predictions are based on the knowledge of the "character" of an entity. Statements about how an entity will behave have almost the same probabilities as the educated speculations made at the subatomic level in physics.

Here the Indian knowledge has an edge over Western scientific knowledge. A truly wise and gifted individual can appear to "cause" things to happen because that person can participate in the emerging event in a way that rarely occurs in Western science. Thus it is that people are said to have "powers," which is another way of saying that their understanding of natural process and their ability to enter into events are highly developed and sophisticated.

The living universe requires mutual respect among its members, and this suggests that a strong sense of individual identity and self is a dominant characteristic of the world as we know it.[11] The willingness of entities to allow others to fulfill themselves, and the refusal of any entity to intrude thoughtlessly on another, must be the operative principle of this universe.[12] Consequently, self-knowledge and self-discipline are high values of behavior. Only by allowing innovation by every entity can the universe move forward and create the future. This creative participation is always personal and has an aspect of novelty.

Respect in the American Indian context does not mean the worship of other forms of life but involves two attitudes. One attitude is the acceptance of self-discipline by humans and their communities to act responsibly toward other forms of life. The other attitude is to seek to establish communications and covenants with other forms of life on a mutually agreeable basis.

Developing responsible self-discipline is not difficult, but it cannot be done in a society in which equality is perceived as sameness and conformity. Sitting Bull, looking with disdain at the white man's educational style, remarked that "it is not necessary that eagles be crows." We would do well to cast a critical glance at our ideas and expectations of democracy, brotherhood, and equality in the light of the demand for self-discipline.

We want to have certain benefits from the physical world. In seeking something for ourselves, we must recognize that obtaining what we want at the expense of other forms of life or of the earth itself is shortsighted and disrupts the balance that the whole fabric of life requires. Instead of the predatory jungle that the Anglo-Saxon imagination conjures up to analogize life, in which the most powerful swallows up the weak and unprotected, life is better understood as a tapestry or symphony in which each player has a specific part or role to play. We must be in our proper place and we must play our role at the appropriate moment. Mutual respect in many ways is a function of a strong sense of personal and communal identity, and it is significant that most of the tribes described themselves as "the people," a distinct group with clearly defined values and patterns of behavior.

The idea of the covenant, clearly articulated in the Old Testament theology of the Prophets, is an early and important concept for tribal peoples. Stories explaining how the people came to hunt the buffalo, how the salmon came to be the major food supply, how bird feathers were incorporated into ceremonial costumes and medicine bundles, all derive from early interspecies communications in which other forms of life agreed to allow themselves to be used in ceremonial and economic ways. A covenant places responsibilities on both parties and provides a means of healing any breach in the relationship.

Thus it was that although Indians hunted and fished wild game, they made it a rule that unless they were starving and needed food for survival, they would not take the animals and birds until these creatures had enjoyed a full family life and reproduced their kind. Even today when taking eagles, the Apaches restrict the hunt to late summer or autumn to ensure that the eagles have the chance to mate, raise a family, and go through the major cycles of life experiences.

Everything Is Related

A living universe within which events and actions have moral content necessarily suggests that all things are related. Not only is everything related, but it also participates in the moral content of events, so responsibility for maintaining the harmony of life falls equally on all creatures.

This principle of relatedness appears most often in the religious realm in the phrase "All My Relatives," which is used as an opening invocation and closing benediction for ceremonies. "All My Relatives," believed by many people, including many Indians, to be merely a devout religious sentiment, also has a secular purpose, which is to remind us of our responsibility to respect life and to fulfill our covenantal duties. But few people understand that the phrase also describes the epistemology of the Indian worldview, providing the methodological basis for the gathering of information about the world.

Western science uses various methods for determining its truths. One of the most common methods is the experimental application of previously derived theories to new kinds of phenomena and the subsequent verification or modification of the theory. But modern science is interested primarily in the physical world and its structure, the search for the ultimate material constituent of the physical universe having been a constant quest since Democritus developed his theory of the atom.

American Indians, understanding that the universe consisted of living entities, were interested in learning how other forms of life behaved, for they saw that every entity had a personality and could exercise a measure of free will and choice. Consequently, Indian people carefully observed phenomena in order to determine what relationships existed between and among the various "peoples" of the world. Their understanding of relationships provided the Indians with the knowledge necessary to live comfortably in the physical world, and to not unduly intrude into the lives of other creatures.

If we could imagine a world in which human concerns were not the primary value, and we observed nature in the old Indians' way, we would observe a plant (or a bird or an animal) for a prolonged period of time. We would note what time of year the plant began to grow and green out; when it blossomed; when it bore fruit; how many fruits or seeds it produced; what animals and birds ate the fruit and when during the maturation process they appeared; what colors its leaves and fruits took on during the various parts of the growing season; whether it shed its leaves and needles and what birds and animals made use of them; and many other kinds of behavior of the plant. From these observations we would come to understand both the plant and its life stages. By remembering the birds and animals who made use of the plant—and when they did so during the calendar year and when in terms of their own growth cycles— we would have a reasonable idea of how useful the plant would be for us.

This knowledge, however, would still be general and would need further refining. At certain times some men and women would receive, either in dreams or in visions, very precise knowledge on other ways in which the plant could be used by humans—information that could not have been obtained through experiment or trial and error use. Some knowledge was so precise that it might only be needed once in a human lifetime.[13] And of course tribes often shared their knowledge of plants or even traded medicinal plants back and forth across large distances so that the knowledge of plants took on an encyclopedic aspect.

All Relationships Are Historical

Part of the experience of life is the passage of time, the fact of personal growth, and the understanding of oneself produced by reflective memory processes. As the universe was known by the Indians to be alive, it followed that all entities had some memory and enjoyed the experience of the passage of time. Thus relationships were understood as enduring in time and were characterized by the same kinds of disruptive historic events as we see in human history. All covenants wore out and changes seemed to occur in the same way they do in human experience. Thus plants might gather together for a long time but then suddenly disappear, beginning to grow in different areas or adapting themselves to new lands and climatic conditions. We call this kind of change evolution today, but the old Indians did not see it that way. They knew that any changes that occurred were already inherent in the creature, or within its potentiality for change—a possibility that some Western scientists are now beginning to accept.

Knowledge of the historical relationships can be exceedingly useful in modern science in providing guidance for ecological restoration projects. The appearance or disappearance of a certain plant can be used to predict similar behavior by related plants and animals. We must note, however, that the relationships established by the Indians are personal relationships between and among other forms of life, and therefore they do not necessarily follow the definitions established by Western scientific systems of classifications. Thus the characteristics that modern botanists and biologists use to define species and genera are not comparable in many respects to the Indian classification by personality types. A good judgment of the accuracy of Indian knowledge and Western scientific knowledge might be made by allowing Indians and scientists to restore similar tracts of land according to different conceptions of what kinds of life can be sustained on the land.

Space Determines the Nature of Relationships

Although the preliminary discussion of the living universe has emphasized spiritual/personality values, the idea that everything is related has definite space/time relevance. Here perhaps we begin to speak mysteriously and vaguely when we try to explain concepts. For most forms of life there appears to be a definite pattern of spatial existence. With plants it is not difficult to see that they are restricted to certain locations, although in fact they can move if they so desire. Most locations of plants can be easily explained by reference to soil, climate, and availability of water. But many medicine men spoke of the places that the various entities were destined to occupy, and of the beginning of a world age as a time when everything was in its proper place.

Some of the language appears to be quasi-Aristotelian in that they attributed a sense of purpose to an entity without having evidence of it. But because each entity has a set of relationships with other entities, all of these relationships were established in a particular geometric pattern and manifested themselves in spatial arrangements. Thus people became concerned when a plant or animal was found in a place where it should not be.

There were basically three major manifestations of space in the Sioux universe: the ceremonial directions; the sacred places that define meaning for the life around them; and the particular place that each species, including particular groups of humans, comes to occupy and live in.

1) The Ceremonial Directions: These were the most abstract expression of the idea of space. Each entity, and by extension each place, was the center of the universe—thinking that fits well with scientific relativity theory. In ceremonies the object was to draw into participation all the powerful elements of the cosmos. So the sacred pipe was offered to the four directions, to the sky and the earth, and acknowledgment was made that at every ceremonial the center of the ritual action is the seventh direction—which is the "here and now." As distance was not regarded as a meaningful obstacle when spiritual powers were invoked, each ceremony began with a representation of the whole cosmos, whether it was a vision quest pit, a sweat lodge, the bowl of the pipe itself, or a Sun Dance arbor.

The object of ceremonial is to make whole again what has now become disassociated and chaotic. In order to accomplish this goal, all possible elements of the universe must be brought within a harmony; sacrifices must be made to heal the injuries of each party, and a new beginning must be made.

Some observers are correct when they describe a ceremony as "world-renewing," as the object of ceremony is to cleanse the participants and offer them a new beginning. But they are wrong when they interpret renewal as simply symbolic in the Western sense of representation. Without the four directions, in the Sioux understanding, the world would not have its physical structure; sky and earth are necessary for human and animal existence, and the center itself represents all possible times taking place simultaneously. In practical terms, relationships are renewed and restored and must be conducted in accordance with the structure of the human universe of the directions once again.

2) Sacred Places: The Sioux also understood the earth to have special places of power and significance, and these places were regarded as sacred in the sense that they required respect and human self-discipline. The Black Hills, for example, were sacred because they were at the center of the Sioux universe (as represented by Bear Butte on the eastern edge of the hills) and because they were set aside by the higher powers as a sanctuary for the birds and animals.[14] Scattered in many different locations throughout the Sioux lands were certain other places where revelations had been given to the people or they had experienced a spiritual presence.

3) Particular Places: Finally there was the idea that particular places were designed for particular species, and, in human terms, for particular peoples. Long ago, even before kinship relations were established, a Sioux man had a dream about the great island hill[15] toward which the people were supposed to migrate. In the course of tribal history, the people wandered through the southeastern United States, into Pennsylvania, and west toward the Great Lakes, until finally they came to the Black Hills where they were destined to live. After finding the proper place, migrations ceased and the people took on ceremonial duties for particular locations.

The importance of finding the proper living space is illustrated by plants and animals. In the Pacific Northwest, for example, tribes would share a river and catch salmon at a bewildering variety of locations, from the mouth of the river to the final spawning grounds. Because the chemistry of the salmon was changing as the fish went upstream, different ways of preserving the catch were used at each location. Each place determined the various life-forms it would support and these creatures then worked cooperatively at their chosen location.

The implications for Western science of the idea of a special place are tremendous. Knowing the sets of relationships between the various plants and animals enables one to predict what kinds of species will be present in a healthy environment, and so failure to locate a species in a particular location will alert people about the condition of the place. Within that place, however, one will also find the most precise examples of species as the place itself affects things.

Time Determines the Meaning of Relationships

Time is a complicated concept in a living universe. The basic pattern seems to be that of growth processes, which is to say that time has qualitative packets of quanta that are regulated by the amount of time it takes an organism or entity to complete a step in maturation. Thus all entities are regulated by the seasons, and their interaction has a superior season of its own that encompasses their relationship and has a moral purpose. Tribes broke human patterns down into several steps: prebirth, babies, children, youths, adults, mature adults, and elders.[16] The idea of the "seven generations" was commonly used by the Plains tribes to describe the relationships existing within a genetic family. If a family was respectable and responsible, its members would be granted old age and a person could live long enough to see and know his great-grandparents and his great-grandchildren. Thus generations, not decades, were the measure of human life.

As there was interspecies communication between humans and other forms of life, people also became aware of larger cycles of time, which can be described as the time jointly shared by all forms of life within a geographic area. This time line seems to have been dominated by the idea of vocation and/or the idea of the fullness of time. In some undetermined manner, the universe had a direction to it: Every entity had a part to play in the creation of the future, and human beings had a special vocation in which they initiated, at the proper time, new relationships and events.

In the experience of the vision quest, people were given the basic outlines of their lives but not specific predictions as to when, in chronological time, certain events might occur.[17] During the ceremonial experiences, as the years passed, humans would be told when and how the larger cosmic time was moving, and would at times be urged to hurry—or counseled to wait until conditions were right for them to play their particular role.

There was a profound sense of determinacy within this aspect of time, but there was also flexibility, so that sequences of action that people knew were to take place did not necessarily have to occur in a manner that people understood or could anticipate. This sense of a determined sequence of specific future actions was seen as evidence that the earth was a living being and that smaller entities were her children and subject to the larger motions of the universe.

On more everyday levels, there was the recognition that over a long period of time human behavior itself changed as the people perceived, or had revealed to them through ceremonials, the occasional behavior of other life-forms that indicated the depth of power contained within them. So, in general, it was recognized that not all information is available to us immediately; some things may simply come into being during the course of time.

Medicine men taught that plants and animals do not become extinct—they go away and do not come back until the location is being treated properly. This belief is being verified today in ecological restoration projects. Lands abused for generations, if treated properly and with respect, will see a flowering of plants that once lived there and that were believed to be extinct, and the birds and animals related to those plants will return. It is worth noting that the plants return first, then the animals, and finally the birds. (Thus antelope have returned to some portions of the Dakota plains, but prairie chickens have still not made a complete return.)

Western science is committed to the doctrine of evolution and consequently sees changes in plants, birds, and animals as responding to the passage of time and changes in the environment. Although science cannot adequately explain the mechanism of evolution, it regards changes as permanent. The Sioux traditional people say that the important thing is the spirit of the creature; that it can and does change aspects of its physical shape in order to deal with change but that basically it remains the same entity. As the Indian interest is in the spirit or soul of the other creature and not in its morphology, some substitutions can be made in ceremonial objects, provided that the substituted materials have the same spiritual relationship to people that the former objects had.

In outlining the Sioux knowledge of the physical universe, and attempting to demonstrate the principles that govern it, we are able to see new applications and interpretations of our existing knowledge. We are also able to reach out and begin to bring emotion and logic back together again. This synthesis is necessary if we are to make sense of our world and our experiences.

NOTES

1. A. McG. Beede, "Western Sioux Cosmology," unpublished paper in the North Dakota State Historical records, Bismarck, and the Newberry Library, Chicago, p. 3.

2. Ibid., p. 4.
3. Ibid., pp. 5-6.
4. Ibid., p. 6.
5. Ibid., pp. 6-7.
6. John C. Neihardt, *Black Elk Speaks* (Lincoln: University of Nebraska Press, 1972), p. 4.
7. Thomas S. Kuhn, *The Structure of Scientific Revolutions* (Chicago: University of Chicago Press, 1962), p. 37.
8. See, for example, Barbara Beddall, "Wallace, Darwin, and the Theory of Natural Selection," in *Journal of the History of Biology*, no. 1 (1968). Also, John L. Brooks, *Extinction and the Origin of Organic Diversity* (Connecticut Academy of Arts and Sciences, Dec. 1972).
9. Willis Harman, *A Re-examination of the Metaphysical Foundations of Modern Science* (IONS Research Report, 1992).
10. Readers should consult especially James Lovelock, *The Ages of Gaia* (New York: W. W. Norton, 1988); and *Gaia: A New Look at Life on Earth* (Oxford: Oxford University Press, 1979).
11. The strong sense of personal identity among the Indians can be exemplified by the frequent changing of names to keep track of the change in the personality as the individual went through life. Most Indians had several names by which they were called, each giving specific information on their talents or accomplishments. Within the family, people would refer to each other by kinship terms in order not to interfere with personality growth and to remind themselves of family responsibilities. Some Indians who did not want to shame their most personal name used secular names to sign treaties that they believed the United States would not keep.
12. Densmore records the explanation of Eagle Shield of the Crow Owner Society of the Teton Sioux regarding the self-discipline of the Indians on this point:

    The Crow is always the first to arrive at the gathering of the animals in the Black Hills. The reason why the Black Hills were so long unknown to the white man was that Wakantanka created them as a meeting place for the animals. The Indians had always known this and regarded the law of Wakantanka concerning it. By this law they were forbidden to kill any of the animals during their great gatherings. (p. 319; emphasis added.)
13. The Lummi Indians who live near the Canadian border in Washington State have a rain dance. It seems ludicrous for people who live in a virtual rain forest to have a rain dance. This dance is used on those rare occasions when it snows so hard that the houses are buried and the people cannot get out of them. The rain melts the snow and rescues the people.
14. See note 12.
15. John Neihardt, "When the Tree Flowered," in *Why the Island Hill Was Sacred* (Lincoln: University of Nebraska Press, 1970).
16. Indians placed considerable emphasis on the prebirth stage of life, believing that it influenced everything else. Charles Eastman recounted

the Indian attitude in his book, *The Soul of the Indian* (Boston: Houghton Mifflin, 1911):

> From the moment of her recognition of the fact of conception to the end of the second year of life, which was the ordinary duration of lactation, it was supposed by us that the mother's spiritual influence counted for most. Her attitude and secret meditations must be such as to instill into the receptive soul of the unborn child the love of the "Great Mystery" and a sense of brotherhood with all creatures. Silence and isolation are the rule of life for the expectant mother. She wanders prayerful in the stillness of great woods, or on the bosom of the untrodden prairie, and to her poetic mind the imminent birth of her child prefigures the advent of a masterman—a hero, or the mother of heroes—a thought conceived in the virgin breast of primeval nature, and dreamed out in a hush that is only broken by the sighing of the pine tree or the thrilling orchestra of a distant waterfall. (pp. 28-29)

17. Roman Nose, the great Cheyenne Dog Soldier warrior, was told that he would be invincible unless he had touched metal before he went into battle, as the metal in his body would then attract bullets. In one fight with the cavalry he deliberately rode three times across the whole line of cavalry in order to encourage them to fire at him and heat their guns. He was not wounded. At Beecher's Island, asked to lead the third charge against the Colorado Volunteers, he knew he would be killed because he had eaten food given to him with a metal spoon. The basic outlines of his life were already given to him in the Vision Quest. But he had a choice when his death would occur if it was to be in battle—and he deliberately chose to end it on behalf of his warriors at Beecher's Island.

▼ Part II ▼

SOCIAL SCIENCE

5

ETHNOSCIENCE AND INDIAN REALITIES

▼▼▼▼

A recent and entirely welcome development in higher education has been the expansion of some traditional fields of scientific inquiry to include the knowledge possessed by tribal peoples about the world they lived in. This change falls under the general rubric "ethnoscience" and includes archaeoastronomy, geomythology, ethnobotany, and the miscellaneous studies of taxonomies and other methods of classification used by tribal peoples. It is comforting for Indian students to learn that their ancestors were correct in some insights into the workings of nature and that some tribes had special systems of classification. It is now clear that gathering and planting food was not an ad hoc activity as anthropological studies once implied. But considerably more work needs to be done to ensure that the whole scope of native knowledge is understood and approached from the proper perspective.

As this movement gathers momentum and becomes an important part of higher education, we should take a careful look at the manner in which the Western scientific community receives tribal knowledge and become particularly alert to the framework it uses in interpreting and understanding this body of information. Western science is wed to the evolutionary scheme of interpretation that suggests that there is an end purpose in everything that is reached by sheer chance. This format is, of course, absurd. It suggests, when discussing human beings, that the task of our species, from the very beginning, was to evolve into tool-making and manufacturing beings who were able gradually to wrest secrets from a reluctant and inert material world of nature.

TRIBAL KNOWLEDGE VERSUS WESTERN WORLDVIEW

The Western worldview places the scientific man at the foundation of evolutionary doctrine. Without this fictional individual, evolution would not make sense. In this format, the so-called primitive peoples were thought to have used a quasi-scientific method, that of trial and error, to understand the natural world. This characterization suggests that primitive people had a discernible goal in mind as they experimented with the phenomena of the natural world. The knowledge of primitives is thus believed to have been born in a struggle to derive a view of the world that avoided superstitions and spirits and which sought to discover in nature abstract principles that were operative in all places at all times.

Anthropological theory, based on observations of recent and modern tribal peoples, suggests that many societies did not abandon the reliance on spirits or beliefs characterized by Western science as superstitious. In fact, they maintained a wholistic understanding of the natural world until forced to change by the intrusions of Western civilization. A recent *Time* magazine issue was devoted to the wisdom of tribal peoples and bemoaned the substantial loss of knowledge about the natural world that is occurring as tribal peoples are being processed into the industrial state.

The development of Western science was based on the idea that human beings could abstract themselves from the observational and experimental situation. They could then devise objective principles that would be applicable at any time or place in reasonably similar situations.

Finally, anyone with proper training could duplicate an experimental or observational situation. This view supposes that primitive peoples felt the same sense of alienation in natural surroundings as do people of the Western industrial society. If the study of modern tribal peoples is the closest we can come to understanding human beings in an earlier stage of evolution, then this basic scenario is wrong, for we do not find a cringing fear of the environment in tribal peoples. Instead they are keenly aware of rhythms and activities that scientific people cannot begin to fathom.

Anthropological literature often suggests that our ancestors spent a great deal of time arranging their information about the world in a systematic fashion so as to gain an advantage and later control of natural forces and processes. According to this fictional narrative, primitive peoples were able to apprehend the complex concepts of modern science that were inherent in the accidental events of their lives, and, having once grasped a scientific principle, they moved steadily toward the modern understanding of it. Eventually one branch of the human family, the Indo-European peoples, overcame their superstitions and developed a technology that enabled them to achieve mastery over the rest of humankind and to order nature to do their bidding.

In this scenario the knowledge possessed by tribal peoples and the nonindustrial societies represents a few valid insights and a considerable number of superstitions that represent earlier stages of scientific endeavor. Western science can examine tribal knowledge to locate interesting tidbits and insights and use these ideas to enhance its own activities, expanding the scope of experiments or increasing the applicability of its existing doctrines and dogmas. In addition, tribal knowledge is often regarded by many educated people as simply "fun" or "quaint" because it is so exotic, suggesting great mysteries that we have not yet unraveled. Very few people accord this knowledge the status it deserves and hardly anyone can articulate the principles that lie at its foundation.

A most encouraging sign today is the number of young Indians who are coming to respect and learn the ancient tribal knowledge. Most discouraging, however, is the rate at which tribal elders who have this knowledge are passing away. These two curves may well intersect in the immediate future, leaving tribes considerably poorer in their ability to deal adequately with their natural resources and to continue their ceremonial life.

Today we should make a concerted effort to gather traditional tribal wisdom into a coherent body of knowledge that can be passed on to the next generation of Indians.

I applaud the efforts of the generation below me to begin to give voice and substance to the revival of tribal knowledge of nature, and I certainly do not want to inhibit the writing and speaking they are now doing. I do think, however, that the effort to preserve and revive the tribal traditions must be placed in the most significant intellectual context possible. I believe firmly that tribal ways represent a complete and logical alternative to Western science. If tribal wisdom is to be seen as a valid intellectual discipline, it will be because it can be articulated in a wide variety of expository forms and not simply in the language and concepts that tribal elders have always used to express themselves.

TRIBAL INSIGHT

One of the difficulties today in speaking about tribal knowledge is the tendency to suggest that when traditional teachings correspond to the findings or present beliefs of Western science, then traditional wisdom is validated. It is comforting to see a reasonable "match" of data and conclusions, but why does that correspondence necessarily validate the tribal insight rather than the other way around? Why do we think that Western science is the criterion of truth and accuracy? Why is tribal knowledge described as striving on an ad hoc basis to rival the information obtained by Western science?

In answering these questions, we should look at the epistemology of Western science and tribal traditions. The first question to be asked, prior to a comparison of the results, is how the two groups gathered information. What makes the data that each group considers in making decisions about the natural world reliable, either in their own eyes or in the view of impartial observers? The initial approach to experience, the process by which we identify data as important or irrelevant, determines how we choose to connect experiences and facts. We formulate the subsequent patterns of arrangement and interpretation that we impose on experience after this initial identification.

In an epistemological sense, there is no question that the tribal method of gathering information is more sophisticated and certainly more comprehensive than Western science. In most tribal traditions, no data are discarded as unimportant or irrelevant. Indians consider their own individual experiences, the accumulated wisdom of the community that has been gathered by previous generations, their dreams, visions, and prophecies, and any information received from birds, animals, and plants as data that must be arranged, evaluated, and understood as a unified body of knowledge. This mixture of data from sources that the Western scientific world regards as highly unreliable and suspect produces a consistent perspective on the natural world. It is seen by tribal peoples as having wide application. Knowledge about plants and birds can form the basis of ethics, government, and economics as well as provide a means of mapping a large area of land. In fact, tribal knowledge systematically mixes facts and experiences that Western science would separate by artificial categories. In tribal systems there is never a sense of disorientation within the tribal understanding of the world.

Western science, on the other hand, discards anything that has a remote relationship with the subjective experiences of human beings and other forms of life. The essence of science is to adopt the pretense that the rest of the natural world is without intelligence and knowledge and operates primarily as if it were a machine. Dreams and spiritual experience are thought to be illusory or delusive and cannot be made a part of the scientific method of gathering data. At the deepest level of thought in Western science, the greatest thinkers rely heavily on intuition, dreams, and visions. But this phenomenon is regarded as evidence of the individual genius of the scientist and not as data derived from external sources or drawn from a reservoir of subjective information available to all individuals.

TWO WAYS OF KNOWING

Let us examine the two approaches to gathering information and transforming it into usable knowledge. The Indian understands dreams, visions, and intraspecies communications, when they are available, as a natural part of human experience comparable in many respects to the mundane daily experiences that constitute his life. Even though data come in a highly emotional context, the task is to make sense of the experience or withhold judgment on its meaning until a sufficient number of similar experiences reveal the pattern of meaning that is occurring. The Indian arrangement of knowledge holds in memory, individually or collectively/communally, many experiences of a similar type. Wisdom—and the number of specific cases—increases with age. As a person gets older he or she is able to remember and understand a wide variety of events or activities that are species-, location-, and time-specific. Instead of matching generalizations with new phenomena, Indians match a more specific body of information with the immediate event or experience. Exceptions to the rule become a new set of specific behaviors that open new classifications for future information.

In Western science the propensity is to classify certain kinds of phenomena under major generalizations and then to accept or reject all additional data according to their proximity to the behavior that the generalization is capable of explaining. Thus Western science develops the "either/or" method of analysis—this creature is either a dog or a cat, it is hot or cold, living or dead, and so on. Each category, and the information stored in it, was devised by many observations and experiments that had as goals the expansion, enhancement, and application of the primary category of classification. The purpose of science is to find that concept or model that best explains all phenomena. Over the centuries the scientific quest focused on locating the "building block" of the physical world.

For a terribly long time people thought that if the atom were understood, the subsequent actions of the physical world could be predicted. Science thus adopted a reductionist epistemology that basically eliminated the world we know and experience in favor of mathematical formulas that described certain kinds of behavior at the subatomic level. Science is thus terribly complex and sophisticated about minute particles that are irrelevant to just about everything we do or want to do. But it was assumed that this information could be used by anyone to predict future manifestations of the same phenomena. Today any new phenomenon is expected to fit into pre-existing categories of interpretation, and scientists are finding that this manner of arranging data is not satisfactory.

These systems of thought—tribal and Western scientific—do not seem to be radically different, but in actual application they diverge radically. A good deal of data are simply discarded by science. To include these data within the experimental framework would mean that nonrational and partially subjective conclusions would have to be drawn and, most important, mathematics would not be the sole criterion of measurement and verification. Data that are individual-specific cannot be reproduced arbitrarily. Consequently, they are often described as "anomalous," falling outside the parameters of the experiment and therefore of science itself.

Western science thus excludes a considerable amount of information that tribal peoples would feel to be a necessary part of understanding the phenomenon.

A good many scientific beliefs and experiments simply produce ad hoc explanations as the focus of the investigation is to give some account of specific phenomena. Thus, at any one time, science has "scientific answers" and explanations, but these ideas do not relate to other parts of science. Presumably when the number of ad hoc answers and anomalies increases to a disturbing proportion, a new scientific paradigm must be called into operation that reduces the number of these dissident and not to be neglected facts. But there is no good guarantee that anomalies and ad hoc explanations will force a change in the interpretation of phenomena.

Western science is now giving way in its strict construction of categories of classification and is beginning to open doors it had firmly closed during the past half millennium. Books describing the life of the unborn child, the use of controlled fires to ensure the fertility of forests, the use of "indicator species" to measure the environmental damage of an area, observations of animal behavior to detect useful plants and secure derivative chemicals and drugs from them, the use of dreams in psychotherapy, and the effect of music on plant growth top the list of anomalous insights into the natural world that are now regarded as valid. That these observations were an integral part of tribal knowledge is surprising to most people.

Unfortunately, these discoveries are coming to light on an ad hoc basis derived from the experiments and observations of new thinkers who are suspect within the scientific community. The information often remains on the periphery of science. Unless a concerted effort is made to understand the basis by which tribal peoples acquired their insights, there will be sparse and sporadic improvement in scientific knowledge because these data will be difficult to connect with the existing body of scientific findings. The common knowledge of Indian tribes, when discovered by non-Indian scientists, is seen as an exciting breakthrough. But from the Indian perspective, it is mere child's play. It is information that traditional people expected youngsters to acquire as a matter of course.

VIEWS OF NATURE—AN EXAMPLE

Let us compare tribal knowledge and Western scientific knowledge in one instance to demonstrate the relative predictability factors that each view of nature contains. If we were to raise a herd of buffalo on an exceedingly large tract of land, we might one day discover we did not know where they were. Turning to Western science, we would scamper through reports on buffalo behavior, we would get a map and try to pinpoint the location of streams and watering places, and we might organize a search for the herd. The data we have would be in every way comparable to the information that the Plains Indians possessed regarding land and buffalo behavior, and there would not be too much difference in the manner in which we approached the problem of locating the herd.

In addition to everything that we can reasonably determine as valid data in locating the buffalo, however, the tribal tradition has a few additional bits of information that would make our task easier. The buffalo loved sunflowers. At times they would gather in a draw where the sunflowers grew and frolic among them, uprooting the plants and tossing them over their heads onto their backs so that they were virtually decorated with these colorful flowers. So we might look more closely at sunflower patches. Grazing buffalo frequently had flocks of blackbirds among them. The birds would sit on the backs of the buffalo, and when the animals grazed and disrupted the insects, the insects would give themselves away, making them easy prey for the birds. We would then narrow our search to locations with sunflowers and many blackbirds.

If we were really sophisticated, we would know that on top of many of the buttes and hills on the northern plains lives a little dun beetle that has two antennae on its head. These antennae always point to the nearest buffalo herd, whether that herd is down in the next valley or fifty miles away. All we need do is pack a picnic lunch and move from one group of beetles to another until we locate the herd. These additional bits of knowledge came as a result of the many other ways that Indians gathered information. Some facts might have come from dreams, others from communication with beetles, and other facts from knowledge of birds that would include their relationship with the buffalo. This information is not extraneous to the knowledge of buffalo, and it is not simply an ad hoc observation. It is included in the teachings of the tribe regarding these animals. And it can be used to predict buffalo, bird, insect, and flower behavior.

Within the Western scientific framework, according to which the natural world is lacking intelligence and personality, it would be exceedingly difficult, if not impossible, to discover these kinds of relationships. The idea that nature is mindless and insensate would have precluded the scientist from observing the proper kinds of behavior and drawing the obvious conclusions.

It does not make sense, when this plenitude of knowledge is available to us from the traditional tribal perspective, to continue to accumulate ad hoc insights into the working of the natural world. Collecting ad hoc bits of interesting data is, at its very bottom, simply unscientific, because no framework of interpretation emerges. To reject sources of information because the scientific mind is not ready to admit them as valid repositories of data or to pretend that part of the natural world has behavior approaching intelligent and deliberate decision making is simply childish. But we are not saying here that anyone can wander out into the landscape and derive these insights and similar bits of information. While this information can be transmitted or communicated in many ways, the specificity of it and the *requirement of personal involvement* eliminate the chance of duplication by anyone through the simple memorization of the mechanics of the phenomenon.

TOWARD ETHNOSCIENCE

As "ethnoscience" continues to expand its reach and attempts to win acceptance within the present scientific body of knowledge, the opportunity for American Indians to speak in a sophisticated manner to the most complicated theories of modern science will be greatly enhanced. Indians now studying Western science would do well to talk with their elders and traditional people and learn to critique the cherished doctrines that their professors and institutions now promulgate. Scholarly papers and dissertations based wholly on the knowledge of the tribe could well hasten the day when our species could deal intelligently with the world in which we live.

6

INDIANS, ARCHAEOLOGISTS,
AND THE FUTURE

▼▼▼▼

I realize that there is still considerable emotional baggage connected with the reburial issue that has been the most recent encounter between American Indians and archaeologists, and although I do not wish to reverse the progress made to date, I do feel a responsibility to represent some of the residual feelings that we see present in Indian minds across the country.

The Society for American Archaeology (SAA) did finally come to a compromise position that supported the Indian efforts to get the Native American Graves Protection and Repatriation Act (P.L. 101-601) passed, although not without some doing. Some representatives of the SAA feel that their final efforts of support should thereby mask what were some dreadfully arrogant attitudes earlier in the struggle. It may well be that we should simply move forward and make the best of the present situation, but we should also recognize that it will take more than a few representatives gathering together in civil conversations to erase the hard feelings on both sides of the issue.

Some of what I can gather as hard feelings from the Indian point of view stem back to the position that the scholarly community has enjoyed for the past century, that is, that only scholars have the credentials to define and explain American Indians and that their word should be regarded as definitive and conclusive. Indians reject that attitude out of hand, and therefore when the reburial issue was first raised and we heard cries of "Science" and its sanctity given as the excuse for not considering the repatriation of Indian human remains and funerary objects, Indians naturally got their backs arched and resentments built quickly. We have been the objects of scientific investigations and publications for far too long, and it is our intent to become people once again, not specimens.

Science today has the edge in establishing itself as the primary source of truth because of the spectacular success of technology, which, in the minds of the general public, is devised by people in white lab smocks busily providing us with more gadgets. Some scholars, particularly people in California, adopted the attitude that the Indian interest in human remains was purely political and had no emotional or religious substance whereas they, as scientists, were impartial and stood above the battle. Nothing could be farther from the truth, of course. Considering the vast financial and status rewards that the academic community bestows on its members, the chances are that scientists would lie, cheat, and steal to advance their personal careers. But the implication of crying out "Science" whenever reburial was mentioned was just the opposite: Indians were made to appear as if they were looting the scientific heritage instead of receiving back the remains of loved ones who had been illegally and immorally taken from them a century or more ago.

Conflicts will always arise and increasingly so, as long as a substantial number of people in the academic establishment insist that their careers and research come before all other human considerations. This conflict is probably inherent in the nature of the academic enterprise itself. We have a society so wealthy that we can pay people outrageous salaries to become experts on butterfly wings and verb tenses of obscure Indian languages and custodians of fragments of old pottery abandoned by earlier people. But in the extreme example, the National Socialist German Workers' party of the 1930s and 1940s in Germany insisted that they alone had the absolute right to use and dispose of human beings and human remains without giving any other people a voice in the proceedings.

I wish some of you could hear the descriptions of the medicine men who conducted the reburial ceremonies for some of the tribes. In these ceremonies the spirits of the people whose remains were being returned appeared. They asked surprisingly practical questions for spirits. Some wanted to know if it was possible to get the indelible ink removed from their bones. Others said that their remains had no feet or no head, and they wondered at the kind of people who would remove these parts of the body and what they thought human life was. I don't much care whether any of you believe in spirits or a life hereafter. I think it is foolish to pretend on the basis of a wholly materialistic science (which can only measure quantities) that there is nothing spiritual and nonmaterial in our universe. It is this attitude, as much as anything, that distinguishes Indians from the rest of American society and most certainly from the scientific endeavor. Whether or not there is sufficient proof of the Indian beliefs and experiences, it is a hazardous thing to assume without good cause that the Indians are lying or simply superstitious. Indeed, large numbers of non-Indians are now embracing the Indian beliefs in increasing numbers, so in some sense materialists are on the losing side of this crest of the historical/emotional wave of sensitivities.

Archaeology has been a suspicious science for Indians from the very beginning. People who spend their lives writing tomes on the garbage of other people are not regarded as quite mentally sound in many Indian communities. And to define Indian civilizations by watching the change of pottery styles, as archaeology once did is not exactly a process of compiling irrefutable knowledge; it is mere white man's speculation and fiction and should be regarded as such. All of us still carry the baggage of former days, and it should be a task in the days ahead for archaeologists who truly want cooperative ventures with American Indians to begin to communicate about some of the new techniques that are being used and the changes in dogmas and doctrines that are occurring as a result of the new instruments and processes available to you.

In this respect, I wonder at the isolation of archaeologists today. I have in the neighborhood of eighty books dealing in one way or another with pre-Columbian expeditions to the Western Hemisphere. These books range from utter nonsense to rather sophisticated and careful review of your own archaeological reports and the addition of new interpretations and efforts to interpret the anomalies that you seemed unable to understand at the time. I began to take this expanding body of literature seriously when I happened to mention Barry Fell's writing to people at the Smithsonian. Before I could even say whether I agreed with Fell or not, William Sturtevant and Ives Goddard got exceedingly heated and began to argue with me about Lydian verb tenses and some translation, or purported translation, of an inscription that Fell had made.

My rule of thumb is that the Smithsonian is the last bastion of nineteenth-century science, so if people there are against any new theory, the chances are they are dead wrong. Thus I have maintained a lively interest in the possibility of proving that some of the theories embraced by lay people regarding pre-Columbian America will some-day be demonstrated. I will willingly grant that we have nothing in the way of small artifacts at some of these sites and that seems puzzling if the other aspects of the site seem to hold. But the "official" explanation I have received about the stone chambers in New England and the ogam inscriptions that seem to abound in other places is simply ludicrous.

Without even examining some of these sites, scholars have told me that they are root cellars or simply marks made by colonists' plows or Indians sharpening their arrows. Now some of the locations where these alleged ogam inscriptions are found are on inaccessible cliffs, and I have great difficulty imagining colonists hitching up their teams and suspending their plows over some abyss in order to make these marks. Moreover, there seems to be an abundance of old coins found in various parts of the country but most noticeably in the eastern United States. If I were to accept the usual scholarly explanation, I would come to believe that the ships that brought immigrants from Europe were stuffed with British, German, and French coin collectors who brought hoards of old coins to this continent and then casually scattered them all over Ohio as a joke. In fact, so many of these sites have been declared to be hoaxes that American society seems to have been filled with practical jokers during most of the three hundred years of European occupation. Looking at the presidential candidates every four years is almost irrefutable evidence for your present interpretation of the alleged pre-Columbian sites but I am still uncomfortable with the idea that *no* contacts were made between Europe and North America before Columbus.

As a side note to this problem, I have been told that there is great debate between diffusionists and others over the interpretation of some digs and that many people feel they cannot advocate pre-Columbian contact, for to do so would mean demeaning the Indians and suggesting that they could not have made discoveries on their own. Strangely, this debate also rages in Indian circles, and a few of my best friends are adamant about maintaining the theory of isolation in order to enhance the achievements of our ancestors. Here I part company with other Indians and urge you to take a good look at all possible theories of pre-Columbian contacts and even the transmission of every cultural trait that is found elsewhere. Samuel Eliot

Morison is now dead, and we need no longer cringe in fear that he will discredit us for believing that someone besides Columbus visited these shores.

Unpleasant though it may be to some Indians, we need to know the truth about North American prehistory, and indeed that of the Western Hemisphere. I personally feel that unless and until we are in some way connected with world history as early peoples, perhaps even as refugees from Old World turmoils and persecutions, we will never be accorded full humanity. We cannot be primitive peoples who were suddenly discovered half a millennium ago. The image and interpretation are all wrong, and we are regarded as freaks outside historical time. During the Wounded Knee trials, I was forced to go along with Bering Strait advocates and argue that Indians had come across from Siberia, during one of those times that you people manipulate by increasing or decreasing the amount of water tied up in the glaciers, and brought along a very sophisticated culture and a protoscientific technology.

Standing in the hall of the courtroom one day, a non-Indian approached me and said, "I am very interested in this Bering Strait theory. It proves we are all natives." I said that being here perhaps 40,000 or even 100,000 years is a little more than having arrived in third-class steerage in 1920. I don't think he got the point since he was a Nebraska intellectual, and we all know that the "N" on Nebraska football helmets represents "Knowledge." But the point I wish to make is that this migration from Siberia is regarded as doctrine, but basically it is a fictional doctrine that places American Indians outside the realm of planetary human experiences. So I hope you will stop being so staid and respectable and begin an era of courageous speculation and openness and try to give pre-Columbian expeditions serious consideration.

Finally, in recent months I have been working hard with the coalition of American Indians seeking to get federal legislation clarifying the status of sacred sites, and naturally archaeology is involved or eventually will become involved in this problem. I must honestly report to you that many Indians are looking to your discipline for specific technical assistance in this struggle. One problem is the requirement of courts, at the present time, to insist that the location be a long-standing sacred site, and so it will make a big difference whether or not continuous or at least consistent use of the site is demonstrated by scholarly means as well as by traditional religious leaders. Some locations have very little evidence of use because they were considered of sufficient spiritual power that few individuals were allowed to go there. Consequently the locations show very little evidence of Indian use. It's not as if annual Methodist picnics and camp revivals were held at these locations.

You will be pleased to know that some very powerful Indian spiritual leaders have decided to find a reliable archaeologist or group of archaeologists who can help them completely cover and record what is present at some of these sacred sites. These people are very worried that if the site is declared sacred it will be invaded by hundreds of New Agers looking for a spiritual experience. So there is concern that plants, paths, shrines, rocks, and other aspects of the site be carefully and accurately recorded in case the place is desecrated by the curious in the years to come.

We can look forward, therefore, to creating a more constructive relationship between scholars and the people they study if we look at the present and future and make an effort to leave the past behind us. One difficulty in making this transition is that we already have a large body of data that represent the efforts of the previous century, and we are stuck with these writings and with the language they use, which is often derogatory and demeaning to American Indians. Students continue to have access to these materials, and consequently old attitudes and stereotypes are perpetuated even in spite of our best efforts. Archaeologists might well consider what the field of law has done in a comparable situation. In law we have what basically amounts to modernization of concepts through the device of scholars and practicing attorneys working to create "restatements" of the law.

One project that might be considered in the decades ahead would be a cooperative effort between archaeologists and interested Indians to rework and restate the findings of major importance in terms and language that eliminate cultural bias and attempt to give an accurate summary of what is known. That task seems formidable, but with some few exceptions it is not only manageable but probably an effort that is easily funded. We may not be able to promote such a project on a national scale, but we can certainly consider the beneficial impact such a recasting would create with respect to specific tribes and scholars and perhaps come up with a solution or alternative way of establishing good relations for the future.

▼ 7 ▼

LOW BRIDGE—EVERYBODY CROSS

▼▼▼▼

It may appear that I have discussed the origins of man and thereby eliminated the Bering Strait theory as a possible explanation of the source of the occupancy of the Western Hemisphere by American Indians and that devoting more time to this idea is superfluous. Nothing could be farther from the truth. Most Americans do not see the connection between the different scientific theories, nor do they understand that a shift or collapse of a major scientific doctrine requires a significant adjustment of all subsidiary doctrines that relied on it for their validity. Thus people accepting the idea that outmoded explanations of human evolution have been modified substantially will continue to hold with the Bering Strait theory even though to do so is a great inconsistency. But another point must be made that requires a chapter of discussion—and that is whether or not the Bering Strait is simply shorthand scientific language for "I don't know, but it sounds good and no one will check."

There are immense contemporary political implications to this theory that make it difficult for many people to surrender. Considerable residual guilt remains over the manner in which the Western Hemisphere was invaded and settled by Europeans. Five centuries of brutality lie uneasily on the conscience, and consequently two beliefs have arisen that are used to explain away this dreadful history. People want to believe that the Western Hemisphere, and more particularly North America, was a vacant, unexploited, fertile land waiting to be put under cultivation according to God's holy dictates. As Woody

Guthrie put it "This Land is your land, this Land is my land." The hemisphere thus belonged to whoever was able to rescue it from its wilderness state.

Coupled with this belief is the idea that American Indians were not original inhabitants of the Western Hemisphere but latecomers who had barely unpacked before Columbus came knocking on the door. If Indians had arrived only a few centuries earlier, they had no *real* claim to land that could not be swept away by European discovery. Aleš Hrdlička of the Smithsonian devoted his life to the discrediting of any early occupancy of North America, and a whole generation of scholars, fearfully following the master, rejected the claims of their peers rather than offend this powerful scholar. Finally, the embarrassing discovery that Clovis and Folsom points abounded in the western states forced the admission that the Indians might have beaten Columbus by quite a few centuries.

These ideas have great impact on how non-Indians view the claims for justice made by Indians. A personal experience may illuminate the impact of the Bering Strait on Indian rights. After Wounded Knee II in 1973, there were a number of trials of the people who had occupied the little village on the Pine Ridge Reservation in South Dakota. Each defendant had as his or her first affirmative defense to the criminal charges an avowed belief that the 1868 Fort Laramie treaty was still valid and that the protest was justified as a means of forcing the United States to live up to the terms of the treaty. This defense was then taken from every case and consolidated as one hearing in Lincoln, Nebraska, that dealt solely with this argument. Had the Indians prevailed in this contention, all the trials would have been rendered moot.

Much evidence was given at Lincoln concerning the relative state of civilized life at the time the treaty was made. The cultural achievements of the Sioux Indians were recited in an effort to demonstrate that, for many purposes, but chiefly for the trial, the Sioux had a clearly defined culture, government, religion, and economics and should have been entitled to the respect and benefits that larger nations enjoyed. In legal terminology, the contention was that the Sioux, in making treaties with the United States, had entered into a protectorate relationship comparable in every way to that enjoyed by Monaco and Liechtenstein with larger nations in Europe. This kind of relationship would then void the widely held belief that Indian tribes were mere "wards" of the government, as a confused portion of the John Marshall *Cherokee* cases had said.

Several traditional people did not want evidence on the Bering Strait offered because they preferred to rely on their own view of how the Sioux people had come to be. Some wanted to talk about an origin from an underground world near Wind Cave, South Dakota; others thought that stories about living in or near the Gulf of Mexico would be sufficient; and still others wanted to discuss the stories about living in the Far North, traditions that Werner Muller had used in his new theory of the human occupancy of North America. None of these accounts would have been understood in a Nebraska courtroom no matter how sympathetic the judge, because they differed considerably from scientific beliefs about the Bering Strait. So some discussion was presented on the Bering Strait.

I was standing in the hallway of the courthouse smoking a Pall Mall (in those wonderful days when you and not your peers chose your vices) and a lady approached me all agiggle about what had taken place that morning. She gushed over what had been said about the Bering Strait as if she were the chairperson of an anthropology department and left me with the comment: "Well, dearie, we are all immigrants from somewhere." After reflecting on her comment for a moment, I wanted to run down the hallway after her and say, "Yes, indeed, but it makes one helluva difference whether we came 100,000 years ago or just out of boat steerage a generation back."

Her remark was symptomatic of the non-Indian response to the pleas of Indians. By making us immigrants to North America, they are able to deny the fact that we were the full, complete, and total owners of this continent. They are able to see us simply as earlier interlopers and therefore throw back at us the accusation that we had simply found North America a little earlier than they had. On that basis, I would suppose, no nation actually *owns* the land its citizens live on, with the exception, if we accept early archaeological findings, of the people of Africa, where human evolution is believed to have begun.

In the 1960s a group of California Indians protested at an Indian Claims Commission field hearing against a ruling that the California claims would be consolidated into one complaint, instead of allowing the individual tribal groups to file specific claims for their lands. The exchange between the Indian protesters and Chief Claims

Commissioner Arthur Watkins got very heated at times. Watkins was a former U.S. senator, and his anti-Indian sentiments were well known. He had introduced the termination policy in Congress during the 1950s (to dismantle reservations and relocate Indians to cities) and was rewarded, after he had lost his Senate seat, with an appointment to the Indian Claims Commission where he could do further damage to Indians. At one point Watkins screamed at the Indians, "Go back where you came from," implying that they had recently traversed the Bering land bridge, perhaps during the Great Depression, and should go back to Asia.

Most scholars today simply begin with the *assumption* that the Bering Strait migration doctrine was proved a long time ago and there is no need to plow familiar ground. Jesse D. Jennings and Edward Norbeck's *Prehistoric Man in the New World* provides a compendium of papers discussing the state of research and field investigations dealing with the earliest sites of human occupation in the Americas. The introductory article has a single sentence on the Bering Strait, and the essays proceed without the slightest doubt that they are being built on a strong foundation. As these scholars were so confident of the validity of the land bridge doctrine, I assumed that there was, somewhere in scholarly publications, a detailed article that cited evidence and arguments that proved, beyond a reasonable doubt, that Paleo-Indians had at one time crossed from Asia into the Western Hemisphere. I was unable to find anything of this nature.

I did locate a splendid book entitled *The Bering Land Bridge*, edited by David M. Hopkins, that appeared to be the answer to my inquiry. Alas, most of the articles dealt with technical geologic and meteorological theories having nothing to do with human migrations. Only two articles even hinted at a discussion of migrations over the strait. H. Muller-Beck wrote,

> *[It has been] established conclusively that glaciers flowing from the Canadian shield coalesced with those originating in the Rocky Mountains during some part of the Wisconsin glaciation: this coalescence may have lasted from as early as 23,000 until as late as 13,000 years ago. During most of this interval, when Alaska was connected with Siberia by a wide Bering land bridge, an ice barrier would have separated Alaska from central North America and contact between*

*Alaska and central North America would have been extremely
difficult for land animals and man.*[1]

Muller-Beck also stated that what scientists were interested in was
"the diffusion of technological traits rather than population migrations in themselves: population movements are difficult to trace and
have little relevance to the present problem."[2] This clarification was
another puzzle, as his article was entitled "Migrations of Hunters on
the Land Bridge in the Upper Pleistocene," and it seemed likely that
population migrations would be important to the topic. Did "traits"
migrate without people?

The second article was "Human Migration and Permanent Occupation in the Bering Sea Area" by William Laughlin. Laughlin had
graciously come to the Wounded Knee trials in Lincoln to discuss
migration across the Bering Strait, so I looked forward to reading his
article. But this article was devoted largely to a discussion of the
Aleutian Islands, whose inhabitants he views as "quite distinct" from
American Indians. No evidence was cited to show that scholars had
proven that Paleo–Indians, or any other kind of Indians, had traversed the Bering Strait at any time. Describing the land bridge,
Laughlin painted a dismal picture:

*The interior landscape was evidently a low rolling plain, for
the most part devoid of relief, studded with bogs and swamps,
frozen much of the time, and lacking in trees or even many
bushes. Grass-eating herbivores may have been present in
fair numbers. The human adaptation to this region must
surely have been that of big-game hunters, living by means of
scavenging dead mammoths and such bovids as caribou,
bison, and musk-ox, and by intentionally hunting live animals.*[3]

But even this boggy, swampy land was not conducive to human
migration. Laughlin pointed out: "Conditions in the interior [of
Alaska] were severe, and likely only a few of its inhabitants found
their way into North America; these wanderers probably became the
ancestors of American Indians."[4]

Notice that Laughlin does not say for certain that any of these
inhabitants crossed the Bering Strait—he only says it was "likely"
that a few people did. We get no evidence at all that any Paleo–Indians

were within a thousand miles of Alaska during this time. No sites, trails, or signs of habitation are cited. And that is it. Laughlin is the acknowledged dean of American Bering Strait scholars, and he offered no concrete evidence whatsoever in support of this theory. I must conclude that generations of scholars, following the so-called scientific method of inquiry, have simply accepted this idea at face value, on faith alone. Here is more evidence that science is simply a secular but very powerful religion.

Scholars and popular science writers, in discussing the Bering Strait doctrine, usually do not address the many real difficulties that this idea presents. They reach a point where they must sound intelligent to their peers and readers and promptly spin out a tale of stalwart hunters trekking across frozen tundra or frolicking in suddenly warm Arctic meadows and then continue with their narrative. Looking at a map of the world, the proximity of Asia and Alaska seems too obvious to reject, but only rarely do scholars look at the map closely enough to see the absurdity of their claim.

We will look at two major geographic factors, the actual topography of eastern Asia and western North America and the barrier presented by the Ice Age, because scholars insist that the Indian migration occurred during a warm period of one of the Pleistocene ice ages. We will then look outside the topical area of Indian studies to see if and how other scholars use the Bering Strait in their work.

Presumably, the Paleo—Indians are living somewhere in eastern Siberia, having migrated there millennia ago. We will begin their journey with hunting bands living along the Kolyma River, at least half of which lies above the Arctic Circle. Looking eastward, they would find two formidable mountain ranges, the Khrebet Gydan and the Chukotskoye Nagor'ye, blocking their migration to the east. If and when they surmount these mountains and find their way to the shores of the eastern tip of Siberia, they must cross over the strait, and here most scholars insist that it was not a strait but a broad plain because the water that would have ordinarily covered it was locked up in the glacial sheet that covers the eastern part of the North American continent. We will allow them to cross, whatever the conditions.

Reaching the area we know as present-day Alaska, the people encounter a forbidding set of mountains both above and below the Arctic Circle. The Baird, Schawat, Endicott, and Shublik chains face them on the north, the Kaiyuh and Kuskokwim mountains are to the south, and on reaching the Canadian border they meet the Richardson Mountains and the Continental Divide of the northern-most chain of the Rocky Mountain group. To the south also are the Ogilvie Mountains and then the massive MacKenzie mountain chain with the smaller Franklin Mountains yet to the east. Finally, the hunt-ers are out on a reasonably flat plain, although one that is not calcu-lated to present a paradise for hunters, as it is, according to many scholars, covered with a thick glacial sheet.

It is theoretically possible for a group of humans, determined to relocate, to push through a seemingly unending set of mountain ranges to reach another location; the question is whether or not this migration really happened. A good practice in testing a theory is to find out what scholars say about a subject when they are discussing another topic and simply mention it as a peripheral part of their discussion. If we were to ask Bering Strait advocates if there were people in Siberia during the glacial interstadials, a time when it was possible for people to move without freezing to death or falling into glaciers, we might be assured that the shores of Siberia were teeming with impatient hunters. Indeed, didn't 98 percent of the Eskimos move from Siberia to Alaska at some point? But suppose we just ask about life in Siberia at this time. Let us see what scholars say about Siberia when they are not addressing the Bering Strait theory.

Kazimierz Kowalski and N. K. Vereshchagin are two important European scholars specializing in eastern Europe and Russia, includ-ing Siberia, in the Pleistocene period. Discussing whether or not Paleo hunters destroyed the mammoth in Siberia, Kowalski wrote that the "mammoth was probably never the principal game of human groups, and the traces of human colonization of Siberia at that time are very scarce."[5] Thus we are talking about a very small group of people even being in Siberia, let alone making the journey to Alaska. And these little groups were hardly a menace to the mammoth or any other megafauna. These few Paleo hunters were not just wandering around Siberia looking for an isthmus. Vereshchagin describes the kind of human occupation of Siberia that existed at the time when Paleo–Indians were supposed to be migrating:

> In the plains of eastern Europe and Siberia the life of primitive
> man was connected with river valleys. Large herds of mammoths,
> rhinoceros, roe, giant deer and reindeer, and boar roamed from

south to north and back along the valleys and flood plains of the rivers. The inhabitants of steppe watersheds preferred meadows and forests of flood plains, especially in dry periods or when the ground was covered with ice crust, because then elk, bison, tur, horse, and even saiga and camel fed upon branches of bushes and trees.[6]

The handful of people who lived in Siberia at this time did not have migratory patterns west to east across mountain ranges and high plateaus. Rather, they spent their time moving from south to north and back again following game who seasonally grazed when the weather was decent. Because these people had more than enough game and so did not hunt any of the species to extinction, there was no good reason for them to pick up their things and begin moving into rugged mountain areas where hunting would be more difficult and grazing animals a minimal resource.

The Kolyma would be the last good river system into which these hunters would have moved. There may have been some temporary expeditions to see what the eastern lands looked like, but the chances that these people would leave good hunting grounds for poorer ones are slim. Assuming, for the moment, that groups of hunters were able to get to Alaska, how would they have fared? Here we will ask a geologist with no doctrine of migration to support. Stephen Taber, writing a geological paper in the *Geological Society of America Bulletin*, gratuitously commented on migrating Paleo–Indians:

Early man would have had difficulty surviving in the non-glaciated areas of Alaska through the first period of deep freezing, and he could not have migrated southward across the ice barrier. During the epoch of deep thawing, conditions were more favorable for the existence of man in Alaska and for his migration southward than at any time since the first deep freezing of Pleistocene sediments; but this warm period was also a time of high sea level, when a land connection between Siberia and America is improbable; and the crossing of Bering Strait on ice is unlikely when the climate was warmer than it is now.[7]

We have only traced the most likely route and given scholars the benefit of the doubt by locating the Paleo–Indians on the Kolyma

River in eastern Siberia. Jared Diamond, discussing the big-game hunter migration that he believes took place around 12,000 years ago, says that "the colonists [of Siberia] probably came from eastern Europe, where Stone Age hunters in what is now the Ukraine built their houses out of neatly stacked bones of mammoths."[8]

If we locate the migrating Paleo–Indians in the Ukraine, then it is necessary to add about a dozen more mountain ranges and a goodly number of high desertlike plateaus, a considerable stretch of tundra, and no one knows how many other obstacles. The point that must be understood is that nobody really knows; they just seem to make it up as they go along. To suggest a Ukrainian origin for people who migrated across the Bering Strait in turn suggests that they had something definite in mind in wandering eastward, and that supposition cannot be substantiated at all. Almost every articulation of the Bering Strait theory is woefully deficient in providing a motive for the movement.

Let us now turn to the second great barrier to human migration over the Bering Strait—the Ice Age. In order to move Paleo–Indians across the Bering Strait, we must have the water level of the ocean drop significantly so that the isthmus will be dry land across which they pass or, alternatively, wander. The Ice Age of North American glaciation has provided a wonderful explanation for most scholars who deal with this subject. They seem to manipulate the water level to whatever depth they need to support their narrative. I have heard of drops of 50 feet, of nearly 300 feet, and, at the maximum, of 500 feet. It all depends on how much land between Alaska and Siberia the scholar needs to prove the case. The water level must drop a minimum of 60 meters, or 200 feet, to have any kind of isthmus at all.

We do not know the causes of the ice ages. They can range from the sudden cooling of the sun to a shift in the poles, the solar system suddenly traveling through an area of intense cold in space, or even a cometary dump of water. Most scientists seem to believe that glaciation was a prolonged process of cooling that enabled a massive ice sheet to build in the Northern Hemisphere and that as temperatures varied over a period of a million years, sometimes less, at least four stages of glaciation affected the Northern Hemisphere. Some scholars today are reducing the traditional four stages to only two, and a few adventurous souls are advocating only one real stage of glaciation with considerable variances in climate affecting the thickness and location of the major ice sheet.

The traditional mechanics of glaciation have snow remaining all summer and precipitating in increasing volume each winter until there is a sufficient amount to become ice and produce glaciers. The actual mechanics of this process are suspect. We need both warming and cooling to an extent far in excess of what we can observe today in order to bring it together. The temperate zones and tropics must evaporate a substantial amount of water in the summer. Indeed, if we are going to drop the water level over 200 feet and create the Bering land bridge, we have to evaporate an incredible volume of ocean water, an estimated 20.82 million cubic kilometers, enough water to cover an area of 5 million square miles with a sheet of ice 1.2 miles thick. All this water must be evaporated in the temperate and tropic zones within a very short time, or a great deal more water, allowing for evaporation, over a considerable period of time, must be evaporated and put into moisture-laden clouds.

Assume that we do get warmer oceans and produce heavy humid clouds; we then have to move these clouds from the temperate and tropical zones in a northerly direction to get them to the latitudes where they can precipitate as snow. Moving moisture north is the most difficult part of the process because there seems to be a kind of natural "dew" line below which cloud humidity would fall as rain and above which it would more likely fall as snow. I would locate this line around the present border of the United States and Canada, although knowledgeable meteorologists might place it higher or lower. We cannot today conceive of a natural process that would evaporate this amount of water and transport it safely from the temperate zones to ensure that it precipitated as ice in Canada.

If a massive cometary "dump" did occur, bringing extraterrestrial water in massive amounts to the Earth, we might be able to trace the fall of the water, torrential rains in the temperate climates and horrendous cascades of ice in the northern and southern latitudes, making the Ice Age almost instantaneous. This scenario is described by Donald Patten in *The Biblical Flood and the Ice Epoch*; it makes a lot of sense and explains many different phenomena. We have always had the problem of locating the source of water in the freshwater Pleistocene lakes in Nevada, Lahontan, and Bonneville. Speculations suggest they were filled by glacial runoff from the Sierra Nevadas, but the magnitude of these lakes prohibits that explanation. So a quick dump of fresh water on the midcontinent might be a good way to fill those lakes.

An annoying technical problem is that on our planet the winds generally move from west to east or east to west depending on the latitude. Constant and reliable winds do not, as a rule, move from north to south or south to north. In the Great Plains we do have the occasional "Alberta Clipper," which brings freezing Arctic air down the east side of the Rocky Mountains and creates serious snow and blizzard conditions. We do have occasional winds from the south that bring unseasonably warm winds north to melt the snow. And there is the very strange "Chinook," or zephyr, wind that heats cold areas unseasonably for a few hours and vanishes. On the whole, however, our winds and weather do follow a west to east pattern in the geographic regions where we find the big glacial sheets, so we must deal specifically with that fact.

To get the Ice Age under way, then, we must violate almost all the present knowledge we have of how our winds, clouds, and humidity work and create a different scenario that has very warm oceans creating clouds that promptly move north, across the dew line, and dump incredible amounts of snow on the Great Plains, the Hudson Bay area, and western Europe. Strangely, as far as we can tell, the snow clouds do not affect Siberia, and no glaciers are found there that remotely resemble what happens in North America and Europe. But there has to be incredible cold in Siberia at this time because we do find frozen mammoths and frozen tundra, and the "deep freeze," of which Stephen Taber wrote, really puts some very cold temperatures into the ground in these areas.

The Ice Age itself, as noted, has been broken up by many scholars into four or more stages, divided by periods called "interstadials," which means that some kind of warming process takes place in the midst of the glacial sheet. The onset of additional cold later then creates more glaciation. No one seems to have a good explanation of why or how the weather warms and subsequently cools. People are satisfied simply to have these interstadials because they make it possible to explain why we find traces of human occupancy in some remote and obscure sites that should have been covered with hundreds of feet of ice. Scholars are also able to introduce the Cro–Magnon people into Europe during the Ice Age by manipulating the data of the interstadial. The scandal at Sheguiandah, Canada, comes about because much evidence seems to point to interstadial settlement of a location. Here excavations, although performed under the most excruciating conditions, revealed significantly old human habitations and resulted in the dismissal of Dr. Thomas Lee.

Scholars also have invented strange concepts that they use to explain deposits that puzzle them. Thus "advances" and "retreats" of glaciers are suggested to account for various kinds of gravels and clays whose presence would raise questions about the validity of a prolonged period of glaciation. A glacier apparently "advances" by moving southward and covering ground where it has not previously been located. By the same token, "retreats" would find the glaciers melting significantly at their southern edge to let a considerable tract of ground dry out and support plant and animal life. It is puzzling just exactly how glaciers do "advance." According to accepted ideas, the snow accumulates to as much as several miles high and, as pressures build, the glacier, or a significant part of it, then begins to stretch out over land that has not previously been affected by glaciation.

This movement of glaciers has always given me problems. It is always presented as if the planet were a Sherwin–Williams paint logo and the glaciers just naturally began to move south, so people have rarely asked how an inert sheet of ice can start to travel.

Present theory would have glacial arms moving away from the Chicago region and traveling southward to the St. Louis, Missouri, area, not an inconsiderable distance. Geologists have primarily studied Alpine, Alaskan, and Greenland glaciers and on that basis have developed the idea of moving glacial ice sheets. But all of these glaciers originate in the mountains. They thus have the assistance of gravity as they move downhill into the flats. It would not seem difficult to move ice downhill in a mountain area, because you would have a solid rock surface underneath the ice, melting waters to lubricate it, and gravity to occasionally coax it along. Melting water would also run downhill, making some movements of the glacier a spectacular leap forward and simply not providing any encouragement during cold seasons.

If we transport this mechanism to the plains and woodlands of Canada, we have a different picture. Ice sheets, no matter how high, are resting on topsoil, so water simply seeps into the ground and finds its way from under the glacier to unglaciated terrain. We have no assistance from gravity at all. Indeed, moving the ice from Hudson Bay to St. Louis would mean moving it uphill many hundreds of feet in elevation. We can simply surmise that ice can and does go uphill if scientists want it to do so.

I have devoted an inordinate amount of attention to the mechanics of glaciation because it is necessary for the reader to see the magnitude of the problem that glaciation presents for our Ice Age Bering Strait immigrants. While eastern Siberia, mysteriously, is not glaciated, the Alaskan mountain chains are victims of glaciation. Existing Alaskan glaciers may be remnants of the original Pleistocene glacial sheet. If we are successful in getting any of the Paleo–Indians across the Bering Strait, they will simply have to remain in the central Alaskan marshlands until the glacial age has subsided and it is safe to travel. Or so we would think. But scientists, being an inventive sort, are not content to leave the settlers alone in Alaska.

The mechanism by which we move the Paleo–Indians from Alaska to the interior of the continent and then to the lower forty-eight is the "ice corridor." Jared Diamond brilliantly articulates this idea in an article in *Discover* magazine:

> At intervals during the ice age, a narrow ice-free, north-south corridor opened through this wall in the glacial ice sheets just east of the Rockies. One such corridor closed about 18,000 years ago, when apparently there were not yet any people in Alaska. However, when the corridor next opened, 12,000 years ago, the hunters must have been ready, for their telltale stone tools appear soon thereafter, not only at the south end of the corridor near what's now Edmonton, Alberta, but also elsewhere south of the ice cap.[9]

We may certainly *need* an ice corridor if we are going to explain how the Paleo–Indians got through the North American glacial sheet, but does that make it a geological certainty or reality?

To be really useful, this corridor would have to extend not only along the eastern slope of the Canadian Rockies. It would have to extend clear into central Alaska so that people then living in those frozen marshlands would be inspired to see where it led. We cannot have Paleo–Indians forsaking the few flat areas where there is game and wandering across range after range of glaciated mountains searching for the corridor that leads them to the south. In addition, it would seem that snow clouds, as they do today in the Rockies, would hit the high mountains and then dump their snow first on the eastern slopes before transporting all that moisture clear across the Canadian plains to deposit it in the Canadian Shield region. So we would have heavy snowfall precisely where scholars want a corridor.

American Indians, as a general rule, have aggressively opposed the Bering Strait migration doctrine because it does not reflect any of the memories or traditions passed down by the ancestors over many generations. Some tribes speak of transoceanic migrations in boats, the Hopis and Colvilles for example, and others speak of the experience of a creation, such as the Yakimas and other Pacific Northwest tribes. Some tribes even talk about migrations from other planets.

The Sioux, Salish, and Cheyenne remember their life in the Far North, which featured entirely different climatic conditions than we find today. The Sioux tradition, related by Thomas Tyon around the turn of the century, states:

> *The seven council fires burned in a land where the trees were small and the leaves fell before the coming of each winter.*
>
> *The seven fires were lighted in a circle (the nations were camped together) and Waziya appeared in the council. He was a large man and clothed in heavy furs. He said, "Why do you stay here where the trees are small and the leaves fall? Come with me and I will show you where the trees grow tall and the leaves are green all winter."*[10]

The Salish account has certain similarities. Ella Clark reports a tradition given to an interpreter in 1923 by four elderly Salish concerning Flathead Lake. To the question of origins, these old people said: "The first Salish were driven down from the country of big ice mountains, where there were strange animals. Fierce people who were not Salish drove them south. So in our stories our people have said: 'The river of life, for us, heads in the north.'"[11] As the memories of American Indians clash directly with scientific speculation, there is little room for compromise here.

Some tribal traditions do speak of ice and snow, which may be memories of North American glaciation, particularly since ice and snow are normal phenomena in the United States and remembering a really big snow would indicate that it was unusual. Most of these tales begin with the supposition that these groups were already present in North America prior to the onset of glaciation and quite possibly were observers of some of the climatic events of the Ice Age. The simplest ice tradition is that recorded by Julian Steward in a collection of Western Shoshone traditions but actually provided by a Northern Paiute person from Winnemucca, Nevada, concerning a large body of ice on the Snake River. As it is short, it can be used to illustrate the casual nature of the account. It seems that Coyote took some of the Paiutes north to the Snake River:

> *Ice had formed ahead of them, and it reached all the way to the sky. The people could not cross it. It was too thick to break. A Raven flew up and struck the ice and cracked it [when he came down]. Coyote said, "these small people can't get across the ice." Another Raven flew up again and cracked the ice again. Coyote said, "try again, try again." Raven flew up again and broke the ice. The people ran across.*[12]

Although there is some involvement with supernaturals, the basic story line is simply that the people went north, saw ice that went to the sky, and tried to cross it.

More complicated is the Chippewa creation story, which says that God tried four times to create the present world, but the first three efforts were doomed to failure because there was too much ice. The fourth time the effort was successful. If this tradition is a memory of the four stages of North American glaciation, it implies that the glaciation occurred within a reasonably short period of time so that people remembered the process. Because the Chippewa flood story relates that the flooding was caused by rapidly melting ice, we might suggest that Chippewa traditions are something to be taken seriously.

The Hopi have a tradition that their clans had to make migrations around the Western Hemisphere at the beginning of this present world. Five clans—the Blue Flute, the Ghost or Fire, the Spider, the Snake, and the Sun—all migrated up the western side of the continent until they reached "a land of perpetual snow and ice." Here they were tempted by Spider Woman to use their special powers to melt the mountains of ice and snow. Sotuknang, nephew of the Creator, then appeared and scolded them, pointing out that if they continued their activities they would melt the ice and snow and destroy the newly created world. They ceased their mischief, but Spider Woman and her clan were punished by becoming the source of evil and discontent in the world.[13] It seems unlikely that the Hopi, living on the Colorado Plateau in northern Arizona, would be able to guess that the northern reaches of the continent were lands of perpetual ice and snow. This tradition must reflect a journey to the north.

The argument over the validity of the Bering Strait doctrine might continue indefinitely, as most scholars are not inclined to take seriously the kinds of objections that skeptics raise. We need some additional evidence on one side or another to tip the scales and force a genuine reappraisal of the idea and the creation of a reasonable alternative. I did not realize how useful the doctrine was until I went outside the anthropological literature and began to look at how the scientists in other disciplines creatively used the Bering Strait for their own purposes. Pending the publication of all the "new" discoveries that Greenman's critics maintained were being made daily, let us now turn to the Bering Strait as it appears outside the Paleo–Indian context.

I was reading Donald Worster's popular historical study, *Dust Bowl*, one afternoon when I came across the following passage: "Horses and camels began their existence 45 million years ago in the North American grassland, migrating later across the Bering land-bridge to Asia. Bison followed the same route in reverse during the Ice Age and discovered a domain in which they could thrive."[14] I certainly wouldn't want to question or denigrate Worster's research or scholarly reputation, but it seems incredible to me that two grazing animals, terribly well adjusted to the grasslands of Kansas and Nebraska, could not thrive there and so would suddenly pick up their things and move north into an increasingly cold climate, where grass is at a minimum, looking for a better place to live.

I can't imagine thousands or perhaps millions of horses and camels struggling to get through the MacKenzie Mountains, or perhaps stampeding up Skagway Pass, crossing over the land bridge, and then being confronted with approximately a dozen rugged mountain ranges that they had to traverse before they found a home in the steppes of Asia. Did they suddenly change their diet, for the purposes of migration, from grass to tree bark and tundra, or yearn for the Asian steppes in some mystical vision?

The bison migration, as some scientists tell it, has a lot more to offer in the way of credibility. I can imagine the scene. *Bison bison* and Mrs. Bison are peacefully grazing in central Asia without a care in the world when they look up and see horses and camels strolling by—the camels perhaps on their way to Egypt. Quick as a wink, *Bison bison* turns to Mrs. Bison and happily exclaims: "Honey, do you realize that there is an ecological niche for grazing animals now open in Kansas and Nebraska?" The whole herd is terribly excited at the prospect in spite of the fact that the monsters *Bison taylori* and *Bison latifrons* already graze most of the central American plains.

Word goes around central Asia and pretty soon the whole *Bison bison* species decides to cross the Bering Strait, knowing full well that a trail has already been made for them by the large herds of horses and camels that have previously made the crossing. The *Bison bison* are very pleased because Indians are also crossing the Bering Strait, and now everything is set for the great American West, 12,000 years hence, when the Plains Indians will hunt them and sell their hides and Buffalo Bill will achieve fame by nearly exterminating them.

Worster may have been a little enthusiastic about his date of 45 million years because Stephen Taber, examining Alaskan muck deposits containing animal remains, suggested that "near the beginning of the Pleistocene, elephants, bisons, goats, moose, wapiti, caribou, bears, wolves, foxes, and other mammals migrated from Asia to America, and horses and camels migrated from America to Asia."[15] It was not just the intuitive feeling that an ecological niche was open around North Platte, Nebraska, then, that encouraged the bison migration. It was the mammal fad of the day, and any socially responsible species in Asia worth its salt was rushing toward the Bering Strait. We can surmise that horses and camels, watching the menagerie come loping across from Asia, decided to vacate North America while there was still time.

A short time later (in relative scientific terms), I found a book by L. Taylor Hansen entitled *The Ancient Atlantic*, which combined orthodox scientific findings about this ocean with some strange anomalies to give a history of geologic and human activities associated with the Atlantic. Hansen confirmed Worster's camel migration and added that "during the Oligocene the Aleutian bridge from Asia to the Americas was dry and functioning as a means for animals and plants to cross."[16] And she said, "While the Aleutian bridge was open in the Oligocene, some American species made their way to Asia. Among these was the baluchitherium, a giant rhinoceros measuring eighteen feet tall at the shoulder. He was therefore four feet higher than the Imperial mammoth and the largest land mammal. He crossed the Aleutian bridge into Asia, probably along with palm, oak and walnut forests of Canada."[17]

Now, I can see John Wayne, Rory Calhoun, and even Bob Hope and Bing Crosby struggling up Skagway Pass because they've done so in the movies. I can even, as a loyal admirer of science, try to visualize herds of horses and camels racing through frozen mountain passes in Alaska and Siberia. I cannot, however, imagine the largest land mammal who ever lived, four feet higher than the Imperial mammoth, moving by the thousands through the western Canadian mountains and trying desperately to get across the Bering Strait to Asia before the sea level rose again.

Nor can I imagine forests of palm, oak, and walnut moving majestically west from Alaska to Siberia. I have great difficulty conceiving of their means of locomotion—other than the fantasy of scholars. Do you suppose that they "threw" their coconuts, acorns, and walnuts as far west as they could reach each fall and in stately procession marched right across the Bering Strait, putting their roots down in tundra and then continuing to lean westward each generation until the migration was complete? Minimally, this scenario would have required that the palms had previously left the Caribbean and Florida areas and moved into the Northwest Territories or come up the British Columbia shores in order to be in a position to take advantage of the land bridge when it finally appeared.

After I saw *Jurassic Park* and was thrilled to learn that most of the dinosaurs featured in the movie were in fact from the Cretaceous period, not the Jurassic, I was determined to learn more about them. Robert Bakker, who was the movie consultant, lives in Boulder, and so some friends called him to see if we could have lunch and learn more about the dinosaurs. He was always quite busy doing important dinosaur work, and, considering the popularity of the movie, it was not difficult to see that he could not take the time to have lunch with fans, no matter how sincere they were.

I eventually did meet him and he is a splendid fellow. But while we were waiting week after week to meet him, I had a chance to purchase and read his excellent book *The Dinosaur Heresies*. Bakker apparently fancies himself the enfant terrible of science and the great paleontological heretic, although his beliefs and theories are quite in line with Stephen Jay Gould and other popular apologists for orthodox science, so the title of the book is a little misleading. He is pretty much a party-line scholar with great personal energy and charisma.

Reading Bakker's book, however, I found chills running up and down my spine. Bakker knows dinosaurs, and, while he identifies literally dozens of great-uncles, uncles, aunts, cousins, and shirttail relatives among the various species of dinosaur, he does not once identify any specific family trees that show evolutionary descent from one species to another. He does know dinosaur muscles, energy levels, diets, and environments intimately, so the book is well worth reading. But what really attracted me about his discussion on dinosaurs was the fact that they also had crossed the Bering Strait land bridge.

My favorite passages are herewith reproduced. Giving us an elaborate description of *Protoceratops,* Bakker says that not one of these creatures "has ever been reported from the rich beds of the American Judith and Laramie Deltas. Swampy meadows and broad humid flood plains were evidently not to Protoceratops's liking, though Canada and Montana did play host to relatives [see!] in late Cretaceous times—the general Leptoceratops and Montanoceratops. Leptoceratops probably was an immigrant from Asia."[18] Bakker elaborates on this tantalizing hint by stating, "There were many advanced mammals and protoceratopsid dinosaurs in the Central Asian Highlands not found in Alberta, Montana, and Wyoming. But very late in the last epoch of the Cretaceous Period, the Asiatic mammals and dinosaurs began appearing in North America. These immigrants could only have passed over the Bering Land Bridge where the northeastern tip of Asia met America."[19]

Fortunately, Robert Bakker does not mince words. He suggests also that South America was once an isolated continent in which mammals and birds evolved into species found nowhere else. Then an isthmus was formed, probably due to the drop in water level of the seas during Pleistocene glaciation, which is now present-day Panama. With this connection made, North American fauna, in particular elephants, jaguars, deer, tapirs, and wolves, rushed into the southern continent. "These North American immigrants devastated the native fauna," Bakker maintains. "Most of the big South American species went extinct, victims of predation and competition from the Northerners, as well as of their diseases."[20]

Bakker is a respected scientist, and so we should take his word on this matter, but it is difficult to believe that deer and tapir can eliminate giant ground sloths twenty feet tall, saber-toothed pouch mammals, and flightless killer birds larger than a lion merely by grazing areas occupied by these animals. Species, particularly grazing herbivores, generally can accommodate themselves to other grazers. Moreover, animals do not, as a rule, transmit diseases across species boundaries. The Panama land bridge is here invoked to explain events (the extinction of large mammals) that scientists cannot otherwise explain—and the explanation simply does not hold water.

Bakker is at least consistent with his arguments regarding land bridges. "The late Cretaceous world contained all the prerequisites for this kind of disaster," he writes. "The shallow oceans drained off and a series of extinctions ran through the saltwater world. A monumental immigration of Asian dinosaurs streamed into North America, while an equally grand migration of North American fauna moved into Asia."[21] From this description it seems likely that every time a narrow body of water was temporarily dry, hundreds if not thousands of species immediately dropped what they were doing and headed for the isthmus before it closed. Even Stephen Jay Gould is not above transporting animals over hypothetical necks of land if the occasion warrants. Witness his description of the Irish elk:

> *The giant deer flourished in Ireland for only the briefest of times—during the so-called Allerod interstadial phase at the end of the last glaciation. This period, a minor warm phase between two colder epochs, lasted for about 1,000 years, from 10,000 to 11,000 years before the present. (The Irish Elk had migrated to Ireland during the previous glacial phase when lower sea levels established a connection between Ireland and continental Europe.)*[22]

Since the interstadial was only 1,000 years long, or about the time between the fall of Rome and the discovery of America, the Irish elk must have been gathered on the shore waiting for the land bridge to open. It does not seem possible, considering the time that most scientists require for species to pass over a land bridge, for the large deer to make the transfer.

When reading these "scientific" explanations we must always remember that in order to have land bridges at all, or even an occasional isthmus, we are basically committed to moving a great deal of water around to create an ice age, or we are making the continents rise and fall a significant distance, or we are otherwise manipulating a monstrous amount of physical material just to make our theories and speculations seem reasonable. If scientists were required to solve these physical problems prior to their rather offhand remarks about migrations, there would be considerably fewer land bridges in scientific literature. Following orthodox methodology, we should not invoke activities of nature that we do not see operative today.

It occurred to me that I might be able to find an essay devoted solely to the question of the validity of land bridges, written when a scholar had no thesis of migrating species to defend and when the Bering Strait migration did not come to mind. And indeed such an essay exists. George Gaylord Simpson was about as close to a living deity in evolutionary biology as Mother Nature herself, and one day he sat down and penned a little piece entitled "Mammals and Land Bridges." We can assume that what was applicable to mammals might be profitably applied to dinosaurs and perhaps even to Paleo people.

Simpson uses a commonsense approach to the subject and suggests that only representatives of genera cross land bridges. A single genus does not by itself cross into new continents. More important, carnivores generally follow the herbivores they have been feasting on. "Where herbivores go, carnivores can and will accompany them, and carnivores cannot go where there are no herbivores. The postulation of land bridges on the basis of one or a few mammals is thus very uncertain. Unless there is a reasonable possibility that their companions have not been discovered, a theoretical bridge based on such evidence is probably unreal."[23] In other words, if we do want to move horses and camels to Asia and bison to America, we will probably want to ensure that carnivores accompanied them if we wish to make our case.

The objection raised earlier regarding human, and then mammal and dinosaur, expeditions across the Bering Strait—that the route had to traverse a set of rugged mountain ranges on both sides of the Bering Strait—is regarded by Simpson as a major barrier even if a land bridge does exist: "For many of these animals, such as the monkeys, the absence of necessary environmental conditions beyond the bridge is an evident reason for their stopping where they did. Others, like the bison, were evidently kept by analogous environmental barriers from reaching the bridge."[24] In other words, the bison simply would not have begun the tedious trip through the Siberian mountains, nor would horses and camels have tried to scale Skagway.

George Gaylord Simpson's conclusion, apparently unread or unheeded by several decades of scientific writers, is that "in the whole history of mammals there are exceedingly few cases (e.g., Lower Eocene between Europe and North America) where the evidence really warrants the inference of a wide-open corridor between two now distinct continental masses."[25] This conclusion supports Werner Muller's Canada to Scandinavia–England–France thesis and does not give much comfort to the myriad scholars who believe in the Bering Strait—for both animal and human migrations.

Not only does the more recent interpretation of human evolution militate against American Indians being latecomers to the Western Hemisphere, an examination of the Bering Strait doctrine suggests that such a journey would have been nearly impossible even if there had been hordes of Paleo–Indians trying to get across the hypothetical land bridge. It appears that not even animals or plants *really* crossed this mythical connection between Asia and North America. The Bering Strait exists and existed only in the minds of scientists.

Dr. Claude Lévi-Strauss, in his article on Brazil, says that "many archaeologists in the United States still subscribe to the dogma that this was the millennium [tenth] when human beings crossed the Bering Strait and set foot in America for the first time."[26] Lévi-Strauss and many European scholars understand that there is no basis for the early dating of the so-called migration. Whether they have discarded the very idea of it is undetermined, but with the admission that various species of hominids coexisted, the way is being cleared for an honest examination of the question of origins on the basis of scientific investigation and not as a dogma that must be uncritically accepted.

NOTES

1. H. Muller-Beck, "Migrations of Hunters on the Land Bridge in the Upper Pleistocene," in *The Bering Land Bridge*, ed. David M. Hopkins (Stanford, Calif.: Stanford University Press, 1967), pp. 380-381.
2. Ibid., p. 374.
3. William S. Laughlin, "Human Migration and Permanent Occupation in the Bering Sea Area," in *The Bering Land Bridge*, ed. David M. Hopkins (Stanford, Calif.: Stanford University Press, 1967), p. 421.
4. Ibid., p. 445.
5. Kazimierz Kowalski, "The Pleistocene Extinction of Mammals in Europe," in *Pleistocene Extinctions*, ed. Paul S. Martin and H. E. Wright, Jr. (New Haven, Conn.: Yale University Press, 1967), pp. 355-356.

6. N. K. Vereshchagin, "Primitive Hunters and Pleistocene Extinction in the Soviet Union" in *Pleistocene Extinctions*, ed. Paul S. Martin and H. E. Wright, Jr. (New Haven, Conn.: Yale University Press, 1967), pp. 372-373.

7. Stephen Taber, "Perennially Frozen Ground in Alaska: Its Origins and History," *Geological Society of America Bulletin* 54 (1943): 1,433-1,548, esp. p. 1,539.

8. Jared Diamond, "The American Blitzkrieg: A Mammoth Undertaking," *Discover* (June 1987): p. 82.

9. Ibid., p. 83.

10. Thomas Tyon, "Spirits," in *James Walker, Lakota Belief and Ritual*, ed. Raymond DeMallie (Lincoln: University of Nebraska Press, 1980), p. 120.

11. Ella E. Clark, *Indian Legends of the Northern Rockies* (Norman: University of Oklahoma Press, 1966), p. 93.

12. Julian Steward, "Some Western Shoshoni Myths," *Bureau of American Ethnology, Bulletin 136*, Anthropological Papers no. 31 (Washington, D.C.: Smithsonian Institution, 1943), p. 299.

13. Frank Waters, *The Book of the Hopi* (New York: Penguin Books, 1963), pp. 39-40.

14. Donald Worster, *Dust Bowl* (New York: Oxford University Press, 1979), p. 72.

15. Taber, "Perennially Frozen Ground in Alaska," p. 1,530.

16. L. Taylor Hansen, *The Ancient Atlantic* (Amherst, Wisc.: Amherst Press, 1969), p. 257.

17. Ibid.

18. Robert T. Bakker, *The Dinosaur Heresies* (New York: William Morrow, 1986), p. 249.

19. Ibid., pp. 440-441.

20. Ibid., p. 443.

21. Ibid.

22. Stephen Jay Gould, *Ever Since Darwin* (New York: W. W. Norton, 1977), p. 90.

23. George Gaylord Simpson, "Mammals and Land Bridges," *Journal of the Washington Academy of Sciences* 30, no. 4 (April 1940): p. 159.

24. Ibid.

25. Ibid., p. 149.

26. Claude Lévi-Strauss, "Saudades do Brasil," *New York Review of Books*, 43, no. 20 (December 21, 1995), p. 20.

▼ 8 ▼

AT THE BEGINNING

▼▼▼▼

As I have already argued, Western science today is akin to a world history that discusses only the Mediterranean peoples. Indeed, the institutionalization of knowledge in the academic setting has made status more important than accomplishments or ideas when determining the canon of truth that will give the best explanation of our planet. We are living in a strange kind of dark ages where we have immense capability to bring together information, but when we gather this data, we pigeonhole it in the old familiar framework of interpretation, sometimes even torturing the data to make it fit.

Discordant facts and experiments are simply thrown away when they do not fit the prevailing paradigm. Once a theory such as the progression of human evolution, the Bering Strait land bridge, or the big game hunters is published, it is treated as if it was *proven* and it is then popularized by people who rarely read the original documents and vigorously defended by scholarly disciplines more fiercely than they would defend our country if called upon to do so. Alfred North Whitehead wrote in *Adventures of Ideas*:

> *When the routine is perfect, understanding can be eliminated, except such minor flashes of intelligence as are required to deal with familiar accidents, such as a flooded mine, a prolonged drought, or an epidemic of influenza. A system will be the product of intelligence. But when the adequate routine*

is established, intelligence vanishes, and the system is main-
tained by a coordination of conditioned reflexes.[1]

No better description can be offered of the big-game hunter hypothesis when we see scholars seriously arguing that the Paleo–Indians killed the megafauna so quickly they didn't even leave large piles of bones.

On the whole, Indian tribes, faithful to their traditions, understand the origin of life on our planet as a creation. The stories may appear childish, but they do describe processes that may well parallel or describe segments of scenarios sometimes put forward by scientists. The perfect-symmetry proposals put forward by Heinz Pagels are not radically different from the Sioux creation story of Inyan the Rock. Some of the other tribal accounts have much in common with the binary theory of quanta evolution developed by Alfred de Grazia. The problem with the Indian traditions is that hardly any open-minded scientist has heard them, and an even fewer number know how to listen to Indian elders, catch the nuances of meaning, and be prepared to elicit the proper information from the story.

I am not a scientist and can only determine the state of our scientific knowledge by reading scholarly articles and popular writers to see what they say science knows. Obviously, from the objections I have raised in [*Red Earth, White Lies*], a great deal of the current popular scientific beliefs and doctrines do not hold up to even the simplest critical review. I hope that the next generation of scholars, Indian and non-Indian, will force open any breaches I may have identified in the wall of scientific orthodoxy and make honest people out of scientists who are now afraid to publish their true beliefs and thoughts out of concern for peer conformity. To that end, therefore, I will now discuss areas where I believe good research and much difficult thinking will produce substantial breakthroughs in the years ahead.

CREATION

Apart from tribes having migration stories as descriptive of their origins, the majority of stories of origin suggest a creation in which people are given, simultaneous with their creation, an awareness that they have been created. These traditions often suggest that there was no essential spiritual/intellectual difference between people and animals. Some tribes report that an entity could change shape and experience what various birds and animals experience in that particular kind of body. Thus stories relate that people and animals married each other. Peter Noyes, an elder on the Colville Reservation in northeastern Washington State, told Ella Clark: "Long ago—I don't know how long ago, the animals were the *people* of this country. They talked to one another the same as we do. And they married, too. That went on for many, many years, and then the world changed."[2] From the Sioux stories of compatible spirits, I feel that this "marriage" must have been a blending of two kinds of individual spirits.

Human beings seem to be the focal point of communication in our world. Many traditions say that we cannot do anything very well except communicate, and consequently we are chosen to be the carriers of ceremonial thanksgiving activities on behalf of all other forms of life. We are not the only primate-shaped creatures, however, since there are peoples larger and smaller than we are, and some of these other peoples at one time coexisted with us, much as Cro–Magnon and Neanderthal are now known to have been contemporaries.

We seem to find cohesive biotic layers in our geologic strata that represent whole life systems with virtually no evolutionary patterns present. It's as if a whole organic interlocking network including prey and predator and creatures dependent on a symbiotic relationship sprang into existence at once. If anything "punctuated," it experienced this spasm along with the creatures it devoured and the predators it fed. Then came the massive deposition of materials, quickly burying the system and preserving the fossils. And then a whole new biota came into existence. We always tread on the verge of "creation," but we cannot bring ourselves to face the probable "fact" of it.

Geologic time scales must inevitably be shortened by scientists. If we have previously allocated millions of years for the decline of the dinosaurs, and consensus is moving toward a quick destruction of these creatures by a meteor hit near Yucatán, do we really need those millions of years any longer? Time estimates on the age of Niagara Falls were once near one million years and are now figured in the thousands of years. Thus we may find ourselves reducing the time span for biotic life by substantial numbers, making it clear that things could not have evolved. I do not think that we will ever reach the short time favored by religious fundamentalists, but we may discover that the planet has a much shorter and more spectacular history than we thought possible.

THE EARLY CLIMATE

Many cultures look back on a golden age; many more see the history of the planet in terms of "ages" that are brought to an end by great catastrophes. Some thinkers have suggested that mountain chains rise quickly and dramatically during these events, building a chain of mountains in months and years rather than in millennia and millions of years.

As we know that the northern lands once had warmth of sufficient duration to grow corals in Greenland, and presumably daisies in Siberia, we have three choices in interpreting these facts: (1) continents shifted dramatically, moving some areas to warm climates and others to cold ones; (2) the planet once had a cloud canopy surrounding it, which provided uniform warm temperatures everywhere; or (3) prior to the tilt of the Earth's axis, there was uniform sunlight hitting the poles and the equator, providing a uniform temperature.

It seems to me that a decent argument can be made for the idea that at one time, when people our size inhabited the Earth, the planet was shrouded with some kind of water canopy. While people could determine light and darkness, the canopy was too thick to produce clear images of the sun and moon. An additional feature of this time was that rain, snow, and thunderstorms, at least as we know them today, were not meteorological phenomena. Instead, the Earth was covered by a mist in which water continuously evaporated from the ground and precipitated again as mist.

Clarence Pickernell, a man with Quinault, Chehalis, and Cowlitz ancestors, said, "When the world was young, the land east of where the Cascade Mountains now stand became very dry. This was in the early days before rains came to the earth. In the beginning of the world, moisture came up through the ground, but for some reason it stopped coming."[3] Genesis also records this phenomenon: "For the Lord God had not caused it to rain upon the earth, and there was not man to till the ground [2:5]. But there went up a mist from the earth and watered the whole face of the ground [2:6]."

We cannot tell which of the possible radical changes in the planet's composition these images might describe. This condition existed prior to the origin of the four rivers in Mesopotamia in the Old Testament, however. I have already noted that Sioux spoke of a time when there was no thunder and lightning and the rivers were dug by giants. So we are talking about a climatic condition in which there were no large rivers because there were insufficient amounts of rain to carve out river beds and provide flow. It is also proper to note in this connection that the appearance of the rainbow made a strong impression on ancient people, and that creates a dilemma, because only the Hebrews connect the rainbow and Noah's flood. The subject of radically different climates is, however, a topic that will require some significant thought.

VOLCANISM

We can surmise that we are talking about some profound volcanism when some traditions speak of the world being destroyed by fire. Ager and Hedge both stated that the lava flows they encountered appeared as if they were fresh. The Sioux traveled to the White River to show their children the plumes of smoke and tell them about the time when they lived in a land of volcanoes. Our experience, and the Indian traditions we have used in *Red Earth, White Lies*, would suggest that volcanism was a local event, and our experiences in recorded history would seem to confirm that idea. Nevertheless, it would be interesting to correlate the various studies on igneous rocks and see if there was a time when widespread volcanism was a major event on the planet, as the destruction of a locale would not necessarily be enough to cause people to believe that the world had indeed ended.

GEOLOGIC STRATIGRAPHIC COLUMNS

Derek Ager raised many questions about the viability of the orthodox interpretations of deposition of strata, his major argument focusing on the fact that many strata regarded as sedimentary had a geographic expanse far in excess of what is possible. Thus the sandstones, limestones, and chalk that spanned whole continents and were found in some places around the world could not have been laid down gradually and calmly by incremental additions of sediment. He pointed out that contemporary measurements of deposition, including the ocean floors, were nowhere near the thickness required to produce the sedimentary rocks we find on the continents. According to Alfred de Grazia:

*If every different statum that was ever labeled were heaped up
in its maximum deposited thickness, the pile would tower into
the stratosphere. According to the accounts rendered of the
world geologic column, there should be 400,000 feet, or 80
miles thick, of sediment. Furthermore, the heap should cover
the globe, unless somebody has been digging rock from the
oceans and carrying it up the continental shelves. For the
ocean bottoms are scarcely sedimented.*[4]

Creation should be excluded from explaining the sedimentary rock in
that it posits a creator who periodically exterminates his biota, leaving
extraterrestrial "dumps" of material from as yet unidentified sources.

Reducing the millions of years required to lay down a bed of sandstone, shale, or limestone, depositing chalk and loess in a quick fly-by
or fly-through of material, and coordinating the lava flows on a global
basis could bring the strata containing flora and fauna much closer
together. We could then explain "living fossils" and the presence of
Jurassic and Triassic flora in the Pacific basin without crossing our fin-
gers behind our backs. With some overlap of the periods having plentiful biospheres on the planet, the monsters of folklore and the giantism
in strata would be seen as part of the early experiences of our species.

While geologists are very conservative, the major problem in
this field is that it is so complicated. Hundreds of thousands of technical reports exist describing very complicated formations. But geologists are trapped in an unrealistic orthodox time scale by the
paleontologists and evolutionists. Geology should properly be linked
with astronomy and not with biology. The Shoemaker and Hale–
Bopp comets suggest that planets, especially ours, are not immune
to cosmic catastrophes of unimaginable size and power. With the
general acceptance of the Yucatán comet/meteor being the cause of
the demise of the dinosaurs and the possibility that the Carolina
bays and the Alaska lakes are remnants of a close fly-by of a comet/
meteor, we can expect geology and astronomy to link ever closer
and lead the way out of our present impasse.

LIVING FOSSILS

In December 1994 a marvelous discovery was made in Australia. David
Noble of the Parks and Wildlife Service of that country discovered

an isolated grove of a rain forest, a grove of what are enthusiastically described as "Wollemi pines," pine trees with dense waxy foliage and knobby bark thought to have disappeared in the Jurassic period. Newspaper accounts suggested that this find was as significant as the discovery of the dawn redwood tree in China in 1944 and the coelacanth fossil fish off Madagascar in 1938.[5] Another instance of living fossils was the discovery of a Temnospondyl, a class of reptiles, found in 1978 by Anne Warren of Latrobe University.[6]

Everyone is pleased at the discovery of the Wollemi pines, but is it such a geologic rarity? L. Taylor Hansen, in *The Ancient Atlantic,* wrote, "There is a botanical fact which demands explanation. The South Sea islands are covered by Triassic plants. These living fossils, not found elsewhere, demand some type of explanation."[7] Furthermore, she pointed out that by the end of the Jurassic, Japan and the Philippines had been isolated from the mainland and consequently have Jurassic flora.[8] So what explanation is given by scientists for these plants that seem to be immune from evolution? How can plants from 150 million years ago not have evolved into something else? How can they be sitting there as nice as can be when completely out of the geologic, paleontological, and evolutionary time scale?

We have become so accustomed to accepting scientific authority that we have lost the ability to understand what scientists are saying. Scientific authorities, on the other hand, casually let fly remarks that drastically undercut their beloved evolutionary doctrines without even realizing what they have done. We have literally hundreds of "fossil creatures" from the past living with us today. In fact, when we begin to compile a list of the animals casually mentioned by scientists, it is alarming. Where is evolution?

Jacob Bronowski, writing about Africa in preparation for telling us about the wonderful fossil ancestors that Louis Leakey, Raymond Dart, and others have discovered there, discusses the alleged human remains, pointing out the great changes that took place over two million years. Then he says: "naturally, we expect the animals of the Savannah also to have changed greatly. But the fossil record in Africa shows that this is not so. Look as the hunter does at the Topi antelope now. The ancestor of man that hunted its ancestor two million years ago would at once recognize the Topi today."[9] If we had never seen a Topi prior to last Christmas, and had been assured by paleontologists that they have been dead for two million years, would we not be surprised and excited if one were discovered in unexplored Africa this past year? Does that make it a living fossil?

Robert Bakker, discussing a large tortoise, Colossochelys, that had been found "everywhere in the Old World tropics, from Kenya to Cape Provine to Java," said that wherever it was found "there was an accompanying rich fauna of big, modern mammals,"[10] indicating that it was probably not really a fossil, simply a species that recently became extinct. "Crocodiles," he noted, "first enter the chronicle of the rocks long after lizards but a few million years before dinosaurs."[11] And not just the crocs: "Alligators are dinosaur uncles—relatives of the direct ancestors of early dinosaurs—and as such they should be living representatives of the ancestral dinosaurs' forelimb arrangement."[12] In other words, many living creatures today should actually be classified as living fossils, representatives of remote geologic eras, because they apparently arose in remote times and have somehow survived all subsequent geologic changes to persist today.

Gordon Rattray Taylor, in *The Great Evolution Mystery*, notes the following examples. (1) Bees: "Bees preserved in amber from the Tertiary period are almost identical with living bees."[13] (2) Bacteria: "Since they reproduce themselves, in favorable conditions every twenty minutes, they might be expected to evolve faster than any other organism—but fossil bacteria going back to three and a half billion years, to the threshold of life itself, have been recovered and are virtually identical with modern forms."[14] (3) Salamanders: "At the start of the Jurassic, there was a sudden and complete change to the modern type of Anuran, a change so successful that they have remained successful for 200 million years and have spread far and wide over the earth."[15] (4) Penguins: "No Antarctic fossil penguins have been found, but there are plenty in Australia, New Zealand, and Patagonia, going back to the Eocene; unfortunately they are very like modern penguins and tell us nothing about their origins."[16] (5) Oysters: "Many bivalves, such as oysters and mussels, have evolved very slowly, changing little in 400 million years." (6) And others: "The king crabs unchanged since the Eriassic and the opossums."[17] And we must not forget the platypus and shark. A large number of familiar mammals and fish, as a matter of fact, have orthodox dates from around the Paleocene—12 million years ago.

It should not take a genius to recognize that the so-called antiquity of these creatures is illusory. We see hundreds of species in our modern world who are, in fact, survivors of previous Earth epochs. If we could find an honest scientist and have him or her make up a complete list of animals, fish, birds, reptiles, bacteria, and plants that "stopped evolving" millions of years ago and are found alive and kicking in the modern world, we would have a pretty good inventory of contemporary fauna and flora. The conifer genus *Metasequoia* was discovered in 1946 in China.[18] The deep sea mollusk *Neopilin galatheae* was found in 1952 off the Mexican coast.[19] The list must be endless. It must be possible, and probably necessary to understand our situation, to collapse these millions of fictional years as much as we can and understand that our planet has a much different history than we have been told.

DINOSAURS

The discussion of living fossils was necessary because a number of tribal traditions describe creatures that may have been dinosaurs. In the worldview of orthodox science, such a suggestion is preposterous at first blush, but as we have seen, a number of fauna originated in very early times and the crocodile and alligator are said to have come on the scene before the dinosaurs flourished. The Tohono O'odham, formerly called the Papagos, live on a large reservation in southern Arizona adjoining the Mexican border. Most prominent on the eastern side of their lands is a large peak, Baboquivari, and this site plays an important role in their earliest traditions. An extremely large animal, personified as the spirit Etoi, was said to have inhabited the mountain and dominated the vicinity.

The Tohono O'odham are very secretive about this creature, but good authority suggests that it was some kind of dinosaur. Several years ago, Tohono O'odham from south of the border in northern Mexico and the American Tohono O'odham gathered for a ceremony to revive ancient customs. It is believed that one object of particular sacredness used in this ceremony was an unfossilized dinosaur bone from one of Etoi's personifications.

Again the Pacific Northwest peoples have a number of stories concerning oversized animals in their lakes and rivers. As the current trend in dinosaur research suggests that these creatures, for the most part, were warm-blooded and had social and instinctual characteristics reminiscent of mammals of today, there is no reason to hesitate suggesting that some of these creatures, described as animals or large

fish by observers, were surviving individuals of some presently classified dinosaur species. That is to say, humans and some creatures
we have classified as dinosaurs were contemporaries.

The best-known story concerns the monster, known as Ogopogo,
who lives in Lake Chelan on the east slope of the Cascades. Lake
Chelan is fifty-five miles long, filling a glacial valley, and reaches
depths of around 1,600 feet. Originally, the Washington area, according to a grandson of Chief Wapato of the Colville tribe, was a
flat, fertile, grassland prairie inhabited by grazing animals. A monster showed up and began devouring the animals, causing the Indians to go hungry. Twice they appealed to the Great Spirit, and he
killed the monster, but it revived. The third time "the Great Spirit
struck the earth with his huge stone knife. All the world shook from his
blow. A great cloud appeared over the plain." And when the cloud finally dissipated, the people could see that the land had been radically
changed: "Huge mountains rose on all sides of them. Among the mountains were canyons. Extending from the northwest to the southeast
for two days' journey was a very deep canyon between high mountains."[20] The monster was buried in this canyon, which was then
filled with water to form Lake Chelan, and this lake was subject to
sudden and intense wave disturbances, leading the people to say
that the monster's tail was still alive and causing problems for them.

Why would we attempt to identify this creature as a dinosaur or
comparable animal? Indians generally speak with precise and literal
imagery. As a rule, when trying to identify creatures of the old stories, they say they are "like" familiar neighborhood animals but then
carefully compare the perceived differences. I have found that if the
animal being described was in any way comparable to modern animals, that similarity would be pointed out; the word "monster" would
not be used.

Only in instances where the creature bears no resemblance to
anything we know today will it be described as a monster. As no
dinosaur shape resembles any modern animal and as the reports are
to be given literal credibility, I must suggest that we are identifying a
dinosaur. Thus, in the story of large animals at Pomme de Terre prairie
in southwestern Missouri, a variant suggests that the western animals
were megafauna and that the creatures who crossed the Mississippi
and Missouri rivers and invaded the lands of the megafauna were
dinosaurs. The dinosaurs thus easily displace the familiar, perhaps

Pleistocene, megafauna and move west, where we find their remains in the Rocky Mountains today.

In numerous places in the Great Lakes are found pictographs of a creature who has been described in the English translation as the "water panther." This animal has a saw-toothed back and a benign, catlike face in many of the carvings. Various deeds are attributed to this panther, and it seems likely that the pictographs of this creature, which are frequently carved near streams and lakes, are a warning to others that a water panther inhabits that body of water. The Sioux have a tale about such a monster in the Missouri River. According to reports, the monster had "red hair all over its body . . . and its body was shaped like that of a buffalo. It had one eye and in the middle of its forehead was one horn. Its backbone was just like a crosscut saw; it was flat and notched like a saw or cogwheel."[21] I suspect that the dinosaur in question here must be a stegosaurus.

Part of the original story implies that the creature was luminous at night, suggesting that someone was combining the memory of this creature with his first view of a steamboat. Frankly, that is a difficult argument to refute, although the Sioux phrase describing the steamboat is entirely different from the phrase used to describe this monster. I have asked various scholars who are familiar with the literature on the Sioux, and many think it was some kind of animal. But their reasoning is somewhat askew. They believe that the Sioux saw a complete skeleton of this animal in the Badlands and then transferred the memory of the shape to account for a creature seen or imagined in the Missouri River.

The problem with this interpretation is that the Badlands are nearly 125 miles from the Missouri River, and consequently it would take a powerful imagination to make this kind of transference. I mentioned this anomaly in a speech at my own reservation, Standing Rock, in North Dakota, adjoining the Missouri River. After my speech a couple of the traditional people approached me and said that the next time I came, if I had time, they would take me to see the spot where the people last saw this creature, implying that it was still possible to see the animal during the last century before the reservations were established. I give their knowledge credence, in part because the spot where the animal was last seen was upstream from the Badlands by about 150 miles.

On both the Standing Rock and Cheyenne River reservations numerous dinosaur bones are found. After spring floods along the

Grand and Moreau rivers, people tell me that bones are washed out of the riverbanks. One of the best *Tyrannosaurus rex* skeletons we have was discovered on the Cheyenne River Reservation a few years back, on the lands of a tribal member. When private excavators tried to take the skeleton to Rapid City, a lawsuit ensued, and the tribe claimed the dinosaur as its heritage. So this part of South Dakota is most definitely dinosaur country.

In September 1996, *The Denver Post* did a feature article on the retirement of Dr. Bruce Erickson, the paleontologist who was in charge of the Wannagan Creek Quarry in the Badlands of North Dakota and who was responsible for discovering fifteen new types of flora and fauna. He spent twenty-six years at this location, and had devised a gigantic wall map with drawings of thousands of bones on it. "That's only about a third of what we found," he was quoted as saying, ". . . the bones that were on the surface. There were twice as many beneath them."[22] His first visit to the location produced about a dozen skulls lying on the surface. According to the article, some alligators and crocodiles found in the quarry were contemporaries of the dinosaurs. But why would bones some 160 million years old be found on or very near the surface?

The dinosaur scenario sounds like overreaching to make a point about the longevity of American Indians, but there is a real basis for making the suggestion. In October and November 1924, a scientific expedition led by Samuel Hubbard, curator of archaeology at the Oakland Museum, and Charles W. Gilmore, curator of vertebrate paleontology at the United States National Museum, and funded by the oil magnate about to be discredited, E. L. Doheny, went to Havasupai Canyon in northern Arizona to search for evidence of prehistoric man. Hubbard and Doheny had visited this area before, Doheny as a young prospector and Hubbard as a scientist.

Following the "Tobocobe Trail" to where it intersects with Lee Canyon, the party soon discovered what they described as "wall pictures," figures scratched long, long ago depicting the local fauna. The most spectacular of these pictures was one of a dinosaur, identified by them as *Diplodocus,* standing upright. The dinosaur figure was "total height 11.2 inches, greatest width 7 inches, length of leg 3.8 inches, length of body 3.9 inches, width of body 3 inches, length of neck to top of curve 3.5 inches, length of tail (approximately) 9.1 inches, length of neck (approximately) 5.1 inches."[23] The desert "varnish," a covering caused by extreme age, had filled in the lines of the figure, indicating a significant age.

Just as spectacular, however, were other discoveries in the canyon. In Hubbard's words:

> On the same wall with the dinosaur pictograph, and about 16 feet from it, we found a pictograph representing an animal which was evidently intended for an elephant, attacking a large man. The elephant is striking the man on the top of his head with its trunk. The wavy line represents water into which the man has retreated up to his knees. Both arms are upraised and the fingers are visible on one hand. . . . Because there are no tusks indicated our surmise is that it is a cow elephant.[24]

This pictograph scene accurately depicts the manner in which scholars believe that man hunted the mammoth—an ambush at a water hole; and in southern Arizona there are several sites that have human and mammoth remains together in an obvious hunting format, with butchering marks on the mammoth's bones.

The scientists of the expedition even tried to identify the species of mammoth represented in the picture: "Figuring the comparative scale of the two figures, if the elephant is identified as an *Elephas imperator* of California, it would be fourteen feet high and the man would also be fourteen feet high—a giant!"[25] In addition, in three different locations within the canyon, pictographs of ibex were found: "One group, showing a male and two females, was right under the elephant picture, but close to the ground."[26] Another picture showed men driving seven ibex and two deer into a canyon. Hubbard submitted the pictures to Roy Chapman Andrews, and he identified the ibex from the knobs on the horns. And on part of the plateau above the canyon floor was found an ancient megalithic fortress.

This whole discussion would seem to beg the imagination, and certainly many scholars, when reminded of it, simply say, "Oh, that old thing," as if it had been satisfactorily explained decades ago. But it has not been explained in any satisfactory manner. Orthodox scholars simply omit it from consideration altogether, as they would with any bit of evidence that shakes the foundations of accepted scientific belief. Is it evidence that people and dinosaurs coexisted? I don't know, but I suspect so. Ibex fossils have never been found in North

America, but there is no reason why lonely explorers from Africa could not have carved scenes from home in the canyon wall. It seems to me that the prevalence of dinosaur remains in South Dakota so near to the surface and this series of pictographs raise important questions that science has not bothered to ask.

RADIOCARBON DATING

Although very little evidence exists that Paleo–Indians were responsible for exterminating the mammoth and no evidence exists regarding the other herbivores, the argument of Paul Martin and his supporters is that radiocarbon dating of human occupancy sites in the United States, particularly sites containing the famous Folsom points, concentrates at around 12,000 years before the present. As these sites are scattered all over the western states, the implication is that the mass extermination was performed by the Indians. In *Pleistocene Extinctions,* Martin discusses various sites that have mammoth remains, discusses radiocarbon dating, and presents a chart that demonstrates that of fifty sites, half fall into the time frame in which he believes the great extinction occurred. Supporters of the theory often cite the radiocarbon dates as if a 50 percent score were proof "beyond a reasonable doubt."

What are the real facts about radiocarbon dating? We have seen that potassium-argon dating of volcanic rocks can go far afield, and we might begin to suspect that if a lava flow from 1800 in Hawaii can be K-Ar dated at 2.96 billion years, we are not getting much accuracy from these "scientific" measuring devices. Charles Ginenthal, in an excellent article on methods used for establishing the age of ancient artifacts entitled "Scientific Dating Methods in Ruins," points out: "J. Ogden, the director of a radiocarbon dating laboratory at Wesleyan University in Ohio, stated that the investigator is first asked what date he will accept for the material he brings to be dated; then, when a figure is obtained that comes near this date, it is duly reported—together with tolerance values—to make the test appear honest."[27] Ginenthal also cites several recent tests that should be more than enough to raise serious questions about the reliability of this way of dating materials:

1. *In the* Antarctic Journal of the United States, *W. Dort wrote that freshly slaughtered seals when subjected to radiocarbon analysis, are dated at 1,300 years old.*

2. In Science, *M. Keith and G. Anderson wrote that shells of living mollusks were dated at 2,300 years old.*
3. In The Physiology of Trees, *Bruno Haber wrote that wood from a growing tree was dated at 10,000 years old.*[28]

This last test is important for our discussion because it seems that the tree was growing next to an airport that had a high level of carbon dioxide from airplane exhausts. (If a mammoth bone had been found nearby, would the tree be as old as the mammoth, or the mammoth as young as the tree?) Finally, Ginenthal quoted R. Stuckenrath from an article in the *Annals of the New York Academy of Science* regarding radiocarbon dating: "This whole blessed thing is nothing but thirteenth-century alchemy and it all depends upon which funny paper you read."[29]

Why don't scientists level with us? Why do they cite measuring techniques that have been found grossly inaccurate, as if they had absolute proof of their theories? Overkill fans piously mention that the debate is closed because radiocarbon dates have demonstrated a connection that cannot be denied. Yet they do not tell us that sometimes lab personnel have been told what dates scientists would prefer to have as the laboratory results. We can thank whatever deity inspires us that these people are in higher education and scientific labs and not in district attorneys' offices.

I discuss this subject because the next generation of people working on these problems, unless they are warned, will simply build on the errors of the famous personalities of the past. We will continue to wander in a darkness of our own making. But also, young Indians are being educated in increasing numbers, and when they try to discuss traditions of their people, even the most logical and credible stories can be turned aside by a mentor just saying, "But we have radiocarbon dates on this." We do indeed—we told the laboratory what dates we wanted and they gave them to us.

CLOVIS POINTS

A favorite game of anthropologists and archaeologists is to pretend that societies of early humans struggled for tens of thousands of years to make the simplest accommodations in the stone tools they made and used. Every change in the shape of arrowheads, pottery, or carving is understood as a radical departure from what had gone before. Thus marvelously poetic essays are written describing early, middle, and late Woodlands peoples, the Beaker and Red Paint peoples, and so forth. If the same technique was applied to explain twentieth-century auto manufacturing, we should have hundreds if not thousands of years intervening between the various models of Oldsmobiles. Today's small cars would be understood as a cultural revival of the business coupe of the late 1940s. All these divisions of sites into early, middle, and late stone crushers are, of course, wholly fictional devices to maintain the value of employing anthropologists when educational funds might be better spent. According to scholars, the Paleo–Indians who marched out of Siberia across the Bering Strait and into America on a blood-lust campaign against megafauna had one superior technological innovation that spelled doom for the animals—the fluted point. No one knows the origin of this startling technology. There is but one fluted point in Siberia, so we must assume that they were developed after traversing the Bering Strait. Alex Krieger, in an essay in *Prehistoric Man in the New World*, said that the date for the invention of these points must be pushed back to around 15,000 years ago because of the immense distribution of these artifacts in the United States. He wrote: "Mason [citation omitted] favors the central part of the eastern United States because Clovis points are most frequent there, and Witthof [citation omitted] believes that the oldest examples came from Pennsylvania." And he argued that the old idea that the fluted point "reached North America from Asia via the Alaska steppingstone must be abandoned because it is not found in Asia."[30] Thus Martin and Diamond, eloquently chronicling the Clovis weaponry, will have to get their big game hunters out of Tennessee, Pennsylvania, and Kentucky rather than bring them from Asia.

Jared Diamond is quite firm in his identification of the Clovis people as the megafauna culprits. But the claim for Clovis is based, he says, on negative evidence: "At excavated Clovis sites, conclusive evidence for artifacts made by other peoples has been found above but not below the level with Clovis tools; and *there are no irrefutable human remains with irrefutable pre-Clovis points anywhere in the New World south of the former Canadian ice sheet* [emphasis added]."[31] I have highlighted this statement because we need to see what Diamond thinks constitutes "irrefutable evidence." And he says:

Mind you, there are dozens of claims of sites with pre-Clovis human evidence, but all of them are marred by serious questions about whether the material used for radiocarbon dating was contaminated by older carbon, or whether the dated material was really associated with the human remains, or whether the tools supposedly made by hand were just naturally shaped rocks . . . .[32]

Applying what we know of radiocarbon dating, it is possible that samples were taken to a laboratory and the lab scientists were instructed to return dates of around 12,000 years ago. Tests were run, and unfortunately the results showed something around 30,000 to 40,000 years ago, far too early to indict the people for mega-cide.

So what is the real state of the Clovis point? Alex Krieger explains that "fluted points are found in all states west of the Rocky Mountains too, but for the most part they are surface finds and have not yet been connected with any particular culture pattern."[33] So this irrefutable evidence of an ice corridor invasion is scattered all over the West, lying on the surface of the ground, and difficult if not impossible to attach to any of the cultures that might have inhabited the area. Actually, the situation is worse than that. Waldo Wedel writes: "It is perhaps worth noting that many of the cutting, scraping and chopping tools of eight to ten thousand years ago differ little from those found on Plains Indian sites of the last five hundred years, and this is true also of such bone tools as awls, needles, etc."[34] So how would Martin, Ardrey, Diamond, or Bakker know whether the Clovis point they had just uncovered was the product of a Paleo–Indian of 15,000 years ago stalking a mammoth or simply a throwaway by a Sioux or Crow Indian in 1887 as they moved to their new reservation? They very likely wouldn't.

ALASKA

In the first edition of *Red Earth, White Lies* I omitted Alaska, even though some articles had been written about the veracity of the oral tradition in that state. I am not familiar with the landscape and do not know any elders with whom the subject might have been discussed. In November 1995 the American Indian Science and Engineering Society (AISES) sponsored a conference on "Origins and Migrations," which dealt with the traditional knowledge of the tribes. Jana Harcharek, an Inupiat, stunned the conference with the stories of prehistory preserved by her people, describing Alaska as a temperate climate suddenly overwhelmed by a great catastrophe. In mid-February the AK MOKAKIT, a Canadian organization devoted to Native science and culture, held a conference that included some southern Athabascans—the White Mountain and Jicarilla Apaches sent delegates, as did the Navajos and Mescalero Apaches. As reported by Richard Pierce, the AISES representative, as stories and languages—actually dialects—were exchanged it became apparent that these people were related but that none of them had any traditions that related to the Bering Strait.

Some scholars have focused on the truth of the oral tradition in Alaska, granting the Natives credibility that is not accorded anyone in the lower forty-eight states. Perhaps the land requires that respect be paid to the Natives' understanding. Julie Cruikshank, in her article "Legend and Landscape: Convergence of Oral and Scientific Traditions in the Yukon Territory," quoted a journalist in 1890: "The Indian names of the mountains, lakes and rivers are natural landmarks for the traveler, whoever he may be; to destroy these by substituting words of a foreign tongue is to destroy the natural guides."[35] For much of Native tradition, particularly that part attached to landscape, some measure of credibility has been recognized, making geomythology much more palatable for scholars.

Cruikshank concentrated on events near the shore and on more recent activities, such as glacial advances and volcanic eruptions, but she rejected earlier accounts of the White River volcanic explosion over a thousand years ago. Over a decade later, D. Wayne Moodie, A.J.W. Catchpole, and Kerry Abel reviewed the tradition and concluded that the Native tradition might very well have been an eyewitness account.[36] Rory B. Egan recently wrote an essay in which he compared the Mediterranean memories of the Thera eruption with the White River volcano and inclined favorably toward recognizing the veracity in both traditions.[37]

The Alaska Natives have already held an important conference on star knowledge at which a representation of Navajos from Navajo Community College, using specially made cylinders, were able to compare Navajo constellations and Alaskan star knowledge. The movement toward revival of traditional knowledge and its comparison with secular Western scientific knowledge is now well under way in the north and promises to produce a methodology for gathering the data needed to verify Native traditions.

CONCLUSION

We do not know the real history of our planet, and we know very little about the historical experiences of the various societies and races that constitute our species. This information is lacking because our scholars and scientists are wedded to an outmoded framework of interpretation and spend their time arranging facts and evidence to fit these old ideas. Our popular science writers seem to do very little thinking before their well-written, poetic, but largely fictional accounts appear in the bookstores. Few of our scholars or scientists seem able to recognize more than one possible explanation for data or phenomena, and they apparently hold in great disdain all traditions except the one in which they have grown up and received rewards.

Nothing can stop these people from filling us with more nonsense except an alert reading public with minds that are not inhibited by the prestigious degrees—a reading public that continues to ask questions and demand sensible answers. Do our scientific writers actually hold us in contempt? Do they feel that we can and should be fed pablum so that "science" can continue? Sometimes they resemble nothing more than priests of a dying religion, making up explanations ad hoc to defend outmoded articles of faith.

Most American Indians, I believe, were here "at the beginning" and have preserved the memory of traumatic continental and planetary catastrophes, keeping the information sometimes in tales deliberately constructed to preserve as well as entertain. When you visit with an elder, you will often get Coyote, Iktomi, and Napi tales that are told in a manner designed to test you as much as inform you. But if the elder thinks you are serious, or that you already know something of the hidden knowledge, he will bow his head for a moment, breathe deeply, and then begin to tell you what his people have taught for thousands of years, giving as closely as possible the literal description of the event. This kind of information is generally not available to scholars who are on a summer research grant and pester people about what they know. That a particular story did not surface decades ago in the work of a Western scholar should not discredit its veracity.

I hope *Red Earth, White Lies* will initiate discussions between traditional people and scholars, and that it will provide a basis for the elders to deal with overeducated younger Indians who have uncritically accepted scientific folklore as fact. Nothing is more annoying than listening to an educated Indian parroting what he or she has been told in a lecture and discovering that tribal traditions have simply been thrown out the window without careful examination. Many non-Indian scholars are ready to accord respect to tribal traditions, but we have to be ready to engage in a free-for-all with them, critiquing their scientific folklore and making them provide the evidence for and basis of their belief. Since the original publication of *Red Earth, White Lies*, I have been challenged many times about my disbelief in the Bering Strait migration, but I have yet to find one opponent who can provide me with one article or book that makes a convincing and reasonable case for believing in this nonsense.

As American Indians have been unjustly accused of exterminating the megafauna, a good test of the question of respect might be to offer an equally silly accusation, based on a slim bit of evidence to counter the overkill thesis. G. Frederick Wright, one of the giants in Pleistocene geology, remarked on something that few people realize. The flora of Europe virtually disappeared during the Pleistocene, the same time period when the megafauna suffered a great reduction in the Western Hemisphere and, incidentally, on the other continents as well. Completely missing in Europe after the Pleistocene are what Wright called Atlantic American types—magnolia, Liriodendron, asimina, nogundo, Aesculus, leguminous trees such as locusts, honey locusts, Gymnocladus, and Cladrastis, Nyssa, Liquidambar, Ericaceae, Bumelia, Catalpa, sassafras, Osage orange, hickory, walnut, hemlock, spruce, arborvitae, Taxodium, and Torreya.[38]

This list is most impressive and indicates that European flora in recent time was a rather drab scene, so that landing in America with its bountiful flora made the New World appear as a paradise rivaling the Garden of Eden. This list is also the equivalent of the listing of megafauna that Paul Martin believes were exterminated by Paleo–Indians. They were all missing or became extinct. Wright noted:

> The capital fact is, that many and perhaps almost all of these genera of trees were well represented in Europe throughout the later Tertiary times. It had not only the same generic types, but in some cases even the same species, or what must pass as such, in the lack of recognizable distinctions between fossil remains and living analogues.

*Probably the European Miocene forest was about as rich
and various as is ours of the present day, and very like it. The
Glacial period came and passed and these types have not
survived there, nor returned.*[39]

Like most of the megafauna bones, there is no evidence that humans had any part in the demise of these flora. However, as Jared Diamond felt that a loosening of the rules of logic and evidence should be suspended in the case of the megafauna, so we must suspend the rules here also. It therefore seems painfully obvious that Europeans were the culprits of this dreadful floracide. With their newfound technology, the single blade point, they migrated up from Africa and west from the Caucasus and engaged in a frenzy of destruction in Europe, dwarfing anything seen in human history until their descendants marched through Tennessee and Kentucky at the close of the eighteenth century, always cutting far more hardwood trees than their homes needed.

Shouldn't we expect the same respect for our thesis that is accorded to the overkill thesis?

NOTES

1. Alfred North Whitehead, *Adventures of Ideas* (New York: Macmillan, 1933), p. 96.
2. Ella E. Clark, *Indian Legends of the Pacific Northwest* (Berkeley: University of California Press, 1952), p. 81.
3. Ibid., p. 25.
4. Alfred de Grazia, *Chaos and Creation* (Princeton, N.J.: Metron Publications, 1981), p. 35.
5. Peter Spielmann, "Botanists Giddy over Rare Find in Australia," *Denver Post*, December 15, 1994, p. 11A.
6. Gordon Rattray Taylor, *The Great Evolution Mystery* (New York: Harper & Row, 1983), p. 89.
7. L. Taylor Hansen, *The Ancient Atlantic* (Amherst, Wisc.: Amherst Press, 1969), p. 201.
8. Ibid., p. 219.
9. Jacob Bronowski, *The Ascent of Man* (Boston: Little, Brown, 1973), p. 26.
10. Robert T. Bakker, *The Dinosaur Heresies* (New York: William Morrow, 1986), p. 77.
11. Ibid., p. 23; note also on p. 160, Bakker observes that water-loving turtles and crocodiles evolve most slowly, changing so little through geologic time that a single genus can be followed for 30 million years or more.
12. Ibid., pp. 207-208.
13. Taylor, *The Great Evolution Mystery*, pp. 24-26.

14. Ibid., pp. 26-27.

15. Ibid., p. 62.

16. Ibid., p. 74.

17. Ibid., p. 84.

18. Editorial Miscellany, *American Scientist* 36 (October 1948): p. 490.

19. Bentley Glass, "New Missing Link Discovered," *Science* 126 (July 1957): pp. 158-159.

20. Clark, *Indian Legends of the Pacific Northwest*, p. 71.

21. Ella E. Clark, *Indian Legends of the Northern Rockies* (Norman: University of Oklahoma Press, 1966), p. 301.

22. Jane E. Brody, "It's Been 26 Years for Fossil Hound at N.D. Site," *Denver Post*, September 8, 1996, pp. 32A-33A.

23. Samuel Hubbard, *The Doheny Scientific Expedition to the Hava Supai Canyon, Northern Arizona*, p. 9. A copy of this privately printed field report exists in the Peabody Museum of American Archaeology and Ethnology, Harvard University, a gift from Dr. A. V. Kidder, a prominent scholar in his own right.

24. Ibid., p. 15.

25. Ibid.

26. Ibid., p. 17.

27. Charles Ginenthal, "Scientific Dating Methods in Ruins," *Velikovskian* 2, no. 1 (1994): 53.

28. Ibid.

29. Ibid., p. 54.

30. Alex D. Krieger, "Early Man in the New World," in *Prehistoric Man in the New World*, ed. Jesse D. Jennings and Edward Norbeck (Chicago: University of Chicago Press, 1963), p. 55.

31. Jared Diamond, "The American Blitzkrieg: A Mammoth Undertaking," *Discover* (June 1987): p. 84.

32. Ibid.

33. Krieger, "Early Man in the New World," p. 35.

34. Waldo R. Wedel, "The Great Plains," in *Prehistoric Man in the New World*, ed. Jesse D. Jennings and Edward Norbeck (Chicago: University of Chicago Press, 1963), p. 198.

35. Julie Cruikshank, "Legend and Landscape: Convergence of Oral and Scientific Traditions in the Yukon Territory," *Arctic Anthropology* 18, no. 2 (1981): p. 79.

36. D. Wayne Moodie, A.J.W. Catchpole, and Kerry Abel, "Northern Athapascan Oral Traditions and the White River Volcano," *Ethnohistory* 39, no. 2 (Spring 1992): pp. 148-171.

37. Rory B. Egan, "Ex Occidente Lux: Catastrophic Volcanism in Greek and *Dene* Oral Tradition." in *nikotwâsik iskwâhtêm, pâskihtêpayih, Studies in Honor of H. C. Wolfart*, ed. John D. Nichols and Arden C. Ogg. Memoir 13, Algonquian and Iroquoian Linguistics, 1996, pp. 196-209.

38. G. Frederick Wright, *The Ice Age in North America* (New York: D. Appleton, 1890), p. 378.

39. Ibid.

9

A FLOCK OF ANTHROS

▼▼▼▼

Anthropology, from Samuel Morton and Lewis Henry Morgan to Frank Cushing and Franz Boas to very recently, was what adult white men did to fulfill their boyhood fantasies of playing Indian. Indeed, Cushing and Boas actually dressed in Indian costumes and pretended they were the real thing. The anthropology literature, therefore, can hardly be regarded as a science, because it reflects the deep psychological problems of its superstars rather than an honest effort to learn something. But it is a luxury of a society so wealthy that a significant institutional support system can be placed at the disposal of members of the elite class to keep them occupied while other members of society produce useful things.

What nomenclature do we assign anthros? Rather, what do we call an identifiable group of them? They are organized into a society called the American Anthropological Association, but some better way of describing them must be found. It has always seemed to me that "herd" is demeaning, "pack" not quite as bad, and "school" absurd because they learn very little. "Pride" may come close, but it attributes a courage rarely seen in their ranks. I suppose that "flock" might be an adequate designation as their collective behavior greatly resembles sheep, but it might be inadequate insofar as they are not shorn like sheep but rather think like them. It is a phenomenon that deserves more attention.

In searching for stories that would provide further evidence of Indian knowledge about geologic events in pre-Columbian North

America, I found anthros to be helpful and enthusiastic, and some of them shared materials with me that they could well have published themselves. When I asked them why they hadn't already published the materials, they would remark, "Oh, God, if I published something like that, I'd get my butt kicked by the profession." If I pressed the point, sweat would break out on their foreheads and they would go quickly to another subject. It was as if the Klan was monitoring their every utterance.

This behavior puzzled me until I remembered the reaction of anthros to my little satire of them in *Custer Died for Your Sins.* Some anthros took offense at the description of themselves, but a number used my piece as a springboard to raise questions within the group about the treatment of their Indian clients. Quite a few of them made me feel like Jesus. That is to say, they came to me "by night" like Nicodemus and confided, after looking fearfully over their shoulders, that they had never been anthropologists, that they had always been "ethnographers." Thus their sympathies were with me, they had tried to bring these same issues forward years ago, but they did not feel they should raise questions among the anthros because they were, after all, ethnographers.

It then occurred to me that anthropology had a very soft underbelly and that careful probing of the anthro psyche, individually and collectively, might prove productive. With some degree of malicious intent I sought out information on the major beliefs of anthropology from a variety of sources to see if my suspicions were true—there was no such thing as a body of knowledge among them, only a body of beliefs, supported by virtually no evidence but held as tenaciously as fundamentalist Christians hold to the six days of creation. By simply asking for evidence, for the best book or article on evolution, the Bering Strait, big game hunters, pre-Columbian expeditions to the Western Hemisphere, and a host of other topics, I learned that much of what is taught in anthropology has no factual basis whatsoever and is supported primarily by the fact that it has always been taught.

After *Red Earth, White Lies* came out, an enthusiastic younger member of the anthropology department at the University of Colorado where I teach suggested that I be asked to speak to the department about my heresy and in fact invited me to speak to his class. But at the department level it was another matter. E-mails flew with reckless abandon, and one of the senior professors vetoed the idea on the grounds that I did not believe in the Bering Strait theory. In other words, far from welcoming another point of view, or even an inquiring mind, the anthros wanted to approve my beliefs before I talked, and if what I thought differed from their point of view, it was "NO GO." I once spoke at a Missouri Synod Lutheran college in Indiana and was allowed to suggest that the days in creation might not have been twenty-four hours, so the Colorado anthro experience became a real highlight of my life.

Reflecting on the dismissal, I remembered many years ago when I was invited to speak at Evergreen State College in Olympia. My proposed appearances triggered a position paper from the evolutionists to the provost arguing that I should not be invited to speak unless I believed in evolution. I was allowed to speak, apparently after some negotiations with the evolutionists, and sometime later was even invited to be the graduation speaker, indicating perhaps that my heresies had not been fatal to the process of memorization that passed for education on that campus. I recount these experiences without rancor and with some measure of exhilaration because they do illustrate the characteristics that support my contention that the anthros should not be an association but a flock.

But what is it that determines what "the profession" thinks? Where are the hidden barriers that prevent frank and open discussion of issues, concepts, and theories and the intellectual structure that is necessary to move the profession along? For nearly a century it has been orthodox doctrine, defended like Mary's virginity, that American Indians came across the Bering Strait in 12,000 B.P. The impetus for that belief is surely the personality and prestige of Aleš Hrdlička of the Smithsonian Institution who wanted Indians to arrive just a few years before Columbus. But following Hrdlička's demise, who ensured that the belief would continue as doctrine?

It seems that there were a group of anthros nicknamed the "Clovis Police" who stood ready to clobber anyone who suggested a new date for human presence in the Western Hemisphere. For many years ordinary laypeople found Clovis points scattered all over the landscape in the West. But these points were not "acceptable" until an anthro dug one up; then they became the "first" solid evidence and hence a part of science. But then people began to dig in South America and were returning dates far earlier than the Clovis Police had accepted. So it was a dilemma for the anthros. How could they continue work with this self-imposed barrier to research? And of course it meant breaking the mold and becoming an outcast.

Beginning in 1977, a team of scientists led by Tom Dillehay of the University of Kentucky began excavating a site at Monte Verde, Chile, and were returning dates that severely disrupted the Clovis barrier. Finally, in 1997, members of the Clovis Police consented to visit the site and examine the artifacts, thus limiting the amount of time they could sit in their offices and write snotty rejections of the reports of people working in the field. Faced with evidence in the ground, the Clovis Police backed off and science leaped forward. In this connection, Dennis Stanford of the Smithsonian was quoted by Maggie Fox on *Infoseek: The News Channel* that he thought "more and more evidence would come out about very early Americans. Scientists who had sites they thought were older than 10,000 years *had been afraid* to come forward for fear of being criticized."

So we discover the real situation. There are apparently already many studies by anthros that contradict, amend, adjust, or radically disrupt existing orthodoxy, and their authors are terrified of publishing them—knowing that they are in conflict with existing dogma. Knowing that their own work refutes what is presented in the textbooks, these scholars continue to teach outmoded ideas and foist these ancient and incorrect beliefs on the next generation of students and scholars. Thus the comparison with sheep. Instead of the fearless scientist pushing the frontier of knowledge ever forward, what we actually have are fat, lazy sheep contentedly grazing at the public trough, fearful that their colleagues will criticize them for thinking something new. BAAAAAAAAAAA!!!!!

Once it appeared that the barrier had been broken, people began to integrate the new knowledge into existing orthodoxy. Maggie Fox quoted a classic statement by Johanna Nichols, a language expert at the University of California at Berkeley who uses computer models to demonstrate how quickly people can migrate. "That's about 8,000 miles once one crossed the ice sheet," Nichols said. "It would have taken about 2,000 years to travel on a beeline at a good clip." Now why on God's green and/or icy earth would these people have made a beeline to Monte Verde, Chile? Well, the answer should be clear: the anthros needed them there. In other words, we are now bickering about virtually nothing. The paradigm has held. Well, it holds until someone invents a new computer program and decides that these Indians could have made it to Chile in five hundred years. The last question then is: How good are sheep at computer programming?

▼ Part III ▼

EDUCATION

10

TRADITIONAL TECHNOLOGY

▼▼▼▼

E ducation today is wholly oriented toward science and secular-ism. At the core of every curriculum is the belief that we can look at phenomena with a completely rational and objective eye and find abstract principles underlying all behavior, from atoms to masses of people. This perspective implies, of course, that the natural world and its inhabitants are wholly materialistic and that even the most profound sentiments can be understood as electrical impulses in the brain or as certain kinds of chemical reactions. We have arrived at this state of affairs through the application of a methodology of reductionism, a tendency to divide, subdivide, and subdivide again in order to find the constituents of an entity or event.

The reductionist view of the world is further enhanced by the spectacular success of modern technology. Natural forces are being brought under human control and cosmic energies bring us both power and entertainment. If a person were to chart the relationships of the various academic disciplines, the resulting outline might find physics and mathematics as coequal partners at the top of a pyramid of knowledge, with chemistry, biology, psychology, and eventually the humanities as imperfect subsets or special cases of the applica-tion of physics to selected phenomena. This outline has dominated most of this century, but recent theoretical developments are now beginning to call this simplistic perspective to account. The Gaia hypothesis, among other new theories, suggests that we should begin to look at things organically and that we might indeed be a minor episode in a larger scheme of life. Whether this hypothesis proves fruitful enough to become a dominant paradigm in the social/scientific future is beside the point; the issue today is that we are no longer bound to use mechanistic models exclusively to tell us how to think about the world.

The knowledge and technology of tribal peoples, primitive peoples, and ancient man do not really appear in the modern scientific scheme unless it is to be found within the minor articulations of the concept of cultural evolution hidden in the backwaters of anthropology, sociology, and history. This knowledge that served our ancestors so well emerges from time to time when modern scientists advocate a novel interpretation of data and, in order to claim some historical roots for their ideas, as new ideas are forbidden in academia, ancient or tribal peoples are cited as societies that once used certain practices or held certain beliefs. But the presentation of the ideas is usually accompanied by the patronizing view that although tribals and primitives did originate the idea or the practice, they could not have possibly understood its significance.

Indian students who come from traditional homes have considerable difficulty assimilating the practices and beliefs that they learned as children with the modernist attitude of science. And among Indian students who grew up in urban areas and whose experience in reservation communities is limited to sporadic summertime visits, an even greater difficulty in assimilating this attitude exists. They believe certain things about tribal knowledge and techniques as a matter of faith many times because their experiences are very limited, but they want to recapture as much knowledge of their own tribal past and practices as possible, so the problem becomes an emotional as well as an intellectual dilemma.

Too often we try to insert various kinds of tribal knowledge into the format of modern science, and the result is that we get a few points for having a historical relationship to the problem area, but the beliefs and practices that our ancestors held about certain things are believed to be merely ad hoc resolutions of the problem or lucky guesses and do not receive the credit that is theirs by right. A good example of this problem is the Six Nations' knowledge of agriculture. With their basically religious knowledge of plants and animals, the Six Nations people traditionally planted beans, corn, and squash together, and these plants were the famous "Three Sisters" who provided the people with food. It was not until this century, when modern Western science discovered the nitrogen cycle, that anyone commented on the fact that the Three Sisters provided a natural nitrogen cycle so that the fields were never worn out from farming. The same problem exists with Indian knowledge of fish habits, the propensity of the Plains and Mountain tribes to herd rather than chase game animals, and the tendency of the tribes to burn brush in certain forested areas to enhance the growth of timber and the perpetuation of meadows. There are many other good examples of Indian technical knowledge of the natural world that could be cited, but to do so would be to engage in additional ad hoc arguments. More important is the understanding that lies behind traditional knowledge and an examination of how it compares with the reductionism of Western science.

CREATION STORIES

If one were to track backward into the past of most of the tribal groups to find how things originated, one would quickly discover that specific instructions were given to the old people regarding plants, animals, birds and reptiles, stones, and technology on how to live in community with them. These instructions came in dreams, visions, and unusual incidents, and more often than not the relationship with plants and animals was a result of interspecies communication. The primary focus of creation stories of many tribes placed human beings as among the last creatures who were created and as the youngest of the living families. We were given the ability to do many things but not specific wisdom about the world. So our job was to learn from other older beings and to pattern ourselves after their behavior. We were to gather knowledge, not dispense it. Western science really traces itself backward to the Garden of Eden scenario in which man is also created last, but it is believed that he is given mastery over the rest of the world. Man is, in the Western scheme of things, the source of knowledge and information, but he is also isolated from the rest of creation by standing alone at the top of the pyramid.

Because we gather knowledge from older beings who have the wisdom of the world within their grasp, we must maintain a relationship with the rest of creation, and consequently the clan and kinship systems that guided the social organization of the world were not only modeled after observed behavior of other beings, they sought to preserve the idea of relationships of the natural world within the technology that arose as a result of our learning experiences. Western science learned its lessons from observation and then from experimentation with the entities of the natural world. There was no sense of community, because man had been placed too far above the rest of creation and there was no hesitancy among Western people to use the rest of creation in any manner it could conceive. But the price of using others as objects was that absolute values had to be maintained and space, time, and matter became absolute concepts within Western science. Both science and its reductionist methods remained absolute as long as these ideas were regarded as absolute.

In a fundamental sense, which many people in science do not yet recognize, the theories of Albert Einstein created tremendous gaps in the Western scientific scheme. Einstein's work challenged the absolute status of space, time, and matter, and his major contribution was to reduce the absolute nature of these ideas to a relative status—he introduced the context into modern science in a way that could not easily be refuted. But the importance of relativity for traditional thinking is that it began to shift the focus from the absolute materialistic framework science had constructed to an idea that things are related. Not many people in the academic community have yet applied this idea to the world as a totality, and certainly many of them would rebel at the idea that science is shifting significantly toward a tribal understanding of the world. They continue to believe that relativity means that there are no absolutes. In fact, it means that things are related in some fundamental ways that had previously been excluded. There may not be as many anomalies and coincidences as we have previously supposed.

Many tribes described relationships in terms of correspondence between two things ordinarily thought to be distinct, isolated, or unrelated. The old saying in religious ceremonies—as above so it is on earth—is such a correspondence; so is the gathering of things for medicine bags, for making drums, weapons, household goods, and clothing, and creating altars and blessing dwellings. In each of these activities a variety of things are used and they are said to "represent" certain things. "Represent" here is not taken as a symbolic gesture but usually means that these things, their power and knowledge, are actually present in the creation of something new.

WISDOM AND VISION—ACKNOWLEDGING THE
LIFE AND POWER IN ALL THINGS

Today we have the artifacts of every tribe lining the shelves of museums and being described as great primitive art. And indeed if we think of these artifacts only as useful utensils and implements, apart from the tribal context, they may be simple instruments, extensions of man's only limbs and desires, as Robert Ardrey once described weapons and tools. The important part of the relationship, however, was that all things were alive, and consequently their own power and wisdom were incorporated with them wherever they were represented. Modern man uses weapons, tools, and instruments to extend the capabilities of his own self, and he uses these things mechanically. Tribal man, in using his instruments, did not simply extend the scope of his own capabilities but enhanced his abilities through the addition of the powers that were inherent in the relationships he had with other living things.

Today we attend colleges and universities in order to learn the principles of how things work and how to use instruments properly. Tribal people learned these things in religious ceremonies, depending on the intensity and scope of the vision a person received or the frequency with which spirits informed him or her concerning the proper attitude to take when exercising certain powers. Thus it was a wholistic understanding that undergirded tribal technology, and the use of technology was vision-specific. That is to say, the knowledge that the old ones attached to their technology demanded that they use their powers sparingly and on the proper occasion. A person could not indiscriminately use powers as we casually use our instruments today. This lesson is important, because today we tend to believe that we can apply technology on a rather indiscriminate basis and we are learning that often we do not really understand the side effects that such use creates.

Correspondences went far beyond the immediate environment. My favorite example of this comprehensive extension in space and time is found in the practices of the Osages. They would plant their corn in the spring of the year along the banks and river bottoms of the Missouri River and then go as far as the Rockies to do their summer hunt. When the leaves of a certain tree began to make initial changes in color in preparation for fall, the people knew it was time to pack up and head back east to harvest their crops. Most of the Plains tribes kept track of where the buffalo herds would be during different times of the spring and summer by measuring time through the use of changes in plant life and star formations far from their traditional winter camps. Many scholars have remarked on the fact that the old Indians, once they had been over a trail, would almost immediately find it even after they had been away from the area for years. Again there was a remarkable sense of how things worked together and what things appeared in relationships and correspondences.

The old anthropology and history of religious schools used to paint tribal peoples as a superstitious lot who cringed in fear of the natural elements and made up simplistic explanations for all things they did not understand in an effort to create some kind of science for themselves. Modern science tends to use two kinds of questions to examine the world: (1) how does it work? and (2) what use is it? These questions are natural for a people who think the world is constructed to serve their purposes. The old people might have used these two questions in their effort to understand the world, but it is certain that they always asked an additional question: what does it mean?

HEALING THE LACK OF BALANCE

The old people, surveying a landscape, had such a familiarity with the world that they could immediately see what was not in its place, and if they discerned anything that seemed to be out of its natural order, a nocturnal animal in the daytime, unusual clouds or weather conditions, or a change in the plants, they went to work immediately to discover what this change meant. Many observers have said that this ability to perceive anomalies meant that the people saw that nature was out of balance and I certainly could not quarrel with this characterization. Presented with the natural ordering of cosmic energies, when the people saw an imbalance they knew that their responsibility was to initiate ceremonies that would help bring about balance once again.

Eventually it was recognized that the world had a moral being and that disruptions among human societies created disharmony in the rest of the world. This belief corresponded to modern professional ethics but differed from them in that the whole tribal society was involved in healing the lack of balance. Today it is only the professional who sees the imbalance and the general society comes to believe that the scientist can create the technology that is needed to bring balance back again. Thus, in spite of a clearly deteriorating physical world brought about by industrial society, we still think in mechanical, technological terms when we discuss restoration of what we have disrupted.

Traditional technology may seem incredibly outdated to many Indian students now undertaking a scientific education. If so, they are not getting the full story from historians and apologists of science. It is said that Albert Einstein had wholistic and sometimes substantial visions of the world and that he spent most of his life looking for the proper mathematics to describe what he had experienced. One need only look at the many instances in which noted scientists had visions or dreams that solved the problem they were confronting. At the very foundations of the world in which we live, it is a unified world and cannot be reduced by techniques and rationality. Where traditional Indians and modern science are quite different is in what they do with their knowledge after they have obtained it. Traditional people preserve the whole vision, whereas scientists generally reduce the experience to its alleged constituent parts and inherent principles.

A great gulf exists between these two ways of handling knowledge. Science *forces* secrets from nature by experimentation, and the results of the experiments are thought to be knowledge. The traditional peoples *accepted* secrets from the rest of creation. Science leaves anomalies, whereas the unexplained in traditional technology is held as a mystery, accepted, revered, but not discarded as useless. Science operates in fits and starts because the anomalies of one generation often become the orthodoxy of the next generation, as witness the continental drift theories.

GIVING TRADITIONAL TECHNOLOGY A CAREFUL LOOK

Indian students would do well to learn about the traditional approach to learning about the world in addition to taking the scientific courses to gain entrance to professions. They should be prepared in their work, as students and later as professional people, to answer the question What does it mean? in addition to answering any other questions that as professional people they will be expected to answer. Traditional technology can be extremely useful because it always reminds us that we must take our cue about the world from the experiences and evidence that the world gives us. We may elicit and force secrets from nature, but it is only answering the specific questions we ask it. It is not giving us the whole story as it would if it were specifically involved in the communication of knowledge. What is given willingly is much more valuable than what is demanded as a matter of force.

Since many Indian students will be working for their tribes once they receive their professional degrees, it would pay them to give traditional technology a careful look. Tribal lands and resources have always been used on a sustained yield basis, and this attitude is in distinct contrast to the American propensity to exhaust resources for short-term gains. Modern technology might indeed be useful in repairing the damages already done to tribal lands so that the lands can once again be put on a traditional use pattern and become productive again. And even this possibility can be learned from the world as it responds to ceremonies and human societies that understand their place in the larger cosmos. As science progresses, so do the ceremonies and as we look ahead there is considerably more to be gained by combining insights than by ignoring them.

11

KNOWING AND UNDERSTANDING:

Traditional Education in the Modern World

▼▼▼▼

M odern American education is a major domestic industry. With the impending collapse of the cold war, education may well become the industry of the American future. Since education significantly impacts Indian communities and has exerted great influence among Indians from the very beginning of European contact, it is our duty to draw back from the incessant efforts to program educational opportunities and evaluate what we are doing and where we are going in this field. It should come as no surprise to people in Indian communities that in recent months one report on Indian community colleges has been released and plans have been announced to conduct yet another study on what is happening in Indian education. We seem to occupy the curious position of being pilot projects and experimental subjects for one group of educators and the last communities to receive educational benefits as determined by another set of educators, primarily administrators. So the time has come to try to make sense of what education has been, presently is, and conceivably might be for American Indians.

European civilization has a determined and continuing desire to spread its view of the world to non-European countries. Within a generation of the conquest of Mexico, the Spanish had founded schools in Mexico City for the education of indigenous youths, and an important part of mission activities for the next three hundred years was education of both young people and adults in the Christian religion and the niceties of European customs. French colonial policy dictated a kind of education in which prominent families within the Indian tribe and the French colonial families exchanged children for a short period of time so that customs would be properly understood and civility between the two groups would not be violated by thoughtless or ignorant actions.

English education, represented first by benevolent members of the aristocracy who gave funds to support Indian schools and later embodied in the U.S. government's encouragement of mission activities among the frontier tribes, represented, and still represents, an effort to effect a complete transformation of beliefs and behaviors of Indians. Education in the English-American context resembles indoctrination more than it does other forms of teaching, because it insists on implanting a particular body of knowledge and a specific view of the world that often does not correspond to the life experiences that people have or might be expected to encounter. With some modifications, and with a considerable reduction in the intensity of educational discipline, the education that Indians receive today is the highly distilled product of Christian/European scientific and political encounters with the world and is undergirded by specific but generally unarticulated principles of interpretation. Because the product is so refined and concise, education has become something different and apart from the lives of people, and is seen as a set of technical beliefs that, upon mastering, admit the pupil to the social and economic structures of the larger society. Nowhere is this process more evident than in science and engineering, fields in which an increasing number of American Indian students are now enrolled.

Education today trains professionals, but it does not produce people. It is, indeed, not expected to produce personality growth in spite of elaborate and poetic claims made by some educators. We need only to look at the conflict, confusion, and controversy over prayer in schools, sex education, and the study of non-Western societies and civilizations to see that the goal of modem education is to produce people trained to function within an institutional setting as a contributing part of a vast social/economic machine. The dissolution of the field of ethics into a bewildering set of subfields of professional ethics further suggests that questions of personality and personal values must wait until the individual has achieved some measure of professional standing.

This condition, the separation of knowledge into professional expertise and personal growth, is an insurmountable barrier for many Indian students and raises severe emotional problems as they seek to sort out the proper principles from these two isolated parts of human experience. The problem arises because in traditional Indian society there is no separation; there is, in fact, a reversal of the sequence in which non-Indian education occurs: in traditional society the goal is to ensure personal growth and then to develop professional expertise. Even the most severely eroded Indian community today still has a substantial fragment of the old ways left, and these ways are to be found in the Indian family. Even the badly shattered families preserve enough elements of kinship so that whatever the experiences of the young, there is a sense that life has some unifying principles that can be discerned through experience and that guide behavior. This feeling, and it is a strong emotional feeling toward the world that transcends beliefs and information, continues to gnaw at American Indians throughout their lives.

It is singularly instructive to move away from Western educational values and theories and survey the educational practices of the old Indians. Not only does one get a sense of emotional stability, which indeed might be simply the impact of nostalgia, but viewing the way the old people educated themselves and their young gives a person a sense that education is more than the process of imparting and receiving information, that it is the very purpose of human society and that human societies cannot really flower until they understand the parameters of possibilities that the human personality contains.

The old ways of educating affirmed the basic principle that human personality was derived from accepting the responsibility to be a contributing member of a society. Kinship and clan were built on the idea that individuals owed each other certain kinds of behaviors and that if each individual performed his or her task properly, society as a whole would function. Since everyone was related to everyone else in some specific manner, by giving to others within the society, a person was enabled to receive what was necessary to survive and prosper. The worst punishment, of course, was banishment since it meant that the individual had been placed beyond the boundaries of organized life.

The family was not, however, the nuclear family of modern-day America, nor was it even the modern Indian family, which has, in addition to its blood-related members, an FBI undercover agent, an anthropologist, a movie maker, and a white psychologist looking for a spiritual experience. The family was rather a multigenerational complex of people, and clan and kinship responsibilities extended beyond the grave and far into the future. Remembering a distant ancestor's name and achievements might be equally as important as feeding a visiting cousin or showing a niece how to sew and cook. Children were greatly beloved by most tribes, and this feeling gave evidence that the future was as important as the present or past, a fact that policy makers and treaty signers have deliberately chosen to ignore as part of the Indian perspective on life.

Little emphasized but equally important for the formation of personality was the group of other forms of life that had come down over the centuries as part of the larger family. Neoshamanism today pretends that one need only go into a sweat lodge or trance and find a "power animal," and many people, Indians and non-Indians, are consequently wandering around today with images of power panthers in the backs of their minds. But there seems to have been a series of very early covenants between certain human families and specific birds, fish, grazing animals, predatory animals, and reptiles. One need only view the several generations of Indian families with some precision to understand that very specific animals will appear in vision quests, sweat lodges, trances, and psychic experiences over and over again. For some reason these animals are connected to the families over a prolonged period of time and offer their assistance and guidance during times of crisis during each generation of humans.

Birds, animals, plants, and reptiles do not appear as isolated individuals any more than humans appear in that guise. Consequently, the appearance of one animal suggests that the related set of other forms of life is nearby, willing to provide assistance, and has a particular role to play in the growth of human personality. In the traditional format there is no such thing as isolation from the rest of creation and the fact of this relatedness provides a basic context within which education in the growth of personality *and* the acquiring of technical skills can occur. There is, of course, a different set of other forms of life for each human family, and so dominance and worthlessness do not form the boundaries between the human species and other forms of life.

Education in the traditional setting occurs by example and not as a process of indoctrination. That is to say, elders are the best living examples of what the end product of education and life experiences should be. We sometimes forget that life is exceedingly hard and that no one accomplishes everything they could possibly do or even many of the things they intended to do. The elder exemplifies both the good and the bad experiences of life, and in witnessing their failures as much as their successes we are cushioned in our despair of disappointment and bolstered in our exuberance of success. But a distinction should be made here between tribal and nontribal peoples. For some obscure reason, nontribal peoples tend to judge their heroes much more harshly than do tribal people. They expect a life of perfection and thereby partially deify their elders. At least they once did. Today, watching the ethical failures of the non-Indian politician, sports hero, and television preacher, it is not difficult to conclude that nontribal peoples have no sense of morality and integrity at all.

The final ingredient of traditional tribal education is that accomplishments are regarded as the accomplishments of the family and not the individual. Early training of children involved some elaborate praise of youngsters carrying out simple tasks, but the praise was directed toward the family, and the individual became a good representative of the family. He or she did not dwell on individual accomplishments. I find this trait a considerable handicap for many Indian students in higher education. They are extremely reluctant to trumpet their accomplishments, and résumés that should be filled with items look exceedingly sparse because of the propensity of some Indian students not to advertise their virtues. But it is a good trait to follow because it helps to distribute both praise and blame over a much larger group of people and again reduces the amount of blame or praise that the individual has to assimilate into his or her self.

Modern education places immense reliance on the standardized tests as a measure of the worth and accomplishments of the individual. Students preparing for college are made to feel that the task is a solitary one and that the measure of their potential is found in the entrance and qualifying tests they take. Most educators, if pressed, will admit that at best tests measure only a potential to successfully undertake a certain course of study. If really pressed to explain the requirement of test scores, administrators will sometimes admit that they require them simply because the forms they use for admission require them—there is a blank left unfilled in the form. I once had a graduate student who we admitted conditionally, since she had not taken the GRE, who was ready to graduate with an M.A. and who was told she could not get her degree because she had not taken the GRE!!

These kinds of institutional barriers become insurmountable if Indian students see themselves as solitary individuals, and here is where the value of traditional education comes into play. We cannot change the American educational system to make it more humane— or even to make it comprehensible to anyone. But we can remember that it is primarily a measure of ability and accomplishments in the narrow field of professional expertise. It really says nothing and does nothing for the whole human being. A solid foundation in the old traditional ways enables the students to remember that life is not scientific, social scientific, mathematical, or even religious; life is a unity, and the foundation for learning must be the unified experience of being a human being. That feeling can only come by remembering the early experiences of the Indian community as it seeks to establish the primacy of personality growth as the goal of life. A student grounded in that context must then always remember that he or she is not and can never become an isolated individual. The community, regardless of its condition, always provides a place for people to return.

Transforming students' perceptions of themselves and the world into a feeling of confidence is a hard task and the frustrations are great. Recently a group of us have been waging a struggle to get the human remains of Indians returned from museums and laboratories. Nothing distresses me more than to be in hot debate over whether Indians are humans and whether our remains deserve reverent burials instead of becoming "specimens" and "teaching devices" and to have an Indian person trained as an anthropologist rise in the audience and say "I'm an Indian, *but I'm also an anthropologist.*" These people are simply the confused products of the American educational system and probably should be put out of their misery. You are *always* an Indian, first, last, and always. You may have a degree in anthropology, law or nuclear engineering, but that is your *profession*, that is how you make your living, it is not you!! So your traditional education should give you guidelines on how to behave. Your first responsibility is to be a human being, an Indian. Once you accept that fact and use it as a positive factor, you can then do whatever professional tasks are required of you, but you will know when to draw the line between professional responsibilities and the much greater responsibility to be a person. You can earn money, but you cannot be happy or satisfied unless you become yourself first.

So there is much to be learned from a traditional education, and we must see it as the prerequisite to any other kind of education or training. Traditional education gives us an orientation to the world around us, particularly the people around us, so that we know who we are and have confidence when we do things. Traditional knowledge enables us to see our place and our responsibility within the movement of history. Formal American education, on the other hand, helps us to understand how things work, and knowing how things work, and being able to make them work, is the mark of a professional person in this society. It is critically important that we do not confuse these two kinds of knowledge or exchange the roles they play in our lives. The major shortcoming in American institutional life is that most people cannot distinguish these two ways of knowing, and for many Americans there is no personal sense of knowing who they are, so professionalism always overrules the concern for persons.

Today we see a great revival of traditional practices in many tribes. Younger people are bringing back crafts, songs and dances, and religious ceremonies to make them the center of their lives. These restorations are important symbols of a sense of community, but they must be accompanied by hard and clear thinking that can distinguish what is valuable in the old ways from the behavior we are expected to practice as members of the larger American society. In this movement it is very important for younger Indians to take the lead in restoring the sense of family, clan, and community responsibility that undergirds the traditional practices. In doing so the next generation of Indians will be able to bring order and stability to Indian communities, not because of their professional expertise but because of their personal examples.

▼ 12 ▼

HIGHER EDUCATION
AND SELF-DETERMINATION

▼▼▼▼

During the 1950s, Congress authorized a program of rapid termination of federal trust responsibilities for American Indians. The policy was ill-conceived, seeking to reduce federal expenditures that were minimal and badly executed, allowing private banks to exercise a restrictive supervision over the assets of tribes that lost their federal eligibility. Virtually no development of tribal assets occurred during this period, and educational programs were generally oriented toward vocational training and relocation of Indian families to designated urban areas. With the New Frontier and the Great Society programs came a radical redirection of Indian programs. Economic development was stressed and the federal government began to provide scholarship funds for Indians in higher education.

We have been living in the era of self-determination since about 1966, and, although appropriations suffered immensely during the Reagan and Bush years, the trend of policy has firmly supported preserving tribal life and enhancing the powers of tribal self-government. The two major thrusts of federal policy from the very beginning have been the education of the next generation of Indians in the ways of the white man and the exploitation and/or development of the reservation resources. Today the government seems intent on stressing the economic aspect of Indian life to the detriment of its educational component, a policy exceedingly shortsighted in view of the continuing economic crisis of the United States and the limited resources that Indian reservations actually contain.

Self-determination grew like topsy over the past three decades, and it never was clearly defined at the onset of the era. It was a concept that originally surfaced in international relations to describe the desire of formerly colonized peoples to break free from their European oppressors and take control over their own lives. These peoples were, for the most part, geographically distinct and distant from their former colonial masters and consequently independence, while painful, seemed more logical because the connections established by colonizing powers seemed and were wholly artificial. Indian tribes, with the possible exception of western and north slope Alaskan villages, have always been viewed as internal to the United States and hence part of its domestic problems. That the Supreme Court has continually characterized Indian tribes as foreign to the United States in cultural and political traditions is difficult for most people to understand, so they make little effort to do so and prefer to consider Indians as simply another racial minority, albeit one with considerable fascinating habits.

Self-determination inevitably had to take on a different meaning when applied to Indian tribes and reservations. Since the original goal of the Kennedy and Johnson administrations was to delay termination of federal services until such time as tribes achieved some measure of economic parity with their white neighbors, self-determination in the Indian context basically has meant that Indians can administer their own programs in lieu of federal bureaucrats. Education was conceived as the handmaiden of development; one need only look at the fields in which Title IV fellowships are being given to understand that federal higher education programs were meant to train a generation of people who could function as low-level bureaucrats in drastically underfunded programs that were intended only to keep Indians active and fearful of losing their extra federal funding.

Two major emphases characterized Indian economic development. Tribes were encouraged to allow major American corporations to control their energy resources in exchange for a few token jobs and a small income. Employment programs were designed to provide temporary wage labor in fringe industries that were themselves in danger of disappearing. Some wage industries, such as the moccasin factory at Pine Ridge, attempted to exploit the public stereotypes of Indians, and others such as recreational ventures placed the Indian workers in the permanent status of servants to a rich non-Indian clientele. Administration and management have thus become the favorite programs of the federal government and private foundations, the belief being that Indians feel more comfortable performing menial jobs or watching their forests and coal reserves being exhausted if some token Indians are involved.

Unfortunately, administration and management have never been areas in which Indians have excelled. They require that people be viewed as objects and that masses of people be moved and manipulated at will in order that programs achieve maximum efficiency. This kind of attitude and behavior is the antithesis of Indians' ways, as is the fact that management and administration are always dressed up in "people" language to make them more palpable. Many Indians did not realize that the programs they were administering were designed to manipulate people and they unintentionally transformed administrative procedures to fit Indian expectations. The result was that program efficiency declined and some programs fell apart even while an increasing number of people were being served. Many programs considered as failures from the non-Indian perspective when considered from the Indian side of the ledger have been outstanding successes even if they have given bureaucrats ulcers.

Indian education of the past three decades has done more than train Indian program chiefs, however. While Indians have been penetrating the institutions of higher learning, the substance and procedures of these institutions have also been affecting Indians. Indians have found even the most sophisticated academic disciplines and professional schools woefully inadequate because the fragmentation of knowledge that is represented by today's modern university does not allow for a complete understanding of a problem or of a phenomenon. Every professor and professional must qualify his or her statements on reality and truth with the admonition that the observations are being made from a legal, political, sociological, anthropological, or other perspective. These statements then are true if confined to the specific discipline and its methodology by which they are formed. That they represent little else may escape the professor or professional, but it does not escape the Indian student who often dismisses theory, doctrine, or interpretation when it does not ring true to his or her experience.

The revolt against social sciences is not simply a few Indian activists criticizing anthros and the suspicion with which Indians in science and engineering view theories in their fields. Rather the problem is the credibility and applicability of Western knowledge in the Indian context. The objections are easily understood. Western technology largely depletes resources or substitutes a mono-cultural approach to a complex natural system. We tend to hide this fact by talking about production rather than extraction but this linguistic acrobatics is not sufficient to escape Indian critique. Social science in the western context describes human behavior in such restrictive terminology that it describes very little except the methodology acceptable to the present generation of academics and researchers. While an increasing number of Indian students are mastering the language and theoretical frameworks of western knowledge, there remains the feeling of incompleteness and inadequacy of what has been learned.

More important, whatever information is obtained in higher education must, in the Indian context, have some direct bearing on human individual and communal experience. In contrast in the non-Indian context, the knowledge must simply provide a means of identification of the experience or phenomenon. It helps to deal with specific examples to illustrate the point. A Western observer faced with the question of how and why certain species of birds make their nests is liable to conclude that it is "instinct." And this identification of course tells us nothing whatsoever, but it does foreclose further inquiry because a question has been answered.

In the Indian context the answer would involve a highly complicated description of the personality of the bird species, be it eagle, meadowlark, or sparrow, and the observed behavior of the bird would provide information on time of year, weather, absence or presence of related plants and animals, and perhaps even some indication of the age and experience of the particular bird. In this comparison Indian knowledge provides a predictive context in which certain prophetic statements can be made. Western science, for all its insistence on reproduction of behavior and test conditions and predictability of future activities, provides us with very little that is useful.

Indian knowledge is designed to make statements that adequately describe the experience or phenomenon. That is to say, they include everything that is known about the experience even if no firm conclusions are reached. There are many instances in the oral traditions of the tribe in which, after reviewing everything that is known about a certain thing, the storyteller simply states that what he has said was passed down to him by elders or that he marveled at the phenomenon and was unable to explain it further. It is permissible within the Indian context to admit that something mysterious remains after all is said and done. Western science seems incapable of admitting that anything mysterious can exist or that any kind of behavior or experience can remain outside its ability to explain. Often in the Western context the answer is derived by the process of elimination. Thus with the theory of evolution: it is accepted primarily because other explanations are not popular or are distasteful.

Western engineering presents a special case. Its validity depends primarily on its ability to force nature to perform certain tasks that we believe are useful to human beings. Its knowledge derives from physical experiments and more recently from complicated mathematical formulas that predict certain kinds of phenomena if certain kinds of things are done under conditions controlled by human beings. There is no question that if we restrict our understanding of the world to particular things we want to do and set up the conditions under which they must occur, we will have some spectacular results. But we do not really understand nature or the natural world, we simply force natural things to do specific tasks and measure the results and construct theories that describe what we have done. We have not yet asked ourselves whether in forcing nature to behave in certain controlled ways we have not set in motion other forces that nature must make manifest so that our demands can be met.

Today there is no question that we are approaching the time of an ecological breakdown. We have identified certain aspects of our interference with nature and believe these things to be the cause of the deterioration we have observed. We have no way of knowing how things relate to deterioration because our context is too small. Would the widespread use of electricity, for example, have anything to do with the ozone problem? Does increased radiation have anything to do with the rapid disappearance of amphibians around the world? Is cancer a function of crowding people together, or is AIDS a function of chemically treated foods and chemical disposal into domestic water supplies? When we begin to ask questions that try to bring by-products of our technology into new combinations so that we can test effects and do further investigations we are virtually helpless because we have no good context within which to ask the questions that should be asked and we must spend immense amounts of time and energy simply identifying the proper questions.

When we take all of the knowledge we receive in colleges and universities along with our certifications for professional work and perhaps even for managerial activities, we are led to believe that we are prepared to exercise self-determination because we are now able to begin to compete with the non-Indian world for funds, resources, and rights. But we must ask ourselves, where is the self-determination? What is it that we as selves and communities are determining? We will find that we are basically agreeing to model our lives, values, and experiences along non-Indian lines. Now the argument can be made that since we are geographically within the United States we must conform to its values, procedures, and institutions. At least we must do so if we are to measure success according to the same standards and criteria. And all of our education informs us that these standards are nationally acceptable and may indeed even be universal throughout the cosmos.

It is increasingly apparent, however, that the myths of Western civilization are also the cause of its rapid degeneration so that it is hazardous to measure ourselves according to those standards. As a nation we no longer produce wealth as much as we borrow from the future. If an individual really wants to make money he or she would do better to master complicated tax laws than to start a new business. Professors stand more chance of getting their ideas accepted if they are immensely popular with their peers than if they actually have something to contribute. The possible existence of a Supreme Being is a great embarrassment to religious people. Poor people are or should be incubators and organ donors for rich people. Wisdom consists of frequent appearances on television shows. Athletes need not be skillful, but they must win regardless of the circumstances. Any form of activity in any other country can be regarded as a threat to the United States—and of course all forms of activity within the United States are threats to its security. It is exceedingly difficult to distinguish between American moral values and bumper sticker slogans.

The practical reality of these insights provides both the criteria for public success and the uncomfortable feeling among educated Indians that something is missing. Most Indians do not see themselves and their relatives within the popular American truisms, and they are greatly embarrassed when other people force them to acknowledge that these criteria really are accepted by a majority of Americans. Minimally, Western mythology describes a society that is not even polite, and that is the key to understanding how to transcend the attitudes and perspectives of non-Indian education so that Indians can determine for themselves and by themselves what they want to be even if they are wholly within the confines of American society.

When we talk of the old days and old ways we frequently place special emphasis on the manner in which people treated each other, the sense of propriety, gentility, and confidence that the elders had. Being polite springs primarily from a sense of confidence in one's self and one's knowledge about the world. Indian narration of knowledge about the world fell into a particular format, and out of a plenitude of data the speaker would choose the set of facts most pertinent to the explanation. He or she would formulate the story so that it ended on a proper note—*oh han*, as the Sioux say. Now, a person cannot bring a teaching to a close, invoke the right response in the listener so that the information is taken seriously, and have some impact without closing off the discussion on a proper note. Real knowledge creates politeness in the personality, and you can see this trait in many wise non-Indians. It is, in fact, their foremost personality trait.

In the past three decades, while the movement for self-determination was proceeding, we have witnessed a drastic decline in politeness and civility in Indian communities. Indian meetings are many times difficult to attend because they consist of little more than people clamoring for attention and people busy impressing each other. The outstanding characteristic of Indian students today is the emergence of politeness as a personality trait. Science and engineering students, more than others, now seem to possess this most precious of all the old traditional personality traits. Here we may have an indication that the current generation of Indian youth is moving beyond the boundaries established for self-determination after the non-Indian pattern and now stands ready to bring something entirely new to the process of applying Western scientific knowledge to Indian problems.

If this observation is correct, then we will witness some very unusual things happening in Indian communities in the future. Indians who are now working at the professional level, particularly in science and engineering, will work their way through corporate and academic institutions and begin appearing as independent consultants and as owners of small technologically oriented businesses working in ecological restoration and conservation areas. Research institutes headed by Indians will begin to appear on certain college and university campuses doing complex research projects. Almost all of this first generation of Indians will be active in traditional religious practices even though many of them will be living away from their reservations. One or two of these people will write extremely sophisticated papers and books that will be highly regarded within their professions.

Indian students in colleges and universities will begin to combine majors, putting together unlikely and unpredictable fields and having some degree of difficulty doing so because of the inability of departments to reconcile the students' interest within traditional Western disciplinary relationships. An increasing number of Indian students will choose very specific new majors that represent non-Indian efforts to do interdisciplinary work and that are almost wholly outside the fields that are being chosen by present Indian students. Indian graduate students will be doing very sophisticated dissertations and, in the hard sciences, highly innovative research projects.

Indian community colleges will begin to show an increasing non-Indian enrollment, some people being nonresidents who come to these schools specifically to study with certain tribal elders. The number of four-year community colleges will dramatically increase, and community colleges themselves will begin to appear on the national scene in scholarly conferences and meetings. Most of the larger community colleges will have their own publishing and TV production programs and some of them will be producing programs for national educational television. Some faculty at reservation community colleges will begin a thriving consultant business as state and private universities far away from the reservation want to establish working relationships with the tribes. Community colleges will play an increasingly influential role in tribal economic and political problems and programs.

Tribal governments will develop new ways to organize the reservation communities and will develop specific programs for a wide variety of land uses. Tribal governments will have a considerably larger role in determining high school curricula, and some reservation high schools will have entirely new formats for study and graduation. Formal and informal networks of elders will begin to resolve some of the reservation problems, radically changing the kinds of topics that tribal councils are asked to handle. New and smaller communities will be built in different parts of the reservation, eliminating the concentrations at agency towns and having new kinds of local governing powers. Self-determination will not be an issue because people will be doing it in forms that even they will not recognize.

Although it appears easy to make vague predictions concerning the future of Indians and education, none of these ideas is an ad hoc concept. Rather everything flows from the original idea of education acting as the motive force in self-determination. The policy makers three decades ago assumed that education would radically change Indian young people while also assuming that they would hold as a constant the value of returning to their tribes to take the lead in development projects. Higher education really was thought to be higher than the knowledge and experiences that Indians brought from their homes and communities. It might have been more complicated, but it was too departmentalized and consequently the chinks in the armor were all too apparent and left most Indian students with the feeling of having incomplete knowledge. Unable to bring academic knowledge to its proper unity, more and more students are supplementing the shortcoming of Western thought by placing it in the context of their own tribal traditions.

Once the process of supplementation began, it would naturally follow that individuals would begin to compare specific items of Western knowledge with similar beliefs derived wholly from the traditions of their tribes, and we see this process now emerging as an identifiable intellectual position of this generation of Indians. It will take considerable time for a new theoretical posture to be developed by this generation, but some individuals are well on the way to doing so. As a new perspective is formed, individual Indians who have moved completely through the institutional structures will pull all conceptions of Indians beyond the ability of Western ideas to compete and this conceptual shift will focus attention on the cultural knowledge of the community colleges. Once community colleges articulate a new conception of what it means to be an Indian and an Indian community, the rest of the shift is apparent and predictable.

In a previous article I discussed the fact that much of American education is really just training and indoctrination into the Western view of the world. Basically this view is held together by the sincerity of its followers. It does not have an internal consistency of its own, except in general methodological patterns whereby information is classified. Indians, over the long run, are exceedingly hard to train because they get easily bored with the routine of things. Once they have understood and mastered a task it seems like a waste of time to simply repeat an activity, and so for an increasing number of Indians the training that is received at institutions of higher learning only raises fundamental questions that are never answered to their satisfaction.

We can visualize the effects of education on Indians as follows. Non-Indians live within a worldview that separates and isolates and mistakes labeling and identification for knowledge. Indians were presumed to be within this condition, except they were slower on the uptake and not nearly as bright as non-Indians. In truth Indians were completely outside the system and within their own worldview. Initiating an accelerated educational system for Indians was intended to bring Indians up to parity with middle-class non-Indians. In fact, it has pulled Indians into the Western worldview and some of the brighter Indians are now emerging on the other side, having transversed the Western body of knowledge completely. Once this path has been established it is almost a certainty that the rest of the Indian community will walk right on through the Western worldview and emerge on the other side also. And it is imperative that we do so. Only in that way can we transcend the half millennium of culture shock brought about by the confrontation with Western civilization. When we leave the culture shock behind we will be masters of our own fate again and able to determine for ourselves what kind of lives we will lead.

▼ 13 ▼

THE TURMOIL OF ETHNIC STUDIES

▼▼▼▼

The activism of the 1960s produced an unexpected development in academia that we have not yet understood or resolved. Students were angered at the isolation of the academy and its callous disregard for the lives of ordinary people. Minorities in particular saw academic studies of their communities as demeaning and paternalistic, and indeed they were. American Indians were the province of anthropologists with occasional archaeological offerings, Mexican Americans and African Americans were the property of sociologists, and Asians were simply not visible at all. Lesbian and gay concerns were much later in developing and almost constituted a second-wave reaction to the ethnic movement.

Breaking out of these intellectual ghettos was a necessity, people believed, if the paternalism was going to be overcome or reduced. Thus there were demands to develop courses on the particular experiences of racial minorities to bolster the images minorities had of themselves and to educate the white majority students about life as racially oppressed people in the United States. Because these requests came in the form of taking over buildings and blocking hallways, the administrations of several California universities agreed to the student demands and colleges and universities in other states, observing the California situation, suddenly decided that Ethnic Studies was a valid academic discipline. Within a very short time, anthropology and sociology classes were cross-listed with the new Ethnic Studies classes and the era of Ethnic Studies was under way.

Finding professors for these new disciplines was a monstrous task as racial minorities had been systematically excluded from the social sciences for decades. Some African Americans had forced their way into urban sociology, there were perhaps three Indian anthropologists, and there was a handful of ethnics in literature, but there was not even a cupboard, let alone a cupboard that was bare. Some courageous white teachers did their best to satisfy the new demand for courses, but many of them, after setting up courses that would begin to focus on ethnic concerns, were driven out of the new discipline on the grounds that only ethnics could understand life as a racial minority. What students really meant was that only an ethnic could feel deeply about the experiences in a personal way but that sympathetic people could certainly imagine the minority condition— at least enough to teach about it.

I never believed that Ethnic Studies would be accepted as a fully respectable discipline for a number of reasons. First, the university administrators, once agreeing that these courses had to be taught by minorities, then had to stock the programs with very inexperienced people. I believe this demand injured a number of good ethnic scholars because they were not allowed to develop themselves intellectually before being placed on the firing line. I joined a new "College of Ethnic Studies" at Western Washington State University in Bellingham in fall 1970. This meant that I had to present a full complement of four basic courses to be taught in my first semester of college teaching. Other minority people faced the same intellectual demands when they arrived on their campuses.

We did our best to create courses for our students, but libraries lacked even basic resources for dealing specifically with courses focusing wholly on racial minorities. Thus assigning long reading lists was useless because there were simply no good bibliographies available. Most of the written materials on Indians used language familiar to Rudyard Kipling, which was hardly suitable for angry students to digest. The expectations of the students were not oriented toward the kind of academic behavior exhibited by the typical professor. That is to say, traditional academic objectivity toward the subject matter enhanced by an atmosphere of aloof snobbishness was not the way to relate to our students. They expected us to be in the midst of community struggle and in many cases to be leading it. I am certain that I met student expectations as I was involved in many of the political activities of the day. But I am equally certain that my courses were lower level in content because I simply did not have time to develop the proper framework for discussing issues in a detached manner.

Another major flaw in the process was the instantaneous way in which the discipline of Ethnic Studies was created. One day there were angry students; the next day there was a list of thirty courses about their group that students could take, almost all of them designed to infuriate the students because of the outmoded content. No other academic disciplines had been asked to develop instantaneously. Rather they were offshoots of existing disciplines. Sociology, anthropology, and other social sciences had evolved slowly as graduate offerings, and then, when the intellectual framework of the topic had been established and the viability of the subject had been demonstrated, undergraduate courses were added as prerequisites and the discipline was regarded as valid and independent of other fields. Criticism of Ethnic Studies by professors in other fields was thus well founded in that ethnics had little time or energy to develop the parameters of their fields. But the motives for attacking the viability of the various ethnic studies offerings were usually based on the desire of the old guard to regain ground lost to Ethnic Studies and to put Euro-American hegemony back in place.

In 1978 I went to the University of Arizona to teach and found the usual paper-thin facade of American Indian Studies. Dr. Edward Dozier, a Santa Clara Indian and one of the few Indians who had a degree in anthropology, had been given a large grant by the Ford Foundation some years before to develop Indian Studies. But he had unfortunately passed on shortly after the grant had been received, and it fell to the anthropology department to administer. The result was as could be expected. Anthropology stocked up with archaeologists to the point that the Ford Foundation asked for the remaining funds back. The new archaeology courses were designed as "American Indian Studies" as well as anthropology.

I remember the day I canceled seven archaeology courses and introduced some courses on contemporary Indian affairs. It was like a minor earthquake as the archaeologists exploded and the phone rang incessantly with calls from the higher administrators who had been harassed by archaeologists seeking to change my mind. But I was able to hold my ground in spite of criticism by the local pet Indian who had lived off the anthropology department for years as its token effort to help Indians. We eventually got the Ford grant restored and developed a set of courses that enabled us to offer a master's degree in American Indian Studies. Today there is a move to expand the offerings to include a Ph.D. In the course of development we were able to attract such Indian superstars as N. Scott Momaday, Leslie Silko, and Joy Harjo to the university.

We did not solve one of the basic questions that all Ethnic Studies programs must consider. Was the content of the program to be about the minority community or about the relationship that the community had experienced with the American political system and American society? Robert K. Thomas, our beloved elder, believed that we could provide enough substance about the reality of Indian communal life so that students would get a taste of who Indians really were.

I did not think this was possible. In my view, we would be on very thin ice if we purported to teach what I regarded as the cultural context of Indian life. My preference was to concentrate on the history of the relationship Indians had with the federal government on the grounds that students would be holding policy-making positions in tribal governments and would need to know the basic outline of the development of federal Indian policy and programs. Bob and I and later professors never quarreled about this division, and each of us taught courses that we believed represented our point of view, allowing the students to decide by enrollment which philosophy they wanted to follow. I must admit that Bob Thomas had a much closer relationship with the students than I did. However, I think my students wrote much more sophisticated theses than did Bob's students.

My last experience with Ethnic Studies was when I moved from Arizona to the University of Colorado in 1990. The program at Colorado was already reasonably developed when I arrived, and the professors were for the most part a younger generation. They already had a technical vocabulary and a framework for discussing ethnicity in an abstract intellectual sense. I was baffled by the variety of big words I had never heard and the complications that these words purported to describe. I realized that some measure of academic respectability had been achieved because I could hardly understand what my colleagues were saying. I was never even sure that they were talking about ethnic problems. That kind of behavior is the best measure of academic respectability—a professor can talk for an hour and only his closest colleagues can understand what he is saying.

So I was fortunate that the history department took me in as an intellectual refugee.

Ethnic Studies did and does meet a great need on the university campus. White students as a rule do want to know about ethnic experiences, and the majority of my students at three different universities were whites. Generally, they were much better students than any of the ethnics and sincerely wanted to broaden their college experience. My ethnic students did not do very well, and from my Colorado experience I can understand the basis of their problem. Both ethnic students and faculty are faced with an impossible task. They must not only study and teach ethnic courses but also remain in good standing with their respective communities. On campus they are, whether they will admit it or not, representatives of their communities. Ethnic faculty must not only meet academic standards in their teaching and publications, they must meet the demands of their students and the outside ethnic community.

One can walk by the offices of white professors and find them comfortably sitting in their chairs casually reading articles and books and occasionally discussing abstract theories with students. The ethnic professor has a dozen phone calls coming in, people from the outside community waiting to talk with them, and students sitting around wanting to hear more about the subject. At any moment they can be invaded by people of their community who have problems in different parts of the state, or even national problems. No white professors are bothered by the Lions Club, Rotary Club or Knights of Columbus the way ethnics are smothered by representatives of their community organizations. Yet public service is rarely accorded any status when promotions and merit raises are considered.

The surge in support of Ethnic Studies has now been reversed by the attacks on affirmative action in the universities, and college administrators, eager to cut budgets, are now wielding financial axes with reckless abandon. The first programs to be cut back will be Ethnic Studies. The trend is so great that I expect Ethnic Studies to disappear in the next decade. It will be a shame as these programs do provide a radical departure from the usual benign middle-class interpretations of life in America. We should be alert to the literature that has been produced during this time that will not be erased with the university budget cuts. It will stand as a constant reminder of the "other" America and will continue to be meaningful wherever thinking people congregate.

▼ 14 ▼

THE BURDEN OF INDIAN EDUCATION

▼▼▼▼

The education of American Indians has always been of major interest to white people with whom they have come into contact. Of the many reasons for devoting time, energy, and money to the task of educating Indian children, but two motives seem to have been primary. Whites believed their way of life, their religious beliefs, and their secular knowledge about the world were correct. They regarded other beliefs as mere superstition. Educating the Indians to truth, be it religious, economic, or scientific, was regarded as the duty of the civilized man.

The Spanish friars who accompanied the conquistadors in their marches through the American Southwest, Florida, and California were certainly the first group to undertake Indian education. Their work, however, died at the end of the California mission era. Our attention, therefore, must be directed to the English colonies and their efforts in Indian education that were adopted and continued by the U.S. government. The first Indians to receive an English education were exchange students. In 1616 the governor of Jamestown, Sir Thomas Dale, sailed for England, taking with him John Rolfe, Pocahontas, and some Powahatan Indians who were to be educated in England.[1] But the experiment was a failure. Most of the Indians died of European diseases, and the remaining students, girls, were hustled off to be married, relieving the Virginia Company of any further expenses.

During the next one hundred twenty years, there were sporadic but continual efforts to educate Indian children in the colonies. Sometimes the colonial legislature would set aside funds for the founding and support of a college to educate Indians, at other times a wealthy English lord would make a bequest for this purpose, or societies interested in the propagation of the Gospel would try to provide educational facilities for Indians. In 1691, William and Mary College was founded to provide Indians of the Virginia colony with an education, and in 1645 Harvard College was given funds to educate two young Indians whom John Eliot had located. In 1650 when Harvard College revised its charter, one of the purposes of the institution was avowed to be the "education of the English and Indian youth of this country in knowledge."[2]

Not all of the Indian tribes saw an English education as the wave of the future. In 1744 at the treaty of Lancaster, the colonists, eager to curry favor with the powerful Iroquois Confederacy, offered to provide schooling for six young boys. The Iroquois representatives, experienced observers of the English educational system, kindly replied:

> We know that you highly esteem the kind of learning taught
> in those Colleges, and that the Maintenance of our young
> men, while with you, would be very expensive to you. We are
> convinced, that you mean to do us Good by your Proposal and
> we thank you heartily. But you, who are wise must know that
> different Nations have different Conceptions of things and you
> will therefore not take it amiss, if our Ideas of this kind of
> Education happen not to be the same as yours. We have had
> some Experience of it. Several of our young People were
> formerly brought up at the Colleges of the Northern Prov-
> inces: they were instructed in all your Sciences; but when they
> came back to us, they were bad Runners, ignorant of every
> means of living in the woods . . . neither fit for Hunters,
> Warriors, nor Counselors, they were totally good for nothing.[3]

It is important to note the expectations of the Iroquois. Their idea of education was an immensely practical one and seemed to concentrate on making the student a useful member of society. The English education, unfortunately, was not designed to produce useful citizens, only to transmit an abstract body of knowledge.

Beginning in 1778 and continuing until 1871, the United States dealt with Indian tribes by treaty, and education was generally an important provision in the negotiations for federal services. The Continental Congress, fearful that the Indians on the frontier might support the British, authorized the sum of $500 to support ten Indian boys who were studying at Dartmouth College when the Revolution began.[4] In 1781 the Congress again appropriated a sum of money to pay the expenses of three Indian students at Princeton College.[5] Both of these expenditures were not made for the benefit of Indian education but to cement good relationships with the tribes on the frontier. Education, therefore, was an instrument of a larger policy involving considerably more elements.

The first mention of educational provisions as such in an Indian treaty is found in the treaty of December 2, 1794, with the Oneida, Tuscarora, and Stockbridge Indians.[6] The United States promised to employ two or three persons to maintain a grist mill and sawmill and to instruct the young men of the tribes in the arts of the "miller and sawer."[7] Succeeding treaties made similar promises, usually for a term of years and generally concentrating on the vocational arts rather than academic learning. It would be repetitious to review all of the treaty promises dealing with educational services since they all are variations on a general theme, but we must note that these treaty provisions meant that Indians were essentially paying for their own education through land cessions.

In addition to specific treaty provisions for particular Indian tribes, the government also appropriated a general fund for the civilization of Indians. A sum of $10,000 per year was authorized by the act of March 3, 1819,[8] and was perennially renewed, becoming the general fund from which Indian educational services were supported if supplemental or incidental educational programs were necessary. Generally, the government would contract with religious missions to provide educational services paid for by the fund. The major difference between the use of the fund and the treaty provisions was one of choice: under the treaties the tribes chose their educators; under the fund the secretary of war and later the secretary of the interior chose the organization that would provide education.

Indian education during the formative years of Indian policy was not a universal program. Schools were open to all children of the tribe, but only a few actually attended. Generally, the school buildings provided the nucleus of settlement in the agency town, particularly if the school was operated by a religious order or society. In

1822 there were eleven principal schools, three subordinate schools, and three schools being built; 508 students attended them, and the cost was $15,827.56.[9] Two years later the student population had increased to move 800 Indian students in twenty-one schools.[10] Although the annual appropriation for education was small, its impact was significant.

Compulsory education began to appear in about 1857 with the treaties of that year with the Pawnees and Poncas.[11] Penalties were provided for any parent or guardian who neglected or refused to send his or her children to school. Generally, these penalties were deductions from annual annuities, although at a much later date the rations of the parent were cut off if the children were not attending school.[12] By 1871, when Congress prohibited the further ratification of Indian treaties,[13] definite formulas had been established. In the 1867–1868 series of treaties, the government promised a schoolhouse and teacher for every thirty children who could be induced or compelled to attend school.[14] In 1871 the Commissioner of Indian Affairs reported school attendance of 6,061 pupils in 286 schools.[15] Although it would appear that Indian education was in good shape, these statistics are misleading. Nearly half of these schools (141) were among the Five Civilized Tribes in Indian Territory and were operated by the tribes themselves and should not have been reported as part of the federal Indian education program.

The first period of intensive federal involvement in Indian education began in about 1873 and lasted until World War II. Its chief features were the establishment of day schools and off-reservation boarding schools such as Carlisle and Hampton. The year 1873 is important because Congress repealed the old provision that allocated $10,000 annually to the "civilization" of Indians.[16] In place of this fund Congress made a special appropriation of $100,000 for Indian education. Under the new emphasis day schools, generally one-room schools with a teacher and twenty or thirty students, reservation boarding schools, capable of educating as many as a hundred older students, and off-reservation boarding schools enrolling several hundred students were instituted. This system was designed to provide education for each and every Indian student who could be enticed, compelled, or convinced to attend school. When the system was finally in place, the reservation agents then used whatever means they had to force the parents to enroll their children.

This new federal system was hardly luxurious. Students performed most of the menial and janitorial tasks of operating the school facilities. In many instances they worked in farmlands connected with the school and grew most of the food for the reservation boarding schools. Actual learning was minimal; these institutions resembled reformatories where culturally deficient inmates struggled to achieve a measure of respectability. Classes were held only in the mornings; the afternoons were devoted to work, hard work, and relentlessly boring routine work.

Discipline was harsh and copied from military life. In most of the schools the children wore uniforms modeled closely after the army uniforms of the day. Runaways were frequent. Illnesses, particularly tuberculosis and fevers, were rampant, and many children died or were sent home fatally stricken with some disease. Every congressional committee sent to investigate conditions of Indians heard more than they wanted to about the operation of the schools and the treatment of children in them. It is perhaps the memory of these schools, passed down over several generations, that contemporary activists complain about. There is no question that this was a thorough, deliberate effort to eliminate tribal cultures and languages and educate the children in the shortest possible time, in the most practical and useful arts.

There was good reason, when we remember the times, for this kind of school system, harsh though it was. After 1887 and the passage of the General Allotment Act, the majority of the children in these schools were actually property owners—they had allotments in their own names. The western spaces were rapidly filling up, and the pressures for further cessions of Indian land continued to increase. There was probably not enough time to preserve Indian culture and Indians also. It was an age when cultural evolution was an article of intellectual faith and the truly educated in American society devoutly believed that the only salvation for Indians could come as a result of cultural uplift. Continued adherence to traditional Indian values, people believed, would only result in death and extinction.

The first erosion of federal responsibility occurred accidentally when a Nebraska congressman discovered that he could authorize the secretary of the interior to transfer a choice tract of land to the local school district in return for that district's promise to educate Indian children. In the act of March 31, 1908, Congress directed the

Secretary to issue a patent for certain lands within the Santee Sioux Indian Reservation to school district number thirty-six in Knox County, Nebraska.[17] Although few people recognized it at the time, and although this device did not immediately become popular, this statute was a fundamental turning point in Indian education. It meant a number of things.

First, the responsibility for Indian education could he transferred from the federal government to a local school district by a simple congressional transaction involving the gift of land. Second, local school budgets, construction programs, and landownership could be immeasurably increased by federal largess if Indian education were used as an excuse. Here was a pork barrel with seemingly bottomless potential. Third, transferring Indian students to state school systems relieved the federal government of enforcing any standards whatsoever. To have insisted on good results would have been an intrusion into local affairs, an act that all good congressmen devoutly abhor.

The legislative record indicates an increasing propensity of congressmen to provide benefits to their white constituents by special statutes that purport to transfer responsibility for Indian education to local school districts and then, having recognized the liberal acts of local schools in assuming this burden, generously compensating them. Thus, to give some specific examples, the Joint Resolution of February 13, 1922,[18] allowed the president to pay the tuition of Montana Indian children in state schools; the act of June 13, 1929,[19] another Joint Resolution of Congress, amended an appropriation for construction of a federal school at Turtle Mountain, North Dakota, to provide "that such school shall be open for attendance by white children and by restricted or nonrestricted Indian children." A proviso attached to this Resolution required the state of North Dakota only to "supplement" federal appropriations for the operation of the school. The dam broke, and by the mid-1930s special educational legislation was passed in every Congress granting lands, funds, or privileges to local school districts in return for their nebulous promises to provide Indian children with an education.

Within this historical framework we can begin our examination of contemporary Indian education issues. The precedents established three quarters of a century ago have now become a way of life. Many local school districts have come to believe that they are *owed* federal support if they enroll Indian children. Recent educational legislation has reinforced that belief, but it did not begin in recent years; it was a tenet of state belief for many decades before the federal government assumed large budgetary commitments in education. For the better part of this century the goal of Indian education has not been education. Indian education has been oriented toward performing other peripheral tasks of a political and economic nature.

The Indian educational landscape before World War II looked something like the following. The federal government had a number of large off-reservation boarding schools that provided the federal equivalent of a bad high school education to children of almost every tribe. The larger reservations had day schools and generally a large boarding school at the agency town. There were scattered in Indian Country a number of mission schools, most of them Roman Catholic. Other denominations participated in Indian education to a much lesser degree. A significant number of smaller tribes did not have federal schools of their own but were expected to send their children either to the off-reservation boarding schools or to public schools. In Oklahoma there were both state schools and federal boarding schools. In Alaska there were primarily federal boarding schools, a few small mission schools, and, where a native village lived in the vicinity of a white settlement, public schools.

Indian education was, however, regarded as the first priority of the Bureau of Indian Affairs (BIA) at this time. Ironically, the situation was so confused as to preclude any realistic efforts by either Indians or federal educators to bring order to the field. Two statutes, the Snyder Act of November 2, 1921,[20] and the Johnson–O'Malley Act (JOM) of April 16, 1934,[21] dealt with Indian education, except at cross-purposes. The Snyder Act authorized the secretary of the interior to "direct, supervise, and expend such moneys as Congress may from time to time appropriate, for the benefit, care and assistance of the Indians throughout the United States for the following purposes: General support and civilization, including education."[22] The Johnson–O'Malley Act provided that moneys appropriated by Congress for Indian education could be turned over to "any State or Territory, or political subdivision thereof,"[23] under a contract by which the recipient agreed to undertake to provide educational facilities in accordance with standards established by the secretary for a specified number of Indian students. Although in theory these two statutes were not in conflict, in actual operation there was a great deal of controversy. States regarded JOM moneys as rightfully theirs; BIA employees regarded the Snyder moneys as rightfully theirs.

The Meriam Report of 1928, a widely recognized study on the conditions of Indians, was not very helpful in resolving the educational pecking order. It suggested that "the task of the Indian Service be recognized as primarily educational, in the broadest sense of that term," and suggested that the BIA "be made an efficient educational agency, devoting its main energies to the social and economic advancement of the Indians, *so that they may be absorbed into the prevailing civilization or be fitted to live in the presence of that civilization at least in accordance with a minimum standard of health and decency*" (emphasis added).[24] Contrary to the beliefs of many Indians today, the Meriam Report did not support Indian self-determination. Instead it counseled benign, efficient, well-funded, and humane programs that, if they would not fit Indians to modern society, would at least enable them to live in a measure of dignity at the bottom of modern society.

The BIA, then, was charged with spending federal funds for the benefit and welfare of Indians under one law; it was directed to subcontract its functions to state and local agencies and subdivisions under another law, and it was admonished to become a superefficient educational agency under a government-sponsored study of the Indian Service that was intended to resolve policy questions once and for all. Nowhere in any of this flowery language and congressional authorization was there a concern for the education of Indian children. They had become peripheral to other considerations, and it now seems clear that this confusion actually represented the preliminary efforts of the federal government to escape the burden of providing educational services to the Indians by any means possible.

World War II was a blessing in a sense because it postponed the collapse of this contradictory structure. Events that occurred during the war foreclosed this confused discussion concerning which agency would provide educational services to Indians and on what basis these services would be delivered. Many small Indian communities simply vanished during World War II as families left the reservations to seek employment in war industries and younger people left home to serve in the armed forces, thereby postponing the creation of new families with children. Consolidation of all federal programs became necessary, and that often meant merging or closing of schools.

With domestic expenditures drastically reduced to enable the nation to wage a two-ocean war, it is little wonder that cost-conscious congressmen who detested the day schools zeroed in immediately on this part of the BIA budget. The congressmen phrased their attack in cultural terms that suggested only a warm concern for the welfare of Indian children. The House Select Committee to Investigate Indian Affairs and Conditions issued a report in 1944 that featured a vicious attack on the day schools. The report implied that the Indian children who attended reservation day schools were subjected to the handicap of "having to spend their out of school hours in tepees, in shacks with dirt floors and no windows, in tents, in wickiups, in hogans where English is never spoken."[25] Had they not been congressmen, whose ability to understand abstract thought is notoriously deficient, they would have understood their report to be in reality a vicious attack on the inability of the federal government to provide decent housing for Indians, not a criticism of the day school program.

So we have another irony of Indian history. Had Indians not rushed to work in the war effort, they would have maintained a sufficient reservation population to make continuance of the day schools a feasible educational and economic alternative to public schools. The day school story is really the story of Indians in a modern setting. Individual decisions, made at different times and different places, have validity in and of themselves that cannot be questioned. Yet the sum total of these decisions produced dire consequences for Indian tribes. Many day schools were closed for lack of students and never reopened. Federal Indian school enrollments declined substantially during the war. Margaret Szasz remarks, "Reservation day schools showed the greatest decline, losing almost two thousand students or 25 percent of their enrollment between 1942 and 1945."[26]

EDUCATIONAL LEGISLATION OF THE 1950s

The changes in federal educational policy in the 1950s were profound, even though they developed incrementally and, like Topsy, grew large before anyone realized it. Indian education programs within the BIA continued on a steady course during this decade, and we can dismiss the few things that occurred with a slight discussion. In the act of July 14, 1956,[27] Congress directed the secretary of the interior to conduct a comprehensive study of Indian education in the continental United States and Alaska and make recommendations concerning the problems of adult education and transferring Indian children to public schools. This report was considered so insignificant that Margaret Szasz, in her study of Indian education in the modern period, did not even mention it.[28] All of the real action, unfortunately, was occurring on another front.

Our story begins in the last year before the war, in 1941, when Congress, knowing that war was imminent, passed the Lanham Act,[29] which was designed to assist communities that had been significantly affected by the rapid development of federal war activities near them or in their midst. Local taxing authorities could not provide municipal services when faced with a large new population living or working on tax-exempt federal lands. Schools could not suddenly provide for hundreds, perhaps thousands of new students in one year. The Lanham Act provided federal funds in lieu of the taxes that would have been forthcoming had these developments been the product of normal growth over a much longer period.

The Korean War began in June 1950, and with cold war ideology gripping the United States the prospect of a long, bitter struggle between ourselves and the communists loomed. To provide for the many new installations that would be required, Congress decided to expand the Lanham Act under two separate statutes popularly called "impact aid." Thus it was that the 81st Congress passed P.L. 81-815,[30] which provided for federal financial support of construction costs for school districts affected by federal activities and P.L. 81-874,[31] which provided for federal assistance in the maintenance and operation of schools affected by federal activities. This double-spouted pork barrel, once tapped, could never be closed again.

The two laws seemed to give preference to certain congressional districts over others. Congressmen from neglected districts began to argue that it was not fair that only defense-related federal activities should receive this kind of subsidy. What about the folks back home who have national parks, national forests, national monuments, federal office buildings, and Indian reservations that are not on the tax rolls? Why should they pay higher taxes just because the federal government is not building bombs in their districts? So the process of amendment began, and each senator and congressman had a thousand good reasons for demanding equal treatment for his constituents.

Indian reservations were included in the 1953 amendments[32] because they were federal activities also.

Indians were not mentioned in the amendments, but it was understood that they qualified as people working or living on federal lands. However, as many states were already receiving federal funds for Indian students under JOM, it was ruled that a state had to declare whether or not it would take P.L. 81-874 or JOM moneys well ahead of the allocation. Thus this source of federal funds simply depended on which agency a governor chose to lie to.

P.L. 81-815 and P.L. 81-874 were amended again in 1958 as P.L. 85-620.[33] This act had two major titles. Title I revised and updated 815 to provide more flexible formulas for figuring the federal contributions to school districts. Title II revised 874 and exempted JOM payments from the definition of "other federal moneys," making it possible for states to receive funds from both sources. The revised statute also gave the commissioner of education considerably more leeway in waiving certain requirements if Indian students were involved in a dispute over the allocation of funds.

The 1958 amendments to impact aid legislation came the same year that Congress authorized the National Defense Education Act, which was designed to make the nation competitive with the Soviets in the production of scientists. Sputnik had frightened the whole country. Everyone realized that only a concentrated effort to produce scientists would enable us to match the Soviets in the space race. Critical for our discussion is that Indians were not included because Congress wished to improve Indian education, not because there was any profound educational goal to be accomplished for Indians. Indians were seen as simply another minority group that should not be omitted from the general benefits flowing from this congressional largess. This inclusion would have the most profound consequences during the 1960s.

EDUCATIONAL PROGRESS OF THE 1960s

No single decade in American history experienced the twists, turns, and turbulence that rocked the 1960s. Indian education was no exception. The decade began with a special Task Force report on the state of Indian programs and policies. John F. Kennedy's New Frontier was as unprepared for Indians as Indians were unprepared for the

New Frontier. Incoming Secretary of the Interior Stewart Udall appointed a special group to tour the reservations and communities and make recommendations regarding the administration's posture on the major issues affecting Indians. Prominent in this group were Philleo Nash of Wisconsin, who had served President Harry S. Truman as a White House assistant on civil rights, and James Officer, an anthropologist from Arizona, Udall's home state. These two men would later play an important role in the Bureau of Indian Affairs, Nash as commissioner and Officer as an assistant commissioner and special Udall confidant. The Task Force report illustrated the middle ground that Interior proposed to take under the Democrats. It recommended a lessening of tensions over implementation of the termination policy, a new emphasis on human and natural resource development, and, curiously, withdrawal of federal services to "Indians with substantial incomes and superior educational experience who are as competent as most non-Indians to look after their own affairs."[34]

Nash and Officer led a generally competent educational team within the BIA but they were never able to recoup the lost years of the 1940s and 1950s when the bureau should have been concentrating on Indian education. When they took office there were a variety of programs, including off-reservation boarding schools and dormitories, adult and vocational education, and a small scholarship program, that had not been revised since its authorization under the Indian Reorganization Act.

In his term as commissioner Nash was able to secure large appropriations for school construction, over and above the 815 funds that were available, because of the presence of Congressman Ben Reifel of South Dakota. Reifel was a Republican from the eastern district of South Dakota and an enrolled member of the Rosebud Sioux tribe of that state. Although Reifel's ideas often reflected the 1930s instead of the 1960s, he did have seniority in the House of Representatives. His success in securing appropriations for Indian schools was best summarized by a fellow congressman who was said to have remarked: "Oh, we let Ben build a new school every year and he goes along with everything else."

The Indian policy articulated by the Kennedy administration sidestepped the subject of termination without providing any clear idea where the administration would stand in a real crisis. Then vigorously advocating termination was Senator Henry Jackson of Washington State, the man who two decades before had demanded justice for Indians when introducing the Indian Claims Commission Act. Jackson's ideas had significantly changed during his years in Congress. Some Indians regarded him as in the same class as Andrew Jackson, the infamous Indian-hater of the previous century. Kennedy was reluctant to irritate Jackson, who was chairman of the Democratic party. Consequently, administration statements on Indian policy had little substance and much style. Although education was a central focus of the administration's effort, it was not given a high profile.

With the ascension of Lyndon Johnson to the presidency and the declaration of a war on poverty, national policy and Interior Indian policy diverged substantially. Interior's purpose was simply to retain control of Indian programs and funds. The newer Office of Economic Opportunity (OEO) saw the task as one of releasing the Indians from an oppressive, colonial, and paternalistic bureaucracy. Interior bureaucrats would generally oppose funding of reservation programs that did not have some provisions for BIA control or veto powers; OEO spent its time seeking to circumvent efforts by Interior to intervene. Indian educational policy fragmented and broke into several identifiable streams of thought and action.

The BIA sought to protect and expand its control over education on reservations within the traditional educational branch of the bureau. The OEO attempted to create an alternative educational system with such projects as Head Start, Follow Through, Upward Bound, A Better Chance, and Neighborhood Youth Corps. Indian educators and politicians, seeking a chance to get additional funds and programs, spent their time harassing both groups, playing on their guilt or supposed guilt and demanding a complete revision of Indian education with themselves and their friends in the driver's seat.

National educational policy, in the interim, moved from the slight intrusions made by 815 and 874 to an all-purpose effort to secure domestic tranquility by making federal education funds available to every constituency that could be identified. The important thing for our purposes is that Indians were able, through skillful and persistent lobbying, to make themselves eligible for special funds in nearly every program that was authorized.

As this process continued into the 1970s, the extent of Indian inclusion in national educational programs can best be shown by a summary of a chart prepared by the Indian Education Task Force of the American Indian Policy Review Commission in 1975. This group, charged with studying Indian education and making recommendations for policy changes, reported that the following education programs had funds that benefited Indians or were attracted by the presence of Indians:

ESEA—Grants for the Disadvantaged
ESEA—Supplementary Services—Nutrition and Health
ESEA, Title VII—Bilingual Education Right to Read
    Follow Through
Drug Abuse Education
Environmental Education
Indian Education Act
874—Maintenance and Operation
815—School Construction
Emergency School Aid
Bilingual Education Projects
Educational Television
Special Programs and Projects
Desegregation Assistance
Education for the Handicapped
Initiation, Expansion, and Improvement of Programs
    Deaf-Blind Centers
Specific Learning Disabilities
Regional Resource Centers
Special Education and Manpower Development
Occupational, Vocational and Adult Education
Basic Vocational Education
Curriculum Development
Educational Professions Development, Teacher Corps
    Educational Professional
Development, Graduate Fellowships and Grants
Adult Education Grants to States
Adult Education: Special Projects
Adult Education: Teacher Training
Ethnic Heritage Studies
Dropout Prevention
Higher Education

Basic Opportunity Grants
Supplementary Educational Opportunity Grants
Work Study
Cooperative Education
Subsidized Insured Loans
Direct Loans
Special Programs for the Disadvantaged
Developing Institutions
Community Service
Library Resources
Library Services and Construction
School Library Resources
Training and Demonstration[35]

There is no question that American education needed some kind of massive financial support to perform its designated task. Nor is there any question that Indian education, which had not received adequate funding since the Collier years, was in need of an infusion of funds. The problem was absorbing all of these programs in a very short time. If we fully understand the condition of Indians as the 1960s began, this situation will take on additional meaning. In 1961 only sixty-six Indians graduated from four-year institutions. In 1968, seven years later and in the midst of this explosion of educational opportunities, only 181 Indians graduated from four-year institutions.[36] The available pool of Indians capable of administering educational programs, then, was very shallow; it did not materially improve over the seven years of most intense and expansive federal program development.

The result was predictable: programs were increasingly administered by people with little if any experience and with minimal educational credentials. Educators in Washington tried a quick fix. Three universities, Harvard, Pennsylvania State, and Minnesota, were chosen by the Indian Desk of the OEO, to become centers of training Indian educators in advanced degrees. Harvard had not shown much interest in Indians since John Eliot; Penn State had no experience with Indians. Only Minnesota had ever shown any interest in Indian education, but its record was not the best among western and midwestern universities. As these programs developed the criteria for admission and successful completion of the coursework became increasingly vague. Harvard admitted almost anyone and graduated people in the shortest possible time with a master's degree.

The graduates of these programs soon banded together and came to dominate the administrative positions in Indian education in the 1970s. The "Penn State mafia" controlled the major positions in the Office of Education allocated to Indians and seemed to have enough political savvy to keep their people installed in office. Yet the cumulative effect of this generation of Indian educators on the quality of Indian education was negligible. Were one to take the total number of scholarly articles written and published by all of the Indian graduates of Harvard, Penn State, and Minnesota during the 1960s and 1970s, the cumulative résumé would still not qualify a non-Indian for consideration for tenure at a Western university.

Because these graduates were certified as having done advanced scholarly work in education, they were considered qualified for important positions in the Office of Indian Education and for the positions in various research and regional assistance centers that were established to work in the field. But because these Indians were administrators, their forte was programmatic, not intellectual. They would attend conferences and answer questions on how tribes or institutions could get waivers of federal rules and regulations. They were never able to begin the important process of articulating directions and substance in Indian education.

What were the articulated goals of Indian education at this time? It all depended on which group was considered a valid voice of Indian concerns. The 1961 Task Force had articulated fairly modest goals for the BIA's Indian education programs. The bureau simply wanted more money, it wanted to build some larger schools on the reservations, and it wanted to expand into scholarships in higher education. Hardly anyone outside of the rather restricted field of Indian affairs knew either the 1961 report or the history of Indian education. Thus when the Office of Economic Opportunity and the Office of Education discovered Indian education, their people believed it to be a novel, neglected, and untouched area where some real progress could be made.

In spring 1967 a number of Indians were invited to Penn State to discuss what could be done in Indian education in the way of research. The conference lasted three days and was marked by incredible confusion. No Indian seemed to know what the agenda was, and speeches droned on interminably. On the second night of the meeting the word was passed that the Office of Education was thinking of giving a grant for a major research project. Did the Indians think it was a good idea? Well, no one had even thought about the project, so the next day there was considerable discussion about why we should have a big research project that no one wanted. The next night word was passed that Dr. Robert Havighurst of the University of Chicago had been chosen to conduct the study.

The Indian delegates left Penn State not believing that they had authorized a study, and few knew who Havighurst was. Some time later a grant of $515,000 was given to Havighurst. The study took two years, was published as *To Live on This Earth,* and promptly disappeared. In the Appendix of the book was an official narrative describing how the study was authorized. Apparently a National Indian Education Advisory Committee had been authorized by this meeting. And the appendix stated: "Through this committee and the staff of the U.S. Office of Education, Professor Robert J. Havighurst of the University of Chicago was asked to become director of the proposed study and to work out the plan for the study."[37]

In relating the actual sequence of events I emphatically do not cast aspersions on Dr. Havighurst's personal and scholarly reputation and integrity. My understanding is that he did not know of the proposed study until after the conference and even then was reluctant to undertake it and needed much convincing to agree to do it. What is important in this scenario is the way in which the Office of Education arranged for Indian participation and got the study authorized. To the observer who did not understand the nuances of obtaining Indian consent in those days, the Appendix version of the meeting sounds like a spontaneous Indian-inspired movement. It was an Office of Education fiasco from its inception. This kind of manipulation of symbols was standard operating procedure for federal administrators during the sixties and shows why the massive amounts of research done on Indian education had little or no impact. The U.S. Office of Education had absolutely no idea what it was doing.

During the hearings on proposed amendments to the Elementary and Secondary Education Act of 1965 in April 1966,[38] the question was raised whether or not the responsibility for the education of Indian children should be transferred to the Department of Health,

Education, and Welfare (HEW) from the Bureau of Indian Affairs. HEW and Interior were asked to report to the subcommittee and filed an interdepartmental report in May 1967. They recommended no transfer, citing recent good relations between the two departments as their reason for rejecting the idea. Senator Paul Fannin of Arizona then wrote to Wayne Morse, chairman of the Education Committee and suggested that a Special Subcommittee on Indian Education be established to investigate further. So Senate Resolution 165 was passed authorizing the special subcommittee. [39]

Robert Kennedy became chairman of the subcommittee. After his death Wayne Morse headed the committee, until he was defeated in a reelection bid and Ted Kennedy assumed control, giving it the popular name, the *Kennedy* subcommittee. The committee filed a report in 1969 entitled *Indian Education: A National Tragedy—A National Challenge.*[40] In its opening summary the subcommittee tried to achieve a high profile by stating: "We are shocked at what we discovered."[41] But the findings were not unexpected or shocking to rank-and-file Indians, who had known all along that things were askew. The report listed sixty separate recommendations covering almost everything that a Congress or an administration could conceivably do for Indians in the field of policy and education. People today remember it primarily for one of its major emphases: it stressed maximum Indian control and participation in education. This idea, self-determination in education, and ultimately in all federal Indian programs, was the articulated will of Indian people beginning with the protest against Stewart Udall at Santa Fe, New Mexico, in 1966, but it had never been given such prominent support by a national political personality.

EDUCATIONAL SELF-DETERMINATION

The new articles of faith decreed that Indian education had failed in the past because of two factors: not enough money had been spent and Indians had not been in control of the programs. The early seventies thus saw a number of successful drives to enact legislation to cure these defects. Kennedy was still regarded as personifying the government in exile, and the fact that he had chaired the subcommittee that recommended these changes significantly contributed to the ease with which the proposals became law.

The most important statute of the seventies dealing with Indian education was the Indian Education Act (IEA) of 1972,[42] which was an amendment to the 815 and 874 impact aid statutes of the 1950 Congress. The IEA established the Office of Indian Education in HEW, now Department of Education. IEA defined "Indians" very broadly to include communities that did not have formal Interior recognition, and no blood quantum or residency requirements were included which would have limited application of the act. In some areas the public schools counted almost anyone who claimed an Indian grandmother for the purpose of reporting to the Office of Indian Education (thus greatly expanding the Cherokee population), and these widely inflated figures meant that the available funds could not conceivably service all the alleged Indian children in school. Efforts throughout the decade to revise the definition of "Indian" were less than successful and generally featured a vicious process of political infighting as representatives of federally recognized tribes sought to exclude nonfederal and urban Indians and the latter struggled to remain within the guidelines.

The IEA had three basic components. Part A provided grants to local educational agencies, including elementary and secondary Indian-controlled schools. Programs under this part ranged from remedial education to cultural enrichment and included bilingual and bicultural programs and guidance and counseling. The funds under Part A were called entitlement because they were based on the number of Indian students enrolled in the school and the average per pupil expenditure in the state rather than on the needs of any school district. Indian students thus became a special bonus item for local school budgets, and every district beat the bushes to increase the number of Indian students to make their grant as large as possible. How much of this special money was actually used to assist Indians with cultural and educational problems over and above the regular offerings remains unknown.

Part B authorized discretionary grants for the improvement of educational opportunities. Typical programs in this part of the IEA included innovative special education, which could be almost anything within the scope of human experience, teacher training, alternative schools, and programs for dropouts. It also permitted the development of special curricula and authorized graduate fellowships in six very restricted areas: medicine, education, law, natural resources, business, and engineering. These fields were chosen because Indians were sparsely represented as professionals in these areas. But this restriction meant that federal support for Indian education in the liberal arts, the arts, and the social sciences was virtually eliminated. The fellowship program was badly administered, although designated for graduate work. Some fellowships were given to undergraduates, fellowships were awarded generally according to family influence and not scholarly potential, and discretionary authority to designate "related fields" was so abused as to make the program a whimsical discretionary fund for Indian bureaucrats.

Part C authorized grants for adult education, to increase literacy and high school equivalency degrees, and for the health, manpower, and social needs of Indian communities. Grants could be given for projects to improve Indian employment opportunities. Part C had minimal funding and therefore not only duplicated existing programs but also had little impact on education. Later amendments, waivers of rules and regulations, and irregular practices made operation of the programs impossible to understand. Rules and regulations were constantly revised to accommodate the inefficiency of staff or the laxity of meeting deadlines or budgetary changes in the larger Office of Education. The act became an administrative nightmare with its various discretionary provisions. Considering that the Office of Indian Education was staffed with Indians who had little experience in administration and powder puff degrees in education, it is a wonder that anything was accomplished at all with this statute.

Congress in 1975 passed the Indian Self-Determination and Education Assistance Act.[43] The chief virtue of this act was its sponsorship, Senator Henry Jackson instead of Senator Kennedy. Title I directed the secretary of the interior to contract with Indian tribes for the administration of Indian programs currently administered by the Department of the Interior, including schools at all levels, and the authorization of supplemental funds for school construction to be used in conjunction with funds already available from the 815 impact aid programs. Apparently Congress had not been keeping track of its other authorizations, because this act duplicated almost every existing provision that was designed to assist Indians.

The final major education act of the seventies was the Tribally Controlled Community College Assistance Act of 1978.[44] Under previous grants from the OEO and the Office of Education the Navajos had established the Navajo Community College (NCC), and although the NCC had innumerable problems, the fact that Indians were establishing an institution of higher education was such a novelty that everyone overlooked the problems and concentrated on the possibility of developing community colleges on the larger reservations.

By 1978 it seemed as if every reservation able to put two hundred students in some kind of building had its own community college. Educators saw this movement as a solution to the dropout problem, tribes saw community colleges as a means of training personnel at home, tribal politicians saw another large pot of patronage funds, and reservation people saw community colleges as a means of upgrading their skills without moving away from home and attending more formal institutions. So everyone was well served by the concept.

The Tribally Controlled Community College Assistance Act authorized the secretary of the interior to make grants for general operating funds to defray expenses at these institutions. These funds were intended to provide the extra income that other independent or non-Indian community colleges would gather from the private sector to assist with their annual budgets. The act did not preclude grants from other federal sources so that figuring the annual budget of a tribally sponsored community college was an exercise in putting together a wide variety of grants eventually bound together by Interior's discretionary but contractual funds.

Most symptomatic of the seventies, however, was the National Advisory Council on Indian Education authorized by the Indian Education Act of 1972.[45] NACIE, as this national council was popularly called, was doomed from the beginning. Appointments were political and not based on educational service or achievements. Persons who wanted to secure an appointment had to muster support among the Indian politicians and then survive a test of national party loyalty, affirming their belief in and support of Richard Nixon, Gerald Ford, and eventually Jimmy Carter. In spite of this rather distasteful aspect of appointment, many Indians eagerly sought a position on NACIE as the council recommended grants and fellowships to the commissioner of education.

The problem with NACIE was that appointees felt obligated to represent their own local, and sometimes personal, interests. The council admitted in its third annual report, "Many have felt that the appointees represent a region, area or constituency. They must be the national voice for native people and serve as advocates for Indian education in the broadest sense in order to make an effective impact on national Indian policy."[46] But no one could live up to this lofty goal, and eventually the council was abolished, its contributions to educational policy virtually nil.

In spite of the generally dismal performance of Indian educators in the federal government and national organizations, on the reservations the people made good use of these programs. Some tribes wanted to operate their own schools, and in time more than one hundred Indian-controlled schools were under contract with Indian school boards. In some instances this change was not as radical as it might appear; the same rigid superintendent administered the school, although Indians filled seats on the school board previously occupied by white ranchers.

Programs for young children such as Head Start were most popular with tribes because they were noncontroversial and therefore easier to get funded and because there was great concern that something be done for the younger generation. When bilingual programs were authorized reservation people saw a chance to create a new kind of curriculum that would emphasize pride in tribal heritage and education in the white man's style. Programs designed to reduce juvenile delinquency were also very popular and made some significant inroads into this perennial problem.

When community colleges began to be funded, the nature of reservation education changed significantly. Many people sought to take advantage of these new programs and the first several years of operation of the community colleges generally saw large enrollments. The need of reservation people, however, was for practical skills that would enable them to secure employment on or near their homes and consequently the academic content of the community college curriculum rarely compared with that offered by similar institutions outside Indian Country. Educators who had hoped that community colleges would ease the adjustment problems of young Indians by enabling them to take the first two years of college at home and then transfer to state colleges and universities were severely disappointed. The reservation community college curriculum was not strong enough to prepare students for success in the four-year institutions. But by the same token, these institutions did provide an education above the high school level for a great many reservation people who would not have continued their education under any other circumstances.

Year-to-year funding was the major difficulty faced by the reservation schools and colleges. Writing grants and traveling to Washington to guide them through the bureaucracy took an intolerable amount of time. Frequently the notification of the award came only days before the school year was to begin. Tribes often had to operate with a letter of credit and the hope that the full budget would eventually be approved. It was obvious that no school system could operate permanently on this basis, yet little was done to ensure that the Indian schools had some financial stability that would enable them to develop their programs with some degree of assurance.

When Title IV of the Indian Education Act came into effect it alleviated this problem slightly as it had entitlement provisions that were almost automatic in determining the amount of funds that would be made available. Yet the inability of the national office of the Indian Education Act to meet deadlines remained a crippling factor in planning tribal educational programs.

With the Reagan administration, federal funds were reduced drastically in nearly every category of assistance. At first Indians hoped that the delivery system of funding would be made more efficient, but it quickly became clear that the new administration intended to eliminate most programs completely. This goal caused a great deal of worry on the reservations. Thus it was ironic that by the time tribes were finally experienced enough to deal adequately with educational institutions the era of federal assistance had ended. This experience was not new to the older generation of Indians who remembered the elimination of the day school system almost four decades earlier.

OVERVIEW OF EDUCATIONAL DEVELOPMENTS

In evaluating the progress and developments in education in the postwar decades, a number of things emerge. Most important for our understanding is the rapid pace at which developments proceeded. In 1961 Indians were still fearful of the termination of their special relationship with the federal government. Just a decade later they were aggressively supporting passage of the Indian Education Act and visualizing a golden age of Indian control of educational institutions, and ten years later they were surveying the ruin of schools and colleges wrought by severe reductions in the federal budget. No group or community can withstand that kind of rapid change and do a credible job of managing institutions or establishing a reputable program for the future. When we consider that during most of this period a much older, less aggressive generation actually controlled tribal governments, the progress that Indians did make is remarkable.

Not only did the pace of developments bewilder most Indians, the Indian community was hardly prepared to deal professionally with the tasks that this rate of development dictated. Trained and experienced Indians who could fill leadership posts were minimal as the sixties opened, and as time passed the number of job opportunities vastly outnumbered the pool of people available to fill them and do a credible job. It is fair to say that from about 1968 until the present the majority of people working in Indian education, particularly at the federal and organizational level, had little experience and had to learn as they went along. Most people had risen so swiftly through the institutional ranks that their experiences were those of grappling with the complex problems of surviving in a vast bureaucracy. It would be years before some of them could actually work in education in the teaching field. One cannot, ultimately, blame these people for their failures in administration, nor can one judge them by standards of another age.

A point that cannot be overemphasized is the fact that most of the programs made available to Indian tribes and communities were derived from national programs conceived and designed to serve urban and suburban populations who subscribed largely to the mainstream ideas of culture and education. Indian education was never really conceived as the education of Indians using the strengths of Indian culture or tradition. Rather Indians were always seen as the most needy and deserving of American minority groups. This theme was prominently played when Indian educators gave testimony before congressional committees, and rather than give new guidance to the Interior Department concerning fundamental redirection of Indian programs, Congress generally tended to shunt aside the Bureau of Indian Affairs and charge other federal agencies with tasks in Indian education for which they had no experience.

Indians were an entirely new experience for most bureaucrats in the Office of Education, and many of these people tended to see in contemporary Indian society the old values and virtues that romantic coffee table picture books attributed to the old chiefs. Unlike most other racial minorities, working with Indians became a personal, almost religious, experience for federal employees. It was a heady experience for a federal bureaucrat to travel to Pine Ridge, Window Rock, Crow Agency, or Red Lake, Minnesota, and evaluate Indian education programs. There he or she might be able to purchase Indian jewelry or buckskin costumes for a fraction of the cost they would pay for similar items in a specialty shop in the District of Columbia. The bureaucrat might be treated to several traditional meals of fried bread, buffalo, venison, or salmon, participate in a powwow, and, if lucky, be made an honorary member of the tribe.

On returning to Washington, the bureaucrat might not only hasten the awarding of an educational grant, he might zealously seek out additional opportunities for "his" tribe. But generally a bureaucrat had in mind as further projects that the tribe might consider those opportunities that a group of whites in similar circumstances might seriously consider. The all-important federal connection might be significantly diverted from its educational purpose by the good intentions of both parties—the bureaucrat in attempting to help the tribe—and the tribe in trying to make the bureaucrat feel at home. When the projects or grants did not succeed, both parties became unusually bitter over what each regarded as a breach of trust on the part of the other party. Here we have cultural conflict rather than corruption, but the result was as degenerating and demoralizing as if the parties had set out to exploit each other.

American education itself deteriorated quite significantly in the postwar decades, and this decline seriously affected Indians in their efforts to obtain a good education. Graduate education suffered some severe dislocations and the number of people seeking advanced work increased dramatically. Theses were no longer required in many master's degree programs and many special courses created to accommodate minority students that purported to speak to their special needs and backgrounds had less substance than some of the undergraduate courses offered at other colleges and universities. Many federal people in the Office of Education told me that they regarded an advanced degree in social science or education achieved after 1963 as suspect and most likely a waste of the student's time. When we consider the fact that the best and brightest Indian students were finally entering graduate school in the early seventies to gain these ephemeral degrees, we can see the problems that Indians faced in attempting to catch up with the rest of American education.

Looking at the variety of educational programs available to tribes, one is struck by the fact that, taken cumulatively, these programs constituted a shadow school system. From kindergarten which was paralleled by Head Start, completely through the school years to the programs operated by Harvard, Penn State, and Minnesota, Indians had an additional program available to cure the defects that traditional institutions were creating. This fact being evident, some consideration should have been given by Congress or one of the administrations to a complete reform or at least the achievement of stability in the BIA's Office of Education. Instead these decades were characterized by the constant rotation of directors of Indian education in both the bureau and the Office of Indian Education. Not only was intellectual leadership lacking, administrative continuity was virtually nonexistent.

It is a wonder, then, that with these dreadful institutional and financial handicaps Indian education made so much progress. If there were only 66 Indians graduating from college in 1961, by the middle seventies there were an estimated 30,000 Indians in some form of higher education. During this period almost 400 Indian attorneys were educated, nearly 100 medical doctors, and numerous engineers and scientists. When confronted with degree programs of substance, Indians seemed to respond well. The many education and business administration programs designed to meet the specific needs of the Indian community were largely failures, however, and there remained as desperate a need for educators and administrators at the end of the period as there had been when the sixties opened.

It is too early to evaluate the effect of drastic budget reductions on Indian education. Many Indians seemed relieved at the prospect of simplified programs; they were exhausted by the annual trek eastward for funds. On the other hand, those programs that were most innovative were generally in agencies that experienced the severest and most immediate reductions in funds. Some people felt that the reductions would enable tribes to set educational priorities instead of being forced to take many programs that were not difficult to fund but which were actually peripheral to long-term tribal needs. Whatever the future may bring to Indian education, it is certain that having experienced the good taste of operating their own programs, most tribes and communities will make every effort to support their educational institutions in the future.

NOTES

1. Alexander Brown, *The First Republic in America* (Boston, 1898), p. 230.
2. Samuel Eliot Morison, *Harvard in the Seventeenth Century* (Cambridge, Mass.: Harvard University Press, 1936), p. 6.
3. *The Papers of Benjamin Franklin,* ed. Leonard W. Labaree et al. (New Haven: Yale University Press, 1961), vol. 4, pp. 481-483.
4. *Journals of the Continental Congress,* vol. 3, pp. 176-177.
5. Ibid., vol. 20, pp. 819-820.
6. 7 Stat. 47.
7. Ibid.
8. 3 Stat. 516, 517.
9. *American State Papers Indian Affairs,* vol. 2, p. 276.
10. Ibid., p. 459.
11. Pawnee treaty, 11 Stat. 7210, Ponca Treaty—12 Stat. 997.
12. 27 Stat. 612.
13. 16 Stat. 544, 566.
14. See, for example, treaty with the Sioux and Arapaho, 15 Stat. 635; treaty with the Navajo, 15 Stat. 667.
15. *Annual Report of the Commissioner of Indian Affairs,* 1871, pp. 606-619.
16. 17 Stat. 461.
17. 35 Stat. 53.
18. 42 Stat. 364.
19. 46 Stat. 9.
20. 42 Stat 208.
21. 48 Stat. 596.
22. 42 Stat. 208.
23. 48 Stat. 596.
24. *Meriam Report,* p. 21.
25. *Report No. 2091,* U.S. House of Representatives, 78th Cong., 2d sess., 1944, p. 9.
26. Margaret Szasz, *Education and the American Indian* (Albuquerque: University of New Mexico Press, 1974), p. 110.
27. 70 Stat. 531.
28. Szasz, *Education and the American Indian.*
29. 54 Stat. 1125.
30. 64 Stat. 967.
31. 64 Stat. 1100.
32. 67 Stat. 530, 536.
33. 72 Stat. 559.
34. *Task Force Report,* 1961, p. 7.
35. *Report on Indian Education, Task Force Five: Indian Education,* American Indian Policy Review Commission (Washington, D. C.: GPO, 1976), pp. 93-97.

36. Szasz, *Education and the American Indian*, p. 134.
37. Estelle Fuchs and Robert Havighurst, *To Live on This Earth* (Garden City, N.Y.: Doubleday, 1972), pp. 329-330.
38. *Indian Education: A National Tragedy—A National Challenge* (Washington, D.C.: GPO, 1969), p. 2.
39. August 31, 1967.
40. 1969 Report of the Committee on Labor and Public Welfare, U.S. Senate, made by its Special Subcommittee on Indian Education, pursuant to S. Res. 80, November 3, 1969 (Washington, D.C.: GPO, 1969).
41. Ibid., p. xi.
42. 86 Stat. 327.
43. 88 Stat. 2203.
44. 92 Stat. 1325.
45. Part D, section 442.
46. *The Third Annual Report to the Congress of the United States,* National Advisory Council on Indian Education, March 1976, p. vii.

▼ Part IV ▼

INDIANS

INDIAN AFFAIRS 1973: HEBREWS 13:8

▼▼▼▼

Whenever an Indian reservation has on it good land, or timber, or minerals," the Commissioner of Indian Affairs stated in his Annual Report for 1876, "the cupidity of the white man is excited, and a constant struggle is inaugurated to dispossess the Indian, in which the avarice and determination of the white men usually prevails."

Ten decades later we discover that while times have changed considerably, ideas about Indians have remained more constant than the Rock of Ages. The feeling still remains that somehow there is a magic key to unlock the aboriginal psyche and that whoever finds this mysterious key can within a reasonable time create from the aboriginal inhabitants a type of person that has rarely been seen during the ages of man's existence.

One can only wonder at the profound inability of the white man to comprehend two factors of human existence that remain in many ways the most important factors of his social existence. These two factors are law and culture. While we all flippantly convince ourselves that we understand law and culture and the manner in which they appear to describe the interworkings of groups of men, a glance at the past century's events and present attitudes should be sufficient to indicate to us that, far from understanding either law or culture, the white man has continued to base his comprehension of society upon what he would like to believe men *should* be rather than what they are.

The predominant—one might say overriding—concern of the influential whites of a century ago was somehow to place the savage tribes on the evolutionary railroad track to civilization. Without examining the popular folklore of social evolutionary theories, whites assumed that nations of men followed inexorable rules of development. Arriving at national consciousness in a hunting state, the embryo nation was supposed to pass eventually to an agricultural state and then gradually evolve into a modern urban society. This process was believed to be part of God's divine plan, and American history was perverted to explain the process. Whether the present collective amnesia that blocks recognition of America's violent past developed during the closing years of the last century is irrelevant compared with the obvious beliefs, found in the writings of the past, that things had happened in a certain way, perhaps revealing a divine plan for America.

The pity of the thinkers of the last century was that they refused to analyze their ideology in logical terms or to expend great amounts of energy observing history to validate the corollaries of their central doctrine. As we glance at the suggestions of such men as Carl Schurz and their view of the divinity of agriculture, and compare the actual performance of the federal government and the American people during the succeeding years, we shall find that the credibility gap is not a phenomenon of recent times. It has been the constant hidden factor at work crushing the possibilities of finding a peaceful and just solution to the problems of American Indians. It exists today in massive doses because it has prospered for four centuries of the white man's existence on the continent and is just reaching national fruition.

From what we can discern of the articles of a century ago, they argued that agriculture was the next step in civilizing the Indian. Thus, the theory went, the Indian reservations should be broken into farming plots and tribal assets should be divided among the tribal members. With the injection of the magical properties of private property, the individual Indians would raise their heads and their sights beyond the limited horizon that hemmed in their tribal existence. The debate, if any existed, was whether the magic of private property could work on the savage psyche. Could Indians be saved, or were they to be exterminated like the buffalo?—a debate hardly above that of a savage mentality even if carried on by people with neckties and high-button shoes.

A glance behind the rhetoric of the time would be astounding even today. In ideological terms the debate was over the feasibility of making the Indian perform the evolutionary feat of leaping from hunting to agriculture in one generation. In practical terms the whites of the western states, cattlemen for the most part, wanted Indian lands. The allotment of the reservations and settlement of surplus lands would allow the sharper whites to gain large ranches for their cattle operations through their manipulation of the homestead acts. In forcing Indians to evolve from a hunting to an agricultural state, federal policy allowed the lower-class whites to continue in their slothful pastoral pursuits. The evolutionary theory did not withstand even a surface analysis of its validity.

Allotment appeared to be inevitable, and the leading exponent of the policy, Senator Henry Dawes of Massachusetts, finally saw his version of the legislation passed in 1887. The act gave policy direction to the president, but it was interpreted by the executive branch as an immediate mandate to allot all tribes, not simply those who applied for allotment. Hurried "agreements" were forced on some of the tribes while exotic inducements were dangled before others; soon most of the tribes of the West had become witting and unwitting victims of the policy.

To indicate how devastating the allotment process was to the tribal land estates, one need only view some of the figures of allotments and "surplus" lands that were reported by the Commissioner of Indian Affairs in 1891 and 1892. The Iowa tribe, for example, at the end of 1891, held 8,658 acres in allotted status and the government had purchased 207,174 acres of "surplus" lands from them—a loss of 90.8 percent of the tribe's landholdings. The Cheyenne and Arapaho tribes of Oklahoma had 529,682 acres left and had sold 3,500,562 acres of "surplus" lands—a loss of 81.5 percent of their lands. It should have been apparent, had anyone cared to understand, that allotment was a contemporary way to strip the tribes of their physical assets by ostensibly legal means.

Had the federal government maintained even a consistent program of allotment many of the tribes might actually have made the evolutionary leap forward that the reformers seemed to visualize. The Allotment Act had hardly been passed, however, when it was amended, and this amendment may have been the single most detrimental act the federal government ever perpetrated on Indians. In

1891 the General Allotment Act was changed so that Indian allotments could be leased out to non-Indians under the supervision of
the Bureau of Indian Affairs.

The leasing amendment was not wholly without justification.
Many Indians were very old and, having been forced to take allotments in their old age, were incapable of farming their lands. Indian
children were given smaller allotments of land according to the provisions of the allotment acts that affected the different reservations.
Generally they received forty acres—a tract insufficient for anything
other than token acknowledgment that they were tribal members at
the time the lands were divided. Giving allotments to children con-
flicted with the federal policy of bundling them off to government
boarding schools early in life, and questions arose concerning the
beneficial use of their lands during their school years.

The change of the allotment law was thus intended to meet these
problems, and the Bureau of Indian Affairs agents were given wide
discretion to lease Indian lands through the development of a federal "trust" over the lands, which grew out of the twenty-five-year
period of restriction on alienation that attached itself to the new
allotments. From this innocent beginning, the present theory of federal trusteeship over Indian lands developed. But the trouble with
vesting absolute discretionary powers in the Indian agents was that
few of them were honest enough to consider the best interests of the
Indians. Many were tied into the local pressure groups that sought
long-term leasing on those Indian lands that they had been unable
to gain through settlement laws. Very shortly, leasing was seen as a
modern means of taking Indian lands.

In the northern plains, where allotment had created thousands
of small tracts, the large ranching and farming combines began
moving onto Indian lands. In 1916, for example, on the 2-million-
acre Pine Ridge Indian Reservation in South Dakota, only forty acres
of land were leased to a non-Indian. A year later nearly 80 percent
of the land was leased to white cattlemen. Other reservations experienced the same phenomenon but at lesser rates of conquest. The
net result of the leasing policy was to reduce the Indians to absen-
tee landlords whose only purpose in life was to frequent the agency
town, drinking and idle, waiting for their lease checks. Allotment,
then, was an effort to force Indians to become white farmers; leasing was a convenient loophole to enable them to survive without

understanding the cultural change that would have enabled them to prosper.

The great social experiment of the nineteenth century became a systematic exploitation of people during the twentieth century. For no sooner had the frontier been declared officially closed by Frederick Jackson Turner than people forgot about the thousands of Indians huddled on the desert reservations of the West. Nostalgia for the frontier overwhelmed public consciousness, and dime novels and the new motion pictures created a West that never was but which everyone *thought* existed. The proper operation of federal laws depended on the continued glare of public understanding and opinion on the actions of the bureaucracy; when Indians were finally submerged as living people and replaced by their fictional counterparts, the bureaucracy moved in and snuffed out all signs of resistance.

Commissioner Francis Leupp, writing in his book, *The Indian and His Problem,* in 1910, declared, "The Indian problem has now reached a stage where its solution is almost wholly a matter of administration. Mere sentiment has spent its day; the moral questions involved have pretty well settled themselves. What is most needed from this time forth is the guidance of affairs by an independent mind, active sympathies free from mawkishness, an elastic patience and a steady hand." If America had not settled the problems of the world, it had at least solved a troublesome and perennial situation with the American Indians.

In the mind of Francis Leupp the solution might have been merely administrative, but the overweening ego of the white man failed to comprehend that such administration had not been a hallmark of present or previous behavior by the federal government. That administrative actions were decisive did not mean that they were moral, proper, or even efficient. Few people thought to inquire behind the actions of the government to determine if goals and results coincided.

It was by some strange intervention of fate that the Indian communities, beaten down with myriad rules and regulations, were placed on the road to cultural recovery. In 1913 a minor case involving the sale of liquor to the Pueblo Indians of New Mexico reached the Supreme Court. The question at issue was whether or not the Pueblos were so far under federal protection as to bar them from drinking. *Sandoval,* the defendant after whom the case was named, maintained that they were. The Supreme Court maintained they weren't. Not only that, the court found that the Pueblos had always been subject to the paramount power of Congress, and the implications of this decision suddenly dawned on everyone. The titles to thousands of acres of land that had been taken from the Pueblos by one method or another over the past half century were voidable.

From 1913 until 1924 the Pueblo lands controversy raged in the Southwest. The Indians organized as the All Pueblo Council to meet the challenge head-on. It was the first time since 1688, when they had thrown the Spanish out of the New Mexico area, that a concerted effort was made by the Indians. The philanthropic groups that had so plagued Indians a generation before rose to the defense of the Pueblos. Under the able leadership of John Collier, a coalition of groups spearheaded by the General Federation of Women's Clubs pushed aside the ranchers and farmers who had gathered under the leadership of New Mexico Senator Bursum and carried the day.

The Pueblo Lands Act set up procedures whereby the white intruders on Indian lands would have to prove their titles to the lands they claimed. The Pueblos were given a special attorney to handle their cases, and over a ten-year period several thousand squatters were expelled from the Pueblo lands. It was a rare instance of laws being used to defend Indian rights to land and communal existence rather than to despoil them.

The fight to protect the Pueblo lands must certainly stand as the turning point in the history of Indian Affairs. For the first time Indians were considered to have rights that could be protected in court. The Cherokees had gone to the Supreme Court to defend their treaty rights in the 1870s with no relief. Again in the 1870s the Indian citizen John Elk had sued to gain the voting franchise without success. Indians had somehow survived a century of disenfranchisement without the ordinary forms of legal protection; in the Pueblo case law was used for the first time to extend, if only by implication, the rights of Indians everywhere.

Collier emerged from the land confrontation as the strong man in the field of Indian Affairs. He spent the remainder of the 1920s needling both Congress and the administration for better conditions for Indians. Having become entranced by the Navajo and Pueblo lifestyle and religions, Collier devoted his energies to rebuilding the Indian cultural base and extending the land base on which the people conducted those ceremonies and lived the life that Collier loved and admired.

With the election of Franklin Roosevelt and the entrance of the New Deal ideologies into American life, Collier became the Commissioner of Indian Affairs. A report done half a decade earlier, by Lewis Meriam, on the administration of Indian Affairs, provided Collier with sufficient documentation and ammunition to drive through the Congress a completely new idea of Indian relationships with the federal government. In 1934 Congress passed the Indian Reorganization Act (IRA) which provided for formally organized and recognized governments for the reservations. Although the final version of the act was not what Collier had conceived, it was a giant step forward in the development of the Indian communities and Collier accepted what he could get and began to build on it.

The past generation has been dominated in one way or another by the work of John Collier. During the 1950s the tribes and Congress fought a bitter battle over the policy of terminating the tribes from federal supervision, services, and responsibilities. The first move by Congress was an effort to repeal the provisions of the IRA in order to cripple the ability of the tribes to fight back. Fortunately, the tribal governments had developed sufficient knowledge about the workings of the federal government to turn back the congressional challenge quickly. Collier's hunch about the continuing struggle between the tribes and the United States paid great dividends when put to the test in the 1950s.

When the War on Poverty was declared, the Indian communities were in an ideal position to exploit the provisions of the legislation. Tribal governments were eligible for grants on the same basis as cities and counties and nearly every tribe had an extensive program developed within a year of the passage of the legislation. Many even admitted non-Indians to their programs in those areas where conservatives dominated local white governments and refused to apply for funds for the poverty war. On the whole it was the ready-made status of tribal governments that enabled Indians to gain many advantages denied to other minority groups during the expansion of social programs in the 1960s.

The mere expansion of programs and opportunities created problems that even John Collier had been unable to foresee. The tribal governments set up under the Indian Reorganization Act were designed for depression conditions. In those days tribal income was exceedingly small; federal programs, even with the expansive nature of the New Deal, were minuscule, and none provided for direct funding of administrative costs to the tribes themselves. Thus the governments of the reservations resembled student governments in the large colleges rather than municipal governments with the ability to expand and contract according to the conditions that existed.

By the late 1960s the problem with the tribal governments was becoming apparent. Times and peoples had changed, but the tribal governments were burdened with an extensive and cumbersome process of amending their constitutions and consequently few had done so. The intangible results of the poverty programs were often to raise the question of Indian identity to a crisis situation. People were being hired partly on the basis of their tribal membership and partly on the basis of their education and professional skills. The two factors seemed to work toward a common middle ground in which the problem of what it meant to be an Indian was the central question.

With the rise of Indian activism in a number of forms, this central question, avoided by both Indians and whites since the days of Carl Schurz, dominated the emotional consciousness of Indians without finding an intellectual context in which it could relate to the modern world. People knew that they were Indians and tried to develop pride in this fact of their existence, but the pride too often expressed itself in antiwhite sentiments, not in a reflection of the basic Indian values that had enabled the tribes to exist during a century of oppression.

In the operations of the poverty programs there was a great deal of wasteful expenditure of moneys. Rather than call the culprit to account to the Indian community for his misdeeds, Indians too often regarded the maladministration of programs as another attack against whites; they refused to call the Indian administrator to account because he would be punished by white-dominated courts and administrative proceedings.

The result for the Indian communities was that instead of regaining the integrity that had been their chief characteristic in former years, the whole system of belief and faith in tribal institutions was so undermined that people began to call for the abolition of tribal governments. The final act of this tragic drama was, of course, the confrontation at Wounded Knee. People of equally sincere beliefs saw the Wounded Knee incident as the beginning of a new era of Indian involvement and the end of an era of inept radicalism during which Indian activists draped themselves in black clothing in order to make a name for themselves.

One would have to conclude that the process of assimilation has created a partial creature that in many ways can never again be made into a whole being. The integrity of law was never very strong when applied to Indians, and with the leasing amendment to the General Allotment Act Congress virtually abdicated its responsibility for Indians and allowed the anonymous and inept bureaucrats to take final control over Indians. The struggles of the succeeding years, while spectacular in some respects and disastrous in others, have been simply the events that could have been expected when central issues were avoided or approached obliquely.

The central issue has been that of culture and civilization. How does one determine the relative value, worth, and reality of culture? What factors are considered in weighing the values by which men live? Does an expanding technology give to one group of men a divine right to force on another group of men behavior patterns, values, laws, and concepts that are foreign to them? What factors finally determine how we understand "civilization" as it appears among men?

Jefferson Davis remarked, "Surely the equitable or humane conclusion would be that it were better the white man, with his larger means and higher intelligence, should have been assigned to the region where artificial appliances were necessary to secure the irrigation which would render the land productive, and science would be available to combat the ravages of destructive insects." The question, then, of mortality, civilization, and culture has been raised previously without creating any great impact.

William Justin Harsha noted, "Law has always availed to settle and civilize society." One can trace throughout the past century the absence of any integrity of the law when applied to Indians. It has rather been, if one reflects on the events that have been reviewed, a curious mixture of sociological theories masquerading as legal concepts that has dominated Indian affairs. The recent disturbances in Indian country have shown simply one thing—Indians are presently repeating the mistakes of the white man by attempting to force law to perform precisely those acrobatics that the whites of the 1880s and 1890s asked it to do.

In reflecting, therefore, on the foibles and follies of the past in the field of Indian Affairs and the learned expressions by policy makers of both red and white heritage, the most profound lesson we can manage is that history teaches nothing and men learn little from generation to generation. If within one generation a few people come to know themselves or to understand the nature of man's experience, it may be a major achievement. But the mixture of thought and emotion that has passed for Indian Affairs has done little for either red men or white men. While white men now own the continent, they are miserable, victims of pathological fears that they will lose their ill-gained wealth, and in the process of destroying the world. Indians have learned little except that they do not understand what has happened to them and have lost their ability even to articulate what that means.

Whether such conflict, when it has occurred in other nations in other ages, can be satisfactorily resolved seems to depend in large measure on an innate sense of proportion—a historical tradition that we have conveniently labeled our sense of "justice." It is the tragedy of our present situation that we cannot find even this sense of propriety, and we are unique among men of all ages in this inability to perceive values by which we can live. It would seem that Indians and whites were somehow destined to be each other's victims in unique and profound ways. And perhaps that is what we ultimately must live with.

▼ 16 ▼

WHY INDIANS AREN'T
CELEBRATING THE BICENTENNIAL

▼▼▼▼

Bicentennial planners are shocked that American Indians are not wildly enthusiastic about the coming anniversary of the United States. In some states there have been angry protests against the committees responsible for the various events, and the focus of the national concerns has been blunted by the refusal of many Indians of national prominence to involve themselves in determinations concerning the celebration.

The undercurrent against Indian involvement in the bicentennial is probably strongest in the traditional Indian communities who have never felt themselves a part of the American system. Their alliance in recent years with the younger activists has been based on a demand for enforcement of treaty rights, and certainly many traditionalists share with the activists a mistrust of the federal government that runs so deep as to preclude even consideration of a role in the anniversary celebration. This development is particularly unfortunate because at the turn of the century the traditional chiefs considered themselves such a part of America that they participated in several presidential inaugurations, particularly that of Theodore Roosevelt.

The activists' ideological stance precludes participation in the bicentennial celebration short of recognition by the United States of the national status of Indian tribes. Wounded Knee and the 1972 "Trail of Broken Treaties" caravan sought a restoration of Indian sovereignty on a quasi-international basis, and the Wounded Knee trials have featured a treaty rights defense that has advocated a hard line on the sovereign status of tribes as governed by traditional Indian customs. It would be ludicrous, therefore, to expect activists to be willing to celebrate the bicentennial year of a nation with which many of them consider themselves to be at war.

Then, too, recent revelations of federal infiltration of Indian organizations have turned many activists and moderates in Indian affairs against any involvement with national concerns. In the recent trial of Dennis Banks and Russell Means at Minneapolis, the U.S. Attorneys swore that the federal government did not have any informers infiltrating the defense planning committee during the trial. In March Douglas Durham, an FBI informer, confessed his role in subverting the U.S. Attorneys' statement to the court concerning informers and announced that he had directed the security of the defense room and had screened all people trying to talk with Dennis Banks, one of the defendants, for more than a year. When a people cannot believe the sworn statement of a U.S. Attorney given in a federal court, they are not particularly eager to celebrate the perpetuation of the government.

Aside from the traditionalists and the activists, however, there are many Indians who are actively participating in federal programs, who depend on the federal bureaucracy for their subsistence, and who have not generally voiced any objection to their conditions. In most instances this group includes the majority of elected tribal officials who have in recent years developed a cozy relationship with the Bureau of Indian Affairs. The strange fact is that even a majority of these Indians feel so alienated in American society that they do not wish to have a role, let alone a prominent role, in the planning for the bicentennial celebration. Their absence is the most conspicuous, and perhaps by analyzing what factors may possibly affect their attitude we can understand why even they are so reluctant to have any role in bicentennial planning and events.

Perhaps the best thing that can be said is that most Indians do not presently know what their relationship to the United States really is. There has not been a clear definition of the status of Indians for more than a generation. The last clear action of the United States was that of the New Deal when President Franklin D. Roosevelt, Secretary of the Interior Harold Ickes, and Indian Commissioner John Collier all supported and articulated the policy of Indian self-government. This policy, which was incorporated in the Indian Re-organization Act of 1934, reversed a trend of nearly sixty years during which the major direction of federal policy was separating Indians from their land through force in some cases and through complicated legislative devices in other cases.

Since the depression years federal policy has fluctuated from a determined but short-lived drive to terminate federal responsibilities for Indians to the present posture of exorbitant funding and benign neglect in articulating the philosophy behind the money. During this period, the initial promise of self-government has been subjected to intense bureaucratic manipulation of rules and regulations so that few tribal governments really understand what their rights and powers are. Court decisions have also been erratic, and although Indians have won many significant cases in recent years involving tribal civil and criminal jurisdiction and treaty hunting and fishing rights, little in the way of corrective doctrines of law has emerged from the mass of litigation that would be of comfort to Indians.

Not only legally but also emotionally, Indians have found no home in American society. Movies, despite Marlon Brando's appeal, still portray the march of the white man across the North American continent as the inexorable movement of God's people. Indian literature is pigeonholed as an exotic and hardly comprehensible childish poetry by American intellectuals, even though the best of American thinkers have not yet achieved a satisfactory understanding of the relationship of lands and peoples that is second nature to the majority of Indian people. Indian music is considered as the primitive ravings of a group of hunters rather than a deliberate and sophisticated form having an integrity of its own.

Except for the fact that federal money pour into school districts enrolling Indian children, local institutions are culturally and emotionally barred to Indian people. And Indians are shamelessly used by local institutions to justify either their superficial liberality or to forestall any solution of racial problems involving Indians, blacks, or Chicanos. In Denver, Colorado, when the federal court announced that Indians would not have to be bused in the new school integration plan, hundreds of whites claimed to have Indian blood to prevent the school district from busing their children. Not one of these families would have accepted the responsibility to work in the Indian center or to help with the usual activities of the urban Indian community or even would have identified as Indians except for this immoral avenue of avoiding busing.

Generation after generation of well-meaning missionaries come to the reservations with the plea that one cannot judge the Christian religion simply because white Christians have killed, raped, and stolen from the Indians. Indians are exhorted to judge Christianity by the ideals preached by the missionaries, not by the deeds of the white Christian businessmen and the local politicians who fill the pews at Christmas and Easter. Yet when Indian religious ceremonies are held, whites feel no hesitation at all in filming, tape-recording, or otherwise intruding into the event and feel slighted if Indians complain at the desecration.

All of these complaints are familiar to most non-Indians today because we have experienced nearly half a decade of Indian protests and occupations of lands and villages in which these accusations have been the chief rallying cry of the Indian activists. To repeat them, therefore, is tedious but not without merit. The last five years have seen an astounding interest in American Indians. Whites have by and large responded to the accusations of cultural and racial genocide by trying their best to repair the damage done by earlier and less understanding generations. How, therefore, can Indians not feel that the non-Indian has done his best? Why are the same charges to be leveled at the non-Indian once again?

Perhaps the problem is the times in which we live. In the last half decade substantial numbers of non-Indians have confessed to their ancestors' sins and made reparations of various sorts, including money, political support, increased community awareness, and demands for justice. Indian activities have received great foundation and public support, and a keen sense of appreciation has developed among many non-Indians for Indian art, literature, and religion. But the results of this concern, in the manner in which they have affected Indian communities, have been the same as the thoughtless and ruthless treatment of Indians a century ago. Wherein lies the difference?

A century ago whites trampled Indian legal rights, religion, and culture because they considered it a primitive and savage form of human existence that no group of people should be forced to maintain. The motivation of injustices past was the strongly held belief of non-Indians that they were given the divine command to civilize the peoples of the earth. In short, they did it because they thought they were right.

The depredations of the past five years have been similar in many instances to those of the past century. As awareness of Indian culture increased, the reservations were plagued with people wanting to help Indians. Amateur archaeologists dug up Indian burial grounds, Indian art prices skyrocketed out of sight, and incompetent filmmakers stalked the Indian homelands seeking a "meaningful" film that would portray the reality and beauty of Indian life. Whereas some filmmakers sought only a profit from filming the sacred places of Indian life, many others sincerely sought to reconcile two ways of life, both of which had a certain reality for the other.

Indian ceremonials were packed with non-Indians who came not to deride or convert but to appreciate and learn. The teachings of Black Elk, the famous Sioux holy man, were avidly read and discussed by a generation of young non-Indians who sought a better understanding of lands and peoples—and themselves. In almost every way the non-Indian peoples reached out for understanding of Indians, and if there was not always sympathy and understanding, there was almost always an acknowledgment that the non-Indian had been wrong and efforts were made to redress the situation.

As we have seen, the results were not basically different from what had taken place a century before. Except that in recent years non-Indians felt that they had been radically and wrongfully at odds with Indian culture, the effects of their concern were the same. So this generation did, out of a conviction that they were wrong, what a previous generation did out of a conviction that they were right.

It is difficult to place blame for recent events on either Indians or non-Indians, even though recent events have tended to push Indians farther into a shell from which many refuse to emerge. A more accurate assessment of the situation would find that neither Indian nor non-Indian has understood the dimensions of change that have taken place in American society in the last two decades. For the non-Indian, the unfolding of the facts of American history, first in the civil rights movement, then in the Vietnam war, and finally in the Indian movement, has triggered a great sense of guilt that has attached itself to everything from ecology to Vietnam orphans.

The first impulse of people suffering this guilt is to rush out in a frantic effort to make amends—a wholly honorable purpose. The results of such concern, however, are not always apparent and are often taken for further intrusion motivated by less admirable concerns. This misunderstanding of non-Indians by Indians has been exploited by Indian activists, thus further frustrating the efforts of non-Indians to make amends. A vicious circle of accusation and amends, recrimination and reparations, has resulted. The net emotional result has been to cause Indians to flee from involvement in anything that would undercut this cycle, for it appears to many people that the cycle bears out the contentions that originally defined it.

Thus Indians and non-Indians have achieved a demonic identity that is dependent on Indians accusing whites of insensitivity and whites responding, in good faith, but in the wrong patterns of behavior, thus fueling the continuing accusations of insensitivity, again triggering a concern for reparations. Both groups, insofar as they are involved in the problems and attitudes of each other, receive their identity from their involvement with each other.

The bicentennial celebration appears to a majority of Indian people as the crowning insult in this vicious cycle and therefore to ask them to celebrate the second hundred years of life of an institution that symbolizes all the uncounted smaller cycles of accusation and reparations is to focus the hurt of four hundred years in one simple concept: the institution of oppression has survived two centuries! Each Indian, many perhaps for individual reasons, views that celebration as something foreign and regretful, as if it were an insult directed at him or her personally.

The missing element in the present situation is that forces of reconciliation and reparations do indeed exist, and those forces that seek peaceful, constructive, and lasting social and economic change in American life continually present us with the opportunity to get involved in the creation of a society more in tune with human needs and highly compatible with the best of Indian and non-Indian beliefs and practices. Perhaps the tragedy of today is that too many Americans see lawyers like William Kunstler, consumer advocates like Ralph Nader, labor leaders like Cesar Chávez, and American poets and writers as disruptive of the old order rather than as precursors of a new order. Indians above all fail to recognize in the reform movements of the present the emerging concern of all peoples for a North American culture, system of laws, ecology, and economic system that must come into being if anyone is to survive in the future.

It is singularly unfortunate that American Indians today do not have the foresight to come to grips with the radical changes that have been accomplished in this country in the past two decades. But their vision is clouded by the inability of non-Indians to become reconciled to themselves and their own history and to go forward with some confidence and humility. The inability of the non-Indian to come to grips with his own identity and the constant search of non-Indians for a true American identity result in continual forays into Indian Country seeking the truth of religion, ecology, social kinship, and other values that are perceived by non-Indians as the strengths of Indian culture. These well-meaning expeditions, the latest of which seems to be the invitation to Indians to join in the bicentennial, with special emphasis on "Indian contributions to America," are again a celebration of the past and simply reinforce the cycle of emotional hurt.

We should be celebrating the goals of the next hundred years instead of the failures and successes of the past two hundred. What is done, is done. It is where we go next that is important. And certainly that is dependent partially on where we have been so that we do not really escape our history. But we should be making a determined effort to move forward in the creation of a continental culture that understands itself as a totality and a novelty whose only concern is developing forms of existence that provide everyone involved with a sense of integrity and identity so that the next hundred years will not force us to look back on mistrust, arrogance, and injustice.

17

THE AMERICAN REVOLUTION
AND THE AMERICAN INDIAN

Problems in the Recovery of a Usable Past

▼▼▼▼

Constructing a commentary on any aspect of American political life, theories, and events is a hazardous enterprise at best. Liberals tend toward self-flagellation in which virtually nothing of the past has a noble bearing when seen in the shadow of contemporary events. Conservatives are outraged when confronted with the facts of history, as if believing that something did not happen erases the past. Furthermore, in contemporary life we have deliberately cut down the old authority figures who once defined our existence, and so unless Walter Cronkite tells us "that's the way it is," we have no guidelines to use in determining who we are, what we are likely to become, and what it will have meant to have survived a rather nebulous and uncontrollable process of growth.

The frightening thing about the celebrations of the bicentennial is that we are tempted to simply increase the velocity with which we manipulate the familiar symbols of our past without coming to grips with a more profound understanding of our history. Things have probably been much better and much worse than we can imagine, and it is only when we enter the arena of discussion of American Indians and the American Revolution that we can determine just how polarized the events of American history have been.

I would like, therefore, to take a very extreme position on the influence of the American Revolution on the American Indian and work from this position to a broader understanding of the meaning of American history. The American Revolution is in a real sense the most radical experiment in the history of human existence, but its radical nature cannot be properly understood unless we get to the roots of honest examination and let the chips fall where they may.

In 1793 the Seven Nations of Canada and a dozen other tribes met in a general council at the foot of the Miami Rapids and drew up a protest against the encroachment of whites in the lands north of the Ohio. The American commissioners had offered, once again, to purchase their lands for settlement, and the chiefs responded:

> *Brothers, money to us is of no value, and to most of us un-*
> *known; and as no consideration whatever can induce us to sell*
> *the lands, on which we get sustenance for our women and*
> *children, we hope we may be allowed to point out a mode by*
> *which your settlers may be easily removed, and peace obtained.*
>
> *Brothers, we know that these settlers are poor, or they*
> *would never have ventured to live in a country which has been*
> *in continual trouble ever since they crossed the Ohio. Divide*
> *therefore this large sum of money, which you have offered to*
> *us among these people; ... and we are persuaded they would*
> *most readily accept it in lieu of the lands you sold to them.*[1]

The Americans, of course, could not conceive of using the money they had brought to purchase the Indian lands to provide social services for their own poor and to allow the Indians to keep their homelands intact. In their failure to conceive of a society in which the whole was responsible for its individual parts lies a great tool for analysis of the meaning of the American Revolution for American Indians. James Axtell hints at this subject when he tells us, "The competition for empire was primarily an educational contest for the loyalty and allegiance of the members of the competing cultures— English, French, and Indian—and therefore a moral contest between competing cultural styles."[2]

The political documents of the American Revolution, especially the Declaration of Independence, proclaim a high moral purpose, and with the success of the recent civil rights movement, many American intellectuals have congratulated themselves and their ancestors on the usefulness of the high sense of morality incorporated in the American state documents. Buttressing our understanding of these documents has been the whole area of natural law, defined in various ways, that seems to justify the events of American history.

But if we conceive of the struggle for jurisdictional supremacy over the continental United States land area as a moral contest, a battle between the agriculturalist and the hunter, the eventual success of the civilized against the barbarian, then let us look at the state of conditions existing in the North American continent at the time of the Revolution and see if the contest, no matter how moral in the abstract, was understood by groups of people capable of performing moral acts or of understanding the moral content of their acts.

First, the immigrants who populated these shores were not exactly the cream of the crop of Europe. For the most part they were the misfits of their day, the losers in political and theological disputes of the day. Some were Manson-like families of 17th- and 18th-century hippies chased from one land to the next until, in desperation, they arrived on these shores determined to reconstruct for themselves the former homelands. New Swedens, New Frances, and New Englands flourished, and one glance at the map of New England will indicate how thoroughly the new settlers wished to relive their former lives in familiar places.

No comprehensive theory of human existence, no profound religious insights, and no universal political ideas came to these shores initially. Rather the ideas that came with the first settlers were the perverted ideas that had failed in Europe; the psychological walking wounded brought with them an irrational fear of the unknown that was slightly less emotional than the fear of extinction that they had known in Europe. All of the ideological failures of European history arrived in the coastal areas with the Pilgrims, and it has taken us many centuries to even comprehend the extent of the disaster that the first settlers presented to the Indians and to themselves.

Second, a large portion of the first generations of settlers were the criminal element of England who had a choice between immediate execution or exile in the wilderness of America. Georgia was a penal colony of the British crown and the first families of Georgia for many generations were descendants of whores and footpads of the Old World. There was not, therefore, an inbred respect for law or human rights that we today attribute to the Founding Fathers. A significant proportion, then and now, was from the beginning devoted to the violation of laws, the disregard of rights of any kind, and the casual murder or rape of those who resisted them. Something in the neighborhood of fifty thousand convicts were transported to the New World in an effort to provide law and order in the Old.[3]

Third, a substantial number of immigrants arrived in the New World with their foreseeable future years already mortgaged to pay for their passage over. "Redemptioners" or "free-willers" booked passage for America and on their arrival were auctioned off by the ship captain to the highest bidder. Many English merchants specialized in this trade and fraudulent practices in recruiting were commonplace. The immigrants were packed aboard like sardines, and a mortality of more than 50 percent during a trip to the New World was not unusual. These people, if they had hope, had a rugged term of servitude before they could realize that hope, and they composed almost half of the total white immigrants before 1776.[4]

Rather than begin with a fairly intelligent, devout, and honest citizenry, therefore, the English settlers were more than 50 percent indentured servants, a considerable percentage of criminals, and a scattering of religious fanatics. It was quite a group to amass under any circumstances.

The major justification used by the Europeans to dispossess the American Indians was that it was God's intent that the farmer should replace the hunter and that civilization should be brought to the shades of primitive chaos. Visualizing the New World as a last chance at living in the Garden of Eden, the early settlers set out to establish roots in the Atlantic coastal areas. But the myth of the European as divine gardener is one of the most ludicrous beliefs that white Americans still cherish.

Instead of being natural farmers, most of the early colonies actually imported food from Europe because they did not know how to farm. The Swedish colony on the Delaware imported food from Sweden for the first twenty years of its existence, and only after nearly a generation had gone by did they learn that crops could be grown in the New World.[5] Finally, it was not the natural genius of the European, his civilized state, or instructions from God that enabled the white settler to survive but his adaptation of Indian techniques in agriculture. The intensive cultivation methods of European farming were finally abandoned by the immigrants and they moved swiftly to the other extreme, farming soils to exhaustion and abandoning them to move on to new fields.

American genius in agriculture until the dust bowl years has really never been its cleverness but its inexhaustible supply of land that could be carelessly exploited and abandoned. Southern planters controlled thousands of acres and ruthlessly exploited labor and land and then sought more land. By the Revolution "the older tobacco areas along the Chesapeake and the great rivers of Virginia were beginning to decay from soil exhaustion."[6] Arthur Schlesinger remarked that even the beginnings of America were the result of a European quest for a more palatable diet, a search for spices to season their coarse foods.

Schlesinger also remarked that the discovery and settlement of the New World resulted in: "a dietary revolution unparalleled in history save possibly for the first application of fire to the cooking of edibles." He continued, "Picture the long centuries when the Old World existed without white and sweet potatoes, tomatoes, corn and the many varieties of beans, and you have some notion of the extraordinary gastronomic advance. Add, for good measure, such dishes as pumpkins, squashes, turkeys, cranberries, maple syrup, blackberries, blueberries, raspberries, strawberries, crab apples, chest-nuts and peanuts."[7]

Schlesinger concludes, "In the four and a half centuries since Columbus blundered into the Western Hemisphere the American has not developed a single indigenous staple beyond those he derived from the Indians. Today, it is estimated, four-sevenths of the country's agricultural output consists of plants (including tobacco and a native species of cotton) which were discovered with the New World."[8]

The argument, therefore, that the Europeans brought the great conception of civilization, conceived as a sedentary agricultural enterprise, to the New World is absurd on its face. That they could not see, in the lifestyle of the Indians, civilization in its best agricultural expression may be another question and certainly one hinted at by our other six papers. "Suppose our fathers had to depend on wheat for their bread," reflected a Tennessean of later days with pardonable exaggeration, "it would have taken them a hundred years longer to reach the Rockies."[9] If ever.

Even the political ideas of the settlers had little or no novelty. They were derived in Europe but bounded by European traditions to such an extent that the settlers had little recourse save a continuous undercurrent of discontent. Economic theory was shifting in Europe from mercantilism, the amassing of gold and silver on a national basis, to Adam Smith's individualistic theories that saw national wealth in terms of the sum of affluent individuals who composed the policy-making portion of the nation. In England all legal theories went to the protection of property from arbitrary actions of the king, and political theory, as filtered through the realism of economics, looked only to the steady operation of law to protect property.

England, from which many of the political ideas had come, was also struggling with the ideas set forth a century earlier by John Locke and Thomas Hobbes, that human government was a creation that was designed and assembled by people in a remote time by a consenual contract of the governed. Projecting backward from present governments to the mists of antiquity, the English thinkers saw but usually did not draw the conclusion that governments could and should be rendered obsolete whenever they infringed on the contemporary conceptions of human rights as articulated in contemporary understandings of the consensual contract that constituted governments.

Undergirding the conception of government as a consensual arrangement was the feeling, derived in part from the successful results of Newtonian physics, that governments are subject to natural law, antedating and superior to all human ordinances, and that natural law projects for humans certain inalienable rights. Government is therefore reducible to a cosmic rhythm that defines a minimum standard of decency that operates in an orderly and reasonable manner with rules readily ascertainable through logic and contemplation.

Finally, merged with these political and economical doctrines was the quasi-religious doctrine that the greatest human motive was that of self-interest and that, properly enlightened, self-interest, through the guidance of common sense, would allow a society to conduct its business with a minimum of interference from governmental institutions. It was safe, therefore, to diffuse the power of groups of people throughout a number of institutions because general self-interest worked spontaneously to provide a social attitude that benefited individual members thereof. The conception of the physical universe working its way efficiently and mechanically toward perfection was transferred to the realm of social thought, and social institutions were attributed a kind of divine guidance that few deities would have recognized.

When this conglomerate of ideologies hit the American shores and filtered among the criminals, religious fanatics, and indentured servants, it appealed to the worst of their instincts, because it was basically a European doctrinal complex transported to a world in which the physical and political and indeed even the religious boundaries of Europe did not exist. Scattered efforts were made to reincorporate the old baronial holdings of Europe into the new continent. Francis Jennings is correct when he says that the American Revolution was essentially a baron's revolt, but even the idea of privileged holdings was tenuous in the New World.[10]

The Carolinas had landgraves and caciques and Maryland had a brief bout with manors owned by lords of quasi-feudal powers, but the nearest thing to Old World landholdings was a patroon system in New York that was as much a concession to earlier Dutch settlers as it was a method of settling large areas fast. It was not long after the Revolution started before the large patroon estates were broken up because of their Loyalist tendencies.[11]

Religious hierarchies were also difficult to transfer to the New World; the old holds exercised by national churches over individual beliefs were not nearly as potent in America. Roger Williams demonstrated very early that religious intolerance in the settled colonies was not absolute as all a dissident had to do was move a few miles down the road and set up an antiestablishment community where he could extend religious freedom or put into place an intolerant regime of his own. Whatever religious unity and discipline existed in the immigrant groups was shattered by the land of America, and the vast expanse of the continent acted as a religious vacuum pulling the souls of men westward and changing them en route.

From 1754 to the Revolution there was continuous change in political institutions, so that although the king of England may well have given royal charters to colonial governments or political favorites, his real exercise of power was negligible and conceptions of political institutions continually changed as Americans began their protests, which ranged from the affirmation that they could not be taxed without their consent to Thomas Paine's ringing rhetoric that nothing short of independence could suffice as an outcome to the struggle between the Americans and the British. American political conceptions evolved from an attachment to rights derived from Parliament to a thin and temporary relationship to the Crown and finally to independence.

Several peripheral considerations must be addressed before I examine the impact of the Revolution on the American Indians. In the period 1750 to 1775, the population of the British colonies more than doubled so that for many of the colonists conflict with the king of England was simply irrelevant.[12] They were themselves newcomers in the New World, seeking only to establish themselves, and either unconcerned with the preoccupation with English political struggle or keenly aware of the possibilities for exploitation unveiled in the struggle of established English settlers with their own problems.

The New World, for many of the immigrants, was not a permanent residence but simply a place where quick fortunes could be achieved which could be transferred back to the mother country as a means of gaining entrance into the social and political institutions they had abandoned to seek their fortunes. Through the last decades of the last century nearly a third of all immigrants to the New World returned to their former homelands with sufficient wealth to enable them to establish themselves as part of the privileged class.[13] There was, therefore, hardly a universal conception of the New World as a place in which to sink permanent roots.

The purely tactical aspects of enforcing English law in the American colonies presented impossible problems so that the Crown really had no option, in the final analysis, than finally to lose its American possessions. At the time of the Revolution, there were nearly three million Americans scattered along a coastline of more than one thousand miles and reaching, in some places, into the interior more than two hundred miles.[14] England had a population of six or seven million people who were surrounded by a European population ten or twelve times as large, many of whom were, at best, neutral.

Logistically, the English military commanders were faced with the problem of transporting war materials more than three thousand miles across the ocean, landing in essentially hostile ports, and equipping armies that could spend years marching up and down the seacoast without ever chancing on a decisive battle. There was no way that this land could be occupied for any length of time by an army of any size in any effective manner. English military men were faced with what appeared to be a war but that, unless the Americans gathered in a convenient spot, was really more of a continuous maneuver. So the coming of armed conflict in the American colonies could have really only one conclusion, and that was separation and independence. During the Civil War, the North faced essentially the same military problem, but the use of railroads and steamboats enabled it to win.

With this background I turn now to the examination of the American Revolution and the American Indian. The Albany conference of 1754 was really the first step of the American Revolution, as Mary E. Fleming Mathur reminds us.[15] The problem was, for the colonies, essentially one of foreign relations—how to treat with the Iroquois—and in June 1754 delegates from New Hampshire, Massachusetts, Rhode Island, Connecticut, New York, Pennsylvania, and Maryland met to agree on a common purpose in settling their relations with the Five Nations. Benjamin Franklin had three years before sketched out a plan of union, and during the conference the delegates went far beyond their original mandate in conceiving how the colonies could meet other problems of government on a commonly shared basis.

Mathur reminds us of the final recommendation of the Albany conference: "Like the Iroquois structure, it recommended an unbalanced representation, but left each colony capable of vetoing the whole effort." She further comments that it was "interesting to see that the colonists could not make the system work, could not function under consensualism, but had to adjust to majority rule."[16] The problem, of course, was that the colonies were in an intellectual halfway house, struggling to confront the realities of the New World, anxious to appear to be representatives of civilization, and yet bound to an intellectual horizon so limited as to leave outside the area of consideration the question of what constitutes a society.

This confusion is further compounded by the fact that the French and Indian War of 1754–1763 is really the first world war in human history.[17] British and French armies fought not only in Europe and the North American continent but also in India and other possessions around the globe, the French losing footholds on two continents. In this context, then, the struggle for North America between colonists and the Indian nation really begins in earnest, and the failure of the colonists to arrive at a satisfactory form of organization at Albany is a problem that has not been solved until the present time. The failure of the colonies, a point that Hendrick fully intuits, is that organization of a society depends more on the internal integrity of lifestyles than on outward structural forms.

I turn next to Crenville's imperial plan for North America, which had been developed in Bute's administration and which carefully articulated eight major points.

1. A line would be drawn, approximately along the crest of the Alleghenies, beyond which settlement and unlicensed trade would be forbidden for the time being.

2. Royal commissioners of Indian Affairs would control relations with the Indians west of the line. They would regulate the commerce carried on by traders licensed by the colonial governors, make treaties with the Indians, and prevent unauthorized settlement.

3. Purchases of land from the Indians would be made only by the Crown for subsequent granting or resale to individuals after a plan for orderly settlement had been worked out.

4. A large force of British regulars would be stationed in North America.

5. New colonies would be organized in Nova Scotia and the Floridas, which would follow in time the existing pattern of the older colonies.

6. Canada would retain for the time being its autocratic government, but with recognition of the right of the French colonists to retain their language, religion, and local laws and customs.

7. With naval assistance, enforcement of the trade and navigation laws and collection of the customs duties would be greatly tightened.

8. A revenue would be raised in the Americas to defray the cost of these services and especially of the troops in the New World.[18]

The whole plan was orderly and sound, and if developed in a bounded land where all factors could remain the same, it would have proved sufficient to handle the problem. But in the New World there was an expanding property base in that people dissatisfied with their status in society, especially with respect to their ownership of property, could simply move into the interior and lawlessly seize new lands and property.

The whole political theory of equal rights for men that was emerging in the colonies in the period 1754–1776 was based on a former European theory of law that protected property. Yet in the New World the last requirement of law was protection of property because property, was the one aspect of society that was geometrically increasing whereas, in comparison, the other factors were remaining relatively stable. During this period, the British policy was to find a means of controlling property through taxation, but the only realistic way in which that could be done was to tax that aspect of property which cemented the relationship of the colonists to the rest of the world.

The Stamp Act of 1764, the Quartering Act of 1765, the Townshend Acts of 1767, and finally the Tea Act of 1773 thus struck at the most important social aspect of colonial existence, their relationship with Europe and their identity as colonies. Were they or were they not Englishmen? Or were they a new breed of men?

In an effort to resolve these questions, which, in the final analysis, were social identity problems, Massachusetts called a congress to meet in New York shortly before the Stamp Act was to go into effect. Nine colonies sent delegates, and their resolutions reflect the confusion present in the minds of the colonists at that time. Resolutions III, IV, and V echo the unarticulated problem of social and national identity felt intuitively by the colonies:

III. That it is inseparably essential to the Freedom of a People, and the undoubted Right of Englishmen, that no taxes be imposed on them, but with their own Consent, given personally, or by their Representatives.

IV. That the People of these Colonies are not, and from their local Circumstances cannot be, Represented in the House of Commons in Great Britain.

V. That the only Representatives of the People of these Colonies are Persons chosen therein by themselves, and that no Taxes ever have been or can be Constitutionally imposed on them but by their respective Legislatures.[19]

The important word in these three resolutions is, of course, "Englishmen," and although the basic theory of American revolutionary theory is contained in these resolutions, it is important to note that the context in which these rights make sense is that of English culture.

The propositions that the Declaration of Independence holds as self-evident are self-evident in a British milieu, which is, in fact, finite in population, in available property, and in the rules and regulations that established guidelines for the protection of property. Once any of these factors are altered or their impact on society is accelerated, the implied social contract underlying the theory of government disappears and the institutions become exploitive in and of themselves.

Yet the colonists did not understand how far from the requirements of their political theories the reality of lands and peoples in the New World had taken them. Still relying on the implied contract of peoples forming a government, they vested major legislative authority in assemblies, even demanding that special conventions be called to ratify the Constitution when they discovered that the Articles of Confederation could not provide a suitable political framework of government. The provision for admitting new states was the reserve of Grenville's plan for development of Nova Scotia and the Floridas and reflected the expectation of the Americans that the social contract of Hobbes and Locke would magically work itself out in the wilderness beyond the original colonies.

The American Revolution can be understood, therefore, as transferring an abstract set of propositions to a physical setting in which there were no real boundaries within which the contract could function. American social and political order has been able to work primarily because it was always had a greater economic opportunity for the mass of people than it allowed expression of political rights or participation. That is to say, during the two centuries of American political existence, there have been few real opportunities to test the validity of political ideas because the relative freedom of economic opportunity has provided an escape valve for discontent.

When things have come to a standstill new ways of opening additional economic opportunities have been found to release the internal pressures that come about because the basic theory of government does not provide an answer to the meaning of human existence or describe properly the function of a society. The American West provides an arena in which the criminal elements of the United States can reenact the drama of a few centuries before until the frontier closed. The struggle of labor and minority groups for political rights always becomes the leverage of getting additional economic benefits, and it is no surprise to us that in the midst of the civil rights struggle of the last decade a "War on Poverty" is declared and an "Economic Opportunity Act" is passed.

Nor should we be surprised at the Full Employment Act of 1946 as an answer to the failure of American society to absorb the returning war veterans, the Social Security Act to counteract the trauma of the depression, or the Homestead Act to disperse the energies of the Civil War period. The American political system has always used economic expansion as a means of providing an additional context in which the political problems of the interaction of human beings can be dissipated in a larger and more chaotic realm.

We return, then, to the council at the foot of the Miami Rapids in 1793 and ask why it never occurred to the American commissioners to accept the Indian offer to use the money proffered for their lands to benefit the poor and hopeless of the United States, leaving the Indian lands intact. And we discover that there really was no conception in the minds of American political leaders, or in American political theory itself, that a society had to confine itself within certain boundaries and that its function was to create a sense of nationality among diverse peoples. They could not provide for their own poor because the only glue that held the American government together was a process of continual expansion, the transference of problems of political importance to the realm of economics.

Growth and its subsequent muting of political controversy kept the American system functioning for two centuries, and it appears to be the only solution to contemporary problems also. Americans now circle the globe exploiting the natural resources of the planet but cannot feed, house, or educate their own people. When territorial expansion becomes a geographic impossibility, people become consumers to provide a quasi-frontier of imagined need that will keep the system continually accelerating.

Bernard Sheehan is absolutely correct when he sees that the native peoples were the victims of the white man's tendency to see the world from a set of universal conceptions.[20] The distinction that he sees between conceiving the world as a paradise and as a howling wilderness underlines the inability of the Europeans to understand the relationship between a nation and the lands on which it lives. The wilderness had to be conquered because the conquest would provide a boundary within which the political theory of the protection of property could become functional. Yet the paradise called people beyond the sterility of the social contract to a new conception of society.

American revolutionary leaders certainly intended, as Bernard Sheehan points out, that "the new republic will be a haven for art and science, where conscience will be free and where the poor and persecuted will find respite."[21] But he also reminds us that "the American passion for liberty was an extension of the American passion to possess the earthly inheritance."[22] What I feel he is telling us is that the American conception of liberty could not function without having as a precondition an infinite potential for material wealth that was already somewhat realized; that liberty was always a function of economic freedom.

Sheehan cites Thomas Jefferson's remark, "The Indians never submitted themselves to any laws, any coercive power, any shadow of government. Their only controls are their manners and that moral sense of right and wrong."[23] And James O'Donnell is right when he says that the world was turned upside down for the American Indians by the Revolution. O'Donnell points out that the "members of the Unitas Fratrum believed that civilization and Christianization went hand in hand, [and] they drew their converts into model communities where they lived in log houses, tilled fields, and went to school and church as white men."[24] The Indian converts were being prepared to function, really, as Englishmen à la the third resolution of the Stamp Act Congress of 1765.

Hendrick may have been the guiding spiritual presence at Albany in 1754 and George Washington may have been the Father of his Country, but a contemporary American has personified American political theory far better than either of these gentlemen. I refer, of course, to John Mitchell, the beloved "Big Enchilada" of the Watergate Follies who warned us, "Watch what we do, not what we say." This attitude has really dominated American political theory in its practical application far better than the Declaration of Independence or the Bill of Rights.

Reginald Horsman reminds us that not everyone saw the world through ideological blinders. "Knox," he tells us, "feared that American expansion over Indian land would be viewed as a sordid episode by dispassionate observers." To quote from Horsman's paper, "How different would be the sensation of a philosophic mind to reflect, that, instead of exterminating a part of the human race by our modes of population, we had persevered, through all difficulties, and at last imparted our knowledge of cultivation and the arts to the aboriginals of the country, by which the source of future life and happiness had been preserved and extended."[25]

We must sadly conclude, however, that there was no knowledge of cultivation and the arts worthy of transmission and that, because American society lacked the substance of a civilized nation, its only recourse was the inexorable working out of an abstract political theme the premises of which have remained unexamined even today. Horsman recognizes that fact and comments that "in its Indian policy, as in so many other areas of American life, the United States from the time of the Revolution began the process of reshaping its European and colonial intellectual heritage to suit the needs of a new, expanding nation-state."[26]

Indeed, American history has been the unfolding of a process by which an abstract idea, devoid of its cultural roots and geographic origins, was forced on an unsuspecting land and its peoples. Axtell's reminder that a cause of converts' recidivism was the imposition of arbitrary authority[27] and Horsman's finding that the legacy of the eighteenth century was violent hatreds and irreconcilable differences[28] only emphasize the determination, which has been present in all periods of American history, to make the theory work, by benign acts if possible, by force if necessary.

Today we are discovering in nearly every area of life that the tenets of civilized existence as demonstrated by the Indian nations were profound and that the solution of American social problems depends in large measure on adopting the Indian style of life. This is true not only with respect to ecology but also with respect to compensation theories of punishment and criminal law, the small, local community as the basic unit of government, and decisions made by consensus rather than by compromise of two irreconcilable differences. In family relationships the commitment nature of marriage rather than the contractual seems to be more promising Big Brother programs are necessary to keep delinquency in check, an echo here of Indian kinship customs. And finally, in this gigantic depression, the function of government must be to provide for its constituents.

The American Revolution, we can conclude, was a jump out of time and place of a conglomerate of people who were willing to abandon participation in history for the opportunity to experiment with a new form of human existence. It was a great historical act of cultural and political patricide; rebellion against the king was also a rebellion against the nature of society and against the reality of human existence. Whether this experiment will prove to have been valid remains an open question. But we can see the tension today in the continual efforts of American foreign policy to force smaller countries of relatively homogeneous racial background and limited geographic and economic resources to conform to the American understanding of social and political existence.

Americans are still, in many ways, and perhaps at the deepest level of the subconscious, atoning for their act of patricide against King George by rushing generously to the aid of any country suffering a disaster while in their foreign policy stubbornly perpetuating the theories that they used to justify their rebellion as Englishmen. How else can we account for our willingness to train Saudis to defend their oil fields against hostile aggression and at the same time be the only nation to openly threaten to invade them?

The American Indian has an intimate relationship to the American Revolution because, of all the peoples in the world, the American Indians have had to bear the impact of the criminality of the United States and to attempt to soften its impact on the rest of the world. In biblical terms, American Indians have had to be the suffering servant for the planet; their role has been to change the American conception of a society from that of a complex of laws designed to protect property to one in which liberty is not a matter of laws, coercive power, or a shadow of government but is characterized by manners and a moral sense of right and wrong.

NOTES

1. Virginia Irving Armstrong, *I Have Spoken* (Chicago: Swallow Press, 1971), p. 37.
2. James Axtell, "The Broken Twig: The Revolution in Indian Education," from a paper presented at the Newberry Library, p. 1.
3. Arthur M. Schlesinger, *Paths to the Present* (Boston: Houghton Mifflin, 1964), p. 65.
4. Ibid., p. 64.
5. Ibid., p. 7.
6. Dan Lacy, *The Meaning of the American Revolution* (New York: Mentor Books, 1964), p. 52.
7. Schlesinger, *Paths to the Present*, p. 220.
8. Ibid., p. 221.

9. Ibid., p. 223.
10. Francis Jennings, "Imperial Revolution," from a paper presented at the Newberry Library, p. 6.
11. Lacy, *The Meaning of the American Revolution*, p. 68.
12. Ibid., p. 73.
13. Schlesinger, *Paths to the Present*, p. 76.
14. Lacy, *The Meaning of the American Revolution*, p. 154.
15. Mary E. Fleming Mathur, "Savages Are Heroes, Too, Whiteman!" from a paper presented at the Newberry Library.
16. Ibid., p. 11.
17. Lacy, *The Meaning of the American Revolution*, p. 74.
18. Ibid., p. 86.
19. Ibid., p. 97.
20. Bernard Sheehan, "The Ideology of the Revolution and the American Indian," from a paper presented at the Newberry Library, p. 1.
21. Ibid., p. 8.
22. Ibid., p. 10.
23. Ibid., p. 10-a.
24. James O'Donnell, "The World Turned Upside Down: The American Revolution as a Catastrophe for Native Americans," from a paper presented at the Newberry Library, p. 13.
25. Reginald Horsman, "The Image of the Indian in the Age of the American Revolution," from a paper presented at the Newberry Library, p. 6.
26. Ibid., p. 18.
27. Axtell, "The Broken Twig," p. 7.
28. Horsman, "The Image of the Indian," p. 18.

18

KINSHIP WITH THE WORLD

▼▼▼▼

It is difficult to present an Indian view of the environment because there is such a difference in the way Indians and non-Indians look at the world. Indians get very confused when non-Indians come up to them and try to engage in a dialogue on nature and the environment. More traditional Indians have a devil of a time communicating to non-Indian audiences exactly what their relationship with nature is.

For the most part Indians do not "deal with" or "love" nature. In the Western European context human experience is separated from the environment. When Indians are told that they "love nature," they cannot deal with this because nature is not an abstraction to them.

Indians do not talk about nature as some kind of concept or something "out there." They talk about the immediate environment in which they live. They do not embrace all trees or love all rivers and mountains. What is important is the relationship you have with a particular tree or a particular mountain.

You can find an extremely intimate connection between the lifestyle, the religions, and sometimes the political organizations of Indian tribes and the land in which they live. The religion of the tribes that live in the woodland area, either the Pacific Northwest or the East, is greatly concerned with dreams and psychoanalysis. If you go to the Plains or the Southwest, you have either ceremonial years or very stark vision quests.

The simple proposition that Indians love nature and embrace it does not tell you why different tribes manifest their relationship to the land in different ways. If you talk to tribal peoples in those particular lands, you will get a better insight into why their religion and their culture developed in certain ways. People in the woodland areas deal with dream analysis and with loss of "soul" because in an intimate relationship with a great deal of vegetation and life you are in danger of losing your psyche among all the other life-forms. This is not articulated in a set of doctrines. But it is alive within a community of people so intimately related to a natural environment that the natural environment shapes the very way they relate to each other and their conception of the world they live in. They do not abstract from that experience to a universal religion or set of universal concepts.

When we talk with non-Indians about nature, there is really nothing that we can say in universal Western concepts that is going to make a lot of sense. I think that Western people who come into an Indian environment and attempt to preach take along their own set of categories and use it to deal with the Indian people they meet. Anthropologists, summarizing what they find in the Indian tradition, always call us animists, and that view is accepted by a great many people in the field of religion. We are put in a cultural evolutionary framework, and then we are supposed to move from animism to some great abstract conception of one god.

The problem with that type of analysis is that it is not an article of faith in any Indian religion that everything has spirit. What happens in the different Indian religions is that people live so intimately with environment that they are in relationship to the spirits that live in particular places. It is not an article of faith; it is part of human experience. I think that non-Indians sometimes experience this also when they are in natural environments.

The non-Indian religious person often acts as if all of the Indian experiences of religion are articles of faith in the same way that Western people have creeds, doctrines, and dogmas. Today, after one hundred years on the reservation, a great many Indians do treat those experiences as creeds, doctrines, and dogmas. It becomes virtually impossible to translate from one culture to another because you end up dealing with a set of experiences on the one hand and a set of concepts on the other.

We need to probe for a minute into the question of why non-Indians think the world is the way they want to see it. We need to begin much farther back in Western European tradition. I would prefer to go as far back as Robert Bellah does in his article on cultural evolution. He raised the question of why, around 4,000 B.C., the civilizations that turned out to be urban civilizations made fundamental decisions about the world. One of those decisions, according to Bellah, was that reality is something "up there" and that everything we deal with in our daily life is considered unreal, ephemeral, and transitory. The religious and political systems, and a type of protoscience, began to evolve as we began to look at reality as being someplace beyond the planet, beyond our daily experiences, and our daily experiences became untrustworthy. As a result of looking at the world in those two ways, those urban civilizations in the river valleys adopted an extremely pessimistic view of the world—that the world was a place of trial, judgment, and punishment and that there was a better place beyond the grave. Such a view encouraged massive, imperialistic wars of conquest.

I want to eliminate all but the tradition out of which Christianity came and add a second division from Greek philosophy that divided the world into the cosmos, which was the mechanical workings of the physical universe, and the *ecumeni*, the world of the affairs of human beings. We now have a pessimistic attitude toward the world and a desire to go out imperialistically and conquer new lands and new people. It is a view of the world that splits it twice: once in terms of eternal verities as opposed to transitory experiences; and once in which it divides the world between science and political affairs.

By the nineteenth century, we had grabbed that quarter chunk of the world of science and said, "We are going to investigate all of human reality, or all of world reality, and we are going to begin interpreting all experiences according to the workings of the physical world. We're going to create social science in which we can treat our own selves and our own psyches as if they were something objective that could be observed and described scientifically."

We have reduced our knowledge of the world and the possibility of understanding and relating environment to a wholly mechanical process. We have become dependent, ultimately, on this one quarter of human experience, which is to reduce all human experience to a

cause-and-effect situation. When we then look at nature and environment through Western European eyes, that is really what we are
looking at. That is not the "nature" Indians understand. Indians never
made any of those divisions.

In the Indian tradition we find continuous generations of people
living in specific lands, or migrating to new lands, and having an
extremely intimate relationship with lands, animals, vegetables, and
all of life. As Indians look out at the environment and as Indians
experience a living universe, relationships become the dominating
theme of life and the dominating motif for whatever technological
or quasi-scientific approach Indian people have to the land.

Indians do not simply learn survival skills or different ways to
shape human utensils out of other natural things. In shaping those
things, people have the responsibility to help complete their life cycles
as part of the universe in the same way they are helping people.
Human beings are not above nature or above the rest of the world.
Human beings are incomplete without the rest of the world. Every
species needs to give to every other species in order to make up a
universe.

Social scientists have badly misunderstood Indian customs. When
they look at Indian customs, particularly in relationship to plants
and animals, and say, "Indians have this great taboo that something
is going to happen unless they do certain things with plant and animal remains," I think that is taking the Western quadrant and projecting onto the Indian psyche a cause-and-effect relationship with
the world.

Different tribes deal specifically with customs and traditions
related to other forms or related to what we call the natural world. In
this cooperative enterprise between humans and other life-forms,
you cannot leave a cycle of relationships undone or hanging loose.
In these relationships both parties must fulfill the ultimate purpose
of the other party. You do not let dogs eat salmon bones or the skin
of the salmon, or chew on the bones of the elk, because your relationship with salmon and elk is such that it precludes dogs. However, in
your relationship with dogs and other animals, you have an inclu-
sive situation wherein you can feed dogs. To violate a relationship,
or to mix up a relationship, would be to introduce a disharmony
into the world that would eventually lead to the downfall of all species. Consequently, what you find in Indian custom is a sensitive

awareness of who other things are and who humans are. It is not a superstitious taboo that says God is going to throw a lightning bolt down on you if you do not behave in a certain way. It is a cooperative need to engage in joint enterprises.

In order to maintain relationships, you do certain things to show respect among beings. Another way of saying it is that these are kin relationships. You are related to different life-forms in different ways. Some are closer to you than others. In the nature of things, some are antagonistic to begin with.

A lot of tribes have stories of how the two-leggeds and the four-leggeds determined their basic division of responsibilities in the world. They held a gigantic race around the rim of the world to determine whether the two-leggeds would supply meat to the four-leggeds or whether the four-leggeds would supply meat to the two-leggeds. The two-leggeds were humans, the grizzly bear, and the birds. The four-leggeds were all of the horned, hoofed, and padded animals. Of course, the birds pulled a sharp one on the four-leggeds. A small bird rode the buffalo horn almost to the finish line and then put in the over-drive and came across first. Otherwise, friends, we would all be in state parks.

That tradition begins to explain the kin relationship between people and animals. It is not a relationship of conquest or of imperialism. It is a relationship in which both basic divisions of the world look back to a time when they had to find some means of allocating responsibilities in the world.

Kin are extremely important in this view of the universe. There are those animals that approach specific human beings and give them specific powers. If you talk to Indians of almost any tribe, and they know their traditions, and they are willing to share them with you, they can take you into communities and point out which persons or which families have had particular relationships with particular medicine animals.

From those animals and their relationships some tribes have developed tremendous systems of psychoanalysis, better and more accurate, I think, than astrology or Jungian psychology or anything else the West has developed. They can look at people and intuitively pick out what medicine animal that person has, or what animal would approach that person and develop a relationship of medicine exchange. From the characteristic of that animal, and how it behaves in its natural environment, the human personality of that person takes on certain parallel or similar aspects. In extremely traditional Indian societies, people finally come to the realization through vision quest or training that they have the medicine of the deer, or the badger, or the antelope, or the raven. That realization opens a whole new avenue of human development through observation of animal adjustments to other life-forms and adjustments of the human personality to the life-forms with which he or she must deal.

The medicine animals become very close kin with human animals. Traditions in many tribes recall a time when all organic forms talked to each other and married each other in an exchange of communication. Since I am no longer an evolutionist, I am investigating whether there really was not a creation when all life-forms became immediately aware of their relationships to each other. Because your kin are individuals and peoples in all of the organic life-forms of the universe, you do not think of passing on your heritage to human beings alone. You pass on your knowledge and heritage to all of creation, and, more particularly, your powers and your insights to your kin in that organic universe, which includes not only human beings but also the medicine animals and the medicine life-forms that you have dealt with while you have been on the planet.

By presenting it this way, I can give you a glimpse of the relationships Indians have to nature and the environment. It is a relationship of specific responsibilities, specific insights, specific knowledge, and a specific task in the world. It is never a community of human beings who go out and "embrace nature." In this situation, what is nature? Nature is too generalized a concept to deal with.

In the modern period, Indians are in tremendous transition because we are going through your educational system, wherein we move away from the specifics of the universe traditional Indians lived with and we move toward the scientific way of thinking. Many Indian people are leaving their culture and traditions in ways they do not suspect. They are developing a schizophrenia. They look at their grandfather, who goes out and talks with birds and coyotes, and they think he is superstitious. And yet they go to school and they learn that they are supposed to love nature and learn from nature. So we are getting, in my opinion, a generation of lost Indians who are going out there, just like lost whites, and trying to embrace trees and think this is doing something Indian.

Lost whites come to the West to love the environment, and they end up paving the damn thing and subdividing it. That is what you end up with. American education is still limited to the fourth quadrant. It does not heal those ancient breaches in the worldview that produce those types of people. Certainly, I would like to keep all of them east of the Mississippi, and let them clean up what they have already screwed up. But there is something that Indians and non-Indians can do well and must do in the future. They must probe these worldviews. We must look at the Indian worldview not as primitive but as one that was generated by experiences in nature. Those experiences proved so intense and so encompassing that Indians did not move away from them.

You have got to look back into your own culture. Why did people six thousand or seven thousand years ago determine that heaven is good and "down here" is bad? Why did they decide to go out and conquer things? Then why did the Greeks later make that other division between history and nature? And why, after Newton and Darwin, did you grab that one quadrant and say that is what the world is about?

I think you have got to ask these questions and start probing them. And when you start working your way through that, I think you will see more of what we are talking about.

▼ 19 ▼

THE POPULARITY OF BEING INDIAN

A New Trend in Contemporary American Society

▼▼▼▼

U nless the increase in the Indian population during the 1970s was due to a remarkable increase in the Indian birthrate, the 1980 census is badly out of kilter and suggests a new social phenomenon of which few people have been aware: The establishment of Indian ancestry as proof of respectability and acceptance in American life has replaced the older concept of American respectability defined by Anglo-Saxon heritage.

In 1980 the federal census allowed people to identify their racial background themselves for the first time. In previous census reports ethnicity was determined by other means. The result of the new method was an increase in the American Indian population beyond anyone's wildest estimate. In 1960 the census reported 523,591 Indians in the United States. That figure jumped to 792,730 in 1970, and the last census showed a count of 1,418,195 Indians in the United States. Obviously this latter figure bears some examination. Let us look first at why there has been such a dramatic increase in the number of people identifying themselves as Indians and then address the more important issue—what are the implications of the significant increase of would-be Indians for the Indian community and its culture?

Traditionally Indians were seen as the ultimate underclass. Original residents of this continent, Indians stood in the way of the advances of Western civilization and consequently had to be extinguished or neutralized in some fashion if settlement were to proceed at its anticipated pace. Many tribes were pushed to remote and barren lands

away from the major centers of population where they were expected to become sedentary agriculturalists, existing as best they
could on fragments of their ancestral lands. The annual reports of
the Commissioner of Indian Affairs testify that the experiment in
farming was not successful in many areas of the West and the Indian population declined precipitiously, reaching an all-time low of
237,196 in 1900. Indians did not prosper under the ministrations of
civilization.

The unpopularity of being identified as an American Indian
affected early census reports. Whenever possible, if a person could
pass as a white, the chances were that he or she did. Unquestionably,
early census reports failed to identify many mixed-blood Indians as
Indians.

It was probably not until the reforms of the New Deal in 1934,
and following, that people began once again to identity themselves
as Indians. With the passage of the Indian Reorganization Act[1] and
the Oklahoma Indian Welfare Act[2] in 1934 and 1936, it became prof-
itable to be an Indian. Certain federal services were made available
to tribal members which had not been part of the Indian's lot in
previous decades.

However, while the New Deal probably emphasized Indian
ancestry for the people who already identified as Indians, there is
little evidence that people crossed over from white to Indian identification simply to take advantage of these services or to seek special
favors from the government because of their racial identification. In
general the number of programs available to non-Indians was considerably greater and more beneficial than that available to Indians.

The Indian population remained at reasonably predictable levels
until 1970, so that while the 1940, 1950, and 1960 census reports
may be slightly undercounted, there is no reason to suppose that
they dreadfully underrepresented the number of Indians. Even the
many programs made available to tribes in the War on Poverty did
not produce much of an increase in the number of Indians in the
United States. One would have expected a large increase between
1960 and 1970 if the sole reason for claiming Indian blood was to
acquire eligibility for services provided for Indians by the federal
government. The halcyon days of the Office of Economic Opportunity were 1964 to 1968, and with the onset of the Nixon administration the tenor of federal policy was to reduce or eliminate social

programs. Although people might have considered themselves Indians in 1964, with the reduction of social programs at the end of the sixties there was no reason to continue the masquerade because the economic benefits inherent in the Indian status were definitely on the decline.

Public opinion was significantly tilted in favor of Indians at the beginning of the seventies. Alcatraz and succeeding activist events may have galvanized the Indian image and made it seem romantic, perhaps even mysteriously exciting, to claim to be an Indian. But the Indian occupation of the Bureau of Indian Affairs in fall 1972 and the occupation and siege of Wounded Knee brought retaliation against Indians by the federal government so that adopting a prominent position as an Indian was not the best way to make one's mark in the world. Continuing cutbacks of federal Indian funds and the withering of reservation and community programs in the late seventies foretold a desperate situation in Indian country for most people, and at the end of the seventies there was no merit—except perhaps some personal emotional stability—that accrued from claiming Indian blood or ancestry.

We must, then, still account for an increase in the Indian population by an astounding 78 percent between the 1970 and 1980 census reports on the basis of nonbiological factors. Never in human history have so many members of the majority undertaken to identify themselves as members of one of the most historically despised minorities of their society. The general tendency of societies traditionally has been to assimilate burdensome minorities quietly and above all to shun identification with them. A glance at Mexico and other nations south of the border will show that, while there is a majority of Indian blood present in the gene pool of those nations, there is hardly an eagerness to identify with that large racial stock of Indianness. On the contrary, people go out of their way to separate themselves from Indian ancestry, denying sometimes even the heritage that is patently obvious on their faces and in their behavior.

In spite of historical animosity toward Indians, Americans apparently consider Indian identity an important factor in maintaining a sense of personal worth. The old verities that once undergirded American social status seem to have eroded substantially, to the point where identification as an Indian is more prestigious and more comforting than continued identification as a member of the majority.

The Anglo-Saxon culture—particularly that of the North Atlantic region—which once defined mainstream American values, heritage, and ancestry, has apparently given way to a new conception of respectability in which a trace of Indian blood adds a sense of stability. This new conception is extremely curious. The conditions of Indian life have not materially improved in recent decades, not so much because Indians have lacked opportunity but more as a result of the increased opportunities for the accumulation of wealth available to members of the majority. Identifying with a group that continues to lag significantly behind the rest of society economically would seem to be a foolish endeavor. Certainly identifying as an Indian also brings with it the assumed but rarely articulated accusation that the individual has not been able to function adequately in this society. So economics alone cannot explain the increased Indian population.

There is some merit in suggesting that identification as an Indian brings with it certain institutional rewards. Colleges and universities today give preference in admission to minorities, and it may well be that non-Indians, eager to obtain admission to law schools or colleges of medicine, are claiming an Indian ancestry in order to leapfrog their fellow applicants who seek admission on the basis of merit alone. The American Indian Law Center in New Mexico reports that it continues to be astounded at the number of alleged Indians attending law schools in various parts of the country. In checking on the applicants, the American Indian Law Center is unable to identify very many as Indians. But a few individuals changing races in order to gain admission to professional schools can hardly have swelled the ranks of American Indians by some 625,000 people, unless law schools are being less than candid about the number of people applying for admission.

Another reason frequently given for the startling increase in the Indian population is the application of Title IV of the Indian Education Act[3] to public schools. Under that law, funds are made available to public school systems that have a certain number of Indians attending them. Though school districts may have greatly inflated the figures in order to receive federal funds, identification under these conditions is a function of the school administrators and not a matter of individual preference or belief when filling out census forms. A school official may certify a certain number of Indians in his school for purposes of receiving federal funds. However, this number remains pretty much a creature of the Department of Education; it generally does not spill over into other statistics. There is no good reason to suppose that temporary identification of a student as an Indian during one school year would carry over into a permanent self-image several years later when the census taker arrived at the door.

Closely related to Indian identification for the purpose of qualifying for federal education funds is identification for the purpose of avoiding forced busing to achieve racial balance. In the late sixties in Denver, a busing plan was put forward which allowed minority children then attending a neighborhood school to escape busing to other parts of town. In a matter of hours the number of Indians in Denver showed a dramatic increase, and there were speculations that Denver might be the world's only wholly American Indian city. Yet forced busing for purposes of integration has not been an imminent peril in people's minds for several years. Claiming an Indian ancestor for the purpose of exempting one's children from busing would again be only a temporary expedient, not a permanent shift from one racial group to another.

Having eliminated biology, economics, admission policies to schools, Title IV funding, and busing as reasons for the increase in Indian identification in the seventies, we now come to the evaluation of personal motives to explain this phenomenon. In American life, the perceived status of the Indian considerably transcends any other status and makes it a desirable complement to one's other personal attributes and accomplishments. The increase in the number of Indians seems to be directly related to the rising interest in religious experience. In the middle sixties, Indians were already acclaimed as the world's first and best ecologists by members of the counterculture. Pop posters proclaimed the Indian reverence for the land, and the protests and occupations almost always featured an Indian activist orating vigorously before the television cameras on some topic advanced as an important religious belief. The demand for restoration of lands, first at Blue Lake in New Mexico and later at Yakima, Warm Springs, and other reservations, laid heavy emphasis on the religious aspect of the land. Since reverence for lands, sacred places, and environment were sadly lacking in Western religions, people began to see their interest in ecology as encompassing important, new religious dimensions.

By 1972, when the Indians occupied the Bureau of Indian Affairs headquarters in Washington, D.C., citing religion as a valid reason for conducting protests was a popular pastime among Indians. The later marches on Washington always featured a number of medicine men who conducted ceremonies and admonished the crowds to follow the old tribal traditions. Since few people had been raised in traditional culture, almost anything that seemed right at the time became a form of traditionalism, and popular ceremonies such as the sweat lodge quickly spread across the country. Indeed, the sweat lodge, conducted under an amazing variety of auspices, became the ritual that united the national Indian movement and provided it with a degree of homogeneity.

In the middle and late seventies the number of medicine men and ceremonies proliferated rapidly. Southern California and the Dakotas in particular experienced an explosion of medicine men, so that it was a rare Indian who did not have access to some form of traditional Indian religious experience. That the medicine man and the ceremonies might have little to do with the actual traditions of any particular tribe seemed not to bother anyone participating in these activities. Few Indians questioned the activities of the contemporary medicine men, and as a result, the divergence from the Indian norm became almost an industry in itself. To be welcomed and sometimes revered by Indians in the neighborhood, an individual needed only bluster to claim a spiritual office in a tribe—generally the more distant the tribe, the more exaggerated were the alleged credentials.

The increased interest in tribal religions did not, unfortunately, influence the ethical behavior of those who professed to have special traditional religious experiences. Both Indians and whites were callously exploited by alleged medicine men who were busy peddling a new form of Indian religion that centered primarily on recycled slogans concerning "Mother Earth." This new statement of the ancient Indian relationship to the Earth asked little in the way of personal commitment and generated a great deal of excitement in the practitioners and participants. People began to feel that they had reestablished the old linkage to the rhythms and revelations of the planet. Heavy emphasis was given to the recitation of pious phrases that people believed would invoke ancient earth spirits and exempt an individual from the guilt that involvement with contemporary industrial society inevitably created.

Books and newspaper articles reinforced the movement of people toward Indian religious experiences. The writings of John Neihardt and Frank Waters on Indian life became immensely popular, and every summer caravans of young whites made their pilgrimages to Third Mesa and Pine Ridge in search of the ultimate reality. People who had little in the way of an Indian heritage found themselves having dreams wherein their past lives, always as Indians, were revealed to them. Upon awakening they adopted Indian names and proudly proclaimed their solidarity with Indians. Once accepted by a circle of Indians, there seemed to be no returning to the life of the ordinary American citizen. The Black Elk phraseology and the Hopi history thereafter seemed to bind together diverse groups of Indians and whites-newly-arrived-as-Indians in a contemporary religious experience that transcended all other considerations. In short, Indian culture became a national culture, not because whites adopted the culture as their own, but because they became Indian and helped to define its contemporary expressions and loyalties.

It is interesting to note what was happening to Indians during this same period. The onset of the War on Poverty saw a strengthening of tribal governments on a scale never imagined by John Collier in the thirties. Prior to 1960 most tribes had what might charitably be called "shadow" governments; they had little income and few programs and did very little business as corporate entities. Beginning with the Area Redevelopment Administration and continuing until the present time, tribal governments have had to take on a great many new responsibilities, almost all of them in the program area. The old Community Action Programs of the poverty war led to more sophisticated institutions that included industrial parks, school systems, and housing authorities. Many tribal governments, in the past twenty years, have become larger than the governments of western towns and counties with a similar population base.

Traditionally Indians conducted their affairs in a highly informal atmosphere. That is to say, formal institutional life was minimized in favor of adherence to customs and kinship responsibilities. With a strong sense of tribal identity, a confirmed isolation from daily intercourse with other groups, and a legend of origin that informed the people that they were specifically chosen from among the peoples of the world to be possessors of a specific religious revelation, tribes did not need to juxtapose the institutions of society against the individual. Social and community disapproval and the shame that mis-behavior might bring to families were sufficient to maintain law and order in all but the most pressing circumstances. Today most of the functions that Indians performed spontaneously according to the cus-toms of their tribe are the subject of an agency or institution, tribally operated to be certain, yet imbued with the impersonality that we see in the modern world with its transpersonal activities.

The primary experience of Indians since they went onto the res-ervations has been one of confronting and resolving their relation-ship with the non-Indian educational system. From allotment, which was supposed to be a practical experience in the handling of prop-erty, to relocation, which was to provide Indian families with first-hand knowledge of the urban areas, almost all federal efforts to assist Indians have been premised on the belief that Indians could and would adopt the educational values of the larger society. In our time, the postwar era, Indians have become considerably more familiar with education of all kinds. Vocational education has expanded sig-nificantly in training programs conducted both on the reservations and in the urban areas. Indians have been admitted to college and graduate professional schools in increasingly greater numbers than at any time in the past. Although still statistically underrepresented, Indians are rapidly becoming accustomed to undertaking difficult educational programs and succeeding in them.

Like other Americans, with the expansion of educational oppor-tunities Indian communities have become subject to the ministra-tions of the professional specialist and consultant. The division of labor and functions in traditional society was an important part of Indian life, but it was not linked to any set of institutional objectives that sought social stability as an end product. Specialist functions were performed for individuals, and it was in the informal setting that specialties were recognized and approved. The expansion of the functions and tasks of the tribal governments today has meant the inclusion of the specialist in the activities of the Indian community. As in other American communities, however, the specialist/professional follows a personal code of ethics and is responsible to the institutional employer. Usually, the specialist/professional is more likely to serve the community on the basis of his or her own skills and activities than on the basis of the needs of the community. Indian communities have accordingly changed significantly in the manner in which they view themselves and their access to the knowledge that enables them to succeed and survive in the contemporary world.

If we take the movement of non-Indians toward the Indian way of life—at least toward identification with a set of behaviors and attitudes that they see as Indian—and the movement of Indians, their tribes, and communities toward the American institutional mainstream, we have a strange phenomenon. Indians seem determined to shed a substantial portion of their heritage even while non-Indians are frantically adopting whatever part of the heritage they can discern and feel comfortable performing. The result of this confusion has been the blurring, almost beyond redemption, of the traditions of the individual tribal groups. It is now enough for a person to be fairly prominent in Indian affairs and have sufficient political clout to turn aside any determined inquiries regarding the extent of his Indian heritage. Leadership in Indian communities has consequently become a matter of media exposure rather than community endorsement or approval. Often it is the individual's connection with non-Indian institutions that verifies his or her Indian identity: If accepted by a well-known non-Indian institution as an Indian, the individual is regarded as an Indian—even by many Indians.

The current ambiguity associated with the Indian community cannot continue indefinitely. The banks of the Indian mainstream have long since overflowed, and as the energies of the Indian movement reach out and include people who have not previously considered themselves Indians or as more people decide to become Indians and willingly leap into the fray, a decided lack of community cohesion results. Loyalties to family, clan, and tribe become faint, and allegiance to political networks and institutional connections become considerably stronger. The Indian landscape takes on the aspect of a charade played out before a bewildered audience that is unable to spot the players or their numbers and has not the slightest idea how one obtains a program for this ritual drama.

A scrutiny of the past may provide clues to the solution of the current problems in the Indian community. The Indian relationship to the United States was originally a political relationship, even though the conflict between Indians and members of the majority was primarily racial in character. In the last two decades the political relationship has matured into a rather precisely defined legal relationship in which rights and responsibilities are determined either by Congress or by the courts. The racial conflict has evolved and for a while appeared to be cultural conflict, but more recently it has become the great counterlifestyle for many people. The specifics of culture have given way to the generalities of fashion, and as the precision of personal behavior becomes less meaningful, a great many things that are simply alternatives to the activities of the majority are considered to be within the sphere of Indian behavior.

Much of what has happened to Indians in the contemporary world was probably predictable once the isolation of the Indian communities was disturbed by the developments of the postwar world. Interstate highways, airplanes, rural electrification, and the entrance of radios, televisions, and telephones in reservations have made a significant difference in the way Indians live their lives and in the manner in which they understand the world. Like other rural people, Indians are presently in a state of deep and profound culture shock, and this trauma cannot easily be overcome. The electric universe continues to transmit more information to Indian communities than they can possibly absorb and understand. And as with other Americans, about all Indians can do is try to fend off the most depressing aspects of contemporary life and hope for better days.

The present situation in Indian country calls for the most intelligent and determined leadership to express itself in an unqualified endorsement of traditions and values that have always been associated with the respective tribes and communities. Today Indians need to speak up but not in the same sense as the sixties and seventies required them to speak. The Indian community needs to address its problems, and it can best perform this task by addressing itself and engaging in new kinds of dialogue within tribes and between tribes. Standards of conduct ought to be reestablished, and individuals should be willing to subscribe to them and follow them. A careful accounting of the tribal cultural heritage is important for every Indian group, and impostors must be driven out. Each Indian tribe has the right, and the responsibility, to determine the criteria for establishing tribal membership. Elected tribal leaders need to develop a new sense of corporate responsibility that can break the present networking with larger institutions and reestablish the old codes of proper conduct and concern that once characterized Indians as a distinct group.

There is every indication that at the grass roots of different tribes this new sense of identity and meaning is emerging. The recent election of Peterson Zah to the chairmanship of the Navajo tribe is a good sign that at the local level the Navajos have chosen to bring their government closer to themselves and force it to perform useful functions for the community as a whole. A new group of Indian leaders seems to be emerging in other places that would demonstrate that the old cohesion that once marked tribes as a people set apart is stirring and making itself felt. Whatever values and beliefs Indians might contribute to American society as a whole cannot be made as long as there is such confusion regarding the real strengths of Indian life. It will be only when Indians begin to speak with a coherent point of view that they will be in a position to assist in the continuing task of improving American society. One cannot hazard exactly what that contribution might be, but it should be of lasting value.

As the attention of the federal government was directed toward Indian communities in the postwar years, a pattern for relationships developed in which Indians recited their problems and a bewildering multitude of bureaucrats, experts, and politicians stepped forward with promises of assistance and assurances of understanding. Considering the situation today, no one standing outside the Indian community is exactly certain what the best approach is for handling the problems of the Indian community. Few people want to dwell primarily on problems, and fewer people still can suggest solutions without identifying the areas where energies must be directed.

Nevertheless, it seems incumbent on us today to discard the mere recitation of wrongs and problems and call people back to a confidence in themselves that can begin to address the areas that demand attention. In the old days—customs, traditions, and whatever institutions were in vogue had a mission to serve the people. If they did not prove useful, they were discarded. That critical sense of utility now seems to be surfacing again. Let us not view it as disruptive but as an opportunity to move forward again toward new horizons and accomplishments. By counting the people who respond to the opportunities of the contemporary world, we will be able to determine how many Indians there really are.

NOTES

1. 48 Stat. 934, 25 u.s.c. § 461 (1934).
2 Act of May 1, 1936, 49 Stat. 1250, 48 U.S.C. § 362 (1940) (now codified 25 U.S.C. § 473A).
3. Indian Education Act, P.L. 92-318, § 401, 86 Stat. 334 (1972).

ALCATRAZ, ACTIVISM,

AND ACCOMMODATION

▼▼▼▼

Alcatraz and Wounded Knee 1973 have come to symbolize the revival of Indian fortunes in the late twentieth century, so we hesitate to discuss the realities of the time or to look critically at their actual place in modern Indian history. We conclude that it is better to wrap these events in romantic notions and broker that feeling in exchange for further concessions from the federal government; consequently, we fail to learn from them the hard lessons that will serve us well in leaner times.

Activism in the 1950s was sporadic but intense. In 1957 Lumbee people surrounded a Ku Klux Klan gathering in North Carolina and escorted the hooded representatives of white supremacy back to their homes sans weapons and costumes. In 1961 a strange mixture of Six Nations people and non-Indian supporters attempted a citizens' arrest of the secretary of the interior, and, sometime during this period, a band of "True Utes" briefly took over the agency offices at Fort Duchesne. The only context for these events was the long suffering of small groups of people bursting forth in an incident that illustrated oppression but suggested no answer to pressing problems. In 1964 the "fish-ins" in the Pacific Northwest produced the first activism with an avowed goal; continual agitation in that region eventually resulted in *U.S. v. Washington,* which affirmed once and for all the property rights of Northwest tribes for both subsistence and commercial fishing.

Indians benefited substantially from the civil rights movement of the 1960s and the ensuing doctrines concerning the poor, which surfaced in the Economic Opportunity Act and more particularly in its administration. The civil rights movement had roots in a hundred small gatherings of concerned attorneys brought together by Jack Greenberg and Thurgood Marshall to determine the legal and philosophical basis for overturning *Plessy v. Ferguson*. Concentrating on the concept of *equality,* a series of test cases involving access to professional education in the border states cut away the unexamined assumption that separate facilities for higher education automatically meant equality of treatment and equality of the substance of education.

In 1954 *Brown v. Topeka Board of Education* stripped away the cloak of indifference and hypocrisy and required the dismantling of segregated schools. By extension, if schools were to be integrated, why not lunch counters and buses, and why not equality under the law in all public places and programs? The *Brown* strategy was created on behalf of the oppressed multitudes of African Americans but did not involve the rank-and-file people until the movement went into the streets and lunch counters of the South. With the announcement of "Black Power" by Stokely Carmichael and SNCC [Student Nonviolent Coordinating Committee] in 1966—made possible in some measure by the insistence of federal War on Poverty administrators that the "poor" knew better than anyone else what poverty was and how to combat it—the civil rights movement became a people's movement.

A people's movement has many benefits—the mass of minority groups are involved, and political strength increases dramatically—but it also has immense vulnerability in that goals that can be seen, articulated, and achieved are surrendered in favor of symbolic acts that illustrate and demonstrate the suffering and frustrations of the people. Symbolic acts demand attention from an otherwise unaware general public, but they also fail to articulate the necessity of specific actions that can and must be taken by the government at the local, state, and federal levels to alleviate the crisis. Consequently, the choice of remedy is given to the institutional structure that oppresses people and to the good and bad politicians and career bureaucrats who operate the institution.

The Poor People's March of 1968 best exemplifies the problem of a people's movement unable to articulate specific solutions and see them through to completion. Organized partially in memory of the slain Martin Luther King, Jr., and partially as an effort to secure increases in the funding of social programs, the march floundered when participants spent their time harassing members of the cabinet about problems that had no immediate solution and demanding sympathy and understanding from federal officials who could not translate these concerns into programmatic responses. Smaller protests had maintained a decent level of funding for poverty programs in past years, but, this time, the march faced the bitter reality of the Vietnam War and the impossibility of continuing to expand the federal budget into unrealistic deficits.

It is important to note that, while the Indian fishing rights struggle maintained itself with measurable goals, Alcatraz represented an Indian version of the Poor People's March. The proclamation presented by the first invaders of the island demanded a bewildering set of responses from the federal government, focusing on transfer of the island's title to an Indian organization and the funding of an educational center on the island for the thousands of Indians who had made the Bay Area their home. The popular interpretation of the occupation was that Indians were entitled to own the island because it was federal surplus property and therefore qualified under a provision of the 1868 treaty of Fort Laramie.

Unfortunately, the treaty provision was a myth. Red Cloud had simply remained in the Powder River country until the government withdrew its troops from the Bozeman Trail and then, satisfied that the trail was closed, arrived at Fort Laramie in November 1868 to sign the treaty. During the Alcatraz occupation, when White House staff and Department of the Interior lawyers looked at the treaty, they could find no phrase that justified returning the island to the Indian occupants; consequently, they were blocked from using any executive powers to resolve the crisis.

The initial group of Indian occupants was composed of students from Bay Area colleges and universities, but, as the occupation continued, these people were replaced with enthusiastic recruits from across the nation and with unemployed people who had nowhere else to go. The mood of the occupants was that they should use the press as often as possible; thus the goal of the movement quickly became confused, with various spokespeople articulating different philosophies on different occasions.

The difference between Alcatraz and the fishing rights fight, and between the *Brown* litigation and the Black Power movement, should be made clear: Behind the sit-ins and the fish-ins was the almost certain probability that, should activists be convicted at the trial court level, they would have their convictions over-turned by a higher court and/or the object of their protest would be upheld at a higher level of litigation. *Brown* and the Medicine Creek fishing rights treaty were already federal law before people went out to protest; the protests were made on behalf of impartial enforcement of existing law. This foundation of legality did not exist for either the Poor People's March or the occupation of Alcatraz. Therefore, in legal terms, these activities meant nothing.

My role in Alcatraz was sporadic and, in a few instances, not welcomed by some of the activists on the Rock. While I was director of the National Congress of American Indians (NCAI), I had worked for several years with people in the Bay Area as part of the NCAI's concern for relocated Indians. I entered law school in fall 1967 and, by the time of the occupation, had already written *Custer Died for Your Sins,* which was released in early October 1969. Some years before, Richard MacKenzie and others had briefly landed on Alcatraz, and, in the years since that first invasion, Bay Area activists such as Adam Nordwall had disrupted Columbus Day celebrations and, with some modest successes, generally tried to focus the attention of Bay Area politics on urban Indian problems. Ironically, some of the people who were now shouting "Red Power" into every microphone they could find had called me a communist the year before for doing a Frank McGee NBC news interview that advocated Red Power.

Adam Nordwall saw that the occupation would flounder unless it was tied to some larger philosophical issue that could be seen by the American public as important to their own concerns for justice. During fall 1969, I was asked several times to come out to Alcatraz to discuss how the people on the island could transform the occupation into a federal issue that could be resolved by congressional action. I favored announcing that not only did Indians want the island, we wanted a federal policy of land restoration that would provide a decent land base for small reservations, return submarginal lands to tribes that had them, and, in some cases, restore original reservation boundaries.

On Christmas Eve 1969, I flew out to California to discuss the land issue with people on the island, but the meeting never got off the ground. Instead of listening to our presentation on land restoration, the activists began quarreling about who was in charge of the operation. Richard Oakes had many supporters, but he also had many rivals. Adam and I were considered intruders because we had not been in the original invasion. About all we got out of the meeting was the sneer that the activists had the whole world watching them, and they were in control of Indian policy. We pointed out that a sensible program had to be articulated so that the administration could act, but we got no positive response.

In January 1970, hoping to highlight a land and treaty issue, I invited Merv Griffin to come out to Alcatraz and do part of a show from there. Unfortunately, many of the people on the Rock had not moved forward in their thinking; Merv got the old response of how the island belonged to Indians under the 1868 treaty and how they wanted to establish an educational and vocational training facility on the island.

In spring 1970, a group of us held a national urban Indian conference on Alcatraz in another effort to provide a context for securing the island. In November 1969 this same urban group had held its conference the weekend before the San Francisco Indian center burned, but now, under different leadership, we were trying to focus everything on the Bay Area in the hope of defining an issue that the public would embrace. The meeting was not long under way when a man and woman began to scream at each other across the room, viciously and seemingly without any provocation. Every time anyone would propose a course of action, one or the other would jump up and let loose a string of curses designed to infuriate everyone. Most people sat there politely listening to the nonsense, but eventually the meeting just dissolved. Later we discovered they were a husband and wife who went through this performance at every meeting they attended.

While our meeting was being held, we learned that Richard Oakes and his supporters had been thrown off the island the day before and that they were likely to confront us when we returned to the mainland. We met only one sullen young man who warned us that he was going to remember our names and faces. Later that evening, as we sat around trying to figure out what to do, we hit on a plan. We had someone call Oakes's headquarters and, in his best reservation English, relate that he was supervising two buses of Navajo boys who were traveling to the Hoopa Bear Dance and wanted to be housed for the night. The Oakes contingent immediately tried to enlist these Navajos as a force to help Oakes recapture the island. They gave us directions for finding their headquarters, and we promised to come help them. A few minutes after hanging up the phone, we decided it would be even better to include buses of Navajo girls, so we had a rather prominent Indian woman call the headquarters and pretend that she was matron over two busloads of girls from Navajo Community College who were looking to make contact with the Navajo boys. This phone call created a dilemma for us and for Oakes's people. They wanted to get the two busloads of girls and lose the boys; we wondered how long we could continue to drive four phantom buses around the Bay Area.

Our pretend Navajo man then called Oakes's people back and said he had gotten lost and was in Oakland, and we got new directions for reaching their headquarters. Our woman then got back on the phone and told Oakes's group that the girls' buses were only a few blocks away. Their response was that they would go out and buy food and get ready to welcome the girls, apparently forgetting that the boys' buses would be along shortly also. We hung up and pondered the situation we had created. The consensus was that we should call back and confess the whole thing before everyone was inconvenienced. We were just about to confess when one of our group said, "Wait a minute! Real Indians would just go their own way and not say a word; we are thinking like responsible, educated Indians." So we just went back to our hotel to bed.

The next morning, as we embarked for Alcatraz to finish the meeting, we were greeted by two surly Oakes supporters. They told us to go ahead and visit the island, but they assured us that we would not stay long because they had reinforcements of four hundred Navajos arriving momentarily and we would be thrown off the Rock along with the anti-Oakes people. Needless to say, our meeting went well, and the Navajos never did arrive. I will not mention the names in our little group, but I can confess that they are still prominent, responsible, national Indian leaders.

The occupation of Alcatraz lingered on. A rougher group of people occupied the island, and it became useless to try to make sense of the occupation. Increasingly, it became a hazard to go out there. Eventually, many of the buildings were burned, and feeble, nonsensical ultimatums were issued by the declining population on the Rock.

Finally, the government swooped down and took the remaining people away. I visited the island about a decade later and heard a surprisingly mild and pro-Indian explanation of the occupation from a Park Service guide. I walked around the grounds and remembered some of the difficult meetings we had held there and how, several times, we almost had a coalition that could have affected land policy. Unfortunately, most of the people involved in the occupation had no experience in formulating policy and saw their activities as primarily aimed at awakening the American public to the plight of Indians. Thus a great opportunity to change federal programs for Indians was lost.

The Trail of Broken Treaties came along in fall 1972. By that time, the activists had devised the Twenty Points, which, in my opinion, is the best summary document of reforms put forth in this century. Written primarily by Hank Adams, who supervised the fishing rights struggle until the Supreme Court ruled in favor of Indians, it is comprehensive and philosophical and has broad policy lines that can still be adopted to create some sense of fairness and symmetry in federal Indian policy.

Then came the Wounded Knee occupation, with its aftermath of trials and further violence. Indians were well represented in the media from the Alcatraz occupation through the Wounded Knee trials, but, unfortunately, each event dealt primarily with the symbols of oppression and did not project possible courses of action that might be taken to solve problems.

The policy posture of Indians at Alcatraz was part of a historical process begun during the War on Poverty when people demanded action from the government but failed to articulate the changes they wanted. With the incoming Nixon administration in 1969, we clamored for an Indian to be appointed as commissioner. Because we failed to support Robert Bennett, who was already occupying the office, the inept Louie Bruce was installed. Bruce's chaotic administration produced an era in which résumé's were enhanced and job descriptions were watered down so that the respective administrations could appoint Indian puppets to symbolize the presence of Indians in the policy-making process. Today the government, under Ada Deer, is at work trying to create a new set of categories—"historic" and "nonhistoric" tribes—so that benefits and services can be radically reduced. When Indians do not clearly articulate what they want, the government feels free to improvise, even if it means creating new policies that have no roots in anything except the fantasies of the creator.

Alcatraz was more than a protest against the oppressive conditions under which Indians lived. In large part, it was a message that we wanted to determine our own destiny and make our own decisions. That burden is still upon us and weighs heavily when contemporary tribal chairpeople are consulted about policy directions. Almost always, immediate concerns or irritating technicalities are regarded as important in the consultative process, and, consequently, it is increasingly difficult to determine exactly where people think we are going. Like the activists at Alcatraz, we often mill around, keenly aware that we have the ears of the public but uncertain what to do next. Until we can sketch out realistic scenarios of human and resource goals, we continue to resemble those occupants of the Rock a quarter of a century ago: We want change, but we do not know what change.

▼ 21 ▼

MORE OTHERS

▼▼▼▼

In the old days when policy makers were describing racial problems in the United States, the primary focus was on African Americans with a quick glance aside at Mexican Americans, and the remainder of the racial minorities conveniently fit into the broad category "others." This practice was perhaps the first trickle-down method of discussing issues. Thus when President Bill Clinton (descendant of a Cherokee grandmother) announced his "Initiative on Race" in 1997, it was not a surprise that Indians fit somewhere under "Others" once again. We have come full circle, it would seem, in our efforts to break clear of anonymity. That is perhaps why we are called the "Vanishing" Americans: We are simply not there when the roll is called.

Stereotypes of Indians have changed a good deal from the image of the bloodthirsty/noble savage, however. Reggie White, ordained minister and Green Bay Packers expert on race relations in the United States, said that Indians had a genius for "sneaking up on people." Mexican Americans were given credit for talent in constructive use of housing, being able to get twenty to thirty people into a one-room house if necessary. Of course, many reservation people would challenge the Mexican-American victory in that category because a reservation house will often house considerably more people in an emergency. But "sneaking up on people"? Before attacking we used to have big dances with drums pounding for hours on end and everyone chanting some weird high-pitched wail guaranteed to drive the foe crazy. I suppose a charitable interpretation of such behavior can be described as "sneaking up," but I don't think it would be convincing.

Over the past four decades it has been fascinating to watch the image of Indians change with the winds of social perceptions. When Indians were an exotic and unknown commodity, boundary lines were enforced rather vigorously, but as more people have become fans of Indian beliefs and lifestyles, a vast middle ground of new stereotypes has emerged that makes it impossible, and politically hazardous, to attempt to reestablish the clear lines of demarcation. Granted, oil-rich Indians have become transformed into Bingo-rich Indians. Belief that each Indian receives a check of jackpot proportions each month still continues in conservative ranks, and all white people still have a Cherokee grandmother in their otherwise pristine Nordic backgrounds. Nevertheless, what is so much fun are the stereotypes Indians have invented for themselves to distinguish between "real" Indians and the fakers down the block.

In 1964 when the War on Poverty was announced, Indians found it fashionable to describe themselves as the poorest of the poor. There was a ready audience who already believed this idea, even though it was plainly evident that African Americans of the Black Belt in the South and various Appalachian communities were obviously in worse condition. Nevertheless, as an identifiable group of people, Indians were not only poor, they were poor as a direct result of federal policies, thereby entitling them to some status in receiving benefits. The Indian Poverty warriors vied to find the descriptive phrase that would draw the most sympathy and support. So began the chorus of "We were so poor that . . . ," and the hands-down winner must have been Dr. Jim Wilson who told, with a breaking voice, how he always pitied white kids when he was growing up because they did not have dirt roofs on their homes and so were unable to grow flowers on top of their houses.

Because most poverty programs dealt with education, one of the standard complaints was that the Indian was forced to attend a Catholic school where nuns regularly beat him for speaking his native language. A rough projection of the percentage of people at a poverty conference claiming nun brutality spread over Indian country would have produced somewhere in the neighborhood of 200,000 nuns flailing away at nearly one million imprisoned Indian children for probably twenty-two hours a day. Many of these same people reemerged in the 1980s claiming they had been brought up "traditional."

With the increase of Indian activism at the end of the 1960s, the symbols of rebellious Americans were projected onto Indians, and when people continued to wear long hair or braids they were then classed as "militants." And it was the fashion to grow hair long as a means of establishing credentials in the movement. In fact, long hair was often sufficient to establish the political correctness of the individual, and this made it easy for younger Indians to wander back and forth between antiwar groups and their own communities with impunity. Many non-Indians joined the movement at this time, including undercover federal agents, and soon long hair was not sufficient to prove Indian identity. So the quest for a tribal background began.

Originally, as we have noted, sympathetic whites could always find a Cherokee grandmother in the family tree. But this claim was so universal that people wishing to change ethnic groups began to claim other tribes. The ploy worked until someone from that tribe unwittingly began to track down mutual relatives, which is a universal Indian trait. The fraudulent Chief Red Fox, in his rewrite of James MacGregor's book on Wounded Knee, laid claim to Oglala Sioux ancestry, and because the book was a best-seller, that encouraged even more people to write and claim Indian heritage and blood. With the tightening of tribal affiliation requirements in arts and crafts, arguments broke out concerning the nature of Indian identities.

If you think about it, the situation is as follows. Go to any Indian crafts store in the Southwest, and you will find hundreds if not thousands of pieces of "Indian" jewelry. Tourist traps in all the western cities have additional thousands of pieces, and even in curio stores near the national parks you find hundreds of pieces of Indian jewelry. But travel to a pueblo and try to locate someone who can do a good piece of Indian jewelry from scratch, and you will be told that hardly anyone makes the stuff anymore. One can only conclude that thousands of Pueblos and Navajos have been kidnapped and held in underground caverns where they are able to make several pieces of jewelry an hour and then these products are sold by the jewelry stores. There is no other explanation for it.

So the race to establish an Indian identity because of the change in federal laws was on. A rather ingenious argument then emerged.

People claimed that they did have Indian blood but that their grand-parents had rejected the federal government out of hand, had moved to the nearest city or fled to the deepest woods, and had nobly and steadfastly refused all federal offers of aid over a period of three or four generations. Thus federal scholarships, the distribution of claims money per capita, and preservation of lands in trust had all been rejected out of hand by these superpatriotic Indians. So prevalent has this explanation become that its claimants have sniped at real blood enrolled Indians as being morally deficient for remaining on the reservations and within the tribes.

Some medicine men were supportive of the occupation of Wounded Knee in 1973, and from this experience came the desire to be seen as a "traditional" Indian. Thus in the late 1970s and increasing greatly in the 1980s, people claimed to have been raised on a reservation but never to have been touched by its institutions. "I was raised traditional," people proclaimed, and by projecting backward to the 1960s, one got the vision that hardly any whites and certainly none of their institutions and practices were present on any of the western reservations until very recently. Thus the nuns vanished and in their place were secret canyons and sacred locations where ceremonies were practiced and ancient wisdom dispersed. No one, it seemed, talked English until they were in their twenties—although if asked to speak their native tongue, most people could only produce a few phrases of Lakota that they had picked up in an urban sweat lodge.

As many reservation Indians were traveling the New Age workshop trail dispensing wisdom and sharing secret ceremonies, reservation Indians, urban Indians, and born-again white converts were now in competition with each other for a New Age clientele. Reservation Indians had the edge, because for the most part they could speak the tribal language sufficiently to impress their new clients. They could also drop the important names at the right time, showing that they had, for the most part, considerable experience with ceremonies. Urban Indians quickly learned the celebrity game and ensured that they spent enough time with reservation people to claim some validation by well-known spiritual leaders. Non-Indian pretenders either sought confirmation from reservation spiritual leaders or invented outlandish names to validate themselves.

About the mid-1980s a real genius, name unknown, invented a gimmick that proved unbeatable and enabled hundreds of people to lay claim to Indian spiritual powers. People claiming to be "Pipe Carriers" now began to hold their version of tribal ceremonies. This idea was very sophisticated. An individual could claim to have been *trained* in the old ways and could perform ceremonies but did not have to take any responsibility. That is to say, he could hold his version of a ceremony and when accused of wrongdoing could then deny that he was a medicine man or spiritual leader, alleging that he was merely a "Pipe Carrier."

In the old days, almost everyone had a pipe. It was considered a common courtesy to enjoy a pipe at the beginning of a visit and to sit quietly and talk while smoking a pipe at the end of the meal or storytelling. Old men would sit together for hours smoking their pipes and reminiscing about the old days. And when praying, ordinary people would use the pipe as part of their activities. The idea, then, that people could be commissioned to be partially spiritual for special purposes was entirely new, and it meant that non-Indians could appear to be an integral part of an Indian ceremony without having to defend their actions. Once this barrier of credibility in the use of the pipe was breached, a great fervor erupted in spiritual circles and ceremonies were opened to many nontribal people on the basis that good things should be shared with anyone who sincerely wanted to experience them. In theological terms, tribal religions often became missionary-minded. It is now approaching total chaos. I was once invited to a Sun Dance to be held on the Navajo reservation, to be conducted by an Aleut. Now that is ecumenical.

While some of the Plains tribal religions were becoming world movements, albeit with European visitors as their missionaries, a new development was occurring far from Indian country that was to have dire consequences for the modern Indian stereotype. The great interest in environment and ecology sparked in the 1960s portrayed the Indian as the original, and often pristine, ecologist. Looking around at corporate rape of the land created considerable concern among the white majority, and many people did not like being compared to Indians when it came to land use. Thus a movement developed to undercut the benign image of the Indian as ecologist.

Actually some inroads had already been made in two areas. In the fishing rights struggle in the Pacific Northwest the best argument used by the Fish and Game departments in Washington and Oregon was that Indians were destroying the salmon runs by overfishing the rivers. Courts did not embrace the reasoning because it was obvious that the Japanese commercial fishing boats were taking the salmon during their three-year cycle in the ocean and that the white commercial fishermen were also taking a significant percentage of the runs before Indians or sportfishing could even begin. But for those people looking for an argument against the Indians, such as long-time Indian foe Slate Gorton, the idea that Indians were the original despoilers was appealing and was repeated continually without regard to the facts of the situation.

In an effort to explain how North America lost its large animals at the end of the Pleistocene era (which can be anywhere from 20,000 to 20 million years ago), Paul Martin concocted the idea that Paleo–Indians rushed across the Bering Strait around 12,000 years ago, invented the Clovis point, and in a blood lust exterminated some thirty-nine species of megafauna. Over the next three decades the thesis gained a few supporters in spite of the glaring lack of any physical evidence and many later studies that undercut even the idea of Bering crossings. But newspaper people loved the idea as it made a swell short Sunday supplement piece and helped to undercut the perceived moral superiority of Indians on the environment.

By the 1990s, people began to devise additional scenarios that were ludicrous on their face but novel in that no fool had ever been taken seriously when he suggested the idea. People followed the dictum What's new is true. Several historians set out to prove that the Indians were responsible for the extermination of the bison or buffalo. Seizing small, isolated incidents, they argued that these few events really described typical Indian behavior and therefore provided a means of affixing the blame. The most absurd of these smear theses was that of Elliott West who argued that the Cheyenne Indians had major responsibility for the demise of the southern buffalo herd because they camped in a little thicket in the western Arkansas valley. In cold winters, he argued, although he did not identify any winters that were actually difficult, the Cheyennes camped in the river bottom where the buffalo would have grazed, thus depriving them of forage and reducing their numbers each year.

The accusation had many flaws. For one thing, there were some thirty million to forty million buffalo roaming the plains, which would put three million to six million in the region where the Cheyennes sometimes wintered. One cannot imagine a very large herd of buffalo standing on the banks of the river, intimidated by a handful of Cheyennes, as there were no more than 3,000 to 4,000 Cheyennes in North America at the time. But even worse, West did not describe the activities of the buffalo hunters. In 1872 the world leather market collapsed because of a drought in South America. The American bison was quickly seen as a substitute, and by spring 1872, the plains were swarming with hunters who were slaughtering buffalo for the hides alone. Some two thousand hunters were in the Dodge City, Kansas, area that year averaging fifteen animals a day killed and skinned. Within three years nearly three million animals were killed and the southern herd was reduced to virtually nothing.

Just how this incredible destruction of the buffalo became the fault of the Cheyennes boggles the imagination, but if one does not discuss the actions of the buffalo hunters and merely talks about the Cheyennes barring the way to winter feed, the idea has an attractive glisten to it. Many of the "New Historians" have been firm supporters of West's thesis, stating that it represents the "New Western History" in which the pimples on everyone are shown. I was unaware that Indians had such a good image in western history that they needed to be accused of something they didn't do in order to prove they were "humans too." But the clincher in the argument is that during the time when they were supposed to be clogging the Arkansas River bottoms and eliminating the buffalo, the Cheyennes and Arapahos were living on a reservation near Fort Sill, Oklahoma, several hundred miles below the Arkansas. I shudder to think of the millions of schoolchildren who will read West's essay, be deprived of the facts of the situation, and conclude that the Indians were no better ecologists than modern destructive extractive industries.

Stereotyping may be the cost of creating a nation composed of individuals—mostly rejects or fugitives—who have little in common with each other. We extol the Constitution as the sacred document that binds us together, but in fact it merely lays down generalized guidelines for the protection of property. With the settlement of the west, government has been changing its role to that of *creator* of property and wealth and consequently tells us little about the manner in which we should conduct ourselves toward other citizens. Both religion and the classical education in the humanities once performed those tasks for us, but they have fallen by the wayside now.

With the exception of Indian reservations, the ethnic ghettos that protected many Americans have been vanishing in the past half century, so that the stereotypes we have today are long since obsolete and should be discarded. In fact, they are generalities that could easily be overcome if our educational system could teach people to think rather than memorize. Today we are faced with subtler forms of discrimination. The recent attacks on affirmative action have within them deep stereotypes, never articulated, that must be removed. The assumption of affirmative action has shifted from the need to have some representation in every activity of life to the tacit assumption that no minorities could ever be employed without special treatment and that all jobs should automatically go to whites without any questions whatsoever.

Reviewing the stereotypes within Indian country is a means of forecasting where the larger society may be headed. The bicentennial inspired much enthusiasm for recapturing individual ethnic heritage, and the intense desire of non-Indians to have some Indian ancestry or activity may be a part of that movement. Unfortunately, we do not seem to have the patience to find both our own heritage and the place in which heritage can make a positive contribution to the larger society. We are in the process of establishing a new kind of American identity, apart from the Pilgrim tradition, and it is a very painful process of sorting out values. We must not take any easy or superficial answers.

22

THE INDIAN POPULATION

▼▼▼▼

One little, two little, three little Indians" is not simply a familiar children's nursery rhyme, it is also a celebration of North American genocide. This little ditty, many Indian militants argue, captures in lyrical form the belief held during the last century by most informed Americans that Indians were vanishing from the face of the earth. This view was popularly symbolized earlier in this century by a small figurine showing an exhausted warrior on horseback, head slumped over and bowed, entitled "End of the Trail," which adorned the mantlepiece of many white homes. The nursery rhyme did not anticipate that in 1994 federal census takers would estimate that 2.2 million people would claim to be Indians and that perhaps four times as many would smile sweetly at each other at cocktail parties and add a Cherokee grandmother to their family tree. Even President Bill Clinton was not immune to this practice, informing a national television audience at a Town Hall meeting that he was a CHEROKEE.

Gathering data on the number of Indians in the United States has always been an inexact science. It is fascinating to trace the various census reports that claim to have properly counted Indians. Indeed, Indian census reports reflect almost every concern except demographics. They are important in every period of American history, however, because federal Indian policy has been based on estimates of the number of Indians for whom the federal government has some responsibility. Without knowledge of the difficulty of determining how many Indians there are, other aspects of Indian life can not be properly understood,

Today's census substantially affects the way Indians look at themselves and is a critical factor in the way federal and state officials, the general public, sympathetic and interested whites, and other racial minorities understand Indians. When tribal governments became eligible for revenue-sharing, tribal leaders began zealously monitoring census returns because part of their income depended on their population. To see how complicated enumerating Indians has been, we need only to review previous efforts to do so.

Perhaps the belief that the Indians were destined to vanish originated in early colonial times as a means of justifying the massacres of Indians by the Puritans. If, as the New England colonists believed, Indians were under a cosmic curse and in a state of rapid decline, killing a few was not really a criminal act and in some instances might actually be doing the Lord's work. It was not all Thanksgiving dinners in those early days. No one questions that the Indian population in the East did decline precipitiously as whites settled the New England area. Many Indians were killed, others hid in obscure places, and still other Indians moved west before the American Revolution.

Many eastern Indians were allies of Great Britain in both the Revolution and the War of 1812. Believing they should not stay behind in the United States when their English friends fled to Canada after the Revolution, they left with the departing British troops, vanishing from the United States but remaining very much a part of things north of the border. The virtual disappearance of Indians east of the Mississippi can be traced directly to Andrew Jackson's policy of removing the tribes of that region to Oklahoma and Kansas, not to some cosmic decree commanding their inevitable extinction. Even then only the largest and most threatening tribes were removed. Smaller tribal groups simply remained in the backwaters of the eastern United States where they had always lived.

The genocidal interpretation of this nursery rhyme usually takes its examples from the massacre of Indians during the wars for control of the Great Plains and Rocky Mountains. Some tribes did suffer significant losses in these incidents. Sand Creek and Wounded Knee are but the most publicized events in a long series of bloody and one-sided engagements. The slaughter of Blackfeet people by Major Eugene M. Baker's troops on January 23, 1870, and the merciless killing of Apaches on December 28, 1872, in Salt Canyon, Arizona, certainly qualify as equally brutal efforts to rid the West of Indians.

But the Apache, Blackfeet, Cheyenne, and Sioux tribes were not wholly exterminated in these battles, cruel and heartless as they were. Perhaps only in California were whole tribes of Indians indiscriminately slaughtered. Ishi, the solitary survivor of his tribe who spent his final years as a living exhibit in the museum at Berkeley, may well represent the fate of many of the West Coast groups. There is some strong supporting evidence of the genocidal attitude of the U.S. government: until World War I, one of the targets on American military shooting ranges was called the "Indian Squaw" and resembled an Indian woman hunched over and running in big skirts.

Strange illnesses were more important than warfare in reducing the population of many tribes in the course of western settlement. The Pequots suffered tremendous population decline in the 1600s, enabling the colonists to defeat them. The Mandans nearly became extinct from smallpox in the 1830s, and on the Pacific Coast during the winters of 1828–1830 an influenza resembling the Asian flu reduced the Chinooks from an estimated 50,000 souls to less than 5,000. On balance it appears that the total Indian population remained rather constant throughout the period of greatest white expansion, so that there was no clear indication whether the Indian population was expanding or declining. If some tribes nearly disappeared or had to merge with larger neighboring tribes to protect themselves, other tribes experienced increases, so that the Indian population continued to reproduce itself.

Estimating the Indian population has always been controversial because people on each side of the question see in population statistics evidence to support their view of other issues that such figures might not otherwise suggest. Conservative historians, particularly those seeking to deny white depredations against Indians, prefer very low historical population figures so they can argue that some of the reported incidents of brutality committed by whites were not as serious as the records indicate. These same people no doubt spend their time disputing the body count of the My Lai massacre. Liberal historians and scholars, in contrast, may inflate the population estimates because a larger aboriginal population makes the brutal products of manifest destiny assume dreadful proportions.

Scholarly debate over the aboriginal population has been with us for some time. In 1928 James Mooney, in a monograph entitled "The Aboriginal Population of America North of Mexico," estimated the total pre-Columbian Indian population north of Mexico to have been 1,152,950. Mooney was followed in 1939 by A. L. Kroeber, the anthropologist who kept Ishi in his museum. As Ishi did not propagate, Kroeber must have felt that Mooney's figures were too high, because he reduced them by nearly 10 percent to 1,025,950. Angel Rosenblatt, a Latin American scholar whose interest in the Indian population of pre-Columbian times seems to have been to discredit the accounts of Spanish depredations against the Indians cited by Bartolomé de Las Casas, joined the discussion in 1945. He reduced the estimate of the pre-Columbian population to an even million north of Mexico and held to this figure until 1967, when he raised it slightly. These low estimates generally reflect the conservative inclinations of these individuals.

Estimates made by scholars on the opposite side of the controversy show the same tendency. Henry Dobyns's 1966 article in *Current Anthropology* entitled "Estimating Aboriginal American Population: An Appraisal of Techniques with a New Hemispheric Estimate" suggested a population of 90,043,000, with a projected high of 112,553,750. To get his estimate, Dobyns used the lowest official federal returns, 490,000 in North America in 1930, and multiplied by an assumed depopulation ratio of 25 to 1 for his high estimate and 20 to 1 for his more modest figure. Other scholars also appeared to prefer the higher figures, although each offered his own version of how the higher estimate should be determined. Harold Driver believed the 1890 census would be a more appropriate base because the Indian population reported was 250,000. Thus using 1890 instead of 1930 would reduce the larger figure by nearly 50 percent, bringing the estimate to 45 million to 50 million, a more comforting figure as genocide cannot be properly conceived when it entails such monstrous dimensions.

Dobyns' estimate of between 9,800,000 and 12,250,00 Indians north of Mexico was cited approvingly by Wilbur Jacobs in an article in the *William and Mary Quarterly* in 1974. Jacobs prudently did not offer a firm figure of his own. He did point out the implications of population estimates:

> *Even if there is a general consensus that reduces the figure
> from one hundred million to fifty million—and some qualified
> investigators concede that we could hardly settle for less than
> that number—we must now accept the fact that the dismal
> story of Indian depopulation after 1492 is a demographic
> disaster with no known parallel in world history. We must
> also acknowledge that the catalyst of all this was undoubtedly
> the European invasion of the New World.*[1]

The estimate of the aboriginal population of the New World not only
has important consequences for American history, it may also force
us to draw some very unpleasant parallels with contemporary events
in Central and South America.

The real problem we have with all estimates of the Indian population, today or in the past, is that they are never made in the same
way. Sometimes we get accurate counts of tribes, other times we get
mere projections, and at still other times we are given estimates based
on what a local observer believes has happened since the last census.
We should be skeptical of statistics gathered by the federal government,
because other considerations are always present. In former years Indian agents were pleased at their progress in civilizing the Indians
over whom they had charge, and annual census taking reflected the
most optimistic descriptions of the work performed by them. The
figures at best represent those Indians with whom the agent had been
working and not the actual number of Indians resident on the reservation. Many times Indians themselves inflated their population count in
order to increase the amount of rations or annuities the tribe would
receive. As the government usually cheated them anyway, the higher
figures probably represented an even trade-off.

The first official estimate of the Indian population we have is a
report by General Henry Knox, secretary of war, submitted to George
Washington on June 15, 1789.[2] Knox estimated the number of Indians
in the United States at 76,000; how he got this figure is unknown.
Apparently the military-industrial complex of that day did not require
large numbers of hostile Indians to justify its annual appropriation
request to Congress. In 1819 the Reverend Jedidiah Morse was commissioned by the secretary of war, John C. Calhoun, to make a complete report on the Indians of the United States. Morse reported as
follows:

Indians in:

New England	2,247
New York	5,184
Ohio	2,407
Michigan & Northwestern Territories	28,380
Illinois & Indiana	17,006
Southern States east of the Mississippi	65,022
West of the Mississippi & north of the Missouri	33,150
Between the Missouri & Red rivers	101,070
West of the Rocky Mountains	171,200
Between the Red River and Rio del Norte	45,370
Total	**471,036**[3]

But Morse's figures were not obtained by a consistent method of estimating. He noted that the population of the Cherokees was 12,935 "by actual enumeration of the Agent in 1809" but also reported that "the pure Seminole Indians, Capt. Bell verbally stated to me are about twelve hundred in number."[4] Morse did the best he could, but he does not say whether the Cherokees were as "pure" as the Seminoles at the time he talked with Captain Bell.

Thomas L. McKenney, head of the Indian Office in the War Department, reported his estimate of Indians to the secretary of war in a report dated January 10, 1825. McKenney did not include an estimate of Indians living in the Missouri valley or the West, which omits a goodly number of Indians. McKenney's figure for the reduced area was 129,366, which compares reasonably well with Morse's estimates of 120,246 covering the same area. Four years later, Secretary of War P. B. Porter estimated the Indian population in 1829 as follows:

New England States and Virginia	2,573
New York	4,820
Pennsylvania	300
North Carolina	3,103
South Carolina	300
Georgia	5,000
Tennessee, Ohio, Mississippi, Louisiana, Illinois, & Missouri	61,997

Peninsula of Michigan	9,340
Arkansas	7,200
Florida	4,000
Country east of Mississippi, north of Illinois west of three upper lakes	20,000
West of Mississippi, east of Rocky Mountains not including Louisiana, Missouri, and Arkansas	94,300
Within Rocky Mountains	20,000
West of Rocky Mountains	80,000
Total	312,933[5]

Porter's estimates showed a large increase in the total Indian population in the United States but suggested a decided decrease in the number of Indians believed to live west of the Rocky Mountains. The estimate for Georgia, which according to other contemporary accounts was infested with Cherokees needing to be expelled from the state, is exceedingly low.

Five years later, in 1834, Lewis Cass, then secretary of war, divided the tribes according to whether or not they had treaties with the United States and estimated 156,310 treaty Indians and 156,300 nontreaty Indians for a national total of 312,610. Two years after Cass's report, when the question of the swift removal of the Indians had become a pressing national issue, C. A. Harris, the superintendent of Indian affairs, reported to the secretary of war the following estimate:

Indians east of the Mississippi	49,365
Indians who have been removed	45,433
West of the Mississippi	150,341
Total	245,139[6]

Just a year later, Henry Schoolcraft, in his *History of Indian Tribes*, gave this estimate for 1837:

Indians east of the Mississippi	49,365
Emigrants (removed Indians)	51,327
Indigenous tribes west of the Mississippi	201,806
Total	302,498[7]

Under the act of March 3, 1847, Congress sought to provide a better organization of the Office of Indian Affairs, and in section 5 it gave authority to the Indian Office to spend $5,000 to gather useful statistics on Indians, assuming that an accurate count of Indians would be included in this information. The census of 1850 listed the number of Indians at 400,764, but it cautioned that the figures for Indians in California, Texas, Oregon, Washington, New Mexico, and Utah were simply guesses and stated that no accurate count existed for the Blackfeet, Sioux, Kiowa, Comanche, Pawnee, and other tribes. These omissions covered a large number of Indians who had previously composed the bulk of the western population estimates. Five years later the commissioner of Indian affairs estimated the number of Indians at 324,622, which appeared to be reasonably reliable except that a footnote at the bottom of the commissioner's report informed the reader that the figures were possibly erroneous and that, with the exception of some Indians who had already assimilated into the general society, the Indian population was somewhere between 320,000 and 350,000. Such precision must have been very comforting to Congress.

Another census was taken in 1860, and the next year the Indian Office estimated the Indian population at 249,965, but the figures were adjusted to account for both "civilized" and "wild" Indians, making the total 254,300. The 1870 census adopted a new set of categories, and General F. A. Walker, superintendent of the ninth census, reported the following:

Sustaining tribal relations (enumerated)	96,366
Sustaining tribal relations (estimated)	26,875
Sustaining tribal relations (nomadic, estimated)	234,740
Out of tribal relations (enumerated)	25,731
Total	383,712[8]

The year 1880 was the last time that estimates of the commissioner of Indian affairs were used. Perhaps stung by the criticism of his former inconsistent estimates and qualifications, the commissioner proclaimed the number of Indians to be 255,938, of which 15,802 represented Indians not under the control of government agents. Thereafter the commissioners' annual reports were careful to cite the previous year's estimates and to explain any discrepancy in figures by noting that certain hostiles had reported in to the agencies or that more accurate methods of counting Indians had been devised.

The great variety of estimates and reports reflects more than the inadequacy of communications and regular record keeping by the federal government during these early years. Most tribes were suspicious of efforts to count their people and tried their best to keep the whites guessing. These figures do suggest that the hysteria over Indians and their danger to the frontier settlements was always greatly exaggerated by federal officials for their own purposes.

Knowing the white population in the territories and having a reasonable means of estimating the Indian population, officials in the Interior and War departments and the governors of the respective territories must have deliberately encouraged the settlers to fear the Indians. It was apparent that the few tribes living in any particular area could not have done much damage to the whites. If the conservative historians studied these old census reports, they might substantially reduce their estimates for the number of warriors present on those occasions when the Indians got the better of the cavalry. Popular novelists and movie producers might well reduce their description of the Indian "hordes" who controlled the West if they reflected on this situation. The census reports would seem to suggest that no more than 200 or 300 Indians were ever available to constitute a horde in most areas of the West in those days.

Beginning with the census of 1890, the year many people regard as marking the end of the real frontier, estimating the number of Indians in the United States became the responsibility of the Bureau of the Census. Unfortunately, the Census Bureau had learned nothing in the intervening years and relied heavily on the Bureau of Indian Affairs (BIA) for gathering its on-reservation statistics. Its method of counting Indians who had left the reservations was simply a matter of visual identification by the census taker. Listed below are the official Indian population figures from 1890 to the present. The numbers are instructive if they represent the growth of the Indian population in this country culminating in today's reported Indian population.

1890	248,253
1900	237,196
1910	276,927
1920	244,437
1930	343,352
1940	345,252

1950	357,499
1960	523,591
1970	792,730
1980	1,418,195
1990	1,959,234
1994	(census estimate) 2,200,000 [9]

The Indian population remained fairly stable until 1960, when the Bureau of the Census allowed self-identification as a means of determining racial ancestry. Self-identification has been used ever since. It was beneficial to have been a recognized Indian during the 1960s when the reservations were receiving money from the poverty programs and one might have expected a great gain, and the figures rose about 50 percent. This increase probably indicates that the 1950 and 1960 census reports had again substantially underestimated the number of reservation Indians. Some of the 1960–1970 increase was no doubt due to a renewed pride in being Indian that Alcatraz inspired, encouraging many mixed bloods to identify with the Indian side of their family tree.

In 1980, 1,418,195 Indians were reported. The Census Bureau later reduced this figure to 1,361,869 Indians, losing some 50,000 Indians in one press release. The 1980 figures present a startling 72 percent increase in the Indian population. The 1990 figures show a 43 percent increase. Although most Indians have a healthy interest in reproduction, these increases cannot possibly be caused by that means alone. A number of factors, taken together, can partially explain this dramatic increase in the Indian population. As this situation will probably never recur, we should try to identify those factors that produced identity changes and helped to create these large numbers.

The census reports for 1960, 1970, 1980, and 1990 all show a marked increase in the number of Indians in the eastern states, particularly in New England. This phenomenon needs further comment. During these decades a number of western Indians moved east for jobs or to get an education and certainly contributed to the increased number of Indians in this region. But these years have also seen the reemergence of the indigenous Indian population of the area. Indians always knew that there were surviving Indian communities in the East, but federal officials had a difficult time accepting the fact that eastern Indians had not vanished or been removed during the 1830s. Stumped when they encountered obviously Indian groups in the East, BIA officials tended to describe them as a small band descended from the Cherokees.

A few of these groups emerged during the Great Depression when Commissioner John Collier authorized employees in the Bureau of Indian Affairs to search out the Indians in the eastern United States and bring them under bureau supervision and protection. The Narragansetts of Rhode Island, for example, were allowed to vote to accept the Indian Reorganization Act; the Chitimacha of Louisiana received formal recognition from the federal government. The Eastern Cherokees of North Carolina and the Mississippi Choctaws were also brought under the BIA when they adopted the Indian Reorganization Act. The tribes with a formally recognized federal status, however, must have been part of the federal census count of Indians beginning in 1940.

The BIA developed a sophisticated way of establishing the Indian identity of these groups. When they visited Pembroke, North Carolina, during the 1930s to identify the ancestry of the Lumbee Indians who lived in that vicinity, BIA anthropologists used a foolproof method of verifying Indian ancestry. Using a study of the Blackfeet Indians that gave the average measurement of their heads, the BIA anthropologists, after much work measuring Lumbee craniums, announced that twenty-two Lumbees qualified as Indians because their measurements perfectly correlated with the average Blackfeet skull. Recognizing these people could not possibly be Blackfeet, the BIA pronounced them to be lost "Tuscaroras," and they were formally recognized as Indians. The possible ancestry of the remainder of the Lumbees, including siblings of the people identified as Indians, remained in doubt. Fortunately, the Blackfeet did not have to satisfy the same morphological criteria.

There is no question that much of the increase of the Indian population in the New England states is a result of Indians now feeling free to identify as Indians. The sudden and dramatic increase in the Indian population in Vermont, Maine, New Hampshire, and Connecticut only redresses a situation in which people found it difficult, if not impossible, to claim their Indian heritage.

Indian educational programs have significantly contributed to the increase in the Indian population, In 1972 the Indian Education Act was passed by Congress. Title IV of the act authorized grants to local educational agencies to operate a broad range of programs designed to improve educational services to any child "who is an enrolled member of a tribe, band, or other organized group of Indians, or *who is a descendant of any such member.*" Schools could identify their Indian students themselves, so the results were predictable. From out of nowhere school districts that had not seen an Indian in a century were able to locate hundreds of Indian students. They were almost literally worth their weight in gold, and as programs became established more and more Indians were uncovered. Undoubtedly, the new census figures reflect a considerable crossover of people from white to Indian as a result of this statute. Whether or not these people will remain Indians now that federal funding has precipitiously declined is another matter. Conceivably, we will see a dramatic decrease in the 2000 census, which would show that the benefits of Indian heritage have run their course.

A number of whites have simply announced themselves to be Indians and proceeded to behave the way they thought Indians did. A personal anecdote will help explain how this kind of personal transformation can occur. I once taught an evening class for the American Indian Studies Center at University of California at Los Angeles. At the beginning of the semester a nice little white lady shyly stopped me and asked if she could come to class and listen to the lectures. I agreed. For a few weeks she sat quietly, occasionally raising her hand at the end of the class period to inquire about books to read. One day in mid-October she arrived for class wearing a headband and sat prominently in the front row, intensely taking everything in. A transformation was occurring before my eyes.

The week that the Indian activists occupied the BIA building in Washington, D.C., she arrived in class dressed in a fancy buckskin costume, heavily laden with Indian jewelry and beads. Class had barely started when she jumped to her feet, greatly agitated, and read me the riot act for proceeding with the lesson when "our people" were facing certain death from the capitol police who had them besieged at the BIA. Before I could respond, she had taken over the class and spent the period reciting the various wrongs committed by the white man against her people the Cherokees, including some incidents that must have been taken from old movies. Class ended with the little white lady accusing the Indians in the class of being "Uncle Tomahawks" for not being in Washington.

This kind of conversion experience is a familiar story to most Indians. Many an Indian leader can remember occasions when they were so eloquent or inspirational that they converted whites in the audience into Indians as they spoke. No one deserves more credit for this kind of increase in the Indian population than the leaders of the American Indian Movement (AIM)—Russell Means, Dennis Banks, and Vernon Bellecourte. During the occupation of the Bureau of Indian Affairs in 1972, they even welcomed a number of federal undercover agents as Indians on the theory that if a person was willing to march to Washington to protest, he must be an Indian.

At one time an FBI undercover agent volunteered to operate a national switchboard in New York City for AIM, suggesting they call in and tell him where they would be protesting, so he could pass the word and ensure a big crowd. This generous hospitality backfired when Means and Banks were indicted and tried for their activities at Wounded Knee. AIM's security chief, the man who watched the door to prevent government spies from entering the defense quarters, Douglas Durham, was himself an FBI undercover agent. Not all the new Indians in the 1990 census returns are federal agents, but as the last three decades have generally been years of unusually paranoid Republican administrations, it is possible that some of the new Indians in the last census are federal agents or informers maintaining their covers.

A final important factor may help to account for the inflated figures in the 1980 census. In 1946 the Indian Claims Commission was established and tribes were allowed to sue the United States for past unconscionable dealings. Some six hundred claims were filed, more than half of which were successful, Congress determined which Indians would be included in the distribution of the moneys, and occasionally there was confusion over which descendants of the original tribe were eligible. In general, judgment funds were distributed fairly and lists of eligible people were prepared with great care. Often the tribal government or the BIA had to advertise through newspapers and radio programs to find missing tribal members. So people who would not otherwise have thought they had Indian blood suddenly became concerned about their roots. Claims judgment funds were usually distributed to the descendants of people who composed the tribe at the time of a particular land cession. So their descendants, whether they saw themselves as Indians or not, were eligible for the funds. Some of these people no doubt listed themselves as Indians in the last several censuses for fear they would be asked to return the funds they had received.

When we speak of Indians today, it is important that we know what information we really want. Indian demographics, indeed the Indian community itself, is a composite of many factors. If we ask how many people racially resemble Indians, we might have less than half a million people. If we seek a cultural identification, the people who really follow tribal traditions, we might be looking at several hundred thousand less. If we counted people who have political relationships with an Indian tribe, we would again substantially increase the number of American Indians. If we dare to ask about socioemotional identification as Indians, then the figure becomes almost astronomical.

Considerable debate exists among Indians concerning which definition is proper. Reservation people prefer to use the most restrictive definition because they realize that if fewer people claim to be Indian, the larger will be the possible benefits and services for reservation residents. Reservation Indians do bear the major brunt of racial discrimination and social ostracism, and so they should reap the lion's share of the benefits. People with only a minimal claim to Indian blood should not be eligible for programs designed to assist reservation residents because the latter need everything they can get.

The other side of the coin has its good arguments also. A greatly inflated population figure means that Indians are given serious consideration at all levels of government. The reservation population in California, for example, is minuscule in relation to the general population of the state and even small in comparison with the state's total Indian population. Restricting the Indian population in California to those people living on the reservation would eliminate any semblance of political strength in the Indian community. Consequently, Indians have an advantage in claiming the large numbers they do in that particular state. And there are an awful lot of real Indians in California.

The people who make up the social and emotional constituency of the Indian community are all too often whites who find a great psychological satisfaction in claiming Indian blood, but they are a distinct handicap for Indians. They often popularize Indian culture so that it becomes the common property of everyone instead of the living customs of a particular group of people. When tribal customs become widespread among non-Indians or even mixed bloods remotely related to the tribal community itself, they are really a part of the larger society and no longer play an integral role in the Indian milieu. If this trend continues, eventually non-Indians will define Indian identity and then no political or blood tie can rescue the tribe from extinction.

The federal census is probably an acceptable way to count Indians today because it does represent a nationally applicable methodology. Creating a composite figure of the enrolled members of federally recognized tribes might be another way to compile reasonably accurate official figures defined solely by political status. But this method would exclude the eastern Indians who have not kept tribal rolls, thus continuing the discrimination they have already suffered at the hands of the federal government. The 2000 census will be eagerly anticipated. The popularity of being Indian should have declined with the reduction of federal Indian budgets, and this count should reflect a more accurate expression of the national Indian community and its various constituent groups than any previous census.

The next census should make every effort to obtain information on reservation Indians, on their health, housing, education, employment, and cause of death. What appears to be happening in the last two census periods is that as the total number of Indians increases, thanks to remotely related people claiming an Indian heritage, the number of people completely within the tribal community—the reservation full-bloods in particular—is declining precipitously. Hence the Indian genetic pool, which was stabilized a century ago with the establishment of the reservations, is evaporating. Unless we are able to find out what is happening to the racially/culturally full-blood Indian, and take steps to improve his or her lot, we may find ourselves with millions of people, all alleging to be Indian, who are indistinguishable from other Americans. Then, of course, everyone will be an Indian—and there will be no more Indians.

NOTES

1. Wilbur R. Jacobs, "The Tip of the Iceburg: Pre-Columbian Indian Demography and Some Implications for Revisionism," *William and Mary Quarterly*, vol. 31, Issue 1 (Jan., 1974), p. 128.

2. Report on Indians Taxed and Not Taxed in the United States (Except Alaska) at the Eleventh Census (Washington, D.C.: Government Publications Office, 1894), p. 4.

3. Ibid., p. 5.

4. Jedidiah Morse, *A Report to the Secretary of War of the United States Comprising a Narrative of a Tour* (New Haven, Conn.: Dais & Force, 1822), p. 309.

5. Reproduced in Henry R. Schoolcraft, *Information Respecting the History, Conditions, and Prospects of the Indian Tribes of the United States*, vol. 3 (Philadelphia: Lippincott, Grambo, and Company, 1853), p. 597.

6. Annual Report of Superintendent of Indian Affairs, Public Documents of the Senate of the United States, December 5, 1836, vol. I (Washington, D.C.: Gales and Seaton, 1837), p. 420.

7. Schoolcraft, *Information Respecting the History, Conditions, and Prospects of the Indian Tribes of the United States*, p. 611.

8. Report on Indians Taxed and Not Taxed, p. 21.

9. Press Release, Bureau of the Census, January 20, 1994.

▼ Part V ▼

RELIGION

23

THE RELIGIOUS CHALLENGE

▼▼▼▼

Indian activists holding religious ceremonies in the Bureau of Indian Affairs (BIA) building concluding their stay by looting the building seems incongruous and ridiculous, unless we probe deeper into the nature of the relationship between Indians and whites. Indian activists accused of fomenting the destruction made a rather weak reply. What about the rape of the North American continent, the destruction of tribal cultures, the wasteful use of human beings, the deprivation of rights to a helpless minority? Do not these crimes make the destruction of a building pale in significance, they asked.

Do they?

In one sense the capture and destruction of the BIA headquarters was a historical anachronism. Watts burned in 1965; the urban areas seethed and burned following the death of Martin Luther King, Jr., in 1968. Was not the Indian occupation of a federal building in the nation's capital an event dreadfully out of time? Was not the sacking of the BIA headquarters and the occupation of Wounded Knee the final spasm of the rugged 1960s when any type of change was considered beneficial and the institutions of society were considered not only obsolete but also malignant? Perhaps it was the last hurrah of an era when people could thumb their noses at established authority without fear of painful reprisal. But the Indian incidents must also be seen within the context of the Indian experience in this nation's history, and in that context the Indian movement raised an entirely different kind of question—that of religion rather than the equal enforcement of the law.

There certainly was an aspect in which the Indian protests were events of the 1960s, although occurring in 1972 and 1973. Since 1968 the major Christian denominations had been pouring funds into social movements of all kinds. They believed deeply in the militant interpretation of black power as continuous confrontations, and grants were made to organizations within the respective minority groups that they were sure would produce the desired protests. A group that snapped and snarled about its social problems stood a much better chance of receiving funds from the churches than did a group that calmly and carefully articulated a problem that they hoped to solve.

Church officials often gauged their relevancy in proportion to the violence of the groups they were funding. Any church not receiving its share of frothing-at-the-mouth demands for money felt isolated from the great events of the American social movement. Thus it was that when the American Indian Movement (AIM) captured a dormitory at Augustana College in Sioux Falls and presented a set of demands carefully worked out by sympathetic Lutherans in secret sessions, the Lutheran churches eagerly embraced the Indian cause. While they had not been overly enthusiastic about helping the blacks during the civil rights movement, some church officials felt that they could get the same kind of action from the Indians without taking a position on a social movement that would antagonize their church members.

Many Lutherans were ecstatic when informed by Indians that they were guilty of America's sins against the Indians, and they embarked on a massive program of fund-raising to pay for their alleged sins. But they were not the only victims. Because the Presbyterians, Episcopalians, and Congregationalists all gleefully responded to the accusation that they had been responsible for nearly all of the problems of American Indians, they also decided that they could purchase indulgences for these sins by funding the Indian activists to do whatever they felt necessary to correct the situation. By early 1971 almost every major Christian church had set up crisis funds to buy off whichever Indian protesters they might arrange to have visit them. Confrontations escalated as each group sought to become more relevant than its competitors, and the path toward destruction was clearly visible to everyone. In a real sense Christian churches bought and paid for the Indian movement and its climactic destruction of the BIA headquarters as surely as if they had written out specific orders to sack the BIA on a contractual basis.

Not every Indian protest, however, was inspired by the financial rewards to be gained from the churches by playing the protest game. Many of the incidents were valid protests by a people who had suffered too much for too long. Even more, younger Indians had seen in the civil rights movement that the institutions of this country respond only when there is a threat to their property, or when disorder in their lives forces them to confront problems that have not been solved for generations. Yet the civil rights issue was peripheral at best when understood in the Indian context. The different tribal groups suffered discrimination and prejudice generally, but more specifically the broken treaties meant immediate hardship for the different communities. Could young Indians enter a civil rights movement and press for removal of discriminatory hiring practices while enjoying preference under federal law for employment in tribal programs based on treaties and agreements? Major institutional differences really did exist among American racial minorities.

Few Indians ever accepted the premises of the civil rights movement. If the tribal chairmen demanded the prosecution of the Indian militants following the departure from the destroyed BIA building, it was a weak response compared to tribal reactions on being asked to join in the civil rights movement and marches half a decade earlier. That the basic goals of the civil rights movement could not attract more than a handful of Indians at any one time should give pause to everyone. What was it that turned Indians off, other than the fear that they might be identified with blacks as a minority group?

American history gives us a partial answer and allows us to raise certain questions that must be asked. The civil rights movement was probably the last full-scale effort to realize the avowed goals of the Christian religion. For more than a century the American political system had proclaimed the brotherhood of man as seen politically in the concepts of equality of opportunity and justice equally administered under the law. Equality under the law, however, was a secularized and generalized interpretation of the Christian brotherhood of man—the universal appeal of individuals standing equally before God now seen as people standing equally before the law and secular institutions. While the National Association for the Advancement of Colored People (NAACP) Legal Defense and Education Fund fought a series of brilliant court battles leading up to the great Supreme Court decisions, in the background certainly lurked the great Christian message of the brotherhood of man. A majority of Americans rejected this secular version of brotherhood and sought to prevent its realization because of long-standing attitudes that people of color were necessarily inferior.

When the struggle in the South reached the point of open boycotts and nonviolent protests, it was the black Christian church leaders such as Martin Luther King, Jr., Ralph Abernathy, and Andrew Young who spearheaded the movement by translating Christian doctrines into political tools of resistance and eventually conquest. In large measure, the civil rights movement was a movement that found its ideology, strategy, and meaning in Christian religious doctrines. King's famous letter from jail in Birmingham was not addressed to the political leaders of the South or to liberals of the North but to the Christian church leaders of the South, who were intent on reducing the Christian religion to a comforting and spineless recital of creeds.

There had to be a point in Western history at which the avowed beliefs of the Christian religion were placed on the agenda to discover if they could become a reality. Could Western Christianity practice the tenets that all people are created equal and that "thou shalt not kill"? The civil rights movement became the acid test in the field of domestic relations. Before the civil rights movement, however, one must look at the Nuremberg trials as the moment of history in which Western Christianity achieved its greatest influence. In those trials the victorious Allied nations presumed to speak for all of civilization and judged the Nazi leaders not as losers but as those who had violated the basic tenets of civilized and religious existence. In setting themselves up as judges, the Western nations had first to overlook the atrocities of their Russian allies and second to affirm before all societies that they themselves stood sinless before all and before history and were fit to judge.

After the Nuremberg trials it became more or less inevitable that the Western nations would fall victim to the moral and intellectual weaknesses in their own societies. Could one really judge Nazi leaders when in one's own nation captured German prisoners of war received better treatment than the black soldiers who had captured them? No, the civil rights movement was inevitable once the Nuremberg trials had taken place. The logic of national identity called for an effort to realize the reality of the Christian religion on a political basis. America had no choice but to embark eventually on a quest for post-Nuremberg meaning. That the civil rights movement began under the benign Eisenhower administration was an indication of the terrible conflicts in which America and its religious sensitivity would engage. If nothing else, Eisenhower personified the good citizen, the American Christian gentleman, the man to whom all good accrues because of his faithful adherence to the American credo. That Dwight D. Eisenhower was compelled by the logic of the law to order federal troops to Little Rock, Arkansas, over the protests of members of his party and the South to enforce a Supreme Court decree seems ironic yet appropriate for the unveiling of the American religious question and its resolution.

It was this terrible inconsistency that many Indians sensed as they approached the civil rights movement. In attempting to distinguish Indian issues from the concerns felt by the black community and understood by their white allies, many Indians began to discover their own culture. They began to trace out the reality of their own religious experiences and to distinguish between the technological superiority of the white man and his moral corruption and the falsity of his religious facade. It was during the Eisenhower years that some of the religious ceremonies of the tribes were first openly performed after many decades of suppression.

Through the 1960s the civil rights movement gained power and strength, calling millions of people to commitments that many had never considered making. One cannot but review the many martyrs of the civil rights movement, black and white, to understand the violence of the time and many religious people's depth of commitment. From the era came writers such as Malcolm Boyd and Harvey Cox, who in retrospect appear as valiant pioneers discerning a break in the ecclesiastical curtain, yet committed and powerless to break out of the deteriorating situation. Their books show a desperate effort to leapfrog American domestic theology and make it speak to the times that were unfolding. *The Secular City*, for example, tries to impress on the mainstream religious community the fact that secularization has all but overtaken them in a tidal wave of change.

Perhaps the civil rights movement held too much promise of a better society. The fervor it inspired in people could not be maintained in the face of exhausting sacrifices for a few intangible accomplishments. Within it was the implicit promise that a better society was but a short distance into the future, and the reality of that society became a means of sustaining the broken heads and broken spirits of the movement. For many young people not in the social movements, the goal of discovering a reality to existence took a different track. The middle 1960s also saw in the rise of the drug culture an immediate release from the complexities of modern life. Timothy Leary's admonition to "drop out, turn on, and tune in" spoke of the same stability of reality in the religious field as did King's dream of a just society, but it was predicated on the idea of individual isolation and a refusal to accept citizenship responsibilities. As the two movements began to intertwine, the formation of a "counterculture" was suggested as a means of explaining the apparent alienation between the two general modes of American existence.

King spoke out against Vietnam. Suddenly a new international dimension impinged on the consciousness of America. True to his Christian ideals, King saw the pervading nature of racism and oppression that led directly from the Christian idea of history. That we were in Southeast Asia at all derived directly from our conception of ourselves as guardians of history against all movements that would upset the balance we had achieved by military and economic power alone. King saw that there could be no solution to domestic problems without a solution to international problems. And solving international problems meant giving up the Western interpretation of history and the role of Western nations in history.

Stokely Carmichael burst on the scene with his cry "Black Power," and the question of community integrity dominated conceptions of measuring social change. No longer was it possible to pass civil rights laws. Now the political and economic stranglehold over local communities had to be surrendered. The idea of forming a unified and homogeneous nation vanished as blacks demanded the right to dissent culturally, and other groups, as if waiting for a signal, charged into the breach in the ideology of integration. Christianity had been built on the individual response to external events, as verified by internal feelings of righteousness and satisfaction. A universal brotherhood of responsible citizens had been conceived in which, with every person acting responsibly in the civil realm, no rupture of the social fabric would occur. Now it was all gone. In its place stood the racial and ethnic communities, demanding the right to national existence in a melting-pot society where there was to be neither Jew nor Gentile.

Finally the ecologists arrived with predictions so chilling as to frighten the strongest heart. At the present rate of deterioration, they told us, mankind could expect only a generation before the species would be finally extinguished. How had this situation come about? Some ecologists told us that it was the old Christian idea of nature: the rejection of creation as a living ecosystem and the concept of nature as depraved, an object for exploitation and nothing more. Almost immediately young whites who were attracted by ecology were accused of copping out on the civil rights movement. A diversion, black activists cried, a means of taking the pressure off the corrupt governmental structures that refuse to give us our rights.

What happened in the 1960s and 1970s is that, in all probability, the logic of Western culture and the meaning of the Christian worldview that supported the institutions of Western culture were outrun by the events of the time. The brotherhood of man may be a noble ideal, but can it be achieved in any society that is not homogeneous? Probably not, we discovered. At a certain point in the struggle for realization, it became apparent that the goals of the civil rights movement could not be achieved because people did not subscribe to them and because the goals were, after all, abstract projections of an ideal world, not descriptions of a real world.

The collapse of the civil rights movement, the concern with Vietnam and the war, the escape to drugs, the rise of power movements, and the return to Mother Earth can all be understood as desperate efforts of groups of people to flee abstract articulations of belief and superficial values and find authenticity wherever it could be found. It was at this point that Indians became popular and the widespread and intense interest in Indians, as seen in the fantasy literature and anthologies, seemed to indicate that Americans wanted more from Indians than they did from other minority groups. For many people, the stoic, heroic, and noble Indian who had lived an idyllic existence prior to contact with whites seemed to hold the key to survival and promised to provide new meanings for American life.

Although Americans who held this view were fooling themselves, they knew what they wanted. Indians who saw this interest doubly fooled themselves because they came to believe that the people were interested in them and not in the intangible experiences they were thought to represent. Thus during the early 1970s and until the mid-1980s at every meeting and convention Indian spokespersons were proudly announcing that the ensuing calendar year would truly be "The Year of the Indian." Ecological advertisements featured Indians paddling or walking across polluted streams and fields with tears running down their faces. Indians were ecstatic—and badly mistaken. People began to inquire about the basic values of Indian life and articulated their version of it to the very Indians they were quizzing. About all the Indians could do was agree and try their best to make corrections that would not insult their white friends or erode their apparent beliefs in things Indian.

The events of summer 1971 should have had much more impact on Indians than they did. Finding a nationwide propensity of whites who wished to dig up Indian graves should have frightened most Indians. Many years before, William Carlos Williams wrote: "The land! Don't you feel it? Doesn't it make you want to go out and lift dead Indians tenderly from their graves, to steal from them—as if it must be clinging even to their corpses—some authenticity."[1] And, of course, on an unconscious level that was precisely what whites did in 1971. That Christian peoples, or even quasi-Christian peoples, could commit such outrages is a measure of their spiritual desperation and unconscious yearning for a feeling of authenticity and emotional stability. But even if these gravediggers posing as amateur archaeologists were not Christian, how could the "true" Christians not have seen the danger in embracing a foreign creed and raised their voices in protest of these acts?

By 1978 the interest in traditional religions was so intense that many experienced older Indians characterized the former activists as the Indian version of "Jesus freaks." Indeed, the late 1970s saw many Americans, Indian and non-Indian, blindly accept various kinds of religious doctrines without the slightest bit of critical appraisal. It was during those confusing days, we must remember, that the Jonestown tragedy took place. Many Indians who had formerly been Christians of one persuasion or another used the Western format as a means of expressing their devotion, and some former AIM members, flying in to Rapid City so they could take part in the Pine Ridge Sun Dance, compared the Sun Dance to taking Communion in the

Christian denomination, a parallel that had absolutely no validity whatsoever.

In the 1980 presidential elections the Western religious fundamentalist right flexed its muscle and elected Ronald Reagan, who stumbled through a confession that, yes indeed, he believed he had had a conversion experience and therefore deserved their votes. While the Indian correlate to the surging religious right was to be found in various Indian communities, it did not have the grim, unrelenting intolerance that characterized the white fundamentalist movement. Instead young Indians began to specialize in ways highly reminiscent of people in the old days who achieved, through visions or hard work, expertise in various badly needed community skills. Only at the fringes of Indian society, where zealous non-Indians sought to participate, was there any friction. Otherwise, the elders were greatly heartened to see the next generation adopting traditional values and customs so readily.

In ideological terms this contrast between Indian and non-Indian religious revival presents a fascinating picture. American whites are victims of a process long predicted. Friedrich Nietzsche and Søren Kierkegaard, European philosophers of the nineteenth century, both foresaw that a tragic breakdown in both vision and values was occurring in the psyche of Westerners. For Kierkegaard, the solution to the problem became the exercise of an incredible power of will that he thought would lead Western peoples back to the fundamental realities as he saw them. Advocating that the individual must have "purity of heart," a solitary and well-disciplined march toward an identifiable goal, Kierkegaard believed that goodness would naturally follow the good if one so willed it.

Nietzsche announced the death of God long before the Anglican bishop John Robinson. Nietzsche's alternative was the creation of the superman, the will to power in this instance being the complete development of human powers and all talents possible. While Nietzsche saw this thrust as an individual decision, the language and temper of his ideas could easily be found in the ecstatic and demonic rantings of Adolf Hitler and National Socialism that simply insisted that the German people were supermen. Unfortunately, these philosophies of will always seem to affect the ordinary citizens by vesting them with an extraordinarily destructive idea of racial superiority.

Both Kierkegaard and Nietzsche attempted to solve the problem of decay inherent with the passage of time within the Western vision of the world by using the Avis approach: try harder by doing the same things that are now outmoded but still seem reasonable. A more commonsense approach to bolstering Western fortunes and moral failures came in the early years of this century when Walter Rauschenbusch (1861–1918) and others promulgated the theology of the social gospel. They visualized the fulfillment of the Christian kingdom on earth in the social reform movements of the muckraker era of American politics. Labor organization, restrictive child labor laws, pure food laws, unemployment compensation, and greatly enhanced educational opportunities became for them the realization of the Western peoples' potential for creating a heavenly society without divine intervention. The New Deal came closer than any other administration in realizing this vision, but the onset of World War II short-circuited its efforts.

When the social gospel was brought into full confrontation with the American political system in the civil rights movement (and there was plenty of social gospel ideology in the War on Poverty), traditional Protestant theology thwarted its realization. While advances were made in civil rights legislation, particularly in the areas of education, employment, voting rights, and housing, most Americans allowed their racial prejudices to overcome their sense of compassion. The first round of retrenchment came with the Richard Nixon/ Spiro Agnew/Billy Graham theology of unquestioning submission to political decisions and the intense concentration of religious energy on achieving a personal relationship with God. This distinction was almost completely erased during Ronald Reagan's terms as president when the values inherent in the personal relationship turned out to be identical to the racist pandering of the Republican party for white voters. George Bush sabotaged constructive social legislation (affirmative action, civil rights commission, etc.), appointed conservative but hardly scholarly Supreme Court Justices, and used subliminal racial themes in his campaigns and speeches. It was no accident that Willie Horton, a black man, became the symbol of the alleged position of Michael Dukakis of being "soft" on crime.

Some non-Indian writers detected a turning point in the mid-1970s. Garry Wills, in two books, *Nixon Agonistes* and *Bare Ruined Choirs*, found sufficient reason to believe that a turn toward secularism within religion itself had taken place. James Michener, usually noted for long, sprawling historical novels about locations, projected a search for a new conception of our position in social history, finding a religious dimension about to be revealed in *A Quality of Life*. Harvey Cox confronted secularism head-on with *The Secular City* and seemed to predict that creature of the Reagan years, the greedy yuppie who had to have it all now. A very naive interpretation of the underlying changes was found in Charles Reich's *The Greening of America*, which conceived of a benign corporate America, transformed by the entrance of movement people into the business world. More to the point, Alvin Toffler's *Future Shock* and Vance Packard's *A Nation of Strangers* forecast the impact on American behavior once computers, the population explosion, dwindling resources, and the change in sexual attitudes really took hold. Toffler and Packard were particularly worried about the increase in the rate of activity on people apart from other predicted developments. Could increasing speed in communications and the flow of information and constant migration include the same religious convictions about the world that people held two centuries ago?

Non-Indian America has fragmented during the past two decades. A small portion of people entered the New Age that has been a smorgasbord of religious experiences derived from any tradition willing to advocate its beliefs and whatever experiences could be packaged for sale to American consumers. Thus astrology, numerology, flying saucers with heavenly "space brothers," past-life regressions, a variety of martial arts techniques, various brands of shamanism, and modern versions of witchcraft fill the empty hours of the affluent fringe groups who reject Christianity but want to have some hold on religious experiences.

An increasing number of Americans have become members of the religious right, the fundamentalists. As mainline churches lose members rapidly through their constant efforts to pander to the unchurched and make themselves relevant, mindless fundamentalism makes amazing strides, even among the educated people in society. When the fundamentalists seized on abortion as an issue, they found the key to political power. Thus was created the irony of modern American life. The fundamentalists could care less about human life after birth. They unquestioningly accept American military ventures around the world and cry for more blood with each

invasion or carpet-bombing of small countries. They steadfastly support the death penalty and see nothing wrong with its one-sided
application to racial minorities. They close their eyes to blatant theft
of American assets by government officials, savings and loan execu-
tives, and bankers, and oppose every social program that is proposed.
Yet on the abortion issue they wax eloquent about the sanctity of
human life as if their salvation depends on it.

Thus through nearly two decades while American Indians were
rediscovering the integrity of their traditional religions, the rest of
American society has torn itself and its religious traditions apart,
substituting patriotism and hedonism for old values and behaviors.
Why was it so easy for American Indians to recapture the essence of
their religious life and so difficult for non-Indians to regain a measure of religious experience and stability? Albert Camus explored
death and suicide in *The Rebel* and gave an incisive analysis of the Western religious problem that bears examining:

> *The profound conflict in this century is perhaps not so much
> between the German ideologies of history and Christian
> political ideologies of history and Christian political concepts,
> which in a certain way are accomplices, as between German
> dreams and Mediterranean traditions . . . in other words
> between history and nature.*
>
> *Christianity, no doubt, was only able to conquer its
> catholicity by assimilating as much as it could of Greek
> thought. But when the Church dissipated its Mediterranean
> heritage, it placed the emphasis on history to the detriment of
> nature, caused the Gothic to triumph over the romance, and
> destroying a limit in itself, has made increasing claims to
> temporal power and historical dynamism. When nature ceases
> to be an object of contemplation and admiration, it can be
> nothing more than material for an action that aims at trans-
> forming it. These tendencies—and not the real strength of
> mediation, which would have comprised the real strength of
> Christianity—are triumphing, in modern times, to the detriment
> of Christianity itself, by an inevitable turn of events.*[2]

If, as Camus would define it, the choice for this century was between history and nature, somehow we made a very bad bargain

when we chose history because it appears history has come to an end. And we are very close to destroying nature.

The religious issue in American society has been developing for several decades. It is not as simple as the old Protestant-Catholic competition, nor does it reflect the former Christian-Jew diversity. American society now has a bewildering variety of sects and religious traditions. The refugees from the Vietnam War and the intense interest in Asian religions, including the martial arts so well publicized by the movies, have made Asian traditions respectable for the first time in American history. The strong interest in the esoteric traditions, astrology, and so on, has broadened the supermarket of possible religious experiences so that people feel quite at home chanting a hymn to Osiris if the occasion calls for it. The religious situation today eloquently reflects the American psyche—we create our own reality and we are absolutely free to do so. This condition, however, suggests that there is no reality and that we live in a completely intellectual world where the free choice of the individual determines the values and emotional content of experiences. We are at ground zero religiously with little possibility of a revelation to enable us to move on.

Reaching into this plate of religious linguini and making an orderly analysis are not as impossible as we might suppose because Camus has properly identified our real choices—history or nature, time or space. While we would like our personal preferences to be realized, if we have any sanity, we must admit that the world outside our perspective has a bit of substance to it and must certainly be constructed on certain principles through which history and nature are related. It is therefore our task to examine with a great deal of seriousness the possible relationships that these two ideas have and the probable configuration that a new understanding of history and nature and time and space would give us.

For the sake of comparison let me suggest the possible representatives of history and nature that we can find in America today and examine what degree of clarity they display that could help us to see new combinations and understandings about the values and directions we must take in solving our social and psychological problems. History must certainly be represented by the Christian churches, the fundamentalists having been disappointed in the recent Gulf War, which many of them felt forecast Armageddon and consequently supported vigorously. Even the old, tired, mainline churches, Episcopal, Presbyterian, United Church of Christ, and others, still preach in glowing terms about the coming of the Kingdom and the prominent part their respectable members will play in it. Add to this mixture the Republican party that, by appointing second- and third-rate scholars and practitioners to the Supreme Court, believes it is now returning to the "original principles" of the Constitution, and we have pretty much the advocates of the idea that history is all-important and nature is merely an inert mass to be exploited.

Identifying the groups that would naturally fall on the side of nature is more hypothetical. American Indians certainly stand out in this respect as the many quotations in anthologies demonstrate. Animal rights activists would seem to qualify as well, and some of the more militant ecological and conservation organizations. It is difficult to distinguish the conservation groups who really see a value in nature and those who simply want it preserved for the sake of human enjoyment. Regardless of motive or perspective, they are more reliable allies in most causes than are the churches or the political parties. Like the groups that believe in the reality of history, those people who see a value in nature and attempt to tailor their behavior accordingly share a general orientation and are not committed to any specific articulation of the idea, if, indeed, they are able to derive abstract principles from their experiences.

Yet there is a profound difference between American Indians and all of these other groups. The Indian is indigenous and therefore does not have the psychological burden of establishing his or her right to the land in the deep emotional sense of knowing that he or she belongs there. Nearly half a century ago Chief Luther Standing Bear of the Sioux tribe commented on the strange feeling of alienation that the intruder experiences and applied his analysis to American whites as follows:

> *The white man does not understand America. He is too far*
> *removed from its formative processes. The roots of the tree of his*
> *life have not yet grasped the rock and soil. The white man is still*
> *troubled by primitive fears; he still has in his consciousness*
> *the perils of this frontier continent, some of its fastnesses not*
> *yet having yielded to his questioning footsteps and inquiring*
> *eyes. He shudders still with the memory of the loss of his*

forefathers upon its scorching deserts and forbidding
mountaintops. The man from Europe is still a foreigner and an
alien. And he still hates the man who questioned his oath
across the continent.

But in the Indian the spirit of the land is still vested; it
will be until other men are able to divine and meet its rhythm.
Men must be born and reborn to belong. Their bodies must be
formed of the dust of their forefathers' bones.[3]

It is significant that many non-Indians have discerned this need to become indigenous and have taken an active role in protecting the environment.

The patriotism of the American conservative may be said to be an expression of the effort to become indigenous. Certainly many Americans chafe at the idea that only Indians should be called "Native Americans," and they argue, quite properly, that anyone born in the United States is a native American. But their allegiance is to democracy, a powerful idea, but it has no relationship to the earth upon which we walk and the plants and animals that give us sustenance. Developing a sense of ourselves that would properly balance history and nature and space and time is a more difficult task than we would suspect and involves a radical reevaluation of the way we look at the world around us. Do we continue to exploit the earth, or do we preserve it and preserve life? Whether we are prepared to embark on a painful intellectual journey to discover the parameters of reconciling history and nature is the question of this generation.

NOTES

1. Virginia Armstrong, *I Have Spoken* (Chicago: Swallow Hill Press, 1971), p. xviii. It seemed to be a startling prediction of what I had thought was developing for years; combined with the series of grave-robbing incidents it is little short of prophetic.
2. Albert Camus, *The Rebel* (New York: Vintage Books, 1956), p. 299.
3. Luther Standing Bear, *Land of the Spotted Eagle* (Boston: Houghton Mifflin, 1933), p. 248.

24

THE CONCEPT OF HISTORY

▼▼▼▼

One of the major distinctions that can be made between the tribal religions taken as a group and the Christian religion that underlies Western secular thought is the extent to which the two views were dependent on the idea of history. The Western preoccupation with history and a chronological description of reality was not a dominant factor in any tribal conception of either time or history. Indian tribes had little use for recording past events; the idea of keeping a careful chronological record of events never seemed to impress the greater number of tribes of the continent. While the Indians who lived in Central America had extensive calendars, the practice of recording history was not a popular one farther north. "The way I heard it" or "It was a long time ago" usually prefaces any Indian account of a past tribal experience, indicating that the story itself is important, not its precise chronological location. That is not to say that Indian tribes deliberately avoided chronology. In post-Discovery times, some tribes adopted the idea of recording specific sequences of time as a means of remembering the community's immediate past experiences. The best-known method of recording these experiences was the winter count of the Plains Indians. A large animal hide, usually buffalo, would be specially tanned, and each year a figure or symbol illustrating the most memorable event experienced by the community would be painted on the hide. Gradually the hide became filled with representations of the years, and it would be maintained as long as there were people who could remember what the figures and symbols meant.

One could not find a very accurate concept of history in the winter counts. In general, they indicated the psychic life of the community—what was important to that group of people as a group. The chances of a continuous subject matter appearing on a winter count were nil. One year might be remembered as the year that horses came to the people, the next year might be the year when the berries were extremely large, the year after perhaps the tribe might have made peace with an enemy or visited a strange river on its migrations. The chances of a series of political or military events being recorded year after year as in the Western concept of history were so remote as to preclude the origination of history as a subject matter of importance. One recent Sioux winter count, for example, does not mention a number of important treaties, and one does not even mention the battle with Custer.

Other tribes devised methods of recording community experiences similar to the winter counts. The Pimas and Tohono O'odhams of Arizona had calendar sticks on which symbols were carved. By remembering what the symbols represented, a reader could recite a short chronology of recent years. But again the ability of the reader limited the extent to which the history could be recorded.[1] Some Indian accounts involved prodigious memories, and recitations of events could take weeks of ceremonial storytelling. The Delaware in post-Discovery times created a long chronology that had many political references called the Walum Olum. It mentioned the tribes immediately bordering the Delawares and with whom they shared a general political fate. In this sense, the Walum Olum can be said to be more complex than the Sioux and Pima/Tohono O'odham systems. However, the accuracy of Western European recounting and recording events was a distant goal for the most history-conscious of the American Indian tribes.[2]

Lacking a sense of rigid chronology, most tribal religions did not base their validity on any specific incident dividing human time experience into a before and after. No Indian tribal religion was dependent on the belief that a certain thing had happened in the past that required uncritical belief in the occurrence of the event. Creation, gifts of powers and medicines, traumatic events, and the lives of great religious leaders were either events of the distant past and regarded as such or the memories of the tribe were still vivid and occupied a prominent place in the people's perspective and understanding of

their situation. Salvation and religious participation in communal ceremonies did not depend on the historical validity of the event but on
the ceremonies and powers that were given to the people in the event.

Culture heroes were plentiful in the tribes. Deganiwidah founded
the Iroquois League some time in the pre-Discovery days. Iroquois
religion and politics did not revolve around him in the traditional
Western religious sense, but the great law of the Iroquois held the
major position in tribal religious and political life. Sweet Medicine,
the Cheyenne religious figure, was believed to have received his powers in historical times, but the ceremonies he brought were important, not Sweet Medicine himself. The story of the White Buffalo
Calf Woman of the Sioux happened in the distant past. The importance in the story was the reception of the Sacred Pipe, not the woman
herself as a personal object of salvation or adoration.

The tribal religions had one great benefit other religions did not
have and could not have. They had no religious controversy within
their communities because everyone shared a common historical
experience and cultural identity was not separated into religious,
economic, sociological, political, and military spheres. It was never
a case, therefore, of *having* to believe in certain things to sustain a
tribal religion. One simply believed the stories of the elders, and
these stories had significance as defining the people's identity. Today
we can say they have specific themes, but that is our interpretation
and not the way the people originally understood them. No tribe,
however, asserted its history as having primacy over the accounts of
any other tribe. As we have seen, the recitation of stories by different
peoples was regarded as a social event embodying civility. Differing
tribal accounts were given credence because it was not a matter of trying to establish power over others to claim absolute truth. To be sure,
tribes that had fallen under the wide-ranging military power of the various confederacies were reminded who ran things. Under the Iroquois
and Creek alliances, weaker allies had no doubt about who was in charge.
But there was no coercion to convert the smaller tribes to an Iroquois or
Creek conception of past historical events and their efficacy.

In the turbulent period of conflict with the whites, speeches
recorded at treaty sessions, statements made to the president of the
United States to remind him of previous promises, and other statements of historical importance made use of chronological references.
But one cannot say, on the basis of these speeches, that a fascination

with historical reality was developed through contact with whites. Rather the speeches reflect negotiations and arguments over specific proposals made by the U.S. representatives.

Perhaps the best articulation of an Indian theory of history is found in the great speech by Chief Seattle at the signing of the Medicine Creek Treaty in Washington Territory in 1854. Recognizing that the loss of lands and establishment of reservations doomed his people, the Duwamish, Seattle sadly remarked as follows:

> *It matters little where we pass the remnant of our days. They will not be many. A few more moons; a few more winters— and not one of the descendants of the mighty hosts that once moved over this broad land or lived in happy homes, protected by the Great Spirit, will remain to mourn over the graves of a people once more powerful and hopeful than yours. But why should I mourn at the untimely fate of my people? Tribe follows tribe, nation follows nation, like the waves of the sea. It is the order of nature, and regret is useless. Your time of decay may be distant, but it will surely come, for even the White Man whose God walked and talked with him as friend with friend, cannot be exempted from the common destiny. We may be brothers after all. We shall see.*[3]

Seattle's theory of history may be much more a recognition of life's cyclical nature than a statement of historical process. For many tribal religions the distinction would be irrelevant. The recognition of growth and decay as limiting factors in a tribe's or nation's existence is worthy of note; it runs contrary to the Western European conceptions of the Heavenly City and the Thousand-Year Reich.

The idea of world ages, held by some tribes, is comparable in many ways to the world age concepts held by people in India. The flood stories, even the most remote, gave rise to the belief that the world is periodically destroyed by flood, fire, or other natural catastrophes, and this idea was held by a number of tribes with stories of some antiquity. Some substance was given to the belief in periodic destruction by particular stories, and in this sense the people could be said to have had a conception of history. For example, the Sioux explanation was framed in familiar terminology. They held that the world was protected by a huge buffalo that stood at the western gate of the universe and held back the waters that periodically flooded the world. Every year the buffalo lost a hair on one of its legs. Every age it lost a leg. When the buffalo had lost all its legs and was no longer able to hold back the waters, the world was flooded and renewed.

The Hopi had the most comprehensive understanding of world ages, as Frank Waters and White Bear recount in *The Book of the Hopi*. These people believed that they had survived three world destructions and that each world had been marked by peculiar circumstances. Before each destruction they were given special instructions for survival, and as each new world began they received songs and ceremonies designed for living in the new world. Their ceremonial life would end with each world destruction. Other tribes had legends of similar content, although a great many tribes now appear to have had prophecies about the whites that have been so garbled and popularized as to confuse efforts to come to any conclusions as to which stories were quasi-histories and which were real prophecies.

Suffice it to say, even the closest approach to the Western idea of history by an Indian tribe was yet a goodly distance from Western historical conceptions. What appears to have survived as a tribal conception of history almost everywhere was the description of conditions under which the people lived and the location in which they lived. Migrations from one place to another were phrased in terms descriptive of why they moved. Exactly when they moved was, again, "a long time ago." The scholars have had a difficult time piecing together the maps of pre-Discovery America because of the vague nature of tribal remembrances. The Iroquois, for example, relate that they once lived on the plains but then migrated eastward. When is not important to them, but their relative hardship on the plains and eventual prosperity in the East are important.

The result of this casual attitude toward history was, of course, that history had virtually no place in the religious life of the tribe. The appearance of the various folk heroes who brought sacred ceremonies and medicines could often not be located in time at all. Only recent and specific events, such as the Cheyennes' loss of some of their sacred arrows to the Pawnees, were remembered and formed a conjunction of history and religion. But the ceremonies, beliefs, and great religious events of the tribes were distinct from history; they did not depend on history for their verification. If they worked for the community in the present, that was sufficient evidence of their validity.

In theory it is entirely possible to construct a chronological history of a tribe. This task would be accomplished by knowing the sacred places within the tribe's geography and all of the stories that are related to these places. By identifying the *before* and *after* of the stories and then arranging them on a time scale, one could project a chronology. Some exceedingly wise people in some tribes can perform this function reasonably well, and some years ago the White Mountain Apaches began to develop a historical atlas of their lands that had something of this flavor. In effect, *The Book of the Hopi* is a reconstruction of a basic Hopi chronology as defined by the migrations and locations that the people remember.

In contrast, Christianity has always placed a major emphasis on the idea of history. From the very beginning of the religion, it has been the Christian contention that the experiences of humankind could be recorded in a linear fashion, and when this was done, the whole purpose of the creation event became clear, not only explaining the history of human societies but also revealing the nature of the end of the world and the existence of heaven, or a future world, into which the faithful would be welcome. Again, we have a familiar distinction. Time is regarded as all-important by Christians, and it has a casual importance, if any, among the tribal peoples.

The contrast between tribal religions and the Christian religion, therefore, can be made painfully clear with a brief and general sketch of the Christian religion itself. In a real sense, the Christian religion can be said to be dependent on the historical accuracy of the Hebrew religion as found in the sacred books of the Jews. After the death of Jesus the remaining disciples began to preach the doctrine that his crucifixion had been more than a simple execution. It was regarded by them as the culminating event in a direct sequence of events going back to the creation of the universe.

[I have previously discussed] how Paul made the connection between a historical man Adam and the historical man Jesus in such a way as to explain how the disobedience of Adam had been canceled with the death of Jesus. It was within the recorded experience of the Hebrew people and the remnant peoples of the tribe of Judah, then known as the Jews, that the Christian innovation of world history took place. Two of the Gospels written to interpret the life of Jesus and his teachings had as their introductory remarks genealogies of Jesus purporting to trace his ancestry back to Adam. That they are different is cause to wonder if a biological history of his family is the intent; if it is not accurate genetics, what is it?

At any rate, the events of the Old Testament were seen as actual events of history in which a divine purpose was gradually unfolding. The idea had been inherent in Jewish religious circles prior to the advent of Christianity, but with the missionary explosion of the Christian religion, the events could be said to have taken on cosmic significance for believers of the new religion. For some time before the lifetime of Jesus, Jewish theological circles had seen the development of a curious type of literature. A large body of literature purporting to have been written by the major folk heroes of the Hebrew past began to surface, and its concern with predictions about the end of the world and the salvation of the Jews appeared to be a common feature. Such writings were called apocalyptic writings, and it is perhaps from these sources more than any others that we derive the Christian idea of a divine purpose in history and a subsequent fascination by Westerners for history.

The religion that took form around the person of Jesus came to regard the events of the past as directly prefiguring his life and teachings. To arrive at such consequences, the books of the Old Testament were scoured for verses that might be interpreted as predicting certain events of his life. What we have in the four Gospels, therefore, is a curious mixture of historical events, parabolic teachings, and tortured proof texts from various sources in the Jewish writings. At best the Gospels, which can be said to be the first Christian effort to define the meaning of past events in terms of humankind's universal history, are exactly that—tortured.

The immediate followers who had known Jesus had come to the conclusion, apparently nurtured by Jesus himself, that their Lord would return within their own lifetime to restore the Kingdom of Israel to the glory known during the eras of David and Solomon. So impending was this feeling that the original commune in Jerusalem, headed by Jesus' brother James the Just, felt no desire or need to gather worldly goods. As a result, they were soon bankrupt, and one of Paul's first acts was to take up collections from converts to bail them out of their financial difficulties.

The whole basis for the Christian belief in life after death was the alleged resurrection of Jesus after he had been dead for three days and his subsequent ascension into heaven. As the Gospels and the Acts of the Apostles were written, there can be little doubt that the primitive Christian community wished its converts to believe that Jesus in his physical body had risen upward to heaven in a cloud. Early converts saw visions in which he returned on the clouds. When Jesus failed to return within the lifetime of those who had been his closest associates, the religion should have folded. But as the original group grew smaller and the religion spread to Asia Minor, the initial prediction was continually modified so that while the basic idea had been an immediate conclusion to history through divine intervention, its immediacy gradually became symbolic, not historic.

It is now nearly two thousand years since Jesus lived and died, and there has been no return. New converts periodically become wildly enthusiastic about the impending return of Jesus, and evangelistic Christianity continuously phrases its message of mission and conversion in terms of a return of Jesus in the not-too-distant future. As the years have passed and certain milestones have been reached, Christianity has gone into traumas with the idea of imminent judgment. The arrival of the year 1000 was particularly disappointing for the thousands of people who sold their earthly goods and prepared to meet their maker. When the crisis passed and the Western world returned to normal, apologists for the religion trotted out their favorite Bible verses, attempting to smooth over the downhearted. "A thousand years is but a day in Thy sight" and other comforting verses were used to cover over the failure of Jesus to reappear.

The Christian religion looks toward a spectacular end of the world as a time of judgment and thus an end of history. It is thus theologically an open-ended proposition because it can at any time promote the idea that the world is ending; when such an event fails to occur, the contentions can easily be retracted by resorting to philosophical warnings about the nature of time. Time thus becomes a dualistic concept for Christians. It is both divine and human; prophecies given with respect to divine time are promptly canceled by reference to human time and its distinction from divine time.

The concept of history became a rather nebulous subject matter as Christianity continued to grow. The events of the Old Testament were regarded as actual historical events, and their miraculous nature was ascribed to divine intervention on behalf of the Hebrews. As the Old Testament came closer to the days of Jesus and the writings became closed to further prophecies, with Malachi the idea of divine intervention in human affairs also appeared to slacken. The first several centuries of the Christian religion appear to have been filled with miraculous acts of God in direct assistance to the Christian martyrs. After several centuries, however, even this tendency ebbed, and with the establishment of the organizational Church as a political power in the crumbling Roman Empire, Christianity adopted the temporary doctrine that Jesus had established a "church" to supervise the affairs of men until he decided to return.

This condition of nearly total Church control over the lives of people was strengthened during the centuries that followed, and for many centuries the political struggles of Western Europe had to have Christian approval to be considered valid. The Protestant Reformation was instrumental in breaking the control of the organized Church structure over the political and economic life of Europe. Since that time, while the political structures have continued to expand their power, the relative influence of the Church has declined.

The original doctrines of Christian expansion, however, did not decline with the waning influence of the Church organization. In the first several centuries of Christian existence, one of the most popular justifications for the failure of Jesus to return to earth was his alleged admonition to his disciples to preach the message of his life to all nations. Thus a substantial portion of the Christians believed that until every nation had heard the message of Christianity, Jesus *could not come*. In almost every generation of Christians, there was somewhere a militant missionary force seeking to convert non-Christian peoples, and this propensity to expand the religion's influence meant in realistic terms an expansion of control by the church structure over non-Christian peoples.

With the rise of secular governmental forms after the Protestant Reformation, the bitter competition between nations for lands in the newly discovered Western Hemisphere, and the very violent struggles between competing interpretations of the religion following the Reformation, missionary activity was seen as an arm of national politics, and the national imperialistic movements were justified on the basis of bringing the Christian religion to the "heathen." What is important for our purposes here is to note that as secular goals became more important, they were clothed in familiar terms of Western cultural attitudes, not in terms of religious reality.

Christian theology also had a direct influence on the development of the manner in which Westerners conceived the nature of the world. In the development of Christian theology, the two Greeks Plato and Aristotle were highly influential. Both of their philosophical systems sought to bring order out of the chaos of the world, and as the two major theologians of Christian history, Saint Augustine and Saint Thomas Aquinas, sought to reconcile Greek philosophy with Christian ideas of history, people in the West became accustomed to thinking of natural processes in terms of uniformity. In the popular mind the Old Testament was filled with highly exciting supernatural events while the story of humankind since the life of Jesus was filled with smaller miracles and lacked the spectacular nature of Old Testament happenings.

Western history as we now have it has failed to shake off its original Christian presuppositions. It has, in fact, extended its theory of uniformity to include Old Testament events so that the history of humankind appears as a rather tedious story of the rise and fall of nation after nation, and the sequence in which world history has been written shows amazing parallels to the expansion of the Christian religion. China, with its history going back far beyond the days of Abraham, thus does not appear as a significant factor in world history until it begins to have relations with the West. India, with even more ancient records, appears on the world scene only when the British decide to colonize it, despite its brief role as a conquest goal of Alexander the Great.

We are faced today with a concept of world history that lacks even the most basic appreciation of the experiences of mankind as a whole. Unless other cultures and nations have some important relationship with the nations of Western Europe, they have little or no status in the interpretation of world history. Indeed, world history as presently conceived in the Christian nations is the story of the West's conquest of the remainder of the world and the subsequent rise to technological sophistication.

Because we cannot understand humankind from a more profound point of view, we have in recent years fallen into a number of easily avoidable difficulties. The original thrust of Christians opposing pagans translated itself many times in Christian history. Shortly after the discovery of the New World, Christianity was thought to be opposed on the one hand to the societies of the New World and on the other to the heretics of Europe. The peoples of the New World were virtually destroyed by the European invaders at the same time that Europe was being ravaged by witch-hunts, the Inquisition, and religious wars.

The tendency of placing Christianity against the social or political forms of man's secular existence continues to this day. After World War II planetary history was seen as a struggle between godless communism and the chosen people of God—the Christian nations. At least part of the involvement of the United States in Southeast Asia was because of the influence of an important figure in the Roman Catholic church, Francis Cardinal Joseph J. Spellman, who sought to bolster the fortunes of the Church and also subscribed to the good guys/bad guys interpretation of world events. Much of the misunderstanding of the role of the United States in postwar worlds involves this tendency to reject the Russians because of their rejection of Christianity.

A major task remains for Western man. He must quickly come to grips with the breadth of human experiences and understand these experiences from a world viewpoint, not simply a Western one. This shift will necessarily involve downgrading the ancient history of the Near East, thus serving to cut yet more subject matter away from the Christian religion. Louis Leakey's discoveries concerning early humans in Africa would seem to indicate that we are reaching a point at which the history of the Old Testament must assume rather minor importance in the whole scheme of development. In addition to surrendering the historical Adam and his successors, we must surrender the comfortable feeling that we can find a direct line from ancient times to the modern world via the Christian religion. This involves, of course, giving up the claim by Christianity of its universal truth and validity.

Already the field of history appears to be reaching a crisis. Ancient history is taken much too casually today because it is assumed that whatever happened within human experiences could not be much different from the mythology that has grown up to explain the relics of history. We have an apparent computer of great sophistication at Stonehenge, England, and yet the traditional conceptions of life during the times when this massive structure was built continue to reflect the Western/Christian idea that nothing of major importance occurred until the advent of Western culture and its religion.

The experiences of the Hebrews do not really take precedence over the experiences and accomplishments of other peoples when viewed with an unjaundiced eye. The world abounds with ruins of incredible proportions relating hardly at all to the history of the Hebraic–Christian peoples. Yet these ruins are passed off with casual and hardly credible explanations based on the old theory of uniformity, which projects that the past had to be experienced in the way in which we experience life today.

The pyramids of Egypt are a case in point. In the popular mind of Western peoples, the pyramids were built à la Cecil B. DeMille with thousands of slaves tugging the large vine ropes up inclines to make a final resting place for the pharaoh. That the only reference to slave labor in the Old Testament remotely connected with building involves the Hebrew slaves making mud bricks is difficult for the popular mind to assimilate. It is when we go to the scholarly mind that we find even greater confusion, so that our sense of human accomplishments and the meaning of history are hardly enhanced by even the best of our educated minds. Walter Fairservis, for example, rejects the concept of slave labor in pyramid building in his book *The Ancient Kingdoms of the Nile.*

> *We know that there were few slaves because foreign conquests were at a minimum. The labor for the pyramids came from the peasant farmers who, at times of high Nile, were comparatively idle and could be used for public projects. In such cases they were maintained at government expense, which in view of the job to be done could not have been meager. The number of pyramids, and the years it took to build each of them, indicates that a stable arrangement between government responsibility and peasant labor had been established.*[4]

The picture appears to be idyllic. In times of unemployment the benevolent pharaoh provided work for his people by having them put together what must certainly be among the most massive structures in history. But is this even a realistic picture of what happened in earlier times? That the U.S. government put forward the make-work projects of the Great Depression years does not mean that the pharaoh did likewise. The very bulk of the pyramids precludes Fairservis's solution to the problem.

The Great Pyramid of Cheops, for example, is incredible. Its base covers

> *13 acres or 7 midtown blocks of the city of New York. From this broad area, leveled to within a fraction of an inch, more than two-and-a-half-million blocks of limestone and granite—weighing from 2 to 70 tons apiece—rise in 201 stepped tiers to the height of a modern forty-story building.*[5]

A construction project the size of this pyramid would have been a task of no mean proportions. Suppose that the workers had placed a minimum of 20 blocks of stone a day in the structure—a feat that would have been virtually impossible, yet still conceivable. Working steadily, they would have assembled the 2.5 million stone blocks in about 125,000 days, or 342 years. In this projection we have still not accounted for cutting the blocks, carrying them down the Nile, and bringing them to the assembly place. And we have projected a straight working project, not a summertime government make-work project as Fairservis and other scholars have assumed. If the Pilgrims had begun building a pyramid the size of the pyramid of Cheops to celebrate their safe landing in America, they would have finished the project in 1962, perhaps just in time to receive a government grant to celebrate. Is the traditional interpretation of history really an exercise in credibility?

At Aswan Dam in Egypt the people of many nations worked to save four sandstone statues from an ancient temple from being destroyed by the waters of the dam. Engineers from nearly one hundred nations pooled their talents to save these priceless treasures. They had the benefit of helicopters, the latest in hydraulic jacks, lifts, cranes, and other modern construction equipment. Yet they had to cut the statues into smaller pieces to move them a mere sixty feet above the waters. In a quarry near Baalbek in Asia Minor, the Hadjar el Gouble stone lies squared and ready for removal. It weighs more than 4 million pounds. And primitive men are going to get their logs and ropes and move it? Hardly.

The world is, as we have noted, literally strewn with ruins of overwhelming proportions, structures that we cannot duplicate today if we wished to do so, yet the Western interpretation of world history is always skirting a straightforward effort to incorporate theories about the origin of these ruins and structures. We are fixed on a rather staid reading of human history because we are emotionally and religiously tied to the assumption, today perhaps subconsciously at least, that everything is pretty much the way people once believed centuries ago.

Even the relatively short time period of American history has been influenced by our religious heritage. There is sufficient evidence that this continent was visited by numerous expeditions prior to the arrival of Columbus. Pottery discovered in South America suggests fairly early contact between Japan and this hemisphere. Ruins in Massachusetts and Arizona may be evidence of early visits by Phoenicians and Romans. Yet up to this time scholars have adamantly refused to believe that any pre-Columbian landing took place. Even the Viking ruins in Minnesota have been buffeted by tremendous criticism and the jeers of skeptics while the Columbian primacy has prevailed.

Cyrus Gordon, a noted scholar at Brandeis University, took a cautious stand in favor of pre-Columbian expeditions in his book *Before Columbus*.[6] He documented two possible pre-Columbian visits to the New World. Gordon's courage in dealing with a controversial subject produced great fruits during the past two decades. Today there are literally hundreds of books dealing with pre-Columbian expeditions to this continent, and many of them make a great deal of sense. The best writing is being done *outside* academic circles because it covers data and theories that are not regarded as orthodox because they make uncomfortable the reigning elder statesmen of anthropology, archaeology, and history.

The reluctance of scholars to consider the possibility of pre-Columbian visits to the Western Hemisphere is but one example of the stranglehold that the one interpretation of history has had. There is, to a certain extent, a political justification in refusing to accept pre-Columbian discoveries. The land title of the United States relates back to the famous doctrine of Discovery, whereby Christian nations were allowed by the pope to claim the discovered lands of non-Christian peoples. To accept a series of pre-Columbian visitations would mean that the lands of the Western Hemisphere were hardly "discovered" by Europeans. It would call into question the interpretations and justifications given to colonization, exploitation, and genocide committed by Europeans during the last five centuries.

Christian religion and the Western idea of history are inseparable and mutually self-supporting. To retrench the traditional concept of

Western history at this point would mean to invalidate the justifications for conquering the Western Hemisphere. Americans in some manner will cling to the traditional idea that they suddenly came upon a vacant land on which they created the world's most affluent society. Not only is such an idea false, it is absurd. Yet without it both Western man and his religion stand naked before the world.

It is said that one cannot judge Christianity by the actions of secular Western man. But such a contention judges Westerners much too harshly. Where did Westerners get their ideas of divine right to conquest, of manifest destiny, of themselves as the vanguard of true civilization, if not from Christianity? Having tied itself to history and maintained that its god controlled that history, Christianity must accept the consequences of its past. Secular history is now out of control and its influence has become a rather demoniac, disruptive force among nations—this is part and parcel of the Christian religion. If the lack of a sense of history can be called a shortcoming of tribal religions, as indeed it can, overemphasis on historic reality and its attendant consequences can certainly be assigned a bad grade for the Christian religion.

NOTES

1. Edward Holland Spicer reproduces a Tohono O'odham calendar stick recording in his book, *A Short History of the Indians of the United States* (New York: Van Nostrand Reinhold, 1969).
2. Spicer also gives a fragment of the Walum Olum.
3. *Uncommon Controversy,* a report prepared for the American Friends Service Committee (Seattle: University of Washington Press, 1970), p. 29.
4. Walter Fairservis, *The Ancient Kingdoms of the Nile* (New York: Thomas Y. Crowell, 1962), p. 89.
5. Peter Tompkins, *Secrets of the Great Pyramid* (New York: Harper & Row, 1971), p. 1.
6. Cyrus Gordon, *Before Columbus* (New York: Crown, 1971).
    Gordon was regarded as something of a traitor because he was willing to consider ideas that were outside the mainstream of doctrine laid down by the "old boy network" of American archaeology. The most telling point in his book, in my opinion, is the fact that *no* ancient peoples could have constructed astronomical tables that would predict eclipses unless they had access to observations spread over 120 degrees of arc in two directions. This suggests that there was a worldwide culture that coordinated information or that our basic ideas of astronomy were given to us as an intact body of knowledge.

25

TRIBAL RELIGIONS AND

CONTEMPORARY AMERICAN CULTURE

▼▼▼

We have seen some examples of the deviations created in religious behavior when a culture defines a religion. In a great many areas, tribal religion defined culture. This aspect of Indian life can be seen fairly clearly in the speeches and attitudes of the old chiefs and warriors. Their refusal to consider land as a commodity to be sold and their insistence that the lands held a great and sacred place in their hearts and the hearts of their people must be understood in its context of the last century, when they faced the momentous decisions of giving up some of their lands in an effort to preserve the remainder of it for themselves and their children.

There can be no doubt that not only times have changed but also cultures since the white man first set foot on the continent. Tribal cultures have shifted to confront the changes forced on the people by the tidal wave of white settlement. The recent Indian activist movement has attempted to recoup the lost ground and return to the culture, outlook, and values of the old days. The fundamental question facing tribal religions is whether the old days can be relived—whether, in fact, the very existence of an Indian community in the modern electronic world does not require a massive task of relating traditional religious values and beliefs to the phenomena presenting themselves.

One small example might indicate the extent to which this problem is a daily irritation to Indian people. In some of the traditional pueblos, modern conveniences are rejected, even electricity. The children of the pueblo attend the public school system, however, and have become accustomed to having cold milk. For the children to have cold milk at home, the pueblo must install electricity. But this innovation will violate the people's religious beliefs. A generation gap of no small distance emerges. What decision do the tribal elders make about the nature of the tribal religion and the demand of the little children for cold milk?

Again and again Indian people are faced with a puzzling unveiling of the distinctions between the Western Christian world and themselves. Sacred bundles of the tribe reside in the state museum; for centuries they were revered by the people, serving to focus their attentions on their religious experience as a people. During the period of religious oppression, the government forbade the practice of Indian religions, and one day the sacred bundle was given or sold to the museum or stolen from the tribe. Everyone had given up on the idea that they would ever again be allowed to practice their own religion, and the sacred bundles were considered the remaining artifacts of paganism. In a scene being played out across the country today the younger people of the tribe, trying to revive the tribal religion, need the sacred bundles. An old man has been found who has preserved the tribal religion. He is old, and unless he can train the young, the religion will be lost. What can be done? The sacred bundles are no longer in Indian hands. Do we storm the museum? Will the whites understand why we need the sacred bundles back?

We have been taught to look at American history as a series of land transactions involving some three hundred Indian tribes and a growing U.S. government. This conception is certainly the picture that emerges when tribal officials are forced to deal with federal officials, claims commissioners, state highway departments, game wardens, county sheriffs, and private corporations. Yet it is hardly the whole picture. Perhaps nearly as accurate would be the picture of settlement phrased as a continuous conflict of two mutually exclusive religious views of the world. The validity of these two religious views is yet to be determined. One, Christianity, appears to be in its death throes. The other, the tribal religion, is attempting to make a comeback in a world that is as different from the world of its origin as the present world is different from the world of Christian origins. Can tribal religions survive? Can they even make a comeback?

Even where the two religious systems have clashed, the picture is not clear as to villain and hero. Father A. M. Beede, a missionary to the Sioux at Fort Yates, North Dakota, told Seton, "I am convinced now that the Medicine Lodge of the Sioux is a true Church of God, and we have no right to stamp it out."[1] Yet they did try to stamp it out while recognizing the wrong they were doing.

Some Christian missionaries successfully bridged the cultural gap and became more important to the tribes than most of their own members. The Reverend Samuel Worcester, a missionary to the Cherokees in the 1830s, remained a faithful friend to the tribe in defiance of the State of Georgia. He persisted in his recognition of the Cherokees as a people, following their cultural development, obeying their laws, and giving continual assistance. For his loyalty he was imprisoned by Georgia, and his appeal for release was heard in the U.S. Supreme Court in the famous case *Worcester v. Georgia*[2] in which Chief Justice John Marshall gave the definitive statement on the status of Indian tribes under the Constitution.

At the opposite end of the spectrum is the Reverend John M. Chivington, an infamous Methodist minister from Denver, Colorado. Chivington served briefly as a colonel in the Colorado Volunteers during the Civil War. Finding no Johnny Rebs to fight, he turned his attentions to the Indians. He planned, led, justified, and celebrated the massacre at Sand Creek, Colorado, in an unexpected dawn attack on a friendly band of Cheyenne and Arapaho Indians in which hundreds of helpless people were needlessly slaughtered. The actions of the Colorado Volunteers remain, even today, as one of the most barbaric examples of human behavior.

Between these two extremes are hundreds of cases of Christian people who reflected well both their religious beliefs and their cultural values in their relationships with Indians. Some were staunch defenders of the tribes they knew; others behaved in a rigid, authoritarian manner without a trace of human feeling. In fairness one cannot judge the religion of the whites as either good or bad when it came into contact with the tribal religions, only that no consistent set of values ever emerged as peculiarly and gloriously Christian.

After four centuries of pressure and religious imperialism, many tribal religions disappeared. Some disappeared because the tribes were destroyed or were reduced to such few members that the survivors, dropping their own religion, joined larger tribes and accepted the practices of the host tribe. It has only been in fairly recent times that a number of religions have emerged that cross tribal lines. Foremost of these has been the Native American Church, which uses peyote in its ceremonies. Although universally respected among Indians, the Native American Church has come afoul of the drug laws of the various states and now faces severe repression. Oppression of the people who use peyote sacramentally, connecting them with the drug war, is ludicrous. Very few people belong to the Native American Church, and its services are always held in the most isolated locations and attended by a handful of people. Traffic in peyote is almost nonexistent, and it has been used successfully in helping Indians escape from alcoholism. But it is, culturally and theologically, foreign to American culture and consequently is seen as a threat to social stability.

The establishment of reservations generally involved the creation of mission stations at agency headquarters. Some of the treaties gave the missionaries lands on which they promised to build schools, houses for teachers, hospitals, and farms. The tribes failed in many cases to appreciate that allowing the missionaries to enter the tribal lands would inevitably result in religious conflict and dissension among tribal members. We have already seen how Chief Joseph refused to have missionaries around, fearing that they would teach the people to quarrel about God.

As the reservations became more permanent, the churches devoted themselves wholeheartedly to converting the people. Religious controversies increased, and missionaries soon became one of the most vocal forces in demanding that tribal political activity be suppressed because it was apparent to them that the religious and political forms of tribal life could not be separated. Soon plans were underfoot to ban tribal religious ceremonies. The ignorance of the Indian agents assisted the missionaries in their endeavors because they interpreted any Indian ceremonial as a war dance.

By the time of the Allotment Act of 1887 (Dawes Act), almost every form of Indian religion was banned on the reservations. In the schools the children were punished for speaking their own language. Anglo-Saxon customs were made the norm for Indian people; their efforts to maintain their own practices were frowned on, and stern measures were taken to discourage them from continuing tribal customs. Even Indian funeral ceremonies were declared to be illegal, and drumming and any form of dancing had to be held for the most artificial of reasons.

The record of Indian resistance is admirable. When people saw that they could no longer practice their ceremonies in peace, they sought subterfuge in performing certain of the ceremonies. Choosing an American holiday or Christian religious day when the whites would themselves be celebrating, traditional Indians often performed their ceremonies "in honor of" George Washington or Memorial Day, thus fulfilling their own religious obligations while white bystanders glowed proudly to see a war dance or rain dance done on their behalf. The Lummi Indians from western Washington, for example, continued some of their tribal dances under the guise of celebrating the signing of their treaty. The Plains Indians eagerly celebrated the Fourth of July because it meant that they could often perform Indian dances and ceremonies by pretending to celebrate the signing of the Declaration of Independence.

In 1934 under the Indian Reorganization Act, Indian people were finally allowed religious freedom. The missionaries howled in protest, but the ban on Indian religious ceremonies was lifted. Traditional Indians could no longer be placed in prison for practicing old tribal ways. Ceremonies began to be practiced openly, and there were still enough older Indians alive that a great deal of tribal religious traditions were regained. The great Black Elk, today perhaps the best remembered of the Sioux holy men, was still alive in 1934. It is said that he had frequent conferences with the holy men from other parts of the tribe living on different reservations.

For several decades the tribal religions held their own in competition with the efforts of the Christian missionaries. But a whole new generation had grown up, educated in mission and government schools and living according to the bureaucrats' dictates; these young Indians rigorously rejected old religious activities as a continuation of paganism. Yet as more Indians went off the reservation, went to war, attended college, and lived in the cities, the situation began to change. The Indian people had always been somewhat in awe of Western technology. It seemed to imply that their god was more powerful than their tribal religions and medicine. The great expansion of the American Indian horizon in the 1950s had a tremendous effect on attitudes toward tribal religions, which provided a very important link with the tribal past. Often through healing ceremonies performed by the holy people of the tribe, sicknesses were cured that urban white doctors could not cure. In one decade many American Indians began to see that whites and their Christian religion had fatal flaws.

In the last several decades tribal religions have seen a renewal that astounds many people. The Pueblos of New Mexico and the Navajos of Arizona managed to retain much of their ceremonial life throughout the period of religious suppression. The Hopi in particular preserved many of their ceremonies with relative purity. The Apaches also kept a number of their tribal ceremonies. In the Northwest some of the tribes kept their ceremonies by holding them in secret on the isolated reservations lacking sufficient federal resident staff to prohibit them. These tribes quite frankly continued their ceremonies by making them once again a total community affair to which everyone was expected to come.

Other tribes have experienced an increasing interest recently as specific ceremonies become the objects of people's affection. Naming ceremonies in some tribes have become more numerous as urban Indians seeking a means of preserving an Indian identity within the confusion of the city have asked reservation people to sponsor naming ceremonies for them. They travel sometimes thousands of miles and spend thousands of dollars to be able to participate in such events.

Religious conflict has become pronounced on some reservations as Christian Indians have had to make room for traditional Indians in tribal affairs. The continuous conflict on the St. Regis Mohawk Reservation in upstate New York is a classic example of such strife. For nearly two centuries the Roman Catholic church dominated the affairs of the Mohawks who remained on this side of the border after the Revolutionary War. Edmund Wilson recounts how he visited a cemetery where many of the Christian Mohawks sat silently in the night, listening to the songs and activities of the traditional Mohawks being held a short distance away. Such was the overt situation until recently.

In 1972 open conflict broke out at St. Regis as the impending wave of traditionalism threatened the political stability of a few figurehead Christian Mohawks who had been dominating tribal affairs for nearly a generation. The largest Indian newspaper in North America, *Akwesasne Notes,* operated by traditional Mohawks on a sharing-the-cost-by-contribution basis, was harassed continuously. Questions were raised about whether Canadian Mohawks and their adopted friends should be allowed to live on the reserve. The fundamental question was that of defining contemporary Mohawk culture and outlook. The traditionals appeared to be strongly appealing to the rest of the people. In 1989 and 1990 violence broke out in Mohawk country as traditional people attempted to forestall the installation of gambling on their reservations. Both the Canadian and U.S. governments were placed in a difficult situation because it appeared as if tribal sovereignty and the viability of the tribal government was at stake. There is no question that the traditional Mohawks held the high moral ground, but there was also the difficulty of recognizing the informal, traditional government because it would not endorse the continued intrusions into community life that the organized tribal council condoned.

As tribal religions emerge and begin to attract younger Indians, problems of immense magnitude arise. Many people are trapped between tribal values constituting their unconscious behavioral responses and the values that they have been taught in schools and churches, which primarily demand conforming to seemingly foreign ideals. Alcoholism and suicide mark this tragic fact of reservation life. People are not allowed to be Indians and cannot become whites. They have been educated, as the old-timers would say, to think with their heads instead of their hearts.

Additional problems face any revival of tribal religions that originated in times when the tribes were small and compact. Whenever a band got too large to support itself and required a large game source to feed everyone, it simply broke into smaller bands of people. The two bands would remain in contact with each other. Often they would share war parties and ceremonials of some importance. At treaty signing times they would congregate and act as a national unit. Their primary characteristic, however, was their manageability. For political decisions, religious ceremonies, hunting and fishing activities, and general community life, both the political and the religious outlook of the tribe were designed for a small group of people. It was a rare tribal group that was larger than one thousand people for any extended period of time.

Today tribal membership is determined on quite a legalistic basis, which is foreign to the accustomed tribal way of determining its constituency. The property interests of descendants of the original enrollees or allottees have become determining factors in compiling tribal membership rolls. People of *small Indian blood quantum*, or those descended from people who were tribal members a century ago, are thus included in the tribal membership roll. Tribes can no longer form and re-form on sociological, religious, or cultural bases. They are restricted in membership by federal officials responsible for administering trust properties who demand that the rights of every person be respected whether or not that person presently appears in an active and recognized role in the tribal community. Indian tribal membership today is a fiction created by the federal government, not a creation of the Indian people themselves.

In the 1860s the Navajo bands who were gathered up and marched to New Mexico to be imprisoned by Kit Carson numbered some four thousand people. The basis of their unity as a people was similarity of language and occupation in a commonly defined area. It was not a political unity. When they were returned to Arizona and given a reservation in the most desolate part of the state, they then fictionally became a distinct tribe, although they had previously composed several distinct independent bands. Today that same tribe numbers close to two hundred thousand people. The Navajo have not had sufficient time to develop an expanded religious or political structure to account for this tremendous population explosion.

The Oglala Sioux once formed a large-numbered tribe but one that was dominated by a series of brilliant and charismatic chiefs such as Red Cloud, Crazy Horse, American Horse, Standing Bear, and Little Wound. They had a number of bands virtually acting independently of each other. Thus Crazy Horse and his people spent most of their time in Montana with the Cheyennes fighting Custer while Red Cloud and his people were living in South Dakota several hundred miles away from that area. It would have been absurd for Red Cloud to have signed a treaty for the Oglala Sioux without having Crazy Horse and the other chiefs also signing for the tribe.

Today the Oglala Sioux number at least fifteen thousand people, perhaps twenty thousand. A substantial number live off the reservation and participate only sporadically in community life. Yet the people must find a way to define what it means to be an Oglala Sioux in today's world. When such a process is rigidly controlled by federal officials fearful that the Sioux may gain control over their lives, then incidents such as the confrontation at Wounded Knee in 1973 are inevitable.

While the AIM [the American Indian Movement] received a lion's share of the publicity at Wounded Knee, it was merely the external symbolic group of which the public was made aware. AIM had been asked to come to the reservation to mount the protest by members of the Oglala Sioux Civil Rights Association, a group formed a year earlier to protest conditions on the reservation brought about by the tribal council's refusal to guarantee civil rights to individual Indians. Cooperating with the two groups was the Black Hills Treaty Rights Council. This council was composed of the elder traditional leaders on the reservation who had tried to preserve the older form of tribal political organization. They had been working all their lives to see that the federal government fulfills its commitments to the Oglalas as promised in the Treaty of 1868 and the Agreement of 1876.

The situation was further complicated by two other organizations supporting the protest. One, the Landowner's Association, was composed of individual Indians who owned allotments of land and wished to use their lands in community cooperatives to form grazing units for the local communities. The BIA [Bureau of Indian Affairs], with the concurrence of the tribal council, had placed their lands in larger grazing units and leased these large units to white cattle ranchers. The individual Indians were thus deprived of the use of their lands and were given small rental checks by the federal government. They were kept in a perpetual state of poverty while the white ranchers enjoyed the benefits of economic prosperity during the great rise in the price of beef.

The fourth group involved in the protest was the Inter-District Council. As the conditions on the reservation grew worse during 1972, the people of the different reservation districts formed their own shadow government known as the Inter-District Council. They had representatives from every one of the eight districts on the reservation and were discussing ways to get a federal law passed to give the people of the local communities political control over their lives through a new constitution. Naturally the existing tribal council and the BIA were violently opposed to such a reform because it would have unseated the tribal council and reduced the power of the bureaucrats. During the Wounded Knee confrontation, the Inter-District Council tried desperately to get the federal government to understand how the conditions on the reservation had led to the protest and how the protest could be peacefully resolved.

Perhaps the most important aspect of the Wounded Knee protest was that the holy men of the tribe and the traditional chiefs all supported the AIM activists and younger people on the issues that they were raising. Some people were fearful of the violence that threatened their lives, but the strong ceremonial life and the presence of medicine men in the Wounded Knee compound diffused a great deal of the criticism that would have been forthcoming from members of the other Indian tribes. No Indian could keep up a sustained criticism of the confrontation upon knowing that the people at Wounded Knee had their sacred pipes and that the medicine men from both the Pine Ridge and the neighboring Rosebud Sioux reservations were performing the ceremonies.

The Wounded Knee protest was dreaded by Indians, but it was not unexpected. The federal government had taken the original rolls of the allotment period and insisted that the descendants of those original allottees be considered members of the tribe whether they had sufficient Indian blood to qualify for membership or whether they lived in the communities on the reservation. The internal social mechanisms that ordinarily would have operated to define community membership were forbidden by federal law—if they operated, they were given no legal status or recognition.

We have just begun to see the revival of Indian tribal religions at a time when the central value of Indian life—its land—is under incredible attack from all sides. Tribal councils are strapped for funds to solve pressing social problems. Leasing and development of tribal lands is a natural source of good income. But leasing of tribal lands involves selling the major object of tribal religion for funds to solve problems that are ultimately religious in nature. The best example of this dilemma is the struggle over the strip-mining at Black Mesa on the Navajo and Hopi reservations. Traditional Indians of both tribes are fighting desperately against any additional strip-mining of the lands. Tribal councils are continuing to lease the lands for development to encourage employment and to make possible more tribal programs for the rehabilitation of the tribal members.

A substantial portion of every tribe remains solidly within the Christian tradition by having attended mission schools. They grew up in a period of time when any mention of tribal religious beliefs was forbidden, and they have been taught that Indian values and beliefs are superstitions and pagan beliefs that must be surrendered before they can be truly civilized. They stand, therefore, in much the same relationship to the tribal religion as educated liberals now stand to the Christian and Jewish religions. Both groups have lost their faith in the mysterious, the transcendent, the communal nature of religious experience. They depend on a learned set of ethical principles to maintain some semblance of order in their lives.

A great many Indians reflect the same religious problem as do the young whites who struggled through the last several decades of social disorder. They are somehow forced to hold in tension beliefs that are not easily reconciled. They have learned that some things are true because they have experienced them, that others are true because everyone seems to agree that they are true, and that some things are insoluble and cannot be solved by any stretch of the imagination.

One of the primary aspects of traditional tribal religions has been the secret ceremonies, particularly the vision quests, the fasting in the wilderness, and the isolation of the individual for religious purposes. This type of religious practice is nearly impossible today. The places currently available to people for vision quests are hardly isolated. Jet planes pass overhead. Some traditional holy places are the scene of strip-mining, others are adjacent to superhighways, others are parts of ranches, farms, shopping centers, and national parks and forests. The struggle of the Taos people to get their sacred Blue Lake away from the Department of Agriculture indicates the tenuous nature of some tribal religious practices in a world of complicated transportation services and radio and television.

If modern conditions were not sufficient to prevent the continuance of traditional ceremonies, the U.S. Supreme Court has made it almost impossible to perform some ceremonies on federal lands. In 1988 in *Lyng v. Northwest Indian Cemetery Protective Association*,[3] the Court dealt with the question of whether the Forest Service could construct a six-mile segment of road for the convenience of the logging industry in the high country of northern California where the Yurok and Karok tribes traditionally conducted religious ceremonies. Relying on the American Indian Religious Freedom Resolution, the Indians demonstrated to the Forest Service and to the lower courts that to construct the road would damage the traditional religion beyond repair. Yet the Court turned away their argument, noting that it could not order the government to protect a religion of this kind. The majority decision compared it to a sudden rush of religious feeling by someone who had gazed upon the Lincoln

Memorial, a dreadful and perhaps deliberate misunderstanding of the religious principles involved.

Education itself is a barrier to a permanent revival of tribal religions. Young people on reservations have available an increasingly complicated educational system. Perhaps like conservative Christians, older Indians see the educational system as basically godless and tending to destroy communities rather than create them. As more Indians fight their way through the education system in search of job skills, their education will increasingly concentrate on the tangible and technical aspects of contemporary society and away from the sense of wonder and mystery that has traditionally characterized religious experiences. In almost the same way that young whites have rejected religion once they have made strides in education, young Indians who have received solid educations have rejected traditional religious experiences. Education and religion apparently do not mix.

Tribal religions thus face the task of entrenching themselves in a contemporary Indian society that is becoming increasingly accustomed to the lifestyle of contemporary America. While traditional Indians speak of a reverence for the earth, Indian reservations continue to pile up junk cars and beer cans at an alarming rate. While traditional Indians speak of sharing the structure of jobs, insurance, and tribal politics, education prohibits a realistic sharing. To survive, people must in effect feed off one another, not share with each other.

In the old days leadership depended on the personal prestige of the people whom the community chose as its leaders. Their generosity, service to the community, integrity, and honesty had to be above question. Today tribal constitutions define who shall represent the tribe in its relationships with the outside world. No quality is needed to assume leadership except the ability to win elections. Consequently, tribal elections have become one of the dirtiest forms of human activity in existence. Corruption runs rampant during tribal elections, and people deliberately vote in scoundrels over honest people for the personal benefits they can receive. Much of the formal resistance to federal programs for increasing tribal independence comes from the Indian people's mistrust of their own leadership, present and future. Many tribes want the tribal lands and assets so restricted that no one can use them to the tribe's detriment—or benefit.

One of the greatest hindrances to the reestablishment of tribal religions is the failure of Indian people to understand their own history.

The period of cultural oppression in its severest form (1887–1934) served to create a collective amnesia in contemporary people. Too many Indians look backward to the treaties, neglecting the many laws and executive orders that have come to define their lives in the period since their first relationship with the United States was formed. Tribal people are in the unenviable position of dealing with problems the origins of which remain obscured to them.

The disruptions of tribal religions for a period of fifty years have resulted in the loss of a well-accepted recent tradition of ceremonies, religious leaders, and other ongoing developments characterizing a living religion. Contemporary efforts to reestablish tribal religions have come at too rapid a rate to be absorbed on many reservations. In some instances ceremonials are considered part of the tribal social identity rather than religious events. This attitude undercuts the original function of the ceremony and prevents people from reintegrating community life on a religious basis.

Most tribal religions, as we have seen, have not felt that history is an important aspect of religious life. Today, as changes continue to occur in tribal peoples, the immediate past history of the group is vitally important in maintaining the nature of the ceremonies. The necessary shift in emphasis to a more historical approach can be seen in the various Indian studies programs that have attempted to fill in the missing tribal history. Indian tribal religions thus find themselves in the position of earlier Christian communities that were forced to derive historical interpretations to account for unfulfilled prophecies.

We may find the incongruous situation of many Indian people leaving Christianity to return to traditional religions, creating a tribal history to solve social problems, and falling into the historical trap that has plagued Christianity. It would seem that history itself is a deceremonial process that continues to strip away the mystery of human existence and replace it with intellectual propositions. As the mainstream of Christianity begins to face ecology and the problems inherent in its traditional doctrine of creation, tribal religions are running the risk of abandoning the traditional Indian concerns about the creation in favor of a more historical and intellectual religion.

Tribal religions in the old days did not create an external ethical system. Cultural considerations involving total tribal life enabled people to merge all societal functions into a unity from which all forms of behavior derived. With tribal members spread across the country today and the conditions on the reservations subject to radical shifting at every change of federal policy, there is not that continuity of experience or homogeneous community of people present that would enable Indian people to avoid creating ethical systems based on traditional values.

The closest parallel that we find in history to the present condition of Indians is the Diaspora of the Jews following the destruction of the temple. A surprising number of Indian activists have made this comparison without considering that the exile of the Jews was for a significant period of time and that the Jewish people almost immediately developed a strong scholarly tradition to preserve their ceremonies and beliefs in exile. The Indian exile is in a sense more drastic. The people often live less than one hundred miles away from their traditional homelands; yet in the relative complexities of reservation and urban life, they might be two thousand or more years apart. It is not simply a spatial separation that has occurred but a temporal one as well.

Many traditional leaders have recognized this problem. In the 1970s an intertribal ecumenical council was formed to meet every summer to discuss ways of keeping the people focused on the nature of tribal religions and their meaning for the future of the tribes. The ecumenical council met most often on reserves in Canada because the Canadian Indians seemed more perceptive in defining the problem of reviewing the traditional way. In summer 1972 some five hundred people attended the sessions. The number of participants grew each year until it was apparent that the gatherings had deteriorated into pleasant sessions of reviewing the past because people were unwilling to forge into the future. Then the council ceased to exist.

One of the chief past functions of tribal religions was to perform healing ceremonies. This function was impaired by lack of any rights to train new people to perform the ceremonies and a general lessening of dependence on tribal medicine men because of the presence of Public Health Service hospitals on the larger reservations. Indian healers were generally considered superstitious magicians by the missionaries and government officials, and healing arts were lost in many tribes.

Today healing remains one of the major strengths of tribal religions. Christian missionaries are unable to perform comparable healing ceremonies, and a great many still regard Indian healers as fakers and charlatans. This particular field is thus open for Indian religious figures who have received particular healing powers, and traditional healing ceremonies are being recognized by the Public Health Service as competent complementary healing practices. Some special grants have been given to train more healers and shamans and to have them work closely with doctors trained in internal medicine.

The modern world has lost a large number of healing medicines because of the arbitrary rejection of Indian religions. Some tribes had special roots and herbs that had amazing properties. Only a few have remained in use in some tribes while the vast majority have been lost for a number of reasons. Restriction of Indian people to the reservations has meant that long trips to particular places to gather specific kinds of roots and herbs have stopped. Gradually people have forgotten which plants were used for what purpose. As the older people have died off, knowledge about a substantial number of medicinal plants has also been lost.

The great orgasm of dam building that hit the West following World War II also destroyed a number of Indian medicines. The dams flooded the smaller creek and river bottomlands where many plants grew, leaving only the higher reservation land above water. Even those plants and herbs that had been remembered and used regularly by the people were thus sometimes lost because the places where they grew were under water. A comparable situation exists on the land that has been reduced to farmland from its original state. Some medicinal plants grew wild on certain parts of the prairie or in certain places in the forests. The prairie in large part has now been reduced to erosion-ridden wheat and corn fields, and in most places the forests have given way to farmlands and cities.

When one remembers that a substantial number of people of each tribe live in urban areas away from the reservation, the problems faced by Indian healers come into sharper focus. Only rather hopeless cases or those presenting an extreme problem will reach traditional Indian healers from people outside the reservation. The task of healing will thus take on an Oral Roberts dimension in the future. People will indeed expect miracles. Unless there is a determined effort to gather individual knowledge of healing plants, herbs, and earths as well as a general acceptance of the necessity of rebuilding tribal use of healing people, the impact of healing on Indian religions will continue to decline in spite of temporary successes. Perhaps religious healing will lose validity as a ceremonial experience in another generation.

A counterpart of the healing ceremonies are the rites performed by the religious practitioners that allow them to predict the future in part or in whole, to give advice on courses of action, and to give general advice and admonitions on a variety of subjects. Divination and foretelling the future were once major parts of religion; with the coming of Christianity, they appear to have lost their respectability. The result of this loss has been the survival of astrology, fortune-telling through cards, and the use of the I Ching in recent years in Western civilization. Discovering the future was once a major function of tribal religious leaders. It remains today as one of the major strengths of traditional religious people.

In the last two decades traditional healers have significantly increased the scope and depth of their ability to foretell the future. The impending earth catastrophes are appearing more and more in these rituals, and this prospect has meant a great increase in the number of Indians returning to traditional ways. Unlike some Western efforts to predict specific personal fortunes, the information received by Indian religious leaders generally describes situations and conditions that are likely to come to pass, given existing circumstances. There is a sophisticated principle of probability here reminiscent of modern explanations of modern physics. So this aspect of tribal religion bears watching and reflection.

One can hardly speculate on either the problems or the changes this field will experience in the immediate future. The most important aspect that stands out is the insufficient number of people who can perform this special function. In many tribes it is a power given to people only after special ceremonies have been undertaken, and it is a power not always given. It would seem to be a gift most urgently needed by Indian people, as decisions of crucial importance are being forced on Indian people daily, particularly on tribal governments. Yet one can be forewarned and do nothing as Julius Caesar did. Learning the future will receive a great impetus if some of the present predictions do come to pass. The big danger is that this gift, which must remain a property of the Indian community, may become part of the popular New Age activities and the Indian religious leaders will lose this talent by secularizing it.

The rapid expansion of the New Age psychic phenomenon has been unusually detrimental to traditional religions. Non-Indians can pay very attractive fees to Indian shamans, and there has been a good deal of pressure on traditional healers to spend their time working with non-Indians and neglecting their own communities. Unfortunately, there have also been an unusual number of Indian fakers who have invaded suburbia offering to perform ceremonies, primarily sweat lodges, for anyone with the money to pay. A regular circuit has been established that these people tour in search of gullible whites. It should be clear to non-Indians that if shamans really had significant powers, they would obtain these powers through constant ceremonial practice in their homeland, and they would not be out hustling the workshop circuits. But the hunger for some kind of religious experience is so great that whites show no critical analysis when approaching alleged Indian religious figures.

A warning light should flash when the Indian practitioners say that their elders told them to go out into the world and teach the traditional ceremonies. If one were to gather the great number of Indians now alleging this divine commission and listen to their patter, it would be clear that they all spent their childhood in the wilderness with traditional people who had never seen whites and they learned secrets that had been hidden for thousands of years. It would be exceedingly interesting to compare this roster with tribal employment rolls of two decades ago, because a good many of the names would be the same. Yet this alleged background is so irresistible to many whites that, even when blatant frauds are exposed, most of them cling to the belief that they have met a real, traditional Indian.

The situation, however, is far from hopeless. On the reservations we are seeing amazing resiliency in restoring the old ceremonies. A massive shift in allegiance is occurring in most tribes away from Christianity and secularism and back toward the traditional ways. A surprisingly high percentage of Native American clergy are also doing traditional ceremonies, and urban area churches are often the scene of traditional healing ceremonies. The Native American clergy are to be congratulated for their efforts to bring the two religious traditions together, but it is clear that no synthesis will take place. In almost every instance the effect of merging the two traditions is to bring attention to traditional ways to the detriment of the particular Christian denomination. The result is that the semblance of a national

Indian religion is being born that incorporates major Indian themes. As people are sensitized to this new religious milieu, being dissatisfied with the lack of specificity in this religious activity, they return to the more precise practices of their own tribes. Thus it appears that traditional religions in some form will transcend the inroads that contemporary American culture has made.

NOTES

1. Ernest Thompson Seton, *The Gospel of the Red Man* (New York: Doubleday Doran, 1936).
2. 6 Pet. 515 (1832).
3. 485 U.S. 439 (1988).

SACRED PLACES AND
MORAL RESPONSIBILITY

▼▼▼▼

When the tribes were forced from their aboriginal homelands and confined to small reservations, many of the tribal religious rituals were prohibited by the BIA [Bureau of Indian Affairs] in the 1870s and 1880s because of an inordinately large number of Christian zealots as Indian agents. I have previously discussed how traditional people had to adopt various subterfuges so that their religious life could be continued. Some tribes shifted their ceremonial year to coincide with the whites' holidays and conducted their most important rituals on national holidays and Christian feast days, explaining to curious whites that they were simply honoring George Washington and celebrating Christmas and Easter. Many shrines and holy places were located far away from the new reservation homelands, but because they were not being exploited economically or used by settlers, it was not difficult for small parties of people to go into the mountains or to remote lakes and buttes and conduct ceremonies without interference from non-Indians.

Since World War II, this situation has changed dramatically. We have seen a greatly expanding national population, the introduction of corporate farming practices that have placed formerly submarginal lands under cultivation, more extensive mining and timber industry activities, and a greatly expanded recreation industry—all of which have severely impacted the use of public lands in the United States. Few rural areas now enjoy the isolation of half a century ago, and as multiple use of lands increased, many of the sacred sites that were on public lands were threatened by visitors and subjected to new uses. Tribal religious leaders were often able to work out informal arrangements with federal and state agencies to allow them access to these places for religious purposes. But as the personnel changed in state and federal agencies, a new generation of bureaucrats, catering to developers, recreation interest, and the well-established economic groups that have always used public lands for a pittance, began to restrict Indian access to sacred sites by establishing increasingly narrow rules and regulations for managing public lands.

In 1978, in a symbolic effort to clarify the status of traditional religious practices and practitioners, Congress passed a Joint Resolution entitled the American Indian Religious Freedom Act. This act declared that it was the policy of Congress to protect and preserve the inherent right of American Indians to believe, express, and practice their traditional religions. The resolution identified the problem as one of a "lack of knowledge or the insensitive and inflexible enforcement of Federal policies and regulations." Section 2 of the resolution directed the president to require the various federal departments to evaluate their policies and procedures, report back to Congress on the results of their survey, and make recommendations for legislative actions.[1]

Many people assumed that this resolution clarified the federal attitude toward traditional religions, and it began to be cited in litigation involving the construction of dams, roads, and the management of federal lands. Almost unanimously, however, the federal courts have since ruled that the resolution did not protect or preserve the right of Indians to practice their religion and conduct ceremonies at sacred sites on public lands.[2] Some courts even hinted darkly that any formal recognition of the existence of tribal practices would be tantamount to establishing a state religion,[3] an interpretation that, upon analysis, is a dreadful misreading of American history and the Constitution and may have been an effort to inflame anti-Indian feelings.

A good example for making this claim was the 1988 Supreme Court decision in the *Lyng v. Northwest Indian Cemetery Protective Association* case that involved protecting the visitation rights of the traditional religious leaders of three tribes to sacred sites in the Chimney Rock area of the Six Rivers National Forest in northern California. The Forest Service proposed to build a six-mile paved road that would have opened part of the area to commercial logging. This area, known by three Indian tribes as the "High Country," was the center of their religious and ceremonial life. The lower federal courts prohibited the construction of the road on the grounds that it would have made religious ceremonial use of the area impossible. Before the Supreme Court could hear the appeal, Congress passed the California Wilderness Act that made the question of constructing the road moot for all practical purposes. But the Supreme Court insisted on hearing the appeal of the Forest Service and deciding the religious issues. It turned the tribes down flat, ruling that the Free Exercise clause did not prevent the government from using its property in any way it saw fit and in effect rolling back the religious use of the area completely.

Most troubling about the Supreme Court's decision was the insistence on analyzing tribal religions within the same conceptual framework as Western organized religions. Justice O'Connor observed,

> *A broad range of government activities—from social welfare programs to foreign aid to conservation projects—will always be considered essential to the spiritual well-being of some citizens, often on the basis of sincerely held religious beliefs. Others will find the very same activity deeply offensive, and perhaps incompatible with their own search for spiritual fulfillment and with the tenets of their religion.*[4]

Thus ceremonies and rituals that had been performed for thousands of years were treated as if they were popular fads or simply matters of personal preference based on the erroneous assumption that religion was only a matter of individual aesthetic choice.

Justice Brennan's dissent vigorously attacked this spurious line of reasoning, outlining with some precision the communal aspect of the tribal religions and their relationship to the mountains. But his argument failed to gather support within the Court. Most observers of the Supreme Court were simply confounded at the majority's conclusion that suggested that destroying a religion "did not unduly burden it" and that no constitutional protections were available to the Indians.[5]

When informed of the meaning of this decision, most people have shown great sympathy for the traditional religious people. At the same time, they have had great difficulty understanding why it is so important that these ceremonies be held, that they be conducted only at certain locations, and that they be held in secrecy and privacy. This lack of understanding highlights the great gulf that exists between traditional Western thinking about religion and the Indian perspective. It is the difference between individual conscience and commitment (Western) and communal tradition (Indian). These views can only be reconciled by examining them in a much broader historical and geographic context.

Justice Brennan attempted to make this difference clear when he observed, "Although few tribal members actually made medicine at the most powerful sites, the entire tribe's welfare hinges on the success of [an] individual practitioner."[6] More than that, however, the "world renewal" ceremonies conducted by the tribes were done on behalf of the earth and all forms of life. To describe these ceremonies as if they were comparable to Oral Roberts seeking funds or Jimmy Swaggart begging forgiveness for his continuing sexual misconduct or Justice O'Connor's matters of community aesthetic preference is to miss the point entirely. In effect, the Court declared that Indians cannot pray for the planet or for other people and other forms of life in the manner required by their religion.

Two contradictory responses seem to characterize the non-Indian attitudes toward traditional tribal religions. Some people want the traditional healers to share their religious beliefs in the same manner that priests, rabbis, and ministers expound publicly the tenets of their denominations. Other people feel that Indian ceremonials are simply remnants of primitive life and should be abandoned. Neither perspective understands that Indian tribes are communities in ways that are fundamentally different from other American communities and organizations. Tribal communities are wholly defined by the family relationships; the non-Indian communities are defined primarily by residence, by an arbitrary establishment of political jurisdiction, or by agreement with generally applicable sets of intellectual beliefs. Ceremonial and ritual knowledge is possessed by everyone in the Indian community, although only a few people may actually be chosen to perform these acts. Authorization to perform ceremonies comes from higher spiritual powers and not by certification through an institution or any formal organization.

A belief in the sacredness of lands in the non-Indian context may become the preferred belief of an individual or group of people based on their experiences or on an intensive study of preselected evidence. But this belief becomes the subject of intense criticism and does not, except under unusual circumstances, become an operative principle in the life and behavior of the non-Indian group. The same belief, when seen in the Indian context, is an integral part of the experiences of the people—past, present, and future. The idea does not become a bone of contention among the people, for even if someone does not have the experience or belief in the sacredness of lands, he or she accords tradition the respect that it deserves. Indians who have never visited certain sacred sites nevertheless know of these places from the community knowledge, and they intuit this knowing to be an essential part of their being.

Justice Brennan, in countering the arguments raised by Justice O'Connor that any recognition of the sacredness of certain sites would allow traditional Indian religions to define the use of all public lands, suggested that the burden of proof be placed on the traditional people to demonstrate why some sites are central to their practice and other sites, while invoking a sense of reverence, are not as important. This requirement is not unreasonable, but it requires a willingness on the part of non-Indians and the courts to entertain different ideas about the nature of religion—ideas that until the present have not been a part of their experience or understanding.

If we were to subject the topic of the sacredness of lands to a Western rational analysis, fully recognizing that such an analysis is merely for our convenience in discussion and does not represent the nature of reality, we would probably find four major categories of description. Some of these categories are overlapping because some groups might not agree with the description of certain sites in the categories in which other Indians would place them. Nevertheless, it is the principle of respect for the sacred that is important.

The first and most familiar kind of sacred lands are places to which we attribute sanctity because the location is a site where, within our own history, something of great importance has taken place. Unfortunately, many of these places are related to instances of human violence. Gettysburg National Cemetery is a good example of this kind of sacred land. Abraham Lincoln properly noted that we cannot hallow the Gettysburg battlefield because others, the men who fought there, had already consecrated it by giving "that last full measure of devotion." We generally hold these places sacred because people did there what we might one day be required to do—give our lives in a cause we hold dear. Wounded Knee, South Dakota, has become such a place for many Indians where a band of Sioux Indians were massacred. On the whole, however, the idea of regarding a battlefield as sacred was entirely foreign to most tribes because they did not see war as a holy enterprise. The Lincoln Memorial in Washington, D.C., might be an example of a nonmartial location, and, although Justice O'Connor felt that recognizing the sacredness of land and location might inspire an individual to have a special fondness for this memorial, it is important to recognize that we should have some sense of reverence in these places.

Every society needs these kinds of sacred places because they help to instill a sense of social cohesion in the people and remind them of the passage of generations that have brought them to the present. A society that cannot remember and honor its past is in peril of losing its soul. Indians, because of our considerably longer tenure on this continent, have many more sacred places than do non-Indians. Many different ceremonies can be and have been held at these locations; there is both an exclusivity and an inclusiveness, depending on the occasion and the ceremony. In this classification the site is all-important, but it is sanctified each time ceremonies are held and prayers offered.

A second category of sacred lands has a deeper, more profound sense of the sacred. It can be illustrated in Old Testament stories that have become the foundation of three world religions. After the death of Moses, Joshua led the Hebrews across the River Jordan into the Holy Land. On approaching the river with the Ark of the Covenant, the waters of the Jordan "rose up" or parted and the people, led by the Ark, crossed over on "dry ground," which is to say they crossed without difficulty. After crossing, Joshua selected one man from each of the Twelve Tribes and told him to find a large stone. The twelve stones were then placed together in a monument to mark the spot where the people had camped after having crossed the river successfully. When asked about this strange behavior, Joshua then replied, "That this may be a sign among you, that when your children ask their fathers in time to come, saying 'What mean ye by these stones?' Then you shall answer them: That the waters of Jordan were cut off before the Ark of the Covenant of the Lord, when it passed over Jordan."[7]

In comparing this site with Gettysburg, we must understand a fundamental difference. Gettysburg is made sacred by the actions of men. It can be described as exquisitely dear to us, but it is not a location where we have perceived that something specifically other than ourselves is present, that something mysteriously religious in the proper meaning of those words has happened or been made manifest. In the crossing of the River Jordan, the sacred or higher powers have appeared in the lives of human beings. Indians would say something holy has appeared in an otherwise secular situation. No matter how we might attempt to explain this event in later historical, political, or economic terms, the essence of the event is that the sacred has become a part of our experience.

Some of the sites that traditional religious leaders visit are of this nature. Buffalo Gap at the southeastern edge of the Black Hills of South Dakota marks the location where the buffalo emerged each spring to begin the ceremonial year of the Plains Indians, and it has this aspect of sacred/secular status. It may indeed be the starting point of the Great Race that determined the primacy between two-legged and four-legged creatures at the beginning of the world. Several mountains in New Mexico and Arizona mark places where the Pueblo, Hopi, and Navajo peoples completed their migrations, were told to settle, or where they first established their spiritual relationships with bear, deer, eagle, and other peoples who participate in the ceremonials.

Every identifiable region has sacred places peculiar to its geography and as we extend the circle geographically from any point in North America, we begin to include an ever-increasing number of sacred sites. Beginning in the American Southwest, we must include the Apache, Ute, Comanche, Kiowa, and other tribes as we move away from the Pueblo and Navajo lands. These lands would be sacred to some tribes but secular to the Pueblo, Hopi, and Navajo. The difference would be in the manner of revelation and what the people experienced. There is immense particularity in the sacred, and it is not a blanket category to be applied indiscriminately. Even east of the Mississippi, though many places have been nearly obliterated, people retain knowledge of these sacred sites. Their sacredness does not depend on human occupancy but on the stories that describe the revelation that enabled human beings to experience the holiness there.

In the religious world of most tribes, birds, animals, and plants compose the "other peoples" of creation. Depending on the ceremony, various of these "peoples" participate in human activities. If Jews and Christians see the action of a deity at sacred places in the Holy Land and in churches and synagogues, traditional Indian people experience spiritual activity as the whole of creation becomes active participants in ceremonial life. Because the relationship with the "other peoples" is so fundamental to the human community, most traditional practitioners are reluctant to articulate the specific elements of either the ceremony or the locations. Because some rituals involve the continued prosperity of the "other peoples," discussing the nature of the ceremony would violate the integrity of these relationships. Thus traditional people explain that these ceremonies are being held for "all our relatives" but are reluctant to offer any further explanations. It is these ceremonies in particular that are now to be denied protection under the Supreme Court rulings.

It is not likely that non-Indians have had many of these kinds of religious experiences, particularly because most churches and synagogues have special rituals that are designed to cleanse the buildings so that their services can be held there untainted by the natural world. Non-Indians have simply not been on this continent very long; their families have rarely settled in one place for any period of time so that no profound relationship with the environment has been possible. In addition, non-Indians have engaged in the senseless killing of wildlife and utter destruction of plant life. It is unlikely that they would have understood efforts by other forms of life to communicate with humans, although some non-Indian families who have lived continuously in isolated rural areas tell stories about birds and animals similar to the traditions of many tribes, indicating that lands and the "other peoples" do seek intimacy with our species.

The third kind of sacred lands are places of overwhelming holiness where the Higher Powers, on their own initiative, have revealed Themselves to human beings. Again, we can illustrate this in the Old Testament narrative. Prior to his journey to Egypt, Moses spent his time herding his father-in-law's sheep on or near Mount Horeb. One day he took the flock to the far side of the mountain and to his amazement saw a bush burning with fire but not being consumed by it. Approaching this spot with the usual curiosity of a person accustomed to the outdoor life, Moses was startled when the Lord spoke to him from the bush, warning, "Draw not hither; put off thy shoes from thy feet, for the place where on thou standest is holy ground."[8]

This tradition tells us that there are places of unquestionable, inherent sacredness on this earth, sites that are holy in and of themselves. Human societies come and go on this earth and any prolonged occupation of a geographic region will produce shrines and sacred sites discerned by the occupying people, but there will always be a few sites at which the highest spirits dwell. The stories that explain the sacred nature of these locations will frequently provide startling parallels to the account about the burning bush. One need only look at the shrines of present-day Europe. Long before Catholic or Protestant churches were built in certain places, other religions had established shrines and temples on that spot. These holy places are locations where people have always gone to communicate and commune with higher spiritual powers.

This phenomenon is worldwide, and all religions find that these places regenerate people and fill them with spiritual powers. In the Western Hemisphere these places, with few exceptions, are known only by American Indians. Bear Butte, Blue Lake, and the High Country in the *Lyng* case are all well-known locations that are sacred in and of themselves. People have been commanded to perform ceremonies at these holy places so that the earth and all its forms of life might survive and prosper. Evidence of this moral responsibility that sacred places command has come through the testimony of traditional people when they have tried to explain to non-Indians at various times in this century—in court, in conferences, and in conversations—that they must perform certain ceremonies at specific times and places in order that the sun may continue to shine, the earth prosper, and the stars remain in the heavens. Tragically, this attitude is interpreted by non-Indians as indicative of the traditional leader's personal code or philosophy and is not seen as a simple admission of a moral duty.

Skeptical non-Indians, and representatives of other religions seeking to discredit tribal religions, have sometimes deliberately violated some of these holy places with no ill effects. They have then come to believe that they have demonstrated the false nature of Indian beliefs. These violations reveal a strange non-Indian belief in a form of mechanical magic that is touchingly adolescent, a belief that an impious act would, or could, trigger an immediate response from the higher spiritual powers. Surely these impious acts suggest a deity who jealously guards his or her prerogatives and wreaks immediate vengeance for minor transgressions—much as some Protestant sects have envisioned God and much as an ancient astronaut wanting to control lesser beings might act.

It would be impossible for the thoughtless or impious acts of one species to have an immediate drastic effect on the earth. The cumulative effect of continuous secularity, however, poses a different kind of danger. Long-standing prophecies tell us of the impious people who would come here, defy the creator, and cause the massive destruction of the planet. Many traditional people believe that we are now quite near that time. The cumulative evidence of global warming, acid rain, the disappearance of amphibians, overpopulation, and other products of civilized life certainly testify to the possibility of these prophecies being correct.

Of all the traditional ceremonies extant and actively practiced at the time of contact with non-Indians, ceremonies derived from or related to these holy places have the highest retention rate because of their extraordinary planetary importance. Ironically, traditional people have been forced to hold these ceremonies under various forms of subterfuge and have been abused and imprisoned for doing them. Yet the ceremonies have very little to do with individual or tribal prosperity. Their underlying theme is one of gratitude expressed by human beings on behalf of all forms of life. They act to complete and renew the entire and complete cycle of life, ultimately including the whole cosmos present in its specific realizations, so that in the last analysis one might describe ceremonials as the cosmos becoming thankfully aware of itself.

Having used Old Testament examples to show the objective presence of the holy places, we can draw additional conclusions about the nature of these holy places from the story of the Exodus. Moses did not demand that the particular location of the burning bush become a place of worship for his people, although there was every reason to suppose that he could have done so. Lacking information, we must conclude that the holiness of this place precluded its use as a shrine. If Moses had been told to perform annual ceremonies at that location during specific days or times of the year, world history would have been entirely different.

Each holy site contains its own revelation. This knowledge is not the ultimate in the sense that Near Eastern religions like to claim the universality of their ideas. Traditional religious leaders tell us that in many of the ceremonies new messages are communicated to them. The ceremonies enable humans to have continuing relationships with higher spiritual powers so that each bit of information is specific to the time, place, and circumstances of the people. No revelation can be regarded as universal because times and conditions change.

The second and third kinds of sacred lands result from two distinctly different forms of sacred revelations where the sacred is actively involved in secular human activities and where the sacred takes the initiative to chart out a new historical course for humans. Because there are higher spiritual powers who can communicate with people, there has to be a fourth category of sacred lands. People must always be ready to experience new revelations at new locations. If this possibility did not exist, all deities and spirits would be dead. Consequently, we always look forward to the revelation of new sacred places and ceremonies. Unfortunately, some federal courts irrationally and arbitrarily circumscribe this universal aspect of religion by insisting that traditional religious practitioners restrict their identification of sacred locations to places that were historically visited by Indians, implying that, at least for the federal courts, God is dead.

In denying the possibility of the continuing revelation of the sacred in our lives, federal courts, scholars, and state and federal agencies refuse to accord credibility to the testimony of religious leaders. They demand evidence that a ceremony or location has *always* been central to the beliefs and practices of an Indian tribe and impose exceedingly rigorous standards of proof on Indians who appear before them. This practice allows the Supreme Court to command what should not to be done, it lets secular institutions rule on the substance of religious belief and practice. Thus courts will protect a religion that shows every symptom of being dead but will create formidable barriers if it appears to be alive. Justice Scalia made this posture perfectly clear when he announced in *Smith* that it would be unconstitutional to ban the casting of "statues that are used for worship purposes" or to prohibit bowing down before a golden calf.

We live in time and space and receive most of our signals about proper behavior from each other and the environment around us. Under these circumstances, the individual and the group *must* both have some kind of sanctity if we are to have a social order at all. By recognizing the various aspects of the sacredness of lands as we have described, we place ourselves in a realistic context in which the individual and the group can cultivate and enhance the sacred experience. Recognizing the sacredness of lands on which previous generations have lived and died is the foundation of all other sentiment. Instead of denying this dimension of our emotional lives, we should be setting aside additional places that have transcendent meaning. Sacred sites that higher spiritual powers have chosen for manifestation enable us to focus our concerns on the specific form of our lives. These places remind us of our unique relationship with the spiritual forces that govern the universe and call us to fulfill our religious vocations. These kinds of religious experiences have shown us something of the nature of the universe by an affirmative manifestation of themselves, and this knowledge illuminates everything else that we know.

The nature of tribal religion brings contemporary America a new kind of legal problem. Religious freedom has existed as a matter of course in America *only* when religion has been conceived as a set of objective beliefs. This condition is actually not freedom at all, because it would be exceedingly difficult to read minds and determine what ideas were being entertained at the time. So far in American history religious freedom has not involved the consecration and setting aside of lands for religious purposes or allowing sincere but highly divergent behavior by individuals and groups. The issue of sacred lands, as we have seen, was successfully raised in the case of the Taos Pueblo people. Nevertheless, a great deal more remains to be done to guarantee Indian people the right to practice their own religion.

A number of other tribes have sacred sanctuaries in lands that have been taken by the government for purposes other than religion. These lands must be returned to the respective Indian tribes for their ceremonial purposes. The greatest number of Indian shrines are located in New Mexico, and here the tribal religions have remained comparatively strong. Cochiti Pueblo needs some 24,000 acres of land for access to and use of religious shrines in what is now Bandelier National Monument. The people also have shrines in the Tetilla Peak area. San Juan Pueblo has also been trying to get lands returned for religious purposes. Santa Clara Pueblo requested the Indian Claims Commission to set aside 30,000 acres of the lands that have religious and ceremonial importance to its people but are presently in the hands of the National Forest Service and the Atomic Energy Commission.

In Arizona the Hopi people have a number of shrines that are of vital importance to their religion. Traditionals regard the Black Mesa area as sacred, but it is being leased to Peabody Coal by the more assimilative tribal council. The San Francisco Peaks within the Coconino National Forest are sacred because they are believed to be the homes of the Kachinas who play a major part in the Hopi ceremonial system. The Navajo have a number of sacred mountains now under federal ownership. Mount Taylor in the Cibola National Forest, Blanca Peak in southern Colorado, Hesperus Peak in the San Juan National Forest, Huerfano Mountain on public domain lands, and Oak Creek Canyon in the Coconino National Forest are all sites integral to the Navajo tradition. Part of the Navajo religion involves the "mountain chant" that describes the seven sacred mountains and a sacred lake located within these mountains. The Navajo believe their ancestors arose from this region at the creation. Last, but certainly not least, is the valiant struggle now being waged by the Apache people to prevent the University of Arizona from building several telescopes on Mount Graham in southern Arizona.

In other states several sacred sites are under threat of exploitation. The Forest Service is proposing to construct a major parking lot and observation platform at the Medicine Wheel site near Powell, Wyoming, that is sacred to many tribes from Montana, the Dakotas, and Wyoming. Because the only value of this location is its relationship to traditional Indian religions that need isolation and privacy, it seems ludicrous to pretend that making it accessible to more tourists and subject to increasing environmental degradation is enhancing it. The Badger Two Medicine area of Montana, where oil drilling has been proposed, is a sacred area for traditional Blackfeet who live in the vicinity. The Pipestone Quarry in southwestern Minnesota was confiscated from the Yankton Sioux in the closing decades of the last century when some missionaries pressured the federal government to eliminate Indian access to this important spot.

Finally, there is the continuing struggle over the Black Hills of South Dakota. Many Americans are now aware of this state thanks to the success of the movie *Dances with Wolves* that not only depicted the culture of the Sioux Indians but also filled the screen with the magnificent landscape of the northern Great Plains. Nineteen

ninety-one was a year of great schizophrenia and strange anomalies
in South Dakota. Local whites shamelessly capitalized on the success of the movie at the same time that they were frothing at the
mouth over the continuing efforts of the Sioux people to get the
federal lands in the Black Hills returned to them. Governor George
Mickelson announced a "Year of Reconciliation" that simply became
twelve months of symbolic maneuvering for publicity and renewal
of political images. When some of the Sioux elders suggested that
the return of Bear Butte near Sturgis would be a concrete step toward
reconciliation, non-Indians were furious that reconciliation might
require them to make a good-faith effort to heal the wounds from a
century of conflict.

The question that must be addressed in the issue of sacred lands
is the extent to which the tribal religions can be maintained if sacred
lands are restored. Would restoration of the sacred Pipestone Quarry
result in more people seeking to follow the traditional religious
life, or would it result in continued use of the stone for tourism
and commercial purposes? A small group of Sioux people have made
a living during this century from making ashtrays and decorative
carvings from this sacred rock; they refuse to stop their exploitation. A major shift in focus is needed by traditional Sioux people to
prepare to reconsecrate the quarry and return to the old ways of
reverence.

A very difficult task lies ahead for the people who continue to
believe in the old tribal religions. In the past these traditions have
been ridiculed by disbelievers, primarily missionaries and social scientists. Today injuries nearly as grievous are visited on traditional
religions by the multitude of non-Indians who seek entrance and
participation in ceremonies and rituals. Many of these non-Indians
blatantly steal symbols, prayers, and teaching by laying claim to
alleged offices in tribal religions. Most non-Indians see in tribal religions the experiences and reverence that are missing in their own
heritage. No matter how hard they try, they always reduce the teachings and ceremonies to a complicated word game and ineffectual
gestures. Lacking communities and extended families, they are unable
to put the religion into practice.

Some major efforts must be made by the Indians of this generation to demonstrate that the view of the world their tradition teaches
has an integrity of its own and represents a sensible and respectable

perspective of the world and a valid means of interpreting experiences. There are many new studies that seem to confirm certain tribal practices as reasonable and sometimes even as sophisticated techniques for handling certain kinds of problems. It might be sufficient to show that these patterns of behavior are indicative of a consistent attitude toward the world and include the knowledge that everything is alive and related.

Sacred places are the foundation of all other beliefs and practices because they represent the presence of the sacred in our lives. They properly inform us that we are not larger than nature and that we have responsibilities to the rest of the natural world that transcend our own personal desires and wishes. This lesson must be learned by each generation; unfortunately, the technology of industrial society always leads us in the other direction. Yet it is certain that as we permanently foul our planetary nest, we shall have to learn a most bitter lesson. There probably is not sufficient time for the non-Indian population to understand the meaning of sacred lands and incorporate the idea into their lives and practices. We can but hope that some protection can be afforded these sacred places before the world becomes wholly secular and is destroyed.

NOTES

1. 92 Stat 469, 42 U.S.C. §1996.
2. See *Wilson v. Block*, 708 F. 2d 735 (D.C. Cir. 1983). Hopi and Navajo sacred sites and shrines on San Francisco peak were destroyed by the U.S. Forest Service to make room for a new ski lift. In *Fools Crow v. Gullet*, 706 F. 2d 856 (8th Cir. 1983), the court upheld intrusions by the U.S. Park Service on Sioux vision quest use of Bear Butte. In *Badoni v. Higginson*, 638 F. 2d 172 (10th Cir. 1980), the court allowed the destruction of a Navajo sacred site at Rainbow Bridge in the Grand Canyon area.
3. The majority decision in *Lyng* even suggested that to recognize traditional Indian religious freedom would make it seem as if the Indians owned the federal lands.

    No disrespect for these practices is implied when one notes that such beliefs could easily require de facto beneficial ownership of some rather spacious tracts of public property. Even without anticipating future cases, the diminution of the government's propety rights, and the concomitant subsidy of the Indian religion, would in this case be far from trivial . . . . (108 S. Ct. 1319, 1327 [1988])
4. At 1327.
5. Justice Brennan's dissent makes this point specifically:

The Court today, however, ignores *Roy*'s emphasis on the internal nature of the government practice at issue there, and instead construes that case as further support for the proposition that governmental action that does not coerce conduct inconsistent with religious faith simply does not implicate the concerns of the Free Exercise Clause. That such a reading is wholly untenable, however, is demonstrated by the cruelly surreal result it produces here: *governmental action that will virtually destroy a religion is nevertheless deemed not to 'burden' that religion.* (At 1337; emphasis added.)

6. At 1332.
7. Joshua 4:6-7.
8. Exodus 3:5.

27

MYTH AND THE ORIGIN OF RELIGION

▼▼▼▼

I f there were gigantic planetary catastrophes in former times, how should they have been described in order to receive credulous consideration by men several thousand years later? What format should the ancients have used so that we could give their descriptions serious attention? Should they have couched their descriptions in mathematical terms? Described the approaches of comets and planets in the astronomical jargon familiar to us today? Should they have raised monuments to the forces of change? Buried "time capsules" for our information?

We tend to project present understandings of the world backward into the ancient records and test their credibility, not by what they describe or narrate, but by what we consider reasonable given our present knowledge of the universe. Certain ruins used to be thought of as religious monuments; today we call them computers.

"Myth" has become a term like "executive privilege"—meaning whatever the thinker wants it to mean when he has decided how ancient accounts are to be interpreted. In order to see this aspect of present-day thinking, I will very briefly compare the use of myths by a number of scholars and then distinguish Velikovsky's methods and approach from theirs.

Émile Durkheim. The sociologist Émile Durkheim, in his famous study of primitive religion, *The Elementary Forms of the Religious Life,* discussed the early efforts by Western European thinkers to interpret the myths of primitive peoples in either animistic or naturalistic terms. The universe was for primitives either a living creature that had a soul and in which millions of souls lived; or else it was a relatively lifeless entity, with stories arising in an effort to humanize its sterility.

Durkheim promulgated his own theory of myth, which he hoped would bridge the extremes that he felt were represented by these two interpretations of myth and religion. Approaching myth via religious stories, Durkheim wrote: "Religious thought does not come in contact with reality, except to cover it at once with a thick veil which conceals its real forms; this veil is the tissue of fabulous beliefs which mythology brought forth. Thus the believer, like the delirious man, *lives in a world peopled with beings and things which have only a verbal existence*" (emphasis added).[1]

This definition of myth, or at least religious myth, excludes the possibility of extracting from myth any historical reality. It finds myth to possess verbal existence only, confining it to the realm of ancient intellectualism or psychological phenomena that occur "in here" rather than "out there" in the world of physical existence. Almost every theory of interpretation of myth since Durkheim, stripped of its rhetoric, accepts this definition.

Franz Boas. Durkheim's reduction of myth to a verbal and quasi-religious reality was echoed by Franz Boas, who focused on the hidden meanings found in myths. Boas wrote in his essay, "Mythology and Folklore" (in *General Anthropology*), "Mythological concepts are the fundamental views of the constitution of the world and of its origin."[2]

The problem with this theory was that it did not get down to specifics regarding particular myths and how they arose. Were all ancient sources to be equally suspect? Or only those with anthropological overtones that could be revisited in surviving aboriginal groups? Were the sacred tales of the Greeks more respectable than those of the Polynesians? Was the Old Testament a series of myths, or history?

In recent years this interpretation of myth has become dominant, and it would appear that almost every ancient source available has fallen under the general category of myth or the mythological. Granted that theologians dance fancy steps to maintain the sacredness and "higher" meaning of myth, the meaning that comes across to the man in the street is that myths are a type of fable designed to comfort, admonish, teach, and inspire but certainly do not refer to historic events and incidents no matter how serious the accounts may appear to be.

R. G. Collingwood. R. G. Collingwood, in his famous book, *The Idea of History,* appears to dismiss ancient accounts whenever they contain any mention of divinity or the activities of the gods intermingling in human affairs:

> *Myth, on the contrary, is not concerned with human actions at all. The human element has been completely purged away and the characters of the story are simply gods. And the divine actions that are recorded are not dated events in the past; they are conceived as having occurred in the past, indeed, but in a dateless past which is so remote that nobody knows when it was. It is outside all our time-reckonings and called "the beginning of things."*[3]

One would think that Collingwood could use this definition to distinguish between ancient accounts reflecting some historical event and those concerned primarily with making a statement about the origin or constitution of the world.

Such is not the case. In the same book, when discussing Homer, Collingwood remarks,

> *The work of Homer is not research, it is legend; and to a great extent it is theocratic legend. The gods appear in Homer as intervening in human affairs in a way not very different from the way in which they appear in the theocratic histories of the Near East."*[4]

It seems incredible that a scholar would attempt to pass off the Homeric legends as theocratic legend, especially after Heinrich Schliemann demonstrated with pick and shovel that Troy was not a fiction possessing verbal reality only. Troy was there whether Homeric verse fit into a definition of history or not.

Mircea Eliade. Among the modern thinkers no man has commanded more respect in the history of religions than Mircea Eliade; his ideas have influenced a generation of students. Eliade finds that myth "is the history of what took place *in illo tempore,* the recital of what the gods or the semidivine beings did at the beginning of time."[5] His approach is basically that of Boas, but with Eliade's scholarly knowledge the definition verges on a commandment from Sinai. It is when we turn to his specific interpretation of myths that we are made uneasy.

"In New Guinea," he writes, "a great many myths tell of long sea voyages thus providing 'exemplars for the modern voyagers.'"[6] But Hawaiians and many other Pacific peoples did undertake long sea voyages and were as much at home on a boundless ocean as they were on any island. The New Guinea myths, if anything, are a fairly accurate account of ancient voyages that can be verified by other data with a high degree of reliability.

Carl Jung. Carl Jung also deals with myth, and his use of myths is quite similar to Eliade's, except that it emerges in practical, psychoanalytic techniques of therapy. Jung frequently uses myths to explain prolonged patterns of psychic behavior. Of his many definitions of myth, the ones that best fit our discussion have to do with the reality behind myth. Jung tells us, "Myth is not fiction: it consists of facts that are continually repeated and can be observed over and over again. It is something that happens to man, and men have mythical fates just as much as Greek heroes do."[7]

Myths seem to be preestablished patterns of emotional behavior when Jung uses them; a predestined sequence of actions and reactions that work out an individual's fate. Jung evidently does not question how myths originate, however, and he remains content to describe the state of his patients according to how far they have progressed through the sequence in which the myth unfolds. A comparison of Jung's use of Greek myths and Velikovsky's analysis of the Oedipus myth in *Oedipus and Akhnaton* will indicate how far apart the two men are. Velikovsky seeks the origin of the mythic story line; Jung is content to see in myths a classic analysis of the manner in which human beings work out their interpersonal relationships. Jung never answers the question of why Greek myths, of all the myths available, seem to work so well in analyzing human personality.

Claude Lévi-Strauss. The most ambitious mythologist in anthropology today is Claude Lévi-Strauss, who has developed a theory of "bricolage." "The characteristic feature of mythical thought," Lévi-Strauss writes in *The Savage Mind*, "as of 'bricolage' on the practical plane, is that it builds up structured sets but by using the remains and debris of events."[8] Exactly what these "remains" consist of is undetermined. Lévi-Strauss makes a vigorous defense of mythical thinking as having a rigor comparable to modern science, but his defense is nearly as much a defense of anthropology as of the validity and reliability of ancient accounts of incidents and events.

"Mythical thought," he explains in *The Savage Mind,* "for its part is imprisoned in the events and experiences which it never tires of ordering and re-ordering in its search to find them a meaning. But it also acts as a liberator by its protest against the idea that anything can be meaningless with which science at first resigned itself to a compromise."[9]

We would have to conclude that myths as we find them have a story line, characters, and a set of descriptive phrases that have been worked and reworked in order to present the best possible tale. But we note that such well-polished stories are the exception, not the rule. Even the creation story of Genesis has the sequence out of phase, with the first day and night occurring before the creation of the Sun, Moon, and stars, an error that should have been eliminated by the ordering and reordering process long before Clarence Darrow pointed it out.

Joseph Campbell. One of the chief mythologists of today, Joseph Campbell takes a rigidly sociological interpretation of myth that probably well suits many modern scholars in both religion and anthropology: "All primitive mythologies serve to validate the customs, systems of sentiments, and political aims of their respective local groups."[10]

Campbell includes the Old Testament under the category of primitive mythology, claiming, "On the surface the books of the Old Testament may appear to have been composed as conscientious history. In depth they reveal themselves to have been conceived as myths: poetic readings of the mystery of life from a certain point of view."[11] Campbell seems to have failed to take into account the historical basis of the Old Testament writings, preferring to avoid the issues of historical experience by viewing the accounts as poetic commentaries on life. A close reading of Kings, Judges, and other books would indicate less poetry and more history.

Alan S. Watts. Alan S. Watts, in his book *Myth and Ritual in Christianity,* advances a definition of myth that all of the previous thinkers should find comforting. It is under his umbrella that we will conclude our survey.

"Myth," Watts writes, "is to be defined as a complex of stories—some no doubt fact, and some fantasy—which, for various reasons, human beings regard as demonstrations of the inner meaning of the universe and of human life. Myth is quite different from philosophy in the sense of abstract concepts, for the form of the myth is always concrete—consisting of vivid, sensually intelligible narratives, images, rites, ceremonies and symbols. A great deal of myth may therefore be based on historical events, but not all such events acquire the mythic character."[12]

MYTH AND HISTORY

The point that seems to escape all of these men is that the ancient sources and accounts that we have in hand today may simply be the way people wrote about the events that affected their lives. Even with Watts's encompassing definition of myth, we find the old Boas "hidden meaning" or quasi-philosophy about the nature of the universe. It seems strange indeed that the ancient peoples would spend so much time writing about the inner mysteries of life and find little time to record the events and incidents of their times. Using the definitions of the various thinkers discussed above, we cannot and will never be able to make any significant statements about the history of the planet, because these thinkers have already ruled out the unusual, preferring to view such accounts as elaborations on religious and philosophical themes.

We are left to wonder whether these men have actually read the myths of the various societies of the past. In many of the myths there is little effort at national glorification; the sins and shortcomings of the heroes are presented in a rather straightforward manner. And the failure of these accounts to exhibit the sequence we would expect of stories possessing only a verbal reality leads us to doubt the notion that they have been carefully polished over many lifetimes. Further, we are confronted with historical facts: many tales of the past, dealing with Troy, Ur of the Chaldees, and other places, are now known to be founded on reality rather than fantasy.

Scholars working with myths seem to rely on two basic assumptions about ancient source materials. The first is that myths are fundamentally religious in content and origin; the second is that they possess primarily a verbal reality, consisting at best of the "debris and remains" of real historical incidents.

With these two assumptions scholars have a great deal of latitude in interpreting ancient source materials. When any historical basis is found for a myth, they can proclaim, "Homer was right." But when the story line verges on the incredible, measured by our present sensitivities, the scholar can fall back on his definition of the "mysterious" nature of human existence and the need felt by ancient peoples to comment poetically on life.

It is precisely at this point in the interpretation of myth that Immanuel Velikovsky has challenged modern thinking. He has taken the story of the Exodus and asked whether or not such a traumatic event as described in the Old Testament could be a rendering of actual history. From this basic question, he then proceeds relentlessly to amass evidence from every possible science, interest area, and source available. Weaving and winnowing his way through an incredible mass of materials, he uses one science to critique another, one document to serve as a guide for interpreting other documents.

THE EXODUS

The result of Velikovsky's method of pursuing, attacking, and interpreting the reality of mythological accounts is that one comprehensive explanation of events begins to emerge in which the many individual strands of knowledge are brought together to describe not only a series of events but also the means by which such events could have taken place and the magnitude of the experience felt by ancient peoples.

Starting with, among other things, a book that is considered basically religious (Exodus), Velikovsky finds in complementary sources—the Papyrus Ipuwer and the Naos of El Arish—support for the idea that something spectacular occurred. Using the Exodus account and cross-checking with these two basic sources, he then proceeds to search for other indications of the reality of the events by posing questions to the various sciences and receiving answers in return as to both the probability and the possibility of events happening in the manner in which they are described.

As this process continues, Velikovsky points out the errors in interpretation, not only of myth, but also of the data compiled by other sciences. The result of Velikovsky's thinking is that a new conception of the nature of the universe comes into being. Instead of sciences going their separate ways, interpreting data in isolation, the sciences become partners in seeking out the meaning of the universe. A relationship is established between the recorded experiences of the ancient Hebrews and the Venus probe of the twentieth century, in that they both illuminate the same realities.

Other mythologists have dealt with the Exodus story, and I will choose three to compare with Velikovsky: Martin Buber, Theodore Gaster, and Johannes Pederson. Each of these men was intimately acquainted with the Hebrew scriptures, the culture of the Hebrews and other Near Eastern peoples, and the history of that region of our planet.

Martin Buber, writing in his book, *Moses,* defines away the Exodus as a historical event early in his interpretation of the scriptures:

> *The Biblical narrative itself is basically different in character from all that we usually classify as serviceable historical sources. The happenings recorded there can never have come about, in the historical world as we know it, after the fashion in which they are described. The literary category within which our historical mode of thinking must classify this narrative is the saga; and a saga is generally assumed to be incapable of producing within us any conception of a factual sequence (emphasis added).*[13]

It has remained a mystery to me how Buber can write that on page 13 of *Moses* and then devote the next two hundred pages to an exegesis that follows the story line of the Exodus remarkably well for a disbeliever.

In describing the passage over the sea of reeds, Buber remarks that a miracle "is not something 'supernatural' or 'super-historical,' but an incident, an event which can be fully included in the objective, scientific nexus of nature and history."[14] Thus it is that Buber's Moses, obediently following the dictates of YHVH, "comes to the shore, he steps on sands that are barely covered by shallow water; and the hosts follow him as he follows the God. At this point occurs whatever occurs, and it is apprehended as a miracle."[15] Such an event would hardly seem capable of producing a religion; people wade in shallow waters quite often without any significant change.

Theodore Gaster, discussing the Exodus story in *Passover,* fails to venture even as far as Buber:

> *It is obvious to any unbiased reader that this story, with its markedly religious coloration and its emphasis on supernatural "signs and wonders," is more of a romantic saga or popular legend than an accurate record. Written down centuries later than the period which it describes, it is clearly more indebted to folklore than to sober fact."*[16]

A question that seems never to have occurred to Gaster is the extent to which the Exodus story is really romantic. When one reads the Book of Exodus, the Hebrews hardly come off as a romantic group. They continually backslide, complain bitterly about their lot in the desert, spend most of their time yearning for the good old days in Egypt, and emerge from the pages of Exodus as a group hardly worth saving. It seems incredible that this story as recorded in Exodus could come from generations of storytellers embellishing, polishing, and glorifying an old migration myth into a romantic epic.

Johannes Pederson, a Scandinavian scholar of no little reputation, wrote a classic study entitled *Israel: Its Life and Culture,* which is one of the monumental works on the Hebrews. Pederson comments on the Exodus story in an appendix:

> *In forming an opinion of the story about the crossing of the Red Sea, it must be kept in mind, as we have remarked above, that this story, as well as the whole emigration legend, is quite obviously of a cultic character, for the whole narrative aims at glorifying the god of the people at the paschal feast through an exposition of the historical event that created the people. The object cannot have been to give a correct exposition of ordinary events, but on the contrary, to describe history on a higher plane, mythical exploits which make of the people a great people, nature subordinating itself to this purpose (emphasis added).*[17]

I remain at a loss to discover what is "history on a higher plane." And, although I admire Pederson's work, I am repelled at the idea that the ancient Hebrews were the prototype of the modern advertising agency, recording history solely for purposes of national self-glori-fication. Indeed, in reading the Exodus account, we find that the Israelites are always getting in trouble with the Lord.

While Pederson projects a "historical event" as the basis for the paschal feast, he apparently rejects any efforts to discover what that event was, calling into question even the emigration legend, which would mean, in realistic terms, that he quite possibly did not believe that the Hebrews were even in Egypt!

The common theme running through the thinking of Buber, Gaster, and Pederson is that it is forbidden to assign the Exodus account any historical basis other than a vague reference to some primeval event that cannot be recovered. They see in the story, the characters, and the descriptions only a primitive effort at public rela-tions on a theological theme.

When we examine Immanuel Velikovsky's interpretation of the Exodus, we find a very careful articulation of the sequence of events, a fine eye for details, an understanding of what the details mean, and a willingness to seek a rigorous confirmation of the theory at differ-ent points in the development of the interpretation. An example of Velikovsky's rigor can be drawn from *Ages in Chaos*. He has already demonstrated the parallels between the Hebrew and Egyptian source materials and is recapitulating:

> *The story of the darkness in Egypt as told in Hebrew and Egyptian sources is very similar. The death of the pharaoh in the whirling waters is also similar in both Hebrew and Egyptian sources, and the value of this similarity is enhanced by the fact that in both versions the pharaoh perished in a whirlpool during or after the days of the great darkness and violent hurricane.*

Following this summary, Velikovsky then pushes his conception of the interpretation of myth to its logical conclusion: "And yet even a striking similarity is not identity. The subject of the two records should be regarded as identical only if some detail can be found in both versions, the Hebrew and the Egyptian, that cannot be attributed to chance."[18]

Velikovsky then proceeds to demonstrate that the place named Pi-Kharoti in the Egyptian source and the place named Pi-ha-hiroth in the Hebrew source are identical. In every case possible Velikovsky sifts the ancient sources to find specific verification of specific details. This method contrasts sharply with the rather blithe manner in which other thinkers, particularly those I have discussed above, dismiss details and work with the generalities of the story line.

NEW ATTITUDES TOWARD MYTH

From a comparison of Velikovsky's approach to myth with that of other scholars, we can derive a few ground rules for interpreting ancient sources, particularly those of an apparently historical nature that have been classified as myths.

Perhaps the first consideration is to recognize that these sources have withstood the critics of their own time and come down to us as respected literature that has had a wide circulation and that has held the imagination of generation after generation of peoples. That recognition marks Velikovsky as more serious than his fellow scholars in a crucial area—respect for one's sources of information.

The second change in approach is to recognize that we are on a small planet; descriptions of unusual or extraordinary events in ancient sources may quite possibly find verification in contemporary sources, or in alternate sources from other nearby societies. Velikovsky demonstrates the necessity for an awareness of this possibility in *Oedipus and Akhnaton*. Taking the Oedipus myth, he follows its details step-by-step, setting the actual conditions in Greece against the historical realities of Egypt. For example, the Grecian Thebes had few gates, hardly the magnificent city of the Oedipus story. Comparing the family of Oedipus with that of Akhnaton, the political situation in Egypt with the story line of the Greek drama, and examining the role of the Sphinx—revered in Egypt and a stranger in Greece—Velikovsky concludes that the Oedipus story was simply transferred from Egypt to Greece by dramatists who saw the tragedy in the events of the royal house of Egypt.

Recognition of the "planetary" nature of human experiences entails a further acknowledgment that geography changes perceptions of real events. If the sun can be visualized as standing still in the Canaan region, extending the daylight hours, then it must also remain hidden from view on the other side of the globe. Attempting to trace out motifs without an acknowledgment of the role of geography in changing the nature of physical phenomena results only in comparing symbolic similarities among the perceptions of human beings, and buttresses the contention that myths express a "higher" history having a verbal reality only.

Given these basic changes in attitudes in approaching myth, we come then to see Velikovsky raising additional questions for the interpreters of myth. Does the process of myth building necessarily result in the glorification or embellishment of the details of the story? Most mythologists seem to feel that the passage of time alters the myth by allowing time for the introduction of editorial comments by succeeding generations. When one considers the nature of our experiences today, one recognizes that the passage of time usually serves to moderate those experiences, softening them and reducing the story line to the bare essentials. Can we suppose that an entirely different process of transmission operated in earlier times?

Velikovsky concentrates his efforts in interpreting the story line of myths on the smallest details of fact. If something appears to have survived generations of storytelling as a factual detail, then he gives it serious consideration. In the Exodus story, for example, he makes great use of the pillar of cloud by day and the pillar of fire by night to show the extent of visibility of the cosmic events that characterized the Exodus experience. Buber, using the same biblical verses, remarks,

> *Quite irrespective of whether volcanic phenomena have or*
> *have not exerted any influence here on either the nucleus or*
> *the development of the tradition, it is to be felt that the primaeval*
> *phenomenon which has found optical expression in the clearly*
> *native, unique picture is the belief of the man Moses in the*
> *leadership of the God whose voice he heard from the fire."*[19]

In other words, Buber finds the language poetic and symbolic of the Hebrews' belief in Moses and Moses' belief in his former experience in the revelation of the burning bush. The Exodus is reduced to an ancient legend designed to produce an infinite number of sermon texts, rather than a historical event that grasped and formed the Hebrew nation. Memories of events are replaced by symbols in Buber's theory of myth; they remain indications of real events in Velikovsky's theory.

The relative constancy of details in myths has a corollary in the relative constancy of the story line. A myth, for Velikovsky, is not simply a collection of symbols brought together for purposes of edification, glorification, and enlightenment but contains within itself a special sequence in which real events can possibly have unfolded. In this attitude Velikovsky and Carl Jung find companionship, but for different reasons. Jung needed the sequence of the myth in order to work out the multitude of psychic relationships that the myth illustrated. Velikovsky adheres to the sequence of events contained in the myth story line because of his belief that the myth contains a description of real events. Velikovsky finds no need to violate the sequence of events and details, because to do so would destroy the whole meaning of the story.

The difference between Velikovsky and Jung is very real, because where Velikovsky welcomes and even relishes specific details within the sequence of events, Jung tends to concentrate on the general format of the story line to the neglect of the details. Place-names, descriptions of natural phenomena, and the possibility of independent verification by use of multiple sources fascinate Velikovsky, whereas they are relatively unimportant to Jung once he has chosen the version of the story line that is acceptable to his needs.

Velikovsky's concentration on details of the story in the sequence in which they occur points to an additional change of attitude. Specific details must be compared and verified if at all possible. Myths must be taken in their completeness as we find them, and the details of the story must not be automatically considered to be elaborations, poetic license, or later additions, unless independent proof that they are such can be obtained. The details of the myth must be confronted in all their inconsistencies or apparent inconsistencies if we are to learn what reality stands behind the myth. This requirement alone could force a new vision of the nature of ancient source materials.

Velikovsky's method creates the possibility of illuminating inconsistencies in myths by adding new materials from other sources or by viewing the descriptions of the stories in a new light. Thus the story of Joshua and the Sun standing still appears to be a poetic flight of fancy of the first magnitude until one understands that *if* the story is correct, then a major displacement of cosmic dimensions must be involved. Recognition of the nature of this displacement requires that one view the planetary nature of human experience and look on the opposite side of the globe for confirming accounts.

An excellent index for evaluating the relative merits of the various approaches to myth would be the extent to which apparent inconsistencies are resolved. This requirement is much preferable to the current scholarly tendency to declare that inconsistencies are either later additions or glosses in the original material. Most probably such an attitude simply indicates what the scholar does not know; his interpretation has at best a verbal or ideological reality of his own construction.

We come, then, to the question of what myth really is. As we have seen in our discussion, most thinkers dealing with myth seem to feel that myth represents a religious reality or an attempt by people less sophisticated than ourselves to explain the origin or constitution of the world. This attitude seems to hold for thinkers from Boas to Lévi-Strauss, from Durkheim to Watts. By combining the knowledge of various sciences and by giving the ancient accounts the utmost respect as conveyors of a historical reality experienced or perceived by people of ancient times, Velikovsky has thrust the question of the origin of religion forward for other thinkers to confront. He has taken the Exodus from its contemporary status as a glorification myth to the much more exalted status of a fairly accurate recording of an important planetary event.

The conclusion that must be drawn is that religions most probably do not originate from the speculations of generations of poets, no matter how profound. In ancient times a great many of them most probably originated from the experiences of a group of people surviving a spectacular planetary event.

It seems doubtful that the other theories of the origin of religion, which see religious beliefs and practices beginning as a result of poetic storytelling, can withstand the rigorous methodology of investigation and interpretation Velikovsky utilizes in developing his thought. The burden of proof should be shifted from Velikovsky, who uses ancient sources for data, to those who so blithely dismiss the details of myths and present their own interpretations—interpretations that reflect a "verbal" reality unrelated to events on our planet.

NOTES

1. Émile Durkheim, *The Elementary Forms of the Religious Life* (New York: Collier Books, 1961), pp. 99-100.

2. Franz Boas, "Mythology and Folklore," in *General Anthropology*, ed. Franz Boas (New York: D. C. Heath, 1938), p. 619.
3. R. G. Collingwood, *The Idea of History* (Oxford: Oxford University Press, 1956), p. 15.
4. Ibid., p. 22.
5. Mircea Eliade, *The Sacred and the Profane* (New York: Harper Torchbooks, 1957), p. 95.
6. Ibid., p. 98.
7. C. G. Jung, *Psychology and Religion: East and West*, essay entitled "Answer to Job" (New York: Pantheon Press, 1958), p. 409.
8. Claude Lévi-Strauss, *The Savage Mind* (Chicago: University of Chicago Press, 1962), pp. 21-22.
9. Ibid., p. 22.
10. Joseph Campbell, *The Masks of God—Occidental Mythology* (New York: Viking Press, 1964), p. 95.
11. Ibid., p. 95.
12. Alan S. Watts, *Myth and Ritual in Christianity* (New York: Beacon Press, 1968), p. 7.
13. Martin Buber, *Moses* (New York: Harper Torchbooks, 1958), p. 13.
14. Ibid., p. 76.
15. Ibid., p. 77.
16. Theodore Gaster, *Passover* (Henry Schuman, 1949), p. 29.
17. Johannes Pederson, *Israel: Its Life and Culture* (Oxford: Oxford University Press, 1959), vols. 3-5, p. 728.
18. Immanuel Velikovsky, *Ages in Chaos* (New York: Doubleday, 1952), p. 43.
19. Buber, *Moses*, p. 76.

28

TRIBAL RELIGIOUS REALITIES

▼▼▼▼

I suggested earlier that the original religious perception of reality becomes transformed over a period of time into philosophies and theologies, which purport to give a logical and analytical explanation of ultimate reality. These explanations, of course, have eliminated the human emotions and intuitive insights of the original experience and in their place have substituted a systematic rendering of human knowledge concerning the natural world. From this process of analysis have come the respective divisions of the natural world into spiritual and material, eternal and ephemeral, this-worldly and other-worldly, and absolute space and time dimensions. Not all societies and traditions reprocessed their religious experiences, however, and we must turn to those traditions, which scholars have labeled "primitive," in order to see wherein the differences lie.

Primitive peoples do not differentiate their world of experience into two realms that oppose or complement each other. They seem to maintain a consistent understanding of the unity of all experience. "Among the primitives," according to Joachim Wach, "there is no clear distinction between the notions of spiritual and material, psychical and physical."[1] Rather than seek underlying causes or substances, primitives report the nature and intensity of their experience. Carl Jung clarified this approach to experience somewhat when he wrote, "Thanks to our one-sided emphasis on so-called natural causes, we have learned to differentiate what is subjective and psychic from what is objective and 'natural.' For primitive man, on the contrary, the psychic and the objective coalesce in the external world. In the face of something extraordinary it is not he who is astonished, but rather the thing that is astonishing."[2]

The traditional picture that Western thinkers have painted of primitive peoples is one of fear, superstition, and ignorance, the intense desire to come to grips with natural forces, and a tendency to attribute powers and intentions to the unusual acts of nature. Jung's suggestion that the astonishment occurs in the objective world rather than in the observer would seem to indicate that primitives have a rather keen sense of observation and are intensely aware of the nature of the physical world in which they live, constantly encountering the unique in everything they meet. Such an attitude is indeterminate, not absolute, and would seem to transcend fear and superstition. At the very minimum, that the astonishment occurs in the objective world means that the identity of the primitive in a personal sense is preserved from destructive psychic disruptions.

But we must not consider the life of the primitive one series of astonishing events after another. Primitive peoples rapidly become accustomed to the apparent periodic movements of nature, and it is the unusual that attracts them. Carl Jung cautioned,

> *Primitive man's belief in an arbitrary power does not arise out of thin air, as was always supposed, but is grounded in experience. The grouping of chance occurrences justifies what we call his superstition, for there is a real measure of probability that unusual events will coincide in time and place. We must not forget that our experience is apt to leave us in the lurch here. Our observation is inadequate because our point of view leads us to overlook these matters.*[3]

The first step in understanding the alternative worldview of primitive peoples, therefore, is to recognize that they do not derive their beliefs out of "thin air" but that all beliefs and institutions derive from experience.

Although Jung warned that we tend to overlook unusual coincidences and relationships that primitive peoples discern, we must recognize that primitive peoples exist on the same planet as we do and therefore have the same basic types of daily experiences as we do. Their insights into the nature of reality, therefore, while occasionally more specific or emotional, or even more intuitive, than ours, refer to the same external reality. Their failure or refusal to differentiate subjective from objective, spiritual from material, seems to form the basic difference that separates them from us. Thus when we examine their system of beliefs, their myths, or their social and political organizations, we must remember that some things that have utmost importance for primitive peoples can be found within the Western scheme of knowledge but perhaps in a differentiated form that makes it difficult to identify properly.

Thus it is with the most common feature of primitive awareness of the world—the feeling or belief that the universe is energized by a pervading power. Scholars have traditionally called the presence of this power *mana* following Polynesian beliefs, but we find it among tribal peoples, particularly American Indian tribes, as *wakan orenda,* or *manitou.* Regardless of the technical term used, there is general agreement that a substantial number of primitive peoples recognize the existence of a power in the universe that affects and influences them. "The mana theory maintains that there is something like a widely distributed power in the external world that produces all those extraordinary effects," Jung explained. And he suggested, "Everything that exists acts, otherwise it would not *be*. It can *be* only by virtue of its inherent energy. Being is a field of force. The primitive idea of mana, as you can see, has in it the beginnings of a crude theory of energy."[4]

It would be comforting, of course, to claim that primitive peoples derived the principles of modern energy theory from their religious experiences thousands of years before Western scientists formulated their complicated explanations, but it is not necessary to be extravagant. It is sufficient to note that the observations and experiences of primitive peoples were so acute that they were able to recognize a basic phenomenon of the natural world religiously rather than scientifically. They felt power but did not measure it. Today we measure power but are unable to feel it except on extremely rare occasions. We conclude that energy forms the basic constituent of the universe through experimentation, and the existence of energy is truly a conclusion of scientific experimentation. For primitive peoples, in contrast, the presence of energy and power is the starting point of their analyses and understanding of the natural world. It is their cornerstone for further exploration.

Western thinkers continually misinterpret the recognition of power by primitive peoples as if it were a conclusion they had reached rather than a beginning they were making. Thus Paul Tillich wrote,

> *The conception of nature that we find earliest in history, so far as we have knowledge of it, is the magical-sacramental conception. According to it, everything is filled with a sort of material energy which gives to things and to parts of things, even to the body and the parts of the body, a sacral power. The word "sacral" in this context, however, does not signify something in opposition to the profane. Indeed, at this phase of cultural development the distinction between the sacred and the profane is not a fundamental one.*[5]

Such an explanation is incorrect, because it is phrased in the traditional language of Western thinkers, which separates spiritual and material into two distinct aspects of reality. Primitive peoples refuse to make such distinctions. We are not dealing, therefore, with a conception of nature in the same way that Western thinkers conceive of things but with a simple recognition of the force field that seems to constitute the natural world.

The implications of understanding the proper sense in which primitive peoples experienced the natural world are important because it bears directly on the manner in which they understand themselves. Ernst Cassirer, writing of the attitudes of primitive peoples, maintained that for them "nature becomes one great society, the *society of* life. Man is not endowed with outstanding rank in this society. He is a part of it but he is in no respect higher than any other member."[6] All species, all forms of life, have equal status before the presence of the universal power to which all are subject. The religious requirement for all life-forms is thus harmony, and this requirement holds for every species, ours included. The natural world has a great bond that brings together all living entities, each species gaining an identity and meaning as it forms a part of the complex whole. If ever there were a truly evolutionary theological position, primitive peoples would represent it.

Primitive peoples somehow maintain this attitude toward the world and toward other life-forms. As long as the bond of life is respected, all species have value and meaning, emotions and intuitions remain a constant factor of experience, and harmony is maintained. The elimination of emotional intensity and intuitive insights into the world, which is accomplished by the great "world" religions, twists this basic apprehension of reality. "No religion could ever think of cutting or even loosening the bond between nature and man," Cassirer wrote. "But in the great ethical religions this bond is tied and fastened in a new sense. . . . Nature is not, as in polytheistic religions, the great and benign mother, the divine lap from which all life originates. It is conceived as the sphere of law and lawfulness."[7]

The great innovation of the world religions is to reduce natural events to a sequence containing some form of predictability, to introduce the conception of law and regularity into the natural world. Such an innovation is wholly artificial and may be understood by primitive peoples as the original sin. Certainly the acquisition of knowledge is understood in Genesis as the original sin, and it is ironic that in attempting to refine religious experiences into a more precise understanding the great world religions commit the sin that alienates our species from the rest of the natural world. Paul Tillich noted that the primitive understanding of reality changes "when the system of powers is replaced by the correlation of self and world, of subjectivity and objectivity. Man becomes an epistemological, legal, and moral center, and things become objects of his knowledge, his work, and his use."[8] This point of departure separates primitive peoples from the rest of the human species; it distinguishes civilized from primitive, and unleashes the energies of our species on a path of conquest of the rest of nature, which has now been reduced to the status of an object.

It is curious that Tillich would support the tendency of the great world religions to reduce the natural world to an objective status, thereby artificially elevating our species above other life-forms. Granted that we seek knowledge continually; knowledge is more than the ability to deal with theories. The curiosity arises because Tillich suggested that the "man who transforms the world into a universal machine serving his purposes has to adapt himself to the laws of the machine. The mechanized world of things draws man into itself and makes him a cog, driven by the mechanical necessities of the whole. *The personality that deprives nature of its power in order to elevate itself above it becomes a powerless part of its own creation.*"[9] It would appear, therefore, that organizing and systematizing religious experiences into reliable and predictable knowledge is a major theological transgression and a movement away from intimate understanding of our place in the world in an epistemological sense.

Arnold Toynbee described the severance of the bond of nature and our species in different terms than did Cassirer, and Toynbee's analysis gives us insight into the problems created by the expansion and sophistication of the great world religions. "The worship of Nature tends to unite the members of different communities because it is not self-centered," Toynbee maintained, "it is the worship of a power in whose presence all human beings have the identical experience of being made aware of their own human weakness." In contrast to the unifying effect that nature has on human communities, Toynbee suggested that "the worship of parochial communities tends to set their respective members at variance because this religion is an expression of self-centredness; because self-centredness is the source of all strife; and because the collective ego is a more dangerous object of worship than the individual ego is."[10]

The characteristic that purports to save members of world religions, while conceived on an idealistic and precise basis, is the very thing that destroys the members thereof—concentrating on the self to the exclusion of the world. Perhaps the best illustration we can find is the comparative status that primitive peoples and adherents of world religions enjoy vis-à-vis each other. Joachim Wach wrote, "In most primitive religions a strong tie binds the members of a tribal cult together, and on the level of great religions, spiritual brotherhood surpasses physical ties between brothers. A 'father or mother in God,' a 'brother or sister in God,' may be closer to us than our physical parents and relatives."[11] This claim may have a certain validity for specific individuals, but on the larger scale it does not appear to be operative. Wach himself noted, "Whatever the prevailing mood, the religious association takes precedence over all other forms of fellowship. Religious loyalty, in theory at least, outranks any other loyalty everywhere except in the modern Western world."[12] The result of the teachings of the world religions, which center on the care and salvation of the individual, is, of course, the creation of the solitary individual, apart from any community of concern.

Most adherents of world religions would dispute the accusation that their tradition isolates individuals; yet their teachings appear to be designed to break the traditional ties that have bound communities together. "In order to create a new and profound spiritual brother-hood based on the principles enunciated by the new faith," Wach explained, "old bonds have to be broken. This break of sociological ties becomes one of the marks of the willingness to begin a new life. To become a disciple of the Buddha means to leave parents and rela-tives, wife and child, home and property and all else, as flamingos leave their lakes."[13] Theoretically, at least, the new community, which is formed according to the principles of the new faith, is superior to the sociological, family, and community ties, which are severed in the primitive community. The product, again, is not what the world religions claim it to be. "Modern Western man is all too prone to think of the solitary individual first and last," Wach wrote, "yet the study of primitive religions shows that, individual experiences not-withstanding, religion is generally a group affair."[14]

The attraction of the world religions appears to be their knowl-edge and idealism, their precise manner of articulating answers to perennial human questions about life, death, and meaning, and their ability to preach and teach methods of living that will enable people to survive in a world that often seems hostile. But clarity in articulating beliefs is not necessarily a benefit. Carl Jung suggested that "it is not ethical principles, however lofty, or creeds, however orthodox, that lay the foundations for the freedom and autonomy of the individual, but simply and solely the empirical awareness, the incontrovertible experience of an intensely personal, recipro-cal relationship between man and an extramundane authority which acts as the counterpoise to the 'world' and its reason."[15] The great bond of experience with nature, no matter how vaguely defined, incorporates the emotional and intuitive dimension of our lives much better than do the precise creeds, doctrines, and dogmas of the great world religions and as such provides us with continuing meaning as long as we treat our apprehension of the great mystery with respect.

The first and great difference between primitive religious thought and the world religions, therefore, is that primitive peoples maintain a sense of mystery through their bond with nature; the world reli-gions sever the relationship and attempt to establish a new, more comprehensible one. Foremost among the religious leaders who fought the great natural bond between our species and the other life-forms and processes of nature were the Hebrew prophets, with their constant warfare against the Baals. "The significance of prophetic criticism," Paul Tillich wrote, "lies in the fact that it dissolves the primitive unity between the holy and the real. To the prophets the holy is primarily a demand. . . . Nature as such is deprived of its sacred character and becomes profane. Immediate intercourse with nature no longer possesses religious significance."[16] In this criticism, therefore, we have a reductionism that severs the holy from its origin and makes it an intellectual ethical requirement. A demand can only originate in a system of duties and responsibilities, a legalism can only produce another legal system and more duties and responsibilities. The collective ego of the new community, which becomes the object of worship, be it the Christian church or whatever, must itself be given structure and a means of operation, and religion becomes a group of humans examining their own beliefs rather than continuing to fulfill a role in the great process of nature.

Primitive relationships with nature have been subjected to criticism from many points of view. They are regarded as remnants of former days when our species had no scientific understanding of the natural world. Tillich defined primitive relationships with nature as "objectification" and suggested that "the objectification of the divine in time and space and in anthropomorphic conceptions, which takes place in myth, is disrupted by prophetic religion, regarded as inadequate by mysticism and dismissed as unworthy and absurd by philosophical religion."[17] Tillich's statement poses important questions for understanding primitive perceptions of religions and, ultimately, natural reality. Our first task is to examine the suggestion that primitive peoples in fact do objectify the divine in time and space.

I have suggested earlier that the major difference between Christianity and Buddhism is that one absolutizes time and human affairs and the other absolutizes natural processes, and ultimately space. By contrast, primitive peoples maintain the unity of space-time and refuse to use either concept as their analytical tool for understanding the world. Ernst Cassirer, writing about the society of natural life that characterizes primitive perceptions of nature, said, "We find the same principle—that of the solidarity and unbroken unity of life—if we pass from space to time. It holds not only in the order of simultaneity but also in the order of succession."[18] Like the modern physicist, the primitive holds the unity of experience in a continuum that transcends traditional Western divisions of space and time.

But there is an additional parallel between primitive peoples' perception of experiences and the theories of modern physics: space may conceivably have priority over time in that time occurs within space and must give way, at least conceptually, to spatial recognitions. "A native thinker makes the penetrating comment," Claude Lévi-Strauss notes, "that 'all sacred things must have their place' . . . . It could even be said that being in their place is what makes them sacred for if they were taken out of their place, even in thought, the entire order of the universe would be destroyed. Sacred objects therefore contribute to the maintenance of order in the universe by occupying the places allocated to them."[19] Far from objectifying the sacred in time and space, here is a recognition that religious perceptions in fact occur in the natural world and go a substantial distance in giving it structure. We have the recognition not only that a divine energy pervades the natural world but also that it is able to reveal itself in particular objects and places. To deny this possibility would be to deny the possibility of an ultimate sense of reality itself. But it is important to note that primitives are dealing with recognitions, not beliefs that have an intellectual content; and recognitions, like perceptions, involve the totality of personality.

Tillich himself admitted that "the holy appears only in special places, in special contexts." But instead of recognizing that the preservation of memories concerning the appearance of the holy is the first stage in structuring the worldview of the primitive, that is, the holy mountain, the sacred river or lake, the point of emergence from the underworld, Tillich argued that "the concentration of the sacramental in special places, in special rites, is the expression of man's ambiguous situation."[20] It is difficult to understand why recognizing sacred places and rites creates ambiguity. Primitive peoples are certainly not confused about the places and rites they consider sacred, for these form the basis of their community and provide an identity that incorporates rather than transcends the space-time dimensions. Ambiguity would only seem to appear if one wished to universalize the sacred nature of experience, thereby, in effect, lifting the sacred from its context of the natural world and holding it in one's mind as a set of concepts. Ambiguity appears only when one attempts to control the appearance of divinity and establish regular guidelines for any relationship that might ensue with divinity.

Whenever we begin to discuss the role of time and space for primitive peoples, we become embroiled in controversy, because Western thinkers have traditionally separated space and time, unconsciously I might suggest, always considering them homogeneous entities in their own right. Thus it is important to clarify the primitive perceptions of space and time so that we can be sure we understand the manner in which primitive peoples perceive experiences. "Primitive thought is not only incapable of thinking of a system of space," Cassirer wrote, "it cannot even conceive a scheme of space." And he continued, "Its concrete space cannot be brought into a *schematic* shape. Ethnology shows us that primitive tribes usually are gifted with an extraordinarily sharp perception of space. A native of these tribes has an eye for all the nicest details of his environment."[21] The primitive easily comprehends the places of his or her experience, but he or she does not abstract from them a scheme of space in a Euclidian or Newtonian sense. The primitive person is thus in direct immediate relationship with his or her environment but fails to extend abstract principles continuously to conceive of "endless" dimensional existence. In view of our discussion of the conceptions of space-time in modern physics, it would appear that primitive peoples, in their religious perceptions of the natural world, coincide with the contemporary conceptual understanding of the world.

This view of primitive peoples provides them with an understanding of the natural world that immediately incorporates all aspects of experience. Thus primitive descriptions of events contain all elements of knowledge that Western scientists have traditionally extracted and organized into distinct academic disciplines. Whenever scholars have attempted to return to the primitive perception and illustrate the wholistic understanding contained in primitive mythologies, they have had to bring in the primitive perception of space as a means of demonstrating their thesis. Thus Lévi-Strauss suggests that there is a symmetry between anthropology and history in primitive thought forms, making the two disciplines parallel, interwoven developments. Lévi-Strauss encounters difficulty with his academic colleagues in advocating this position, and he complains, "This symmetry between history and anthropology seems to be rejected by philosophers who implicitly or explicitly deny that distribution in space and succession in time afford equivalent perspectives. In their eyes some special prestige seems to attach to the temporal dimension, as if a diachrony were to establish a kind of intelligibility not merely superior to that provided by a synchrony, but above all more specifically human."[22]

When we admit the equivalency of temporal and spatial dimensions as perspectives for understanding, we can answer the accusations of the prophets, the mystics, and the expositors of philosophical religion. Perceptions of experience articulated in predominantly spatial terms incorporate the immediacy of the situation without including prior causations and future projections as part of the original experience. Thus the immediate event is passed forward as it occurred, without editorial reordering, and primitive peoples preserve "chunks" of experience, not interpretive patterns of activity. Rather than a demeaning manner of understanding, which fails to comprehend cause and effect and temporality, the primitive form of apprehension may be more sophisticated. Marshall McLuhan comments on this possibility in *Understanding Media,* suggesting that, although "our ideas of cause and effect in the literate West have long been in the form of things in sequence and succession," such a way of understanding the world is "an idea that strikes any tribal or auditory culture as quite ridiculous, and *one that has lost its prime place in our own new physics and biology.*"[23]

We conclude that primitive peoples' perceptions of reality, particularly their religious experiences and awareness of divinity, occupy a far different place in their lives than do the conceptions of the world religions, their experiences, and their theologies, philosophies, doctrines, dogmas, and creeds. Primitive peoples preserve their experiences fairly intact, understand them as a manifestation of the unity of the natural world, and are content to recognize these experiences as the baseline of reality. World religions take the raw data of religious experience and systematize elements of it, using either the temporal or the spatial dimension as a framework, and attempt to project meaning into the unexamined remainder of human experience. Ethics becomes an abstract set of propositions attempting to relate individuals to one another in the world religions while kinship duties, customs, and responsibilities, often patterned after relationships in the natural world, parallel the ethical considerations of religion in the primitive peoples. Primitive peoples always have a concrete reference—the natural world—and the adherents of the world religions continually deal with abstract and ideal situations on an intellectual plane. "Who is my neighbor?" becomes a question of great debate in the tradition of the world religions, and the face of the neighbor changes continually as new data about people become available. Such a question is not even within the worldview of primitives. They know precisely who their relatives are and what their responsibilities toward them entail.

As we attempt to devise a new metaphysics for our time, we face the question of integrating social existence around a new set of questions and beliefs that have planetary application and can transcend the parochial historical, racial, geographic, economic, and religious traditions. The vision once held out by the world religions—the equality of every person before the deity and in human society, peace and prosperity, and a universal brotherhood of life—is usually cited by their adherents as a partial justification of their existence and as the benchmark of intellectual accomplishments that distinguishes them from primitive peoples. As ideals, these goals are admirable, but are the doctrines, beliefs, and ethical systems of the great world religions capable of bringing about such conditions? Judging by their historical performance, we would conclude no.

Can the primitive peoples do better? Paul Radin (1883–1959), an American anthropologist who studied many different primitive peoples, wrote,

> *[If asked] to state briefly and succinctly what are the*
> *outstanding positive features of aboriginal civilization, I,*
> *for one, would have no hesitation in answering that there are*
> *three: the respect for the individual, irrespective of age or sex;*
> *the amazing degree of social and political integration*
> *achieved by them; and the existence there of a concept of*
> *personal security which transcends all governmental forms*
> *and all tribal and group interests and conflicts.*[24]

Insofar as it is possible to conceive three attributes of a society that we would like to emulate, these characteristics of primitive peoples look appealing. Primitive peoples, in their system of social organization, were hardly unsophisticated, and they do not deserve the scorn that Western thinkers, philosophers and theologians especially, have heaped on them. If they did not construct massive scientific technologies and immense bureaucracies, neither did they create the isolated individual helplessly gripped by supraindividual forces.

But how can we incorporate the primitive modes of perception, both religious and secular, into our understanding of the world, especially in a world now emerging from the Darwinian-Newtonian era of scientific absolutism? Quite obviously, we cannot return to the primitive forms of religion that once dominated the worldview of small tribal groups. The modern tendencies to discover a guru or medicine man as a spiritual teacher all collapse of their own inadequacies. Efforts of tribal peoples to retribalize and return to their original posture toward the world collapse in the face of an affluent technology that rips them apart. We live in a modern, electronic age in which blood sacrifices, ceremonies, and even kinship ties cannot withstand the future shock of a rapidly changing style of life.

Our task in searching for a new metaphysics is not one of picking and choosing from a variety of applicants those elements of any human tradition that are either very appealing or that seem to describe reality in properly respectable terms. The major accusation that can be made against Christianity is that it is a conglomerate, a syncretism of divergent views, held together by faith and the expenditure of intellectual energy—I believe, therefore what I believe is true. Thus we cannot suggest that there is anything we can "borrow" from primitive peoples in the way of a view of the world, ceremonies, beliefs, customs, or traditions. We face the future immediately, and although we can be aware of the sound basis for primitive beliefs and customs, we can never return to them or take them up, expecting them to save us.

It is not necessary, however, to do so. Our examination of the *oikumene* indicates that the most fruitful avenues of development today are directing us toward a new type of social existence that parallels primitive peoples', perhaps incorporates some of their insights or unconsciously adopts some of their techniques, but which will be fully modern and capable of providing a meaningful existence. The importance of these movements for primitive peoples is that as modern industrial society becomes aware of new ways of structuring its understanding of the world, economic and political decisions will begin to reflect a more comprehensive and intelligent view of the world and of our species, thereby taking the pressure, in a political and economic sense, away from the surviving primitive and tribal peoples.

Aside from recognizing that primitive religious perceptions affirmed a divine and universal power or energy inherent in the world of experience, what can we learn from the primitive tradition that would be relevant today? I have suggested that primitive myths and traditions contain a memory of historic events from which we can extract, for the benefit of various disciplines, additional knowledge concerning the history of our planet. Indeed, one of the chief characteristics of primitive mythology is that it originates in the prehistoric period before the invention of writing and alphabets and has the potential to enable us to extend our knowledge of human affairs to that dimly understood time.

There are two substantial issues raised by the literal use of primitive myths to describe unusual planetarywide happenings. Much of the material in myths, legends, and traditions deals with catastrophes and disasters on a scale nearly inconceivable to modern minds. Can we accept a literal rendering of these stories when we do not observe the same processes at work in the physical world today? Mingled with these stories of catastrophes are themes concerning the actions of gods and goddesses, similar in many respects to the ancient astronomical knowledge; that is, the gods and goddesses who play important roles in the stories of catastrophes, not coincidentally, also represent planets, suggesting that the stories recount an astral catastrophe in our solar system. Do we interpret these dramas of the gods literally or as religious themes of some moral importance?

As the myths and legends of both primitive peoples and the distant ancestors of our present Western industrial nations had such a uniformity of concern about catastrophes, and feared the influence of heavenly bodies in their affairs, we must examine the basis on which it may be possible to derive important knowledge from these stories.

NOTES

1. Joachim Wach, *The Comparative Study of Religions* (New York: Columbia University Press, 1961), p. 93.
2. C. G. Jung, "Archaic Man," in *Civilization in Transition*. Collected Works, vol. 10 (Princeton, N. J.: Princeton University Press, 1970), p. 63.
3. Ibid., p. 60.
4. Ibid., p. 69.
5. Paul Tillich, *The Protestant Era*. Abridged ed. (Chicago: University of Chicago Press, 1957), pp. 99-100.
6. Ernst Cassirer, *An Essay on Man* (New Haven, Conn.: Yale University Press, 1944), p. 83.

7. Ibid., p. 100.
8. Tillich, *The Protestant Era*, p. 120.
9. Ibid., p. 123. Italics mine.
10. Arnold Joseph Toynbee, *An Historian's Approach to Religion* (New York: Oxford University Press, 1956), p. 34.
11. Wach, *The Comparative Study of Religions*, p. 125.
12. Ibid., p. 139.
13. Ibid., p. 128.
14. Ibid., p. 121–122.
15. C. G. Jung, "Religion as the Counterbalance to Mass-Mindedness," in *Civilization in Transition.* Collected Works, vol. 10 (Princeton, N. J.: Princeton University Press, 1970), p. 258.
16. Tillich, *The Protestant Era*, p. 108.
17. Paul Tillich, "Myth and Religion," in Pelikan, Jaroslav (ed.), *Twentieth Century Theology in the Making*, vol. 2. Translated by R. A. Wilson (New York: Harper & Row, 1969, 1970), p. 346.
18. Cassirer, *An Essay on Man*, p. 83.
19. Claude Lévi-Strauss, *The Savage Mind* (Chicago: University of Chicago Press, 1966), p. 10.
20. Tillich, *The Protestant Era*, p. 111.
21. Cassirer, *An Essay on Man*, p. 45.
22. Lévi-Strauss, *The Savage Mind*, p. 256.
23. Marshall McLuhan, *Understanding Media: The Extensions of Man* (New York: McGraw-Hill Publishing Co., 1965), p. 86. Italics mine.
24. Paul Radin, *The World of Primitive Man* (New York: Grove Press, 1953), p. 11.

29

THE RELIGIOUS CHALLENGE

Freedom of Religion in Scalia's America

▼▼▼▼

Recently, the Supreme Court wrought a marvelous revolution in constitutional rights that will affect religious individuals and communities far into the next century. In *Employment Division v. Smith* (1990), the Court decided that two men, active participants in the ceremonies of the Native American Church, which uses peyote in its rituals, were not eligible for unemployment compensation if they had been discharged from their jobs as individuals using a prohibited drug. The governor of Oregon has since signed a law that allows the defense of "sacramental use" for anyone caught in a similar situation in the future. But the impact of the reasoning of the law has caught a New York and a Seattle church in the web of municipal ordinances and stripped away their immunity from harassment by local government.

It is no secret that recent appointments to the Supreme Court, and the appointment now pending, have been made with the primary purpose of rolling back all human rights decisions made by the Court in the past three decades. Instead of nominating outstanding judges and acknowledged experts on constitutional law, the tendency has been to find nominees who have done so little in the way of scholarship and decision writing that no objections can be made to their elevation to the Court. The result has been the rapid ascent of second-rate minds and third-rate writers to the highest tribunal of the land. Not only has the reasoning of recent decisions been appalling (for example, the recent step backward into the Middle Ages in the ruling permitting forced confessions), but also the substance of judicial reasoning has created a bizarre direction for future efforts to bring sanity and balance to America's religious sensitivity.

The majority churches all have a bevy of lobbyists in our nation's capital. The collective wisdom of these people suggests that the best solution to the problem raised by the *Smith* decision is to seek an amendment to existing law that would allow the major Protestant denominations to escape the logic and application of *Smith* and force the Indian religions to bear the consequences of the case (or to conform their ceremonies and rituals to acts and substances that are approved by the government). Such a change in the law, of course, would then raise the question of whether or not Congress has established certain kinds of religion and prohibited certain others. Such a move would itself be unconstitutional. Unfortunately for the religious American, the intellectual landscape is so devoid of leadership that the challenge thrown down by the Supreme Court has not been understood, much less confronted.

People read but they rarely understand, so it is not unexpected that the full meaning of Justice Antonin Scalia's decision has escaped notice. In a seemingly casual but ultimately important sentence early in the decision, Scalia writes: "It would doubtless be unconstitutional, for example, to ban the casting of 'statues that are to be used for worship purposes,' or to prohibit bowing down before a golden calf." Only those Americans who have an acquaintance with the Old Testament would know that worshiping the Golden Calf was anathema to Moses (and also sat uncomfortably with Joshua) and that it has been symbolic of both secularism and pagan superstition for the better part of 3,500 years. That it would now be the primary form of religious activity protected by the United States Constitution seems ludicrous—but ironically just—considering the inroads made by secularism in this century.

Considering that he is an avowed Roman Catholic, the Scalia contention is amazing. But even more stunning is the absence of any sense of outrage from American Christians. Instead, they are wallowing in the subtleties of sexual behavior—the mainline Protestant denominations debating it and many right-wing evangelicals and television preachers engaging in it. So we have the strange situation of a society thought to be morally informed by Christianity and Judaism being able to protect constitutionally only one religious form—and that one a practice prohibited by both Christianity and Judaism!

The Indians, of course, come as an afterthought. Their religions are considered exotic, primitive, and precisely the kind of spirituality that many Christians wish they could find in their own rituals. Indeed, annually we are treated to many conferences in which American Indians are asked to speak about spirituality. We see Episcopal bishops garbed in outlandish purple vestments, with war bonnets on their heads, trying to hold a communion service that is partially Christian and partially powwow. We see hundreds of Christian clergy coming to the reservations like Nicodemus at night, trying to get into sweat lodges and sun dances so they can have some kind of religious experience. It is all too sad.

After the *Smith* decision, a coalition of American Indians was formed to seek remedial legislation that would once and for all protect the various forms of traditional tribal worship. These forms include the use of peyote in ceremonies as a sacramental substance; the use of eagle and other bird feathers and animal parts in healing ceremonies and medicine bundles; access to sacred places that are presently "administered" by federal agencies; access by Indian prisoners to traditional ceremonies in penitentiaries; reburial of Indian human skeletal remains from museums and curio shops; and repatriation of sacred objects from these same museums and collections.

The Association on American Indian Affairs and the Native American Rights Fund are raising both money and issues in an effort to get redress from Congress on the religious freedom issue. A new omnibus religious freedom act for American Indians is now ready to be introduced in Congress, which has plenary powers in the field of Indian Affairs according to an earlier Supreme Court ruling. Ranged against Indian religious freedom are mining and grazing interests; a large coalition of federal agencies that seek to administer federal lands free from any interference or public scrutiny; and the general ignorance and lethargy of the American public, which seems to be fascinated with holding Desert Storm parades and to remain uncritical of anything the government does.

Some time ago, Robert Bellah warned us about the rise and possible triumph of secular religion. Pious intellectuals debated the fine points as church bodies turned to other issues, because they were, for the most part, comfortable with government and, in some instances, receiving federal grants to operate social programs. Scalia's opinion demonstrates that not only has civil religion overcome traditional religious expressions, it is now in danger of being superseded by very ancient forms of idol worship—a fitting legacy of the Reagan years.

The challenge to religious people is overwhelming. First, the moral and intellectual leadership of the various church bodies must be replaced if it can't move on from its adolescent fascination with sexual mores. Second, if there is going to be any acknowledgment of the existence of higher spiritual powers, the religious community must once again stand against secular values and advocate and articulate the beliefs and values of the religious life. Third, divergent or even competing religious traditions must be protected in their entirety. (Reactionary Supreme Court Justices who seek to suppress tribal and other religions must reach far into the religious freedom clauses to prohibit religious behavior. The result is oppression for all religious expressions.) The ultimate goal of religious people today must be to establish, in belief and behavior, a clear difference between religion and secularism.

I mourn for any Americans who don't care to protect their own religious traditions and are content with worshiping the Golden Calf, as recommended by the Supreme Court. But of *New World Outlook* readers I ask more: Help American Indians secure federal legislation that will enable us to continue ceremonies and practices that are thousands of years old. We still believe in higher powers and communicate with them in ceremonies and prayers. *Just in case* we are right, it would be a prudent thing to help us.

▼ CREDITS AND PERMISSIONS ▼

▼▼▼

The following is previously published material appearing in this volume:

"Low Bridge—Everybody Cross" and "At the Beginning," from *Red Earth, White Lies: Native Americans and the Myth of Scientific Fact* (1997, pp. 67–91, 211–234); "The Religious Challenge," "The Concept of History," "Tribal Religions and Contemporary American Culture," and "Sacred Places and Moral Responsibility," from *God Is Red: A Native View of Religion* (1994, pp. 46–61, 98–113, 236–253, 267–282), published by Fulcrum Publishing, Golden, Colorado.

"Kinship With the World," in *Journal of Current Social Issues* (vol. 15, no. 3, Fall 1978), pp. 19–21.

"Tribal Religious Realities," in *Metaphysics of Modern Existence*, originally published by Harper & Row, New York: Harper & Row, 1979, pp. 151–161.

Grateful acknowledgment is made to the following for permission to reprint previously published material by Vine Deloria, Jr.:

"Perceptions and Maturity: Reflections on Feyerabend's Point of View," originally published in German, Versuchungen Aufsatze zür Philosophie, Paul Feyerabend, Edition, Surkamp, Germany, 1980.

"Relativity, Relatedness, and Reality" (Autumn 1992, vol. 7, no. 4), pp. 34–40; "Ethnoscience and Indian Realities" (Summer 1992, vol. 7, no. 3), pp. 12–18; "Traditional Technology" (Spring 1990, vol. 5, no. 2), pp. 12–17;

▼ INDEX ▼